THE PRACTICE OF CONCEPTUAL HISTORY

Cultural Memory

in

the

Present

Mieke Bal and Hent de Vries, Editors

THE PRACTICE OF
CONCEPTUAL HISTORY

Timing History, Spacing Concepts

Reinhart Koselleck

Translated by Todd Samuel Presner and Others

Foreword by Hayden White

STANFORD UNIVERSITY PRESS

STANFORD, CALIFORNIA

Stanford University Press
Stanford, California

Printed in the United States of America
on acid-free, archival-quality paper.

Library of Congress Cataloging-in-Publication Data

Koselleck, Reinhart
    The practice of conceptual history : timing history, spacing concepts /
Reinhart Koselleck ; translated by Todd Samuel Presner, with others.
        p.   cm. — (Cultural memory in the present)
    Includes bibliographical references.
    ISBN 0-8047-4022-4 (cloth : alk. paper) — ISBN 0-8047-4305-3 (pbk. : alk. paper)
        1. History—Periodization.   2. History—Philosophy.   3. Historiography.
4. Semantics, Historical.   5. History—Methodology.   I. Presner, Todd Samuel.
II. Title.   III. Series.
D16.15 .K67   2002
901—dc21   2002001374

Original Printing 2002
Last figure below indicates year of this printing:
16

Typeset by James P. Brommer in 11/13.5 Garamond

The publication of this work was subsidized by a grant
from the Goethe-Institut Inter Nationes, Bonn

Contents

Foreword

Hayden White

It is a great honor to be invited to present this collection of Reinhart Koselleck's essays and addresses. Some Anglophone readers will already know his *Futures Past*, a seminal work of historical theory. This collection of essays is much more far-ranging and evidences Koselleck's status as one of the most important theorists of history and historiography of the last half-century. Koselleck's work has implications for contemporary cultural studies that extend far beyond discussions of the practical problems of historical method. He is the foremost exponent and practitioner of *Begriffsgeschichte*, a methodology of historical studies that focuses on the invention and development of the fundamental concepts (*Begriffe*) underlying and informing a distinctively historical (*geschichtliche*) manner of being in the world.

If this formulation of Koselleck's project seems somewhat intimidatingly Hegelian to Anglophone sensibilities, it is because his work is itself deeply grounded in the tradition of *Geisteswissenschaften* that extends from Kant and Hegel through Marx, Dilthey, and Nietzsche, down to Weber, Heidegger, and Gadamer. But there is nothing insular about Koselleck's work. He has a profound knowledge of the British, American, and French contributions to philosophy of history, and he takes the whole sweep of European history, from the Greeks to the present, as his field of inquiry.

It is, however, to the study of the concept of history itself that Koselleck has devoted most of his scholarly life. It is not that Koselleck treats history's concept as some kind of Platonic paradigm against which every individual "idea" of history can be measured. On the contrary, he believes that the notion of history itself had a long period of historical development, extending from Herodotus to Gibbon, before it achieved conceptualization as a fundamental mode of human existence in the nineteenth century. Before this epoch, men certainly possessed a number of ideas about "history," viewing it as a method of research ("inquiry"), a place ("the past"), a process (temporality), a practice (memorialization, celebration, remembrance), a literary or, more precisely, rhetorical genre (history writing), and even a manifestation of an ontological category (humanity). But they did not, on the whole, or except very rarely (as in Vico), conceive a difference between natural temporality and historical temporality which, according to Koselleck, is crucial for understanding the role played by the concept of history in the identity of modern European society and culture.

For Koselleck, the modernity of our epoch differs from all of the other modernities of past epochs of social transformation, technological revolution, and cultural renaissance by virtue of European culture's achievement of "the concept of history." While European culture has always been characterized by a sense of history, a sense of having a history, a sense of being a historical phenomenon, only in its modern phase—sometime between 1750 and 1850—did European society begin to think and act as if it existed in history, as if its "historicity" was a feature, if not the defining feature of its identity. So Koselleck argues, and the essays in this collection so ably translated by Todd Presner and his colleagues bear out this contention with impressive force and amplitude.

These essays should not be thought of, however, as a contribution to "philosophy of history" in the speculative and prophetic mode of Hegel, Marx, and Spengler. They are intended, rather, as contributions to the theory of history, without which, Koselleck insists, historical studies must remain something less than a true science even if they continue to produce more and more truthful information about the past.

Modern professional historical studies were born in the nineteenth century—of a desire for a knowledge of the past free of all theological, metaphysical, and ideological preconception and productive of detailed information about the natures of those peoples aspiring to nationhood in the wake of the French Revolution. History was to be studied in an objective and disinterested manner in order to construct a picture of historical reality by which to measure the falsity of various ideological constructions thereof. But since ideology was thought to be a result of theory overriding the gathering of information about the past—as witnessed by the nefarious effects of philosophy of history on social and political thought—historical studies remained caught on the horns of a dilemma: in order to become a science, they had to have a theory; but an interest in theory appeared to foreclose that interest in particular facts about the past on which historical studies was focused. The resolution of this dilemma was, however, implicitly contained within what came to be called the historist (or historicist) vision of historical reality, which posited historicity as not only a specifically social mode of being in the world but also a social mode of being in the world marked by a particular experience of temporality. Thus, the "content" of history could be grasped as social reality undergoing changes quite unlike those that mere nature underwent. Historical change could be seen to differ from natural change by its heterogeneity, multileveledness, and variability of rate of acceleration. With the discovery that the time of history was different from the time of nature, men also came to believe that historical time could be affected by human action and purposiveness in ways that natural time could not, that history could be "made" as well as "suffered," and that a historical knowledge true to its "concept" provided the prospects for a science of society that balanced the claims of experience with the insistencies of expectation, hope, and faith in the future.

Anglophone readers may have some difficulties with a few of Koselleck's key terms and especially with that of "concept." Permit me to try to unpack the term by contrasting it with some other terms occupying the same semantic field. Consider the phrase "the concept of history." This phrase can be differentiated from affine phrases such as "figure of history," "idea of history," "theory of history," "philosophy of history," and so on. Examples of figures of history would be mythical representations of the muse Clio, the Fates, or Destiny; Machiavelli's "fortuna," Walter Benjamin's "Angel of History," Hegel's "rose in the cross of the present," or the classical "historia magistra vitae." These are metaphorical expressions intended to bring the notion of history before the mind's eye by endowing it with the attributes of some conventionalized image or symbol.

An "idea of history," by contrast, would be an intuition (or perception) of historical phenomena submitted to rationalization by the application of categories of thought deemed adequate to their analysis. Thus, for example, Thucydides may be said to have had an idea of history different from that of Herodotus by virtue of the specific categories of thought he used to order his materials, assess conflicting accounts of the same phenomena, emplot his story, and present it in a manner uniquely his own. Thucydides uses many of the same categories used by Herodotus, but he adds a number of other categories—borrowed, for example, from Hippocratean medicine—in order to work up the materials of his subject and present its truth as different in kind from that of Herodotus. And so too for Polybius, Livy, Tacitus, Orosius, Commynes, and Salutati, down through Machiavelli and Guicciardini, Scaliger, Bayle, Voltaire, and Gibbon. Each of these historians brings to his labors a different "idea" of history—considered as a sequence of actions and events occurring in a given space over a given span of time—by which to distinguish between what will count as a historical as against some other kind of event, between significant or important events and insignificant or unimportant events, and between truthful accounts of these events and a merely imaginary, fictional, mythical, duplicitous, or simply erroneous account thereof.

What none of these purveyors of "ideas" of history provides, Koselleck suggests, is a proper "concept of history," by which he means a model of a structure of logical relationships by which to distinguish between a properly historical account of reality and a nonhistorical or ahistorical or antihistorical account thereof. A concept of history will specify the common content of all of those ideas of history informing the works of the master historians of the world: the content of history's subject matter, on the one hand, and the content of the forms of historical writing, on the other. A concept of history will identify the shared contents of all the ideas of history that have contributed to the definition of a distinctively historical way of knowing reality as history.

I will not further block the reader's access to the essays that follow, and that spell out all of this in persuasive detail, but will only add that, in general, Koselleck's theory of the concept of history features the following theses.

First, historical process is marked by a distinctive kind of temporality different from that found in nature. This temporality is multileveled, is subject to differential rates of acceleration and deceleration, and functions not only as a matrix within which historical events happen but also as a causal force in the determination of social reality in its own right.

Second, historical reality is social reality, an internally differentiated structure of functional relationships in which the rights and interests of one group collide with those of other groups and lead to the kinds of conflicts in which defeat is experienced as an ethical failure requiring reflection on "what went wrong" in order to determine the historical significance of the conflict itself. Koselleck makes the interesting argument that historical knowledge (as against information about the past) is driven forward by the kind of theoretical reflection to which the vanquished in a conflict of world historical significance may be driven (he cites Thucydides, Tacitus, Machiavelli, and Niebuhr as cases in point) by the need to ask "What went wrong?" or: What is the nature of historical reality, that the best laid schemes of mice and men so often go astray? In the domain of historical theory, Koselleck tells us, nothing succeeds like failure in a combat in which both sides feel they represent the right. The victorious have little reason for theoretical reflection. At most, they only need to know the facts. The vanquished, on the other hand, must inquire into the nature of a reality that permits expansive hope only to dash it to despair. Thus, the pattern of "rise and fall" is intrinsic to a genuinely historical thinking, but another pattern, that of "progress," is discernible to the historical consciousness capable of distinguishing between a defeat and the new knowledge of reality that the experience of defeat makes possible.

Thirdly, a "critical historical consciousness" is born of an awareness of a gap between historical events and the language used to represent them— both by the agents involved in these events and by historians retrospectively trying to reconstruct them. Awareness of the disparity between language and historical reality is the basis of history's prime auxiliary discipline, source criticism (philology, paleography, diplomatic, heuristics, hermeneutics in general). It is also the basis of the recognition that every historical account is a construction in discourse of past reality rather than simply a translation of the facts contained in the evidence into contemporary language. The disparity between our experience of reality and the language we have available for representing both this reality and this experience is what infuses the concept of history with the realization that history is an open-ended process rather than a closed science and a fatality. The critical historian must proceed on the basis of the realization that she has to invent a language adequate to the representation of historical reality for her own time and place of work.

The history of historiography, in Koselleck's view, is a history of the evolution of the language of historians, a language that is ever more conceptually self-conscious, ever more aware of the difficulty of grasping the experience of others in terms adequate to its reality. In this respect, Koselleck's work converges with that of Barthes, Foucault, and Derrida, all of whom have stressed the status of historiography as discourse rather than as discipline and featured the constitutive nature of historical discourse as against its claims to literal truthfulness.

Finally, and this is the fourth aspect of Koselleck's notion of the concept of history, a properly historicist concept of history will be informed by the realization that what we call "modernity," "modernization," and "modernism" are nothing other than aspects of the discovery of history's concept in our age. The Enlightenment program of modernization, with its expectations about the possibility of bettering society through the progressive extension of the hegemony of reason, science, and technology over nature and culture, presupposes the concept of history as its condition of possibility. Our difference from all earlier eras and epochs of our history consists precisely in the belief that we exist in history understood as a process of progressive development in which both society and our knowledge of it are historical in nature. The aporias of modernism—in arts and letters as well as in the human and natural sciences—are a function of the discovery of the historicity of both society and knowledge.

The idea that our knowledge is subject to the same rule of evolution as our objects of study generates a kind of relativism, to be sure, insofar as epistemic validity has to be seen as grounded in the time, place, and social circumstances of its production. But Koselleck insists that this relativism provides no grounds for nihilism or a crippling skepticism. Historical relativism, he concludes, avoids Pyrrhonism by virtue of its substitution of the relative certainty of the knowledge we can have of our society and culture for the absolute certainty promised by all forms of idealism. The concept of history includes a concept of historical knowledge that knows itself to be always provisional and open to revision. As historical knowledge dissolves the myths, lies, and falsifications of history, it secures a stable base from which to assess and augment that "space of experience" in which men build a notion of a human reality that is both always changing and ever more becoming itself.

ROME, JULY 14, 2000

THE PRACTICE OF CONCEPTUAL HISTORY

1

On the Need for Theory in the Discipline of History

Ever since the era of neo-Kantianism, our academic field has been caught in a self-definition: history has to do with what is individual and specific, whereas the natural sciences concern themselves with what is general. The history of science has passed this antithesis by. The hypothetical character of its statements and the intertwining of subject and object in its experiments have introduced an element of relativity into the natural sciences that can justly be called "historical." At the same time, many of the social sciences and the humanities have placed themselves under systemic constraints, which have long since cut through the unifying tie of the historical worldview. As the dispute over Popperianism shows, a battle line no longer divides the paired opposites of the natural sciences and the humanities. This has hardly affected our research practice, however, and in consequence the historical profession finds itself isolated. History has been thrown back upon itself and no longer occupies a clear place within an academic world that has in the meantime become dehistoricized.

We can escape from our isolation only via a new relationship to other disciplines. This means that we must recognize our need for theory or, rather, face the necessity of doing theory if history still wants to conceive of itself as an academic discipline. This is not an attempt to borrow theorems from neighboring disciplines to establish hyphenated alliances. It would be rash to couple sociology and history in a way that would set the conditions for deriving our own disciplinary concept from a social science

(*Gesellschaftswissenschaft*) somehow conceived in sociological terms. Instead, I would propose that we can push our way out of our own characteristic bottlenecks only by concentrating on those points that are themselves in need of theory or that promise theoretical insights.

1. It is an irony of the semantic history of "history" that "history itself" (*Geschichte selber*) or "history pure and simple" (*Geschichte schlechthin*) originally meant the need for theory within our discipline. As soon as people gave up thinking "history" in conjunction with certain subjects and objects that were assigned to it, the discipline of history was obliged to conform to a system. When the terms "history itself" and "the philosophy of history" (*Geschichtsphilosophie*) first appeared around 1770, they were identical in meaning. In the course of time, the metahistorical component of these expressions was absorbed by the newly coined term "historicity" (*Geschichtlichkeit*).

Recent discussions of historicity face the theoretical challenges that have resulted from the crisis of historicism. The concept of historicity is used to halt the permanent process of relativization for which historicism was reproached. Historicity absolutizes relativity, as it were, if I may use this nonconcept. The influence of Heidegger cannot be overlooked here, even though he did not exactly promote this discussion within our field. As early as *Being and Time*, there is an almost complete abstracting from history. Historicity is treated as a category of human existence, yet no intersubjective or transindividual structures are thematized. Although Heidegger points the way from the finitude of *Dasein* to the temporality of history, he does not pursue it any further. That is why, on the one hand, the danger of a transhistorical ontology of history (as, for example, devised by August Brunner) lurks behind the fruitful category of historicity. On the other hand, when Heidegger applies his philosophy to history—where it receives an eschatological coloring as the history of Being—,it is no accident that traditional historical-philosophical schemata of decay and ascent become visible.

Historicity and the categories assigned to it open onto a historics (*Historik*) and onto a metahistory that investigate mobility instead of movement and changeability instead of change in a concrete sense. There are many similar formal criteria concerning historical (*historisch*) acting and suffering, which are basically "timeless" across history and serve to unlock history (*Geschichte*). I am thinking of such criteria as: "master and servant"; "friend and foe"; the heterogony of purposes; the shifting relations of time and space with regard to units of action and potential power; and the anthropological substratum for generational change in politics. The list of such categories could be extended; they refer to the finitude that sets history in motion, so to speak, without capturing in any way the content or direction of such movements. (Often enough, Christian axioms—like those of negative theology—are hidden behind such categories; they appear again and again in Wittram's book on interest in history, for example).

Historicity is supposed to outline both the conditions of possibility for histories (*Geschichten*) as such and the place that historical research occupies within them. It clears the historian of the charge of a putative subjectivity; one cannot escape this subjectivity to the extent that "history" (*die Geschichte*) constantly passes both the historian and the writing of history (*die Historie*) by. Here, the "transcendence" of history signifies the process of overtaking that continuously forces the researcher to rewrite history. Thus, the rewriting of history becomes not only the correction of mistakes or a compensatory act, but part of the presuppositions of our profession—provided that *Geschichte* is transcendent with regard to *Historie.* We can therefore say that just as in the past history (*Historie*) as the art of narration developed its own historics (*Historiken*), the discipline of history today has conceptualized historicity as outlining the conditions of possibility both for history in general (*Geschichte überhaupt*) and for the discipline of history (*Geschichtswissenschaft*) more narrowly defined.

The problematic of historical anthropology demonstrates how difficult it is to introduce metahistorical categories into concrete research. Nipperdey has recently pointed this out, and no doubt our western neighbors, with their structuralist, ethnological, and psychosociological approaches, are ahead of us in this respect. Again and again, one is faced with the aporia that enduring formal criteria are themselves historically conditioned and remain applicable only to phenomena that can be delimited historically. In other words, in the course of research, all metahistorical categories will change into historical statements. Reflecting on this change is one of the research tasks of historical anthropology in particular and of any kind of history in general.

2. Discussion of the systematic premises of "history in itself" (*Geschichte an sich*) leads to a reversal of the question, to a turn toward the need for theory in the practice of research. A specifically historical question

can legitimate itself academically only by going back to the historics that inhabits or precedes it; for the purpose of research, it has to unfold its own theoretical premises.

The individual disciplines that have distanced themselves from the assumption of a historical experience of the world have all developed particular systematics relative to their own objects of research. Economics, political science, sociology, philology, linguistics: all can be defined in terms of their objects of study. By contrast, it is much more difficult for history to develop a historical systematics or a theory referring to an object of study based on its actual objects of research. In practice, the object of history is everything or nothing, for history can declare just about anything to be a historical object by the way in which it formulates its questions. Nothing escapes the historical perspective.

Significantly, history "as such" (*Geschichte "als solche"*) does not have an object—except for itself, which does not solve the question of its object of research but only doubles it linguistically: the "history of history." Here, the extent to which "history pure and simple" (*Geschichte schlechthin*) originally was a metahistorical category becomes clear. The question, then, is whether defining an object of study will help the discipline of history regain the historical character that distinguished it up to the eighteenth century. Certainly not. Our concept of history remains ambivalent: in reference to an object, history becomes a historical category; without an object, it remains a metahistorical quantity—and a reservoir of theological, philosophical, ideological, or political classifications that are accepted more or less uncritically.

I would therefore like to narrow down my thesis: history conceived as ubiquitous can only exist as a discipline if it develops a theory of periodization; without such a theory, history loses itself in boundlessly questioning everything. I assume that metahistorical and historical categories will be forced to converge in the question of periodization. Such a question has both a systematic and a historical character. This can be demonstrated by means of a few examples.

a) Let me first refer to a topic of our study group for modern social history, namely, *conceptual history*. Conceptual history, as we attempt it, cannot manage without a theory of periodization. We do not mean temporality of a general kind, which can be procedurally stylized into historicity and which has to do with history in a fundamental way. It is, rather, a question of theoretically formulating in advance the temporal specifics of our political and social concepts so as to order the source materials. Only thus can we advance from philological recording to conceptual history. One hypothesis regarding our dictionary of fundamental historical concepts is that, despite continual use of the same words, the political-social language has changed since the eighteenth century, inasmuch as since then a "new time" has been articulated. Coefficients of change and acceleration transform old fields of meaning and, therefore, political and social experience as well. Earlier meanings of a taxonomy that is still in use must be grasped by the historical method and translated into our language. Such a procedure presupposes a frame of reference that has been clarified theoretically; only within such a frame can these translations become visible. I am speaking here of the "saddle period" (*Sattelzeit*), as it was called by the study group. This period thematizes the transformation of the premodern usage of language to our usage, and I cannot emphasize strongly enough its heuristic character.

We cannot master our task if we try to write a historical-philological history of words at a comparatively positivistic level. We would then get bogged down in the mass of source material and could at most provide an incomplete glossary of sociopolitical expressions. In doing so, we would have to record the history of a lexical item with different meanings or be forced to trace word by word what are supposedly constant meanings. Such an additive description, by which we proceed hand over hand through history, requires a temporal indicator, which, drawing on the sum of the linguistic findings, points out to us that there is a history at all. The theoretical anticipation of the "saddle period" between about 1750 and about 1850 amounts to a statement that during this period the old experience of time was denaturalized. The slow decline of Aristotelian semantic content, which referred to a natural, repeatable, and therefore static historical time, is the negative indicator of a movement that can be described as the beginning of modernity. Since about 1770, old words such as *democracy, freedom,* and *the state* have indicated a new horizon of the future, which delimits the concept in a different way; traditional topoi gained an anticipatory content that they did not have before. A common denominator of the sociopolitical vocabulary can be found in the increased emergence of criteria pertaining to movement. The productivity of this heuristic anticipation is demonstrated by a series of ideas that thematize concepts of movement themselves, such as progress, history, or development. Although these words are old, they are almost neologisms, and since about 1770, they have had a temporal coefficient of change. This offers a strong incentive to read and interrogate other old concepts of the political language in terms of features indicating movement. The hypothesis of a denaturalization of the historical experience of time, which also affects the semantics of sociopolitical expressions, is supported by the emergence of the modern philosophy of history, which appropriates these terms.

In other words, only a theoretical anticipation that uncovers a specific time period can open the possibility of working through certain readings and transposing our dictionary from the level of positivistic recording to that of a conceptual history. Only theory transforms our work into historical research. This presupposition has so far proved its worth. The entire linguistic space of sociopolitical terms has—while retaining the identity of many words—moved from a quasi-static tradition that changed only over the long term to a conceptuality whose meaning can be inferred from a future to be newly experienced. This presupposition does not have to hold for all words, however.

Once the natural constants determining the old historical experience of time have been destroyed—in other words, once progress has been set free—a wealth of new questions emerges.

b) One of the most important concerns the theoretical premises of *structural history*. The answer can be found only by asking about the historical determination of time in statements that are supposed to indicate duration. If one assumes that historical time remains embedded within natural time without being entirely contained in it; or, put differently, that whereas the time of day may be relevant for political decisions, historical connections cannot be measured with a clock; or, put differently yet again, that the revolution of the stars is no longer (or not yet again) relevant for historical time, we must find temporal categories that are adequate to historical events and processes. Categories of the type developed by Braudel can therefore be introduced into empirical research only if we are clear about the theoretical significance of what can last. This consideration leads us into a fundamental dilemma.

We are always using concepts that were originally conceived in spatial terms, but that nevertheless have a temporal meaning. Thus we may speak of refractions, frictions, and the breaking up of certain enduring elements that have an effect on the chain of events, or we may refer to the retrospective effects of events upon their enduring presuppositions. Here, our expressions are taken from the spatial realm, even from geology. They are undoubtedly very vivid and graphic, but they also illustrate our dilemma. It concerns the fact that history, insofar as it deals with time, must borrow its concepts from the spatial realm as a matter of principle. We live by naturally metaphorical expressions, and we are unable to escape from them, for the simple reason that time is not manifest (*anschaulich*) and cannot be intuited (*anschaulich gemacht werden*). All historical categories, including progress, which is the first specifically modern category of historical time, are spatial expressions by origin, and our discipline thrives because they can be translated. "History" originally also contained a spatial meaning, which has become temporalized to such a degree that we refer to the doubling of "structural history" if we wish to (re-)introduce statistics, duration, or long-term extension into our concept of history.

In contrast to other modes of study, history as a discipline lives by metaphorical expression. This is our anthropological premise, as it were, for everything that must be articulated in temporal terms is forced to rely on the sensory bases of natural intuition. The impossibility of intuiting pure time leads directly into methodological difficulties concerning whether meaningful statements about a theory of periodization can be made at all. A specific danger lurks behind these difficulties: namely, that our empirical research naively accepts metaphors as they come to us. We must rely on borrowings from everyday linguistic usage or other disciplines. The terminology borrowed and the necessity of using metaphorical expressions—because time does not clearly manifest itself—requires constant methodological safeguards that refer to a theory of historical time. This leads us back to the question of "duration."

Evidently, certain long-term processes prevail, whether they are supported or opposed. One can, for example, ask whether the rapid industrial development after the Revolution of 1848 happened despite the failed revolution or because of it. There are arguments for and against; neither side is necessarily convincing, but both sides indicate a movement that establishes itself across the political camps of revolution and reaction. In this case, the reaction may have had a more revolutionary effect than the revolution.

If revolution and reaction are both indicators of one and the same movement, sustained by both camps and driven forward by both, then this pair of ideological concepts evidently indicates a continuous historical movement, a structure of irreversible, long-term progress, which transcends the political pros and cons of reaction and revolution. Progress itself is thus more than an ideological category. Even the category of the reasonable middle way, which was habitually invoked at the time, is only meaningful if a stable coefficient of change is introduced. The scope of action for a movement that is already pregiven makes it impossible to statically grasp any reasonable middle way, for this middle way is forced to oscillate between "right" and "left." Its meaning changes by itself over time. When we ask about their temporal meaning, spatial metaphors thus necessitate prior theoretical considerations. Only then can we define what, for instance, is meant by duration, delay, or acceleration in our example of the process of industrialization.

c) The destruction of natural *chronology* leads to a third issue. Chronological sequence, by which our history is still guided at times, can quite easily be exposed as a fiction.

In the past, the natural course of time served as the immediate substratum for possible histories. The calendar of saints and sovereigns was organized by means of astronomy; biological time provided the framework for the natural succession of rulers, on which self-reproducing legal titles in the wars of succession depended—until 1870, symbolically enough. All histories remained rooted in "nature," directly embedded in biological pregivens. The mythological superelevation of astrological and cosmic time, which contained nothing ahistorical in the prehistoric age, pertains to the same experiential realm. But since the triad of antiquity, the Middle Ages, and modernity has structured chronological succession, we have succumbed to a mythical schema that tacitly structures all of our scholarly work. This schema is obviously not of any immediate use for the relation between duration and event. We must, rather, learn to discover the simultaneity of the nonsimultaneous in our history: it is, after all, part of our own experience to have contemporaries who live in the Stone Age. And since the large-scale problems of the developing countries are coming back to haunt us today, it becomes imperative to gain theoretical clarity about the nonsimultaneity of the simultaneous and to pursue related questions. The seemingly metahistorical question about historical structures of time has again and again proved relevant to concrete research questions. Among these, there also belongs

d) the interpretation of *historical conflicts*. Historical processes are driven forward only so long as the conflicts inherent in them cannot be solved.

As soon as a conflict dissolves, it belongs to the past. A historical theory of conflicts can be sufficiently developed only by bringing out the temporal qualities inherent in the conflict. In historiography, conflicts are usually dealt with by introducing opponents as stable subjects, as fixed entities whose fictive character can be recognized: "Hitler" and "Hitler within us."

The historical subject is an almost inexplicable quantity. Think of any famous personality or of the "people," which is no less vague than "class"; think of the economy, the state, the church, and other such abstract entities or powers. Perhaps only in psychological terms can we understand how "effective forces" come about and how they are reduced to subjects. If one applies the temporal question to such subjects, they dissolve very quickly, and it turns out that intersubjective connections are the proper topic of historical research. Such connections, however, can be described only in a temporal way. The desubstantialization of our categories leads to a temporalization of their meaning. Thus the scale of past or future possibilities can never be outlined on the basis of a single modality or unit of action or from one unit of action. Such a scale refers, rather, to that of one's opponents. Therefore only temporal differences, refractions, or tensions can express the trend toward a new structuring of reality. In this way different temporal relations and factors of acceleration and delay unexpectedly come into play.

When one thematizes long, average, and short periods of time, it is difficult to establish causal relationships between the temporal layers thus singled out. We recommend working with hypotheses that introduce constant factors, against which variables can be measured. This does not prevent us from seeing the constant factors as themselves dependent on variables or other constant factors. Such historical relativism, if well thought through, seems to lead to the functional method. This method excludes infinite regress. Once temporal differences among the intersubjective connections have been thematized, it is difficult to hold on to the supposedly scientific character of causal chains, on whose basis we are accustomed to interrogate the past so as finally to arrive at the absurdity of linear questions of origin. Perhaps lines of direct derivation from past pregivens hide a secularized derivative of the Christian doctrine of creation, living on undetected.

In the course of nineteenth-century research, the categories of spontaneity, of historical uniqueness, and of historical forces, which were originally designed with an eye to genuine historical time, became bound up in substances such as personality, the people, class, certain states, and so on.

This made possible historically naive statements at which we smile today. Nevertheless, there is a hidden difficulty here as well. Though I am not in a position to evaluate it, I would like to direct attention to it. I mean

e) *temporal series.* Schumpeter once said that one can only make historically meaningful statements if there is a possibility of comparison in sufficient temporal depth. Comparisons based on temporal series, however, presuppose a subject conceived as being continuous. Only when measured against such a subject can changes be discernible at all.

I feel that these subjects, thought to be continuous, should be introduced only hypothetically. Here I would invoke the New Economic History. What is exciting about these researchers' view of history, in my opinion—if I judge the work of Fogel correctly—is that they gain genuinely historical insights via theoretical premises that are not characteristic of our discipline. Fogel once presented calculations based on his theories that refute the argument that slave labor in the United States was economically unprofitable before the outbreak of the Civil War. The number sequences were verified empirically, and they indicate that the efficiency of black labor rose in relation to westward migration. Through such an insight, the moral significance of liberal propaganda gains a tremendous weight *per negationem,* for the purely moral argument that no human being must be a slave increases in conclusiveness to the degree that the supposed economic proof loses power (a proof that the liberals, of course, also used in a subsidiary fashion).

This is an example of how determinable phenomena emerge more clearly thanks to a theory that excludes certain data from consideration. Moreover, excluding certain questions under certain theoretical premises makes it possible to find answers that would otherwise not have come up: a clear proof of the need for theory in our discipline. If one supposes the necessity of forming theories—and such theories must not be restricted to temporal structures—it follows from previous examples that we must become aware of the hypothetical character of our method. This will be demonstrated by way of further examples, which can instruct us about the naive use of historical categories and about the similarly naive criticism of these categories.

f) Our discipline works under a tacit presupposition of *teleology.* We all know a book that is disreputable today, Treitschke's history of Germany in the nineteenth century.[1] In this book, Treitschke presented the glorious path of Prussian history, which led to the unity of the German Reich, ex-

cluding Austria. In so doing, Treitschke deployed a teleology that organized and oriented the wealth of his recorded references, like a magnet.
The unity of the German Reich, excluding Austria, was the premise ex post
facto under which he read his sources. In this, he openly admitted that his
statements were conditioned by his position. And in the preface, he made
clear that he intended to show that everything had to happen the way it
did and that those who had not comprehended this yet could learn it from
his book. Three theorems are contained in this bundle of statements:

1. The teleological principle as the regulating idea of his statements
   and as the organizing principle for the selection of sources;
2. Consciously admitted positionality; and
3. The historical-philosophical certainty with which Treitschke
   claimed to have history pure and simple on his side.

He thus wrote a history of victors who, on the basis of their own success, reproduce world history as the Last Judgment. These three theorems
—knowing history to be on one's side, the teleological principle as a regu-
lative idea of analyzing sources, and the historian's positionality—cannot
be tackled as easily as someone who accuses Treitschke of bias or nationalism might believe.

If every historian remains rooted in his situation, he will be able to
make only observations that are framed by his perspective. These, however,
evoke final causes. A historian can hardly escape them, and if he disregards
them he relinquishes the reflection that teaches him about what he is doing.
The difficulty does not so much lie in the *final causality* deployed but in
naively accepting it. It is possible to come up with as many causes as one
wishes for any event that ever took place in the course of history. There is no
single event that could not be explained causally. Whoever gets involved in
causal explanations will always find reasons for what he wishes to demonstrate. In other words, causal derivations of events do not themselves contain any criteria for the correctness of the statements about them. Thus
Treitschke, too, was able to come up with proofs for his theses. If one reads
the same sources from different angles today, Treitschke's political position
will be found to be outdated, but its theoretical premise, which triggered the
causality he was searching for, will not. We must keep this reservation in
mind when we seek to reject explanations of final causality in an ideological-
critical way.

Any history, because it is ex post facto, is subject to final constraints. It is impossible to do without them. Yet one can escape the schema of causal addition and narrative arbitrariness only by introducing hypotheses that, for example, bring into play past possibilities. Put differently, perspectivism is tolerable only if it is not stripped of its hypothetical and, therefore, revisable character. Stated more concisely: everything can be justified, but not everything can be justified by anything. The question of which justifications are admissible and which are not is not only a matter of the sources at hand, but above all a matter of the hypotheses that make these sources speak. The relationship between the circumstances, the selection, and the interpretation of the sources can only be clarified by a theory of possible history and, therefore, a possible discipline of history.

Chladenius was probably the first to reflect upon *positionality* as a premise of our research. He wrote a theory of the discipline of history, which, although it was conceived before historicism, contains many ideas that surpass Droysen's historics. Because of its dry and didactic language, it has unfortunately not yet been republished, but it remains a treasury of insights untouched by historicism. Chladenius defined all historical statements as reductive statements about a past reality. "A narrative completely abstracted from one's own point of view is impossible." But Chladenius did not historically relativize point of view or regard the formation of judgments as subject to revision. Consequently, he believed that he could discern a reality congealed within past objects. Statements about such a reality were, in his opinion, however, necessarily subject to rejuvenation, given that no past totality could completely be reproduced. The expression "rejuvenated" is already conceived in temporal terms and is no longer spatial. For Chladenius, what is "young" is what is present, and the past is interrogated from this epistemological-formal perspective of progress. History becomes visible only through the lens of the present. Such a teleology dispenses with a criterion of direction that points toward the future, as it is sought within the horizon of the philosophy of history.

The third theorem that Treitschke brought into play, namely, having history on his side, is an ideological fiction. This fiction thrives on the category of *necessity*, which Treitschke tacitly introduces in order to represent as inevitable the course of German history to the point at which the German Reich excluded Austria. The determination of necessity hides a flat tautology, which is not only deployed by Treitschke but by any historian who refers to it. Identifying an event as necessary amounts to a double statement about that event. Whether I say that something happened or whether I say that it happened by necessity is identical from an ex post facto perspective. Something did not happen more so only because it had to happen. By making a statement about an event and by adding that it had to have happened, I vindicate for this event a necessary causal chain— a necessity that in the end derives from the omnipotence of God, in whose place the historian is acting.

Put differently, the category of necessity continuously obscures the necessity of forming hypotheses, which alone can allow for causal chains. We can risk making statements of necessity insofar as we formulate them with reservations. Cogent reasons can be devised only within the framework of hypothetically introduced premises. This does not exclude the possibility that different ways of asking questions will bring into view completely different causes. Correctness in interpreting sources is not only assured by the source data but, first of all, by making the question concerning possible history theoretically evident.

Thus teleological questions and the questioner's positionality cannot be eliminated; rather, any statement about reality involving a claim of necessity is subject to our critique. This critique refers to temporal determinations: it is directed against the uniqueness and the unidirectionality of historical processes, which in some respect are a secularized derivative of providence, of a providence that for us remains hidden in the declaration of urgent necessity. A theory of periodization that is adequate to the complex historical reality requires multilayered statements.

g) This leads to the well-known discussion about (vulgar) Marxist *monocausality*, a discussion in which Western historians often congratulate themselves on their own superiority. The charge that history cannot be interpreted in a monocausal way, however, can easily be reversed. Whether I introduce one cause, two, five, or an infinite amount of causes says nothing at all about the quality of my historical reflections. A monocausal schema permits statements that are very reasonable from a hypothetical point of view. Let me call to mind the works of Schöffler; their insights often rest upon monocausal explanations—which is the very source of their fruitfulness and their surprising accuracy. When Marxists offer monocausal constructions—for example, when they indicate dependencies of the "superstructure" upon the "base structure"—this is a legitimate procedure of hypothesis formation. The real objection that can be raised against Marxists is not to be found in monocausality as a possible historical category but, first, in the facts that they use this category naively (though precisely on this point they agree with many of our historians); and, second and more importantly, that they are often forced to formulate their statements upon command and are not allowed to question them critically. Properly seen, the objection against monocausality is an objection against blindness to hypotheses; on a different methodical level, it is also directed against any subjection to political directives. The reflection on positionality and the determination of goals is thus politicized and eludes scholarly verification. This touches on a tricky problem; everyone is familiar with the ambiguous ground on which, for example, Communist historiography operates as a discipline. Yet we must keep in mind, with regard to Marxist problematics, party-political ties and the compulsion both to change one's goals (when the situation changes) and to self-criticism. I come thus to my concluding section.

3. The Communist camp has the specific political advantage of a continuous reflection on the relationship between *theory and practice* in scholarly work. However valid objections against the control of historiographical guidelines by party politics in Marxist countries may be, every historiography does in fact perform a function within the public sphere.

Yet we must distinguish between the political *function* that a discipline serves and the particular political *implication* that it may or may not have. Thus the pure natural sciences do not have any political implications if judged by their subject matter: their results are universally communicable, and, taken by themselves, they are apolitical. That does not preclude the fact that the political function of these sciences—let me call to mind the utilization of nuclear physics or of biochemistry—can be far more influential than that of the humanities or the social sciences. The discipline of history, by contrast, always performs a political function, albeit a changing one. Depending on whether it is conducted as church, legal, or court history, whether it is political biography, universal history, or something else, its social place changes, as does the political function exercised by the results it achieves as an academic discipline. The political implications of historical research are not adequately determined in this way, however. They depend on the kinds of questions posed by a given line of research. However trivial it may sound, one must bear in mind that topics in music history, for instance, do not involve political questions in the same way as do topics in diplomatic history. Not even the ideological reduction of historical activity to political interests can substitute for the disciplinary evidence of a given method and the results thereby achieved. Political function and political implications are not enough. Those who blur the distinction transform history into lessons in ideology and deprive it of its critical task, a function it may (but need not) have as a discipline.

Turning away from our initial question about the theoretical premises that guide us on our path to the sources, the question of how dependent we are on forming hypotheses, let us take a path that leads from our sources back into the public sphere. Marxist reflection always takes this path into consideration, whereas in our profession it is followed for the most part naively or merely verbally invoked. Here, we take on the worn-out issue of didactics, which can certainly be discussed scientifically, in a way analogous to our specialized research. I assume that we can talk meaningfully about the didactics of history only if history as a discipline uncovers its own theoretical premises. The discontent with history as a school subject might then turn out to have the same roots as the lack of a capacity for theoretical reflection that characterizes our discipline. Stated positively, if we accept the compulsion to do theory, didactic consequences that "didactics" itself is unable to locate will impose themselves.

Although we have refined and mastered our philological-historical tools over a century and a half, historians all too easily let their path from the sources to the public sphere be mapped out for them by particular constellations of power. Precisely the great successes achieved on the positivistic level served to encourage an arrogance that has been especially susceptible to national ideologies.

The path from research into the sources back toward the public sphere has different ranges: in the university, it remains comparatively close to research; at school, it leads further away; at a greater distance, it reaches the public sphere of our political spaces of action; it finally extends to the public in the global sphere of addressees of historical statements.

Here we must remember that historical statements can reproduce past states of affairs only in a reductive or rejuvenated way, for it is impossible to restore the totality of the past, which is irrevocably gone. Strictly speaking, the question of "how it really was" can only be answered if one assumes that one does not formulate *res factae* but *res fictae*. If it is no longer possible to restore the past as such, then I am forced to acknowledge the fictive character of past actualities so as to be able to theoretically safeguard my historical statements. Any historical statement is a reduction if measured against the infinity of a past totality that is no longer accessible to us as such. In the vicinity of a naive-realistic naively realist theory of knowledge, any compulsion toward reduction is a compulsion to lie. However, I can dispense with lying once I know that the compulsion toward reduction inherently belongs to our discipline. In addition, this both involves a political implication and allows didactics to gain a legitimate place within the realm of the historical discipline. We must ask ourselves continually what history means, what it can be and what it is supposed to be for us today: at the university, at school, and in the public sphere. This is not to say that research activity ought to have its aims prescribed from the outside in political and functional terms, but we should always be aware of the specific political implications that our field of research does or does not have, and of the propositional form that we must develop accordingly. Then we can better define the political function that history has or ought to have on the basis of the discipline of history itself. It is important to dissolve the aporia of historicism—its adherents were convinced that one could not learn anything from histories any more, even though the discipline of history counted as teaching. For this reason, I would like to bring out four *practical consequences* of the previous considerations:

(a) The types of systematic questions concerning "historicity" mentioned at the beginning and the demand for a historics directly lead to today's methodological dispute within the discipline of sociology. Methodologically, the compulsion to form hypotheses, once it has been articulated, moves the discipline of history closer to the social sciences in general—closer, that is, than has perhaps been recognized so far. In any case, it appears to me that the commonalities go so far as to suggest combining *social studies (Gemeinschaftskunde)* and *history lessons (Geschichtsunterricht)* in school.

(b) The supposed wealth of historical material and the difficulties of theoretical premises concerning it discussed above both suggest studying the discipline of history as a *single major*. This is not to say that minors are to be dispensed with. Rather, minors ought to be studied for the very reason that they offer different theoretical approaches, but as *subsidiary* and *complementary subjects*, which are of particular benefit to historical questions. Foreign languages are certainly subsidiary subjects of this kind, and so are linguistics, law, and economics, or any other subjects that promote specialization within the subject area of history and, above all, widen the angle of vision.

For schools, this would mean that such subsidiary subjects could nonetheless be subjects for teaching. Why, for instance, should French be taught only by philologists but not—for a certain stretch—also by historians of French constitutional history or by experts on political or philosophical texts in the French language?

At the university level, all minors would accordingly be utilized in different ways, which would be subsidiary or complementary to the respective majors. Foreign languages for history majors would have to be taught differently to some degree; instead of remaining truncated majors (which they are), foreign language instruction would need to specifically thematize historical or sociological types of questions.

Conversely, history as a subsidiary subject for a student of linguistics ought not to be taught as merely a thinned-down extract from Plötz [a standard reference work for historians]. Bridges ought to be built in interdisciplinary tutorials and discussion sections. Only experiment can succeed here.

(c) A further practical consequence results from the theory of periodization alluded to above. Neither a course of study determined by chronological sequences, which lives by filling in their gaps, nor the triad of introductory seminars in ancient, medieval, and modern history, which is derived from a mythical schema, is methodologically cogent. Furthermore, thus far professorships have been organized in a way that stems from the humanistic myth of Cellarius, which is no guarantee of its correctness.

In addition, the purpose of a university degree required for the teaching profession must not be prescribed in political and functional terms— by reference to didactics—from the outside; rather, this purpose can only be defined anew by adhering to the necessity of theory formation in our discipline. So long as the still customary three introductory seminars differ only in terms of the areas of linear chronology studied and their respective means of analysis, their organization will remain implausible. The sequence of ancient, medieval, and modern history plus "contemporary history" is legitimated neither by the general historical-philological method that they share nor by a theory of different temporal levels. The necessity of forming hypotheses is also common to all three areas. In accordance with ongoing planning at Bielefeld University, let me therefore suggest a new *canon of undergraduate education.*

A first course ought to serve as an introduction into the historical-philological methodology that interprets sources from all time periods comparatively. Continual use of the same method would be conducive to identifying differences in source and temporal conditions in a particularly clear way.

A second course could be defined as a seminar on "analyzing problems" (Blumenberg). Here it would be important to develop a wealth of historical questions that cannot be derived from the sources directly; answering them would require that information and hypotheses from all areas of the social sciences be consulted.

It goes without saying that both introductory courses will need to be planned in conjunction; they could be merged in practice.

In a third—elective—introductory course, it would be important to acquire the knowledge base and the fundamental principles of a subject that is subsidiary or complementary to the discipline of history. This would be the place to prepare for future specialization in ancient and medieval history, for example, by studying Greek or Latin literature and linguistics. It would also be the place to begin studying other, auxiliary disciplines, depending on the main emphasis of one's interests. Statistics, economics, or an introduction to jurisprudence might be recommended as subjects to complement modern history. Obviously there would be an infinite number of possible combinations. It remains crucial that the subsidiary or complementary subject contain its own theory and also its own systematics, and that it not be exclusively shaped by historical-philological methodology. The refraction of different questions constitutes the stimulation in this third introductory course. To me, it seems inevitable that such a program can only be fulfilled if the discipline of history is studied as the only major, if subsidiary subjects are also tested in oral examinations, and if they become subjects that can be taught in schools. Our theoretical considerations have thus led us quite informally to a new canon of undergraduate education that does not abolish the traditional topics of teaching but reconfigures them in a disciplinary and didactic way.

(d) A final conclusion results from didactic considerations themselves. It aims at what is often evoked as *exemplary teaching* and concerns the ways in which such teaching can be accomplished academically and in terms of personnel policies. Exemplary teaching concerns not only the issue of developing examples for past situations, conditions, or epochs but also the task of making teaching exemplary for us as well. In order to grasp the double-sidedness of exempla—namely, being exemplary both for something and for us, we need to go back before German Idealism, which has distorted exemplarity in a philosophical-historical way.

The question of meaningful selection continues to impose itself. Examples of social-historical and structural-historical phenomena for teaching cannot be sought on a short-term basis. Here, schools and universities must complement each other. It is important to stimulate the interaction between schools and universities, and it appears to me that no one is more suited for this than the secondary-school teacher who is teaching in a university. These schoolteachers ought not to form a nonprofessorial teaching staff, which is the worst of all possible solutions. Rather, such teachers really ought to be able to come from schools and also return there or, upon proof of their academic qualifications, be able to change over altogether to university teaching or to adult education in general. Secondary-school teachers at universities ought to do both at the same time: teach school at half load and teach at the university by conducting two- to four-hour seminars. Disciplinary and didactic questions could then be blended together. Thus, an osmosis between schools and universities would be established, which would prevent a new, negative type of professorship from forming among the nonprofessorial teaching staff when old full professors retire. The real threat is not the democracy of secondary-school teachers, but the democracy of secondary-school teachers already looming behind plans for an integrated university (*Gesamthochschule*). Secondary-school teachers who alternate between teaching at a university and teaching school certainly produce conflicts in social status and prestige, but it seems more important to me that we face difficulties where they actually emerge instead of insisting on total solutions whose very wording is suspicious.

Translated by Kerstin Behnke

2

Social History and Conceptual History

Anyone who is concerned with history—whatever this may be—and defines it as social history is obviously delimiting his topic. Anyone who specifies history as conceptual history is obviously doing the same. Nevertheless, the two definitions are not the usual delimitation of special histories within a general history. The economic history of England, for example, or the diplomatic history of the early modern age or the church history of the West are special topics of such a kind, predetermined as worthy of investigation via their subject matter, time period, and region. In such cases, we are dealing with special aspects of general history.

Social history and conceptual history are different. On the basis of their theoretical self-justification, they make a general claim, one that can be extended and applied to all special histories. All history deals with intersubjective relationships, with forms of sociability or with social stratifications; therefore, the characterization of history as social history makes an enduring, irrefutable, and, so to speak, anthropological claim that lies concealed behind any form of historiography. And which history would not have to be comprehended as such before it congeals into history? Investigating concepts and their linguistic history is as much a part of the minimal condition for recognizing history as is the definition of history as having to do with human society.

Historical Retrospective

Both social history and conceptual history have existed as explicit modes of questioning since the Enlightenment and the discovery of the historical world it included, that is, since the time when previous social formations became porous and linguistic reflection also came under pressure to change from a history that was being experienced and articulated as something new. Anyone who follows the history of historical reflection and historical representation since then encounters both approaches again and again, whether they explicate one another, as in Vico, Rousseau, and Herder, or whether they exist in isolation from one another.

The claim to reduce all historical utterances concerning life and all changes in them to social conditions and to derive them from such conditions was asserted from the time of the Enlightenment philosophies of history up to Comte and the young Marx. Such claims were followed by histories that, methodologically speaking, employed a more positivistic approach: from histories of society and civilization, to the cultural and folk histories of the nineteenth century, up to regional histories that encompassed all aspects of life, from Möser to Gregorovius to Lamprecht, their synthetic achievement can aptly be called social-historical.

By contrast, since the eighteenth century there have also been deliberately thematized conceptual histories (*Begriffsgeschichten*)[1]—the term apparently derives from Hegel—which have retained a permanent place in histories of language and in historical lexicography. Of course, they were thematized by disciplines that proceeded in a historical-philological manner and needed to secure their sources via hermeneutic questioning. Any translation into one's own present implies a conceptual history; Rudolf Eucken has demonstrated its methodological inevitability in an exemplary fashion for the humanities and all the social sciences in his *Geschichte der philosophischen Terminologie.*[2]

In practical research, reciprocal references that bring together social-historical analyses or analyses of constitutional history together with questions of conceptual history are ubiquitous. Their mutual connection, more or less reflected upon, has always been present in the disciplines concerned with antiquity and in research on the Middle Ages: especially where minimal sources are available, no fact can be recognized without taking into account the manner of its former and present conceptual assimilation. Obviously, the reciprocal interlacing of social and conceptual history was systematically explored only in the 1930s; we are reminded of Walter Schlesinger and, above all, of Otto Brunner. In neighboring fields, Erich Rothacker was a similar force in philosophy, as was Carl Schmitt in jurisprudence and Jost Trier in linguistics.

In the political aspects of research, social and conceptual history were conjoined against two very different tendencies, both dominant in the 1920s. On the one hand, there was a parting with concepts concerning the history of ideas and of spirit (*ideen- und geistesgeschichtliche*), which were pursued outside a concrete sociopolitical context—for their own sakes, as it were. On the other hand, history ceased to be regarded as primarily a political history of events, and instead its longer-lasting presuppositions were investigated.

As Otto Brunner emphasized in the second edition of *Land und Herrschaft*,[3] he wanted "to ask about the concrete presuppositions of medieval politics, without, however, representing it itself." He sought to focus on long-term structures of social conditionality (*Verfaßtheit*) and changes in these—which were never merely of the moment—doing so by thematizing particular linguistic self-articulations of social groups, associations, or strata and the history of their interpretation. It is no accident that the *Annales*, which emerged from an analogous research interest, established in 1930 the rubric "Things and Words." For Lucien Febvre and Marc Bloch, linguistic analysis was an integral part of social-historical research. In Germany, Gunther Ipsen did pathbreaking work in modern history by complementing his social-historical, specifically demographic investigations with linguistic research. All these ideas were taken up by Werner Conze when he founded the Workshop for Modern Social History in 1956–57.[4] Thanks to Conze's initiative, conjoining social-historical and conceptual-historical questions became one of its enduring challenges, as did the differential determination between them, which will be the topic of the following pages.

The Impossibility of an "Histoire Totale"

There is no history without societal formations and the concepts by which they define and seek to meet their challenges, whether reflexively or self-reflexively; without them, it is impossible to experience and to interpret history, to represent or to recount it. In this sense, society and language belong to the metahistorical premises without which *Geschichte* and *Historie* are unthinkable. Social-historical and conceptual-historical theories, questions, and methods thus refer to all possible areas within the discipline of history. Thus, too, the wish to conceive a "total history" occasionally sneaks in. Though for pragmatic reasons the empirical investigations of social or conceptual historians concern limited topics, this self-limitation does not lessen the claim to generality; it follows from a theory of possible history, which must presuppose society and language.

Social-historical and conceptual-historical approaches necessarily proceed in an interdisciplinary fashion, because they work within specializations that are methodologically mandated. It does not follow from this, however, that their theoretical claim to generality could be posited as absolute or total. It is true that they operate under the constraint of having to presuppose the totality of societal relations, as well as their linguistic articulations and systems of interpretations. But the formally irrefutable premise that all history has to do with society and language does not allow the farther-reaching conclusion that it would be possible, so far as content is concerned, to write a "total history" or even to conceive it.

As numerous and plausible as the empirical objections against a total history are, an objection against its possibility follows from the very attempt to make it conceivable. The *totum* of a social history and the *totum* of a linguistic history can never be completely projected onto one another. Even if we make the empirically unrealizable assumption that both areas could be thematized as a finitely delimited totality, there would remain an unbridgeable difference between any social history and the history of comprehending it.

Linguistic comprehension does not catch up with what takes place or what actually was the case, nor does anything occur without already being changed by its linguistic assimilation. Social history (*Sozialgeschichte oder Gesellschaftsgeschichte*) and conceptual history stand in a reciprocal, historically necessitated tension that can never be canceled out. What you do will only be told to you by the following day; and what you say becomes an event by eluding you. What occurs interpersonally or socially and what is said during that event or about it gives rise to a constantly changing difference that renders any *histoire totale* impossible. History takes place in the anticipation of incompleteness; any interpretation that is adequate to it therefore must dispense with totality.

Characteristically, historical time again and again reproduces the tension between society and its transformation, on the one hand, and its linguistic processing and assimilation, on the other. Any history lives by this tension. Social relations, conflicts, their solutions, and their changing presuppositions are never congruent with the linguistic articulations by which societies act, comprehend, interpret, change, and reform themselves. This thesis can be tested on two counts: history occurring *in actu,* and history that has happened and is past.

History, Speech, and Writing As They Occur

When social history and conceptual history are referred to each other, the differential determination between them relativizes the claim of each to generality. History neither becomes resolved in the mode of comprehending it, nor is it conceivable without such comprehension.

The connection between everyday events is pregiven in an undifferentiated way, for humans, being endowed with language, are co-originary with their societal existence. How can this relation be determined? As they occur, individual events depend on linguistic facilitation; this is comparatively clear. No social activity, no political deal, and no economic trade is possible without accounting, without planning discussions, without public debates or secret talks, without commands—and obedience—without the consensus of those involved and the articulated dissent of conflicting parties. Any everyday history in its daily course is dependent on language in action, on talking and speaking, just as no love story is conceivable without at least three words—you, I, we. Any societal event in its manifold connections is based on advance communicative work and on the work of linguistic mediation. Institutions and organizations, from the smallest association to the United Nations, must depend on them, whether in oral or in written form.

As self-evident as this observation may be, it is equally self-evident that it must be qualified. What actually takes place is, obviously, more than the linguistic articulation that has led to the event or that interprets it. The command, the cooperative resolution, or the elemental cry to kill is not identical with the act of killing itself. Lovers' figures of speech are not resolved in the love that two people experience. The written rules of organization or their spoken modes of performance are not identical with an organization's acts.

There is always a difference between a history as it takes place and its linguistic facilitation. No speech act is itself the action that it helps prepare, trigger, and enact. Admittedly, a word often triggers irrevocable consequences; think of the Führer's command to invade Poland, to mention a striking example. But precisely in this case the relation becomes clear. A history does not happen without speaking, but it is never identical with it, it cannot be reduced to it.

For that reason, there must be further advance work and performative modes beyond spoken language in order for events to be possible. There is an area of semiotics that transcends language. Think of bodily gestures in which language communicates only in an encoded form; of magical rituals, including the theology of sacrifice, which has its historical place not in the word but on the cross; of modes of group behavior habituated by symbols or by modern traffic signs. All are matters of a sign language that is comprehensible without words. All of the signals mentioned can be verbalized. They can be reduced to language, but it is particular to them that one has to do without spoken language in order to trigger or control appropriate actions, attitudes, or modes of behavior through them. Let me call to mind further extralinguistic preconditions: spatial nearness or distance; distances that either harbor or delay conflict; temporal differences between age groups within a generation or due to the bipolarity of the sexes. All these differences contain in themselves events, conflicts, and reconciliations that are made possible prelinguistically, even if they can, but do not have to, take place by virtue of linguistic articulation.

There are thus extralinguistic, prelinguistic, and postlinguistic elements in all actions that lead to a history. They are closely attached to the elementary geographical, biological, and zoological conditions that, via the human constitution, all have an effect on societal events. Birth, love, and death; eating, hunger, misery, and diseases; perhaps happiness, but in any event robbery, victory, killing, and defeat—all are also elements and performative modes of human history, reaching from the everyday to the identification of political power structures. Their extralinguistic pregiven data are difficult to deny.

Certainly, the analytic distinctions made here can hardly be comprehended in the concrete context of the actions that constitute events. All prelinguistic pregiven data are linguistically recovered by human beings and are mediated in concrete conversation through their doings and sufferings. The spoken language or the writing that is read, the particular conversation that is effective—or overheard—intertwine in the topical performance of what happens to form an event that is always composed of extralinguistic and linguistic elements of action. Even if conversation ceases, linguistic preknowledge remains present—it is inherent in human beings and enables them to communicate with those confronting them, be they human beings or things, products, plants, or animals.

The more highly aggregated the human units of action—for instance, in modern processes of labor and their economic interconnections, or in the increasingly complex political spaces of action—the more important conditions of linguistic communication become for maintaining the ability to act. Linguistic mediation extends from the audible range of a voice through communication devices—writing, the printing press, the telephone, and broadcasting to the screen of a television set or a data processor—including the institutions of their modes of transmission, from the postman and print media to the news satellite, including the consequences that intervene in any linguistic codification. People have always tried either to fix the range of spoken language permanently or to expand and accelerate it so as to anticipate, trigger, or control events. This comment may suffice to demonstrate the intertwining of any social history and any conceptual history in their respective enactment of speaking and acting.

Spoken words, writing that is read, or events that take place cannot be separated *in actu* but can only be divided analytically. Someone who is overwhelmed by a speech will experience this not only linguistically but all over his body, and someone who is being silenced through an action will experience his dependence on language all the more, so as to be able to move again. This personal interrelation of speech and action can be transferred to all levels of the social units of action, which are becoming increasingly complex. The interrelation between "speech acts" and "actual" happenings ranges from individual instances of speaking and acting to the multiple social interrelations through which events, in all their interconnections, occur. Despite all historical variation, this finding constitutes any history that occurs, and it has considerable effects on the representation of past histories, especially on the difference between social history and conceptual history.

Represented History and Its Linguistic Sources

The empirical connection between action and speech, acting and speaking, as demonstrated so far, breaks up as soon as we shift our view back from the history occurring *in eventu* to past history, with which the professional historian deals *ex eventu*. The analytic separation between an extralinguistic and a linguistic level of action gains the status of an anthropological pregiven datum, without which no historical experience can be transferred into everyday or academic statements at all. What has happened, and has happened beyond my own experience, is something that I can experience merely by way of speech or writing. Even if language may—in part—have been only a secondary factor in the enactment of doings and sufferings, as soon as an event has become past, language becomes the primary factor without which no recollection and no scientific transposition of this recollection is possible. The anthropological primacy of language for the representation of past history thus gains an epistemological status, for it must be decided in language what in past history was necessitated by language and what was not.

In anthropological terms, any "history" constitutes itself through oral and written communication between generations that live together and convey their own respective experiences to one another. Only when, with the passing of older generations, the orally conveyed space of recollection melts away, does writing become the primary carrier of historical imparting. It is true that numerous extralinguistic remainders indicate past events and conditions: ruins left over from catastrophes; coins that are evidence of economic organization; buildings that bespeak communities, political rule, and services; streets that bespeak trade or war; agricultural landscapes that testify to age-long labor; monuments that testify to victory or death; weapons that indicate struggle; tools that indicate invention and use. These are all "relics" or "findings"—or images—that can testify to everything at the same time. Everything is processed by special historical disciplines. Certainly, what "actually" may have taken place can, beyond all hypotheses, only be guaranteed by oral and written records, that is, by linguistic evidence. Only at the linguistic sources does the path divide between what is to count as "linguistic" and what is to count as "actual" in the events of the past. Under this aspect, genres and their differentiations can be related anew to one another.

What belonged together, and how it did so, *in eventu* can only be determined by linguistic evidence *post eventum*; depending on how these linguistic records, this oral or written tradition, are handled, the most different genres move more closely together and others move apart.

Myths, fairy tales, dramas, epics, and novels all presuppose and thematize the original connection between speech and action, between suffering, speaking, and being silent. Only this making present of history as it occurs establishes a meaning that remains worthy of memory. All histories do just this, using true and fictitious utterances to do justice to events worth remembering or retrieving words congealed into writing that testify to the combination of speaking and acting.

Unmistakable situations bring about their own changes; behind them, something like "destiny" can appear. It remains a challenge for any self-interpretation and interpretation of the world to find them out and hand them down. In a more or less accomplished fashion, all memoirs and biographies belong to this genre; in the English language, they emphasize the interrelation between language and life—"Life and Letters." In addition, all histories that follow events in their immanent dynamics belong here. "He said this and did that; she said that and did something else; something surprising, something new followed from it that changed everything"—many works are structured according to this formalized schema, especially those, like histories of political events or of diplomacy, that make it possible to construct *in actu* the course of events by virtue of the state of the sources. Viewed as linguistic achievements, these histories enter into a series that ranges from myths to novels.[5] Only when they claim academic status do they depend on the authenticity—which needs to be checked—of the linguistic sources; these sources need to vouch for the interrelation of speech acts and actions, an interrelation that previously had to be presupposed.

What can be distinguished analytically, the prelinguistic from the linguistic, is brought together again "in analogy to experience" thanks to the work of language: it is the fiction of the (f)actual. Viewed in retrospect, what has actually taken place is only real in the medium of linguistic fiction. In contrast to the speech that acts in history as it takes place, language thus gains an epistemological primacy that urges it continuously to make decisions about the relationship between language and action.

When submitted to this alternative, some genres articulate themselves in a very one-sided way. There are annals, which only register results— namely, what happened, but not how it came to happen. There are handbooks and "narrative" works of history, which concern actions, successes, and failures, but not the words or utterances that led to them, only that great men act, or that highly stylized subjects of action become active in a speechless fashion, as it were: states or dynasties, churches or sects, classes or parties, or whatever else is hypostasized as a unit of action. Rarely, however, are linguistic patterns of identification investigated; without them, such units of action would not be able to act at all. Even where spoken speech or its written equivalents are included in the representation, linguistic evidence comes under ideological suspicion or is read only instrumentally with pre-given interests and evil intentions in mind.

Even investigations made from the perspective of the history of language, which primarily thematize the linguistic evidence itself, tend to refer it to a "real" history that must first itself be linguistically constituted. But the methodological difficulties of referring speaking and language to social conditions and changes, to which sociolinguistics in particular is exposed, cling to the aporia of having to constitute linguistically the field of objects of which they are about to speak, an aporia that is shared by all historians.

For that reason, the other extreme will also be found in the future: editing the linguistic sources as such, the written remains of formerly spoken or written utterances. The accident of tradition will then have thematized the difference between extralinguistic and linguistic action. And everywhere, it is the task of the good commentator to track down the sense of the document that could not be found at all without the differential determination of speech and facts.

Thus we have established three genres, which, given the alternative of speech act and actual act (*Tathandlung*) either refer to each other or, in the extreme case, are thematized separately. Epistemologically, a double task always falls upon language: it refers to the extralinguistic connections of events as well as—by doing so—to itself. Conceived historically, it is always self-reflexive.

Event and Structure—Speaking and Language

Although we have so far spoken only about history as it occurs and history as it has occurred, asking how speech and action relate to each other *in actu*, in a synchronic section, as it were, the question expands as soon as diachrony is thematized as well. Here, as in the relation of speaking and acting in the enactment of events, synchrony and diachrony cannot be separated empirically. The conditions and determinants that, in a temporal gradation of various depths, reach from the "past" into the present intervene in particular events just as agents "simultaneously" act on the basis of their respective outlines of the future. Any synchrony is *eo ipso* at the same time diachronic. *In actu*, all temporal dimensions are always intertwined, and it would contradict experience to define the "present" as, for instance, one of those moments that accumulate from the past into the future—or, conversely, that slip as intangible points of transition from the future into the past. In a purely rhetorical manner, all history could be defined as a permanent present in which past and future are contained—or as the continuous intertwining of past and future that makes any present constantly disappear. If we focus on synchrony, history deteriorates into a pure space of consciousness in which all temporal dimensions are contained at once, whereas if we focus on diachrony, the active presence of human beings would, historically speaking, have no space of action. This thought experiment is designed only to refer to the fact that the differential determination between synchrony and diachrony, introduced by Saussure, can everywhere be analytically of help without being able to do justice to the complexity of the temporal intertwinings in the history that is taking place.

With these reservations, we shall use the analytic categories of synchrony, which aims at the topical presentness of events, and diachrony, which aims at the temporal dimension of depth that is also contained in any topical event. Many presuppositions have a long-term or a medium-range effect—as well as a short-term one—on a history that is taking place. They delimit the alternatives of action by making possible or setting free only certain alternatives.

Characteristically, social history and conceptual history both, in ways however different, theoretically presuppose this connection. It is the link between synchronic events and diachronic structures that can be investigated historically. An analogous connection exists between spoken speech, synchronically, and the diachronically pregiven language that always takes effect in a conceptual-historical way. What happens is always unique and new, but never so new that social conditions, which are pregiven over the long term, will not have made possible each unique event. A new concept may be coined to articulate experiences or expectations that never existed before. But it can never be too new not to have existed virtually as a seed in the pregiven language and not to have received meaning from its inherited linguistic context. The two lines of research thus broaden the indispensable diachronic dimensions, variously defined, of interplay between speaking and acting within which events occur, and without which history is neither possible nor conceivable.

A series of examples can elucidate this. Marriage is an institution that, regardless of its prelinguistic biological implications, is a cultural phenomenon with numerous variants across the history of humanity. Since it is a form of sociality between two or more human beings of different genders, marriage belongs among genuinely social-historical research topics. At the same time, obviously one can talk about it in a social-historical manner only when written sources inform us about various kinds of marriages and the ways in which they have been conceptualized.

Two methodological approaches can be constructed, in the simplified form of a model. One is primarily directed at events, at acts of speech, writing, and action; the other is primarily directed at diachronic presuppositions and their long-term changes. The latter approach seeks to find social structures and their linguistic equivalents.

1. This way, an individual event can be thematized: for instance, the marriage ceremony of a ruler, about which dynastic sources offer us ample information, including the political motives that were in play, the nature of the contractual conditions, the kind of dowry that was negotiated, the way in which the ceremonies were organized, and suchlike. The course of this marriage can also be reconstructed and narrated anew, including the sequence of events, up to such terrible consequences as when, for instance, following the death of a spouse, the contractually determined inheritance led to a war of succession. Today an analogous, concrete history of a marriage can also be reconstructed from the circle of people making up its subhistories—an exciting topic in the history of the everyday, which uses numerous sources that have not been deployed before. Both concern unique, individual histories, which may contain some unparalleled suspense between happiness and misery, and which both remain embedded in their religious, social, and political contexts.

2. Social history and conceptual history cannot manage without such individual cases, but it is not their primary interest to investigate them. To characterize the second methodological approach—again, in a model-like simplification—both focus on the long-term conditions that are effective

diachronically and that make possible each individual case. Both inquire into the long-term occurrences that can be derived from the sum of individual cases. Put differently, they inquire into the pregiven linguistic conditions under which such structures have entered into social consciousness and under which they have been comprehended and also changed.

Let us first follow specifically social-historical and then specifically conceptual-historical modes of procedure.

The synchrony of individual marriage ceremonies and of the speeches and letters exchanged in connection with them is not omitted by social history. Rather, it is embraced diachronically. Thus, for example, numbers of weddings can be statistically ascertained from the perspective of social-historical questions so as to prove population increases for each social stratum. Questions to be asked include: When did the number of weddings expand beyond the number of the houses and farms pregiven by estates that had a specified amount of food? How can the number of weddings be related to wage and price graphs, to good and bad harvests, so as to make it possible to weigh the economic and natural factors relating to the reproduction of the population? How can numbers of marital and extramarital births be related to each other so as to measure social situations of conflict? How do numbers of births and deaths of children, mothers, and fathers relate to each other, so as to explain long-term changes in "typical" married life? How does the graph of divorces run, allowing us to draw conclusions about the typical marriage? All these questions, which have been singled out almost at random, have in common that they help construct "actual" long-term occurrences that are not directly contained as such in the sources.

Laborious preparatory work must be done to render source statements comparable in order to aggregate series of numbers from them, and systematic reflection is needed, both beforehand and afterwards, to interpret the aggregated series of data. Longer-term structural statements cannot be derived directly from the linguistic sources. The sum of the concrete individual cases that occur synchronically and that are verified is itself mute and unable to "verify" long-term, medium-range, or in any way diachronic structures. In order to derive permanent statements from past history, preparatory theoretical work and the employment of a subject-specific disciplinary terminology are necessary. These alone enable one to track connections and interrelations that could not yet have been perceptible to the people affected by them.

What has "actually"—and not linguistically—occurred in history in the long term remains an academic construction, viewed in social-historical terms; evidence for it depends on the plausibility of the underlying theory. Any theoretically based statement must submit to methodological control by the sources in order to claim past actuality, but the reality of long-term factors cannot be sufficiently justified on the basis of individual sources. For that reason, ideal types can be formed, following Max Weber, for instance; they combine various criteria of describing reality in such a way that the connections that are to be presupposed can be interpreted with consistency. To take a case from our series of examples, it is possible to develop typical marriage and family trajectories for peasants and those below them, together with the average number of births and deaths, in correlation with wage and price series or with the sequence of crop failures, working hours, and the tax burden, to determine how marriage and family trajectories at the peasant level can be distinguished from those at lower levels, and how both changed in the transition from the preindustrial age to the industrial age.

The factors in individual cases, not the cases themselves, can then be structured in such a way that the economic, political, and natural presuppositions—depending on the importance of the wage and price structure, the tax burden, or harvest results—become understandable for a marriage typical of a certain social stratum. Questions to be asked are: Which factors are homogeneous and for what period of time? When are they dominant and when recessive? The answers make it possible to determine time limits, periods, or thresholds of epochs, according to which the history of peasant marriages and of those below the peasant level can be organized diachronically.

So far our series of examples has been consciously selected for clusters of factors that allow primarily extralinguistic series of events to be structured diachronically and to be related to each other. Establishing them presupposes a social-historical theory. Aided by a subject-specific terminology (here that of demography, economics, and finance), it permits a determination of permanence and change that cannot be found in the sources as such. The theoretical claim thus grows in proportion with the distance it must keep from any "self-proclamation" of the sources so as to construct long-duration limits or typical societal forms.

Certainly, quite different clusters of factors than those mentioned so far also enter into the history of marriages posited as "typical." Such factors cannot be investigated without an interpretation of their linguistic self-articulation. We thus arrive at the conceptual-historical procedures required to distinguish between topical speech and its linguistic pregiven data, a distinction analogous to that between event and structure.

Theology and religion, law, custom, and tradition each posit the framework conditions for any concrete marriage that antedate the individual case diachronically and that generally outlast it. Altogether, institutionalized rules and patterns of interpretation establish and delimit the lebensraum of a marriage. In this way, "extralinguistic" patterns of behavior are also determined, but language remains the primary instance of mediation.

A marriage can neither be entered into nor conducted without certain linguistically articulated pregiven conditions (although their number and stringency are decreasing). These range from traditions to legal acts to sermons, from magic to the sacraments to metaphysics. What therefore needs to be investigated are the kinds of texts, of various social classifications, in which particular marriages have been conceptualized. These texts may have come into existence spontaneously, like diaries, letters, or newspaper reports, or, at the other extreme, they may have been formulated with a normative intent, as were theological treatises or juridical codifications and their interpretations. In all cases, language-bound traditions diachronically establish the life sphere of a possible marriage. And when changes become apparent, they do so only when the notion of marriage has been conceptualized anew.

The theological interpretation of marriage as an indissoluble institution ordained by God is dominant right into the eighteenth century; its main purpose is to preserve and propagate the human race. Depending on the rules that determined the prerogatives of particular social groups, a marriage was authorized only when the economic basis of the home was sufficient to feed and bring up children and to guarantee mutual spousal support. Thus numerous people were legally excluded from the prospect of marrying. As the nucleus of the home, marriage remained embedded within estate prerogatives. This changed in the wake of the Enlightenment, which in a new departure, dealt with marriage in the *Allgemeines Landrecht* in terms of contractual law. The economic tie was loosened, and the freedom of the spouses as individuals was so much expanded that divorce—which had been theologically prohibited—became permissible. The common law did not give up the theological determinations and those pertaining to estate prerogatives, but the concept of marriage—and this can only be registered by way of a conceptual history—shifted decisively in favor of greater freedom and self-determination for both spouses.

At the beginning of the nineteenth century, we finally find an entirely new concept of marriage. Theological justification is replaced by an anthropological self-justification; the institution of marriage is divested of its legal framework so as to give space to the moral self-realization of two loving people. The Brockhaus of 1820 emphatically celebrates this postulated autonomy and innovatively conceptualizes it as a marriage of love. With this, marriage loses its previous primary purpose of begetting children; the economic tie is cut; and Bluntschli later goes so far as to declare a marriage without love to be immoral. As such, it comes under the obligation of being dissolved.[6]

We have thus sketched out three conceptual-historical stages; each has structured the inherited normative economy of argumentation in different ways and innovatively altered its decisive points. Seen in terms of linguistic history, common law and romantic-liberal conceptual formations both had the character of an event. They affected the entire linguistic structure on whose basis marriages could be conceived. It was not that diachronically pregiven language as a whole had changed, but its semantics and a new linguistic pragmatics had been set free.

One cannot derive from the conceptual-historical procedure any history of the actual wedding ceremonies and marriages that may have occurred alongside this linguistic self-interpretation. The economic constraints stressed by the social-historical viewpoint continue to remain in force to restrict certain marriages, to make them more difficult, and to weigh them down. Even if the legal barriers were lowered, social pressures continued to remain in effect so as not to turn marriage for love into empirically the only, normal case. Certainly, much could be said in favor of the hypothesis that, in a case of temporal anticipation, as it were, the concept of the love marriage, once it was developed, found prospects for its realization that improved in the long term. Conversely, it cannot be denied that already before the romantic conceptual formation of the love marriage, love as an anthropologically pregiven datum had entered even into marriages that, being defined by estate prerogatives, do not mention it.

What follows, for determining the relationship between social history and conceptual history, is that they need each other and relate to each other, yet cannot ever be made to coincide. What, in the long term, was "actually" effective and did change cannot be completely derived from sources handed down in written form. That requires preparatory theoretical and terminological work. Yet what can be demonstrated, from the written records, as conceptual history involves the linguistically delimited space of experience and testifies to innovative ventures that might have registered or initiated new experiences. This, however, does not permit conclusions about an actual history. The difference between acting and speaking, which we have documented with reference to history as it takes place, also in retrospect prevents social "reality" from ever converging with history in its linguistic articulation. Even if speech acts and actual acts (*Tathandlungen*) remain intertwined in a synchronic section (which is itself an abstraction), diachronic change, which remains a theoretical construct, does not take place in the same temporal rhythms or temporal series with regard to "real history" and conceptual history. Reality might have changed long before the change was conceptualized, and concepts might likewise have been formed to set free new realities.

Yet there is an analogy between social history and conceptual history, to which I will refer in closing. What, in each case, takes place as unique in history as it occurs is possible only because presupposed conditions repeat themselves with a longer-term regularity. A wedding ceremony may be subjectively unique, but repeatable structures express themselves in it. The economic conditions of a wedding ceremony depend on harvest results, which vary every year, or on longer-term economic changes, or on the tax burden that disrupts planned budgets every month or every year (apart from the regular services required of the peasant population). All these presuppositions are effective only by virtue of regular, more or less steady repetition. The same is true for the social implications of a marriage ceremony, which can only be grasped in a specifically linguistic way. The pregiven data of traditions, of the legal setting and perhaps of theological interpretation—all these institutional bonds are only effective *in actu* by repeating themselves periodically. They change only slowly, but their structures of repetition do not break as a result. What is called "long duration" is only historically effective if the time of the events, unique in each case, contains repeatable structures whose speeds of transformation are different from those of the events themselves. The topic of all social history is contained in this interrelation, which is only insufficiently defined by "synchrony" and "diachrony."

The interrelation between topical speech and pregiven language is to be determined in an analogous, but not homogeneous fashion. When a concept, for instance that of "marriage," is used, experiences of marriage, which have a long-term effect and which have entered into the concept at and as its foundation, are linguistically stored in it. And the linguistic context, which is also pregiven, regulates the range of its semantic content. With any topical use of the word *marriage*, the linguistically determined pregiven data that structure its sense and its understanding repeat themselves. Here, too, linguistic structures of repetition are set free, yet also delimit the scope of speech. And any conceptual change that becomes a linguistic event occurs in the act of semantic and pragmatic innovation, which makes it possible to comprehend what is old in a different way and to understand in any way what is new.

Social history and conceptual history have different speeds of transformation and are based in distinguishable structures of repetition. Therefore, the academic terminology of social history remains dependent on the history of concepts, so as to access linguistically stored experience. And equally, conceptual history remains dependent on the results of social history, so as to keep in view the difference between vanished reality and its linguistic evidence, which can never be bridged.

Translated by Kerstin Behnke

3

Introduction to Hayden White's *Tropics of Discourse*

The theory of the discipline of history asks about the conditions of possible history. Two smaller questions are always contained in this question. What are the empirically verifiable conditions that have made possible and are making possible actually occurring history in its temporal extensions? This question aims at facts. The other question is directed toward the linguistic work undertaken by historians when they formulate and seek to answer questions of fact. In what ways do historians constitute their history (*Geschichte*) when they fix it, orally or in writing, and offer it to a circle of listeners or readers? In both cases—but from different perspectives—the questions concern the mediation of being and saying, happening and recounting, *Geschichte* and *Historie*.

During the last decades, the debate over theory within the historical profession has surely placed the emphasis more on the first—factual—question. This is understandable from the internal perspective of the discipline, for what could be more obvious for an academic institution than securing the general rules by which it marks out, competently and appropriately, its subject? Whatever the political occasions or ideological intentions that in the past provoked debate over theory in the discipline of history, its result has been disillusionment. No serious dispute can be aroused anymore over the idea that every narrated story (*erzählte Geschichte*), just like every explanatory, justifying, and thus represented history (*dargestellte Geschichte*), is implicitly or explicitly interwoven with or guided by theoretical premises.

Not the possibility but rather the kinds and applications of theory are in dispute. Accordingly, in Germany the debate over theory has primarily taken place in the medium of historical safeguarding in order to maintain or substantiate positions that have proven themselves in the context of previous research. We need only to think of names like Droysen and Jacob Burckhardt, Dilthey and Nietzsche, Marx and Max Weber, Simmel and Troeltsch to indicate the extent to which historicism, despite all the criticism, has still not been fundamentally left behind. The debates, given comparatively scant reception in the West, treated the writing of history (*Historie*), in terms of disciplinary theory, as just a special case. The same is true for the excitement that Hempel and Oppenheimer's all-embracing explanatory model triggered, and it is also true for the numerous effects that the work of analytic philosophy of language has had on all textual studies. Finally, the same holds true for the different tendencies of French structuralism, whether articulated in linguistic, anthropological, or even historical terms. In this context, the twelve essays that Hayden White offers us provide an auspicious point of entry from which to more intensively resume our disciplinary and theoretical disputes with Western positions.

Hayden White's primary interest is not the discipline of history (*Geschichtswissenschaft*) as a research discipline with its own methodology, nor is it primarily the writing of history (*Historie*) as a literary genre. Hayden White takes a step back, as it were, both chronologically and factually: chronologically back to rhetoric as an old grammar encompassing all types of texts and as an art of appropriating the world through language. Factually, White considers historical texts primarily as *texts*, regardless of their scholarly or artistic achievements. He investigates the linguistic constitution of human experience as such, insofar as it is reflected in all areas of the humanities (*Geisteswissenschaften*), as opposed, in German terminology, to the natural sciences (*Naturwissenschaften*). Hayden White's investigations primarily thematize works of historical theory and representation, but his approach reaches much further. He asks how the cultural treatment of historical experience is linguistically made possible at all. In this respect, his claim moves into proximity with Gadamer, for whom historics (*Historik*) is an ancillary case of general hermeneutics. And he also proceeds similarly to Hans Blumenberg, for whom the power of linguistic metaphors discloses experience and precedes all historical statements. Although neither author is referred to by Hayden White, we may nevertheless expect a link here.

By returning the writing of history (*Historie*) once again to its former definition as a part of rhetoric, White first of all gains a new systematic perspective. With regard to the linguistic appropriation of the world, this perspective includes texts of poetry, literature, philosophy, psychology, psychoanalysis—as well as texts of history (*Historie*). His own bold premise is that the linguistic conditions of possibility for experiencing the world are tropologically delimited. Investigated since Aristotle, Cicero, or Quintilian, figures of speech, which are in no way rationally imperative or logically cogent, open up horizons of interpretations that, according to Hayden White, reach far beyond syntactical figures. No matter what kinds of texts are in question, behind them, White argues, there are always prior tropological decisions. These concern regularities of linguistic articulation that at once open up as well as restrict patterns of interpretation in all imaginable historical situations, time and again, consciously or not, in a more or less encoded way. Hayden White turns the attention of his readers here, to where, according to him, key decisions occur. For example, he poses the question: Into what parts do historians split their subject matter, and which parts do they relate, and in what way, to each other? Or, he asks: How do parts relate to the whole, which parts are singled out as representative, or what is separated out, and in what way, in order to be able to be compared? Or he asks: How are temporal continuities and discontinuities established? All these preliminary questions arising in theory are tested by White in terms of the linguistic decisions out of which they arose. Knowingly or not, linguistic options always thus stand behind theoretical decisions. It is the pictorial nature of the figures of expression that prejudges supposedly pure theoretical concepts. Within the field of rhetoric, these figures can be traced back to the tropes of metaphor, metonymy, synecdoche, and irony. Hayden White does not merely scrutinize individual linguistic passages in order to track down such tropes; rather, he discerns patterns of interpretation in the prior tropological decisions that impregnate the entire text. This is valid regardless of the open question of whether language is implemented only instrumentally with regard to the author's intentions, or whether figures of language already unconsciously fix the possibility of thinking these intentions.

It is obvious that with this approach, the writing of history (*Historie*) moves together with all such texts concerning the transformation of experience into sense. And it is also obvious that, with this, the old Aristotelian division between history, poetry, and philosophy becomes invalid, or at least subject to scrutiny. Thus the frequent proposals to find a place for history between art and science reveal themselves as a spurious problem. Instead, in the fashion of the rhetorical tradition, White interrogates the historians, or to be more precise, their texts, as to how they can socially mediate their claim to truth. He does not ask himself the internal disciplinary question of whether historical statements are correct or incorrect, but rather insists that the linguistic achievement of a historical representation must rise to the societal challenge of being good and not bad, understandable and not incomprehensible. A historical statement is only meaningful when it speaks to its addressees in such a way that the otherness of past or foreign experiences can be integrated into their own experience.

In this respect, Hayden White appears to be near Theodor Lessing, who puts a subjective interpretation on the chaos of pregiven facts or data. But precisely here, White has gone a step farther methodologically. He shows how what is tropologically pregiven in a language—its traditional "figures," similes, and updatable comparisons—finitely delimit the boundless space of possible data. Even the so-called plot, presumably underlying the narrative treatment of a sequence of events, belongs to the conditions of possible mediation that facilitate the task of deriving meaning from historical statements in the first place. In this respect, White leaves the subjectivist interpretation behind in order to investigate the linguistic criteria of objectivization in whose wake the disciplinarity of history can be justified from a linguistic perspective. One of the intentions of White's essays is to achieve this.

Certainly, the objection can be raised that linguistic options, such as how a history (*Geschichte*) should be presented and interpreted, are only consequences of factual considerations formulated by historians in their work as scholars. Questions such as which pregiven historical experiences lead to which sort of theoretical conceptualizations, or which theoretical anticipations, in principle, constitute what kinds of interrelations among events, are resolved within the discipline according to the self-understanding of historians. This also determines what data are considered important at all in the explanation of remote or unexpected findings in order to extend meaning and derive an internally meaningful sense of connection from events. Hayden White is inclined to classify this question as secondary, and he is here both more skeptical of the theoretical claim of historians but also more certain with regard to the linguistic constitution of all representations of history. He aims at an analysis of, as it were, the normative patterns that possess a linguistically demonstrable status. Historians who refer to their theoretical explications as constitutive of their histories are thus pressed for an additional level of reflection. They are confronted with the question of whether there are not linguistic patterns of interpretation hidden behind their theoretical considerations; they think less about reflecting on these patterns because the execution of the representation itself is all too often classified as secondary by historians, in particular as a consequence of their research. Here, Hayden White steers against the self-understanding of the profession even though he levels many a polemic against a naive realism in historical epistemology, something by which present-day historians should hardly feel affected anymore.

In every case, in good humor and with hearty polemics, Hayden White makes it clear how quickly prior metaphorical decisions lead to the linguistic circle of communication before they have even been justified theoretically and scientifically. Whether a history (*Historie*) is developed causally or functionally, comprehensively or partially, whether it is primarily oriented toward comparisons or more toward individual differences—behind all these formalizable options, there always stands the pregiven, metaphorical potentiality of every linguistic articulation.

As already mentioned, the four linguistic figures that Hayden White examines are not only explanatory patterns for individual sentences but also for entire historical designs. Whether they are holistic or causal, materialistic or idealistic, can already be shown within language before a perspective of criticism of ideology, itself always remaining entangled in the linguistic patterns of interpretation, has to be applied. Thus it can definitely be the case that the theoretical self-assessment or critical perspective of an author in no way corresponds to the linguistic devices and forms of which he makes use.

Hayden White offers a metahistorical pluralism of linguistically facilitated interpretations of the world without thereby sinking into a historicizing relativism and without validating techniques of reduction based on criticism of ideology as final statements. In the end, his basic tenor stems from a humanistically conceived rhetoric, which examines how interpretations of the world can both mediate and facilitate political and ethical decisions.

As such, it becomes explainable why certain historians have been able to reach the status of classics: classics depend on the linguistic evidence with which historical experiences have been transformed into meaningful statements. Even if individual errors are detectable in the sphere of interpreted facts, historical (*historische*) texts can negotiate historical (*geschichtliche*) truths. Analogous to poetic or philosophical truths, these remain retrievable and worth discussing regardless of their origin and initial conditions.

Secondly, apart from the systematic approach, Hayden White also makes use of diachronic patterns of interpretation; he derives them from the temporal sequence in which figures of speech succeed each other. He is inclined to track down a temporal logic, beginning with the figure of strict metaphor, so as to let the figures of metonymy, followed by synecdoche, and finally, the figure of irony, emerge from it. In this respect, Piaget's developmental model of how children learn to appropriate the world, for example, is interpreted tropologically in the sequence mentioned above as a linguistic acquisition of experience and its enrichment. Even Foucault's periods, intended to be antihistorical, are converted into a meaningful, diachronic schematic order of events. Foucault is decoded as a legitimate heir to Western philosophy of history who, according to White, can under no circumstances only be read in post-historical or poststructuralist terms. And even Thompson's history of the English working class, consciously geared toward purely empirical considerations, is interpreted by White as a sequence testifying to the increasing self-awareness and power of reflection of acting subjects within society. Prudently, Hayden White leaves open the question of to what extent Thompson himself projected a linguistic pattern of interpretation onto the historical stages of the English workers' movement, or (and what would empirically be a harder thesis to argue) whether he in fact empirically confirmed the stages of increasing self-awareness corresponding to the alternating tropological figures of speech.

Thus, interpretations of history are not just composed of the free choice between always available linguistic options but are instead subject to a sequential constraint of metaphorical language. This interpretation, made plausible with reference to Vico, definitely adds a historical thesis to the systematic one, which recognizably approaches Hegel. Certainly, the question remains to be answered whether the sequence of social, cultural, and political facts, conflicts, and changes leads to processes in the so-called sphere of subject matter that can be interpreted as analogous to sequential patterns intrinsic to language. To be sure, Hayden White is more cautious here than in his systematizing approach. However the difference between so-called actual history and its interpretation is determined, the determination of the difference itself can only be made by linguistic means. Whatever the content of the factual theories brought forward by historians, Hayden White offers them a linguistic metatheory. There may still be no science of historiography as a factual genre; however, there is a linguistically justifiable metahistory. In these exaggerated terms, one could outline Hayden White's position. He does not go so far in this respect as the French poststructuralists who want to dispose of the historical (*historische*) text as a historical (*geschichtliche*) mediator of truth. According to Hayden White, the pictorial figures of speech, constituting both intuition and thinking, are finitely limited—the field of what needs to be researched in the domain of history remains open. Hayden White knows how to reformulate forgotten questions into new ones, or how to forge new approaches with old ones.

Translated by Todd Presner

4

Transformations of Experience and Methodological Change

A HISTORICAL-ANTHROPOLOGICAL ESSAY

What is sought after, found, and represented as historical truth never depends solely on the experiences that a historian has, or solely on the methods that he uses. Certainly, as a historical work is being written, experience and method interrelate with one other. However, determining their relation is difficult, first because in the course of history it has constantly changed, and second, because as yet we have neither an anthropologically grounded history of historical experience nor a comprehensive history of historical methods.[1] The following essay is therefore a proposal that asks more questions than it supplies answers.

I. Semantic Prelude

In one of his most insightful articles, Jacob Grimm discusses the meaning of "to experience" and "experience" (*erfahren/Erfahrung*) and the changes that have occurred in these terms. He stresses the originally active, even processual connotation that they once had. "Experience" primarily meant exploration, inquiry, trial. Thus its earlier meaning is close to the Greek *historein*, which also includes, apart from secondary narration, "to explore," "to inquire." With regard to certain phenomena and their exploration, "experience" converged to a great extent with "history" (*Historie*) and even with "historical method," insofar as it registered the procedures of inquiry and trial. Hence, "he who experiences is thought of as someone going where he will inquire."[2] To have experience means "to conduct inquiry" (*Nachforschung halten*). But Jacob Grimm also noted a shift in, or even a differentiation of the concept "experience" in the modern period. A more passive, receptive meaning emerges: "at a considerable remove from the original meaning of 'experience' is the one that is now frequently employed, the mere perception or registration of objects, without a sense of movement and inquiry" (*fahren und forschen*).[3] For this reason, as Grimm notes with regret, *Erfahrenheit*—originally the concrete result of active experience—could be absorbed or displaced by the neutralized sense, so to speak, of *Erfahrung*.

In the course of the early modern period, then, "experience" was stripped of its active, inquisitive dimension; the "methodological" pathway of trial was weeded out and lost. Even if we acknowledge that Grimm quotes only literary and theological sources, a restriction in the general linguistic use begins to emerge: "experience" (*Erfahrung*) comes to concentrate on sensory perception, lived experience (*Erleben*). "Experience" is "reality" and enters into opposition to "mere thought."[4] Both experience as the experience of lived reality and the mental activity previously included in the meaning of premodern "historical" inquiry are thus separated from one another in linguistic-historical terms. Since the eighteenth century, the term "experience" includes the sense of "good and bad, as it is meted out to us"; whereas the process of exploration and inquiry as the pacemaker of knowledge, is no longer covered by the concept of experience. Grimm laments this differentiation, which prefigures the continuing challenge of historicism in German culture, the problem of how "life" and "history as academic endeavor" (*Historie als Wissenschaft*) are related to each other. In the subdued words of the old Jacob Grimm: "It is difficult, however, always to distinguish between inquiry and knowledge, between active and passive perception."[5]

Grimm was right. He tried to rescue the comprehensive unity of the old concept of experience because the receptive experience of reality and the productive exploration and inspection of this lived reality condition each other and belong together inseparably. He rebelled against the analytical distinction between sensory perception, seeing and hearing, and the conscious activity of exploration and inquiry, which Herodotus still characterized as *historia*, and to which the German word *Erfahrung*, with both its active and passive connotations, lent itself.

It is all the more surprising that Jacob Grimm dismisses Kant's definitions as technical terms tantamount to "empiricism." For Kant semantically rearranged the differences between perception, experience, and judgment in such a way that experience is simply not possible without sensory perception and the faculty of judgment. As Grimm quotes him: "Before perception is turned into experience, an act of judgment has to occur; the given intuition has to be subsumed under a concept."[6]

Although his definitions take their point of departure from the history of philosophy and natural history, Kant restored the old semantic fullness to the concept "experience," namely, its being both receptive and active, or, as Grimm put it, both cognition and inquiry. All knowledge begins with experience, as Kant writes, but experience in turn necessarily relies on the faculty of judgment and on the concepts in order to exist at all.[7]

The epistemological ambiguity of Kant's concept of experience, embracing both reality and its knowledge, finds a surprising analogy in the new concept "history" (*Geschichte*), as it emerged at the same time. Since around 1780 the concept "history," hitherto only referring to events, has absorbed the corresponding concept of *historia*. Since then, colloquial language contains only one shared concept for experienced reality and for its cognition and scientific knowledge: "history" (*Geschichte*). With respect to Grimm's definition of the older concept "experience," we can observe that the modern concept of history has assumed that unity of "experience," referring both to the sensory-mediated cognition of reality and its investigation. In this sense, the modern concept "history" has sublated the old "experience" and, with it, also the Greek *historia* as exploration and inquiry.

We can see how these data from linguistic history point to a remarkable continuity behind all the terminological changes and transformations. "History" is and remains a "science of experience," whether it is defined in line with Herodotus's history (*Historie*) as cognition and inquiry, or, in modern parlance, whether it transforms a pregiven reality into historical enunciations through sophisticated methods. In both cases "history" refers experience and knowledge to one another. Neither one can exist without the other.

What has become colloquially intertwined to the point of being indistinguishable must be separated analytically, if only to highlight the mutual constitution of experience and investigation. It is significant that the differentiation between the two terms, as observed by Grimm, occurs during the time when history begins to be constituted as an autonomous discipline in German culture. At least since then, the experience of reality had to be separated methodologically from its scientifically controlled treatment.

But the semantic evidence also refers us behind that threshold time during which our modern concept of history arose. Precisely its analytical flexibility, meaning both reality and its knowledge, also makes it possible to apply it—with all the necessary methodological reservations—to all previous histories and their modes of comprehension, that is, the *res gestae* as distinguished from *historiae*.

The following thoughts, therefore, start from the hypothesis that beyond all transformations of experience and methodological change, there are certain irreducible anthropological commonalties that allow us to relate them to each other, without relinquishing the unity of what is called "history."

II. Methodological Prelude

Once we accept the semantic difference between *pragmata, res gestae*, events, on the one side, and histories (*Historien*) or historical knowledge (*Geschichtskunde*), on the other, we could—purely theoretically—determine their relation from their respective vantage points. In their respective temporal perspectives as autonomous processes, two possibilities might offer themselves for analyzing the transformation of experiences and of methods so as to privilege them as the primary factors of change. Usually historians are inclined to give priority to the transformation of experience and define themselves merely as the recording narrator or analyst. But there can be no doubt that a methodologically framed experience of history can itself become an independent causal factor with great consequences. Without the Christian church's theological-clerical interpretation of the world in terms of salvation history, neither the Investitures Dispute together with its political consequences, nor the Crusades, nor the trans-Atlantic colonialism resulting from Christian sea voyages, nor, of course, the history of religious civil wars in the early modern period, would have been possible. Machiavelli's direct influence may be seen as relatively small, even if indirectly it is omnipresent; but it is beyond any doubt that Marx's methodologically derived vision of history (however cogent) has influenced the course of world history in a way that without him would be hard to imagine.

Accordingly, we could immediately discount an immanent history of methods primarily sustained by its innovations. Despite all the presuppositions that enter into every new formulation, innovations are not entirely derivable from one another. In the end, such a history would be organized around its great discoverers: from Herodotus as the father of historiography (*Geschichtsschreibung*) and Thucydides as the discoverer of the political world, to Augustine as the inventor of a salvation history determined by God, perhaps to Niebuhr as the master of philological methods of making present an alienated past; from the Scottish Enlightenment historians via Marx to Max Weber, in order to explain history from its sociological conditions. It would be possible to fill in all the details of this almost random series so as to identify the methodologically immanent, irreversible progress that undoubtedly exists.

The second possibility would be to derive methodological change from the prerequisite transformations of experience via a sociology of knowledge. It is easy to prove that observable transformations in the social and political sphere correlate with methodological innovations. Concrete experiences pose new questions, new questions lead to new methods. Such a reasoning surely has some plausibility. But just as easily one could deduce new experiences from new methods: the argument from the sociology of knowledge is bound to be circular and ultimately irrefutable.

Both approaches can achieve a certain plausibility. On the one side, the methodologically secured progress of epistemology, driven by itself or by significant innovations, would be thematized. On the other side, the historical transformation of experience, which undoubtedly exists and has led to the formation of new methods, would be emphasized. Both approaches are based on hypothetical, final causes that cannot be questioned as such. But they remain one-sided and arbitrary modes of explanation, just like the possible reduction of methodological change to internal *or* external factors.

This essay does not aim at determining such final causes. Instead I will attempt to correlate the terms of experience and method through an anthropological differentiation based on the assumption that *Geschichte* and *Historie*, reality and its conscious treatment, are always already related and mutually determined by one another, without being entirely derivable from each other.

The following thoughts, then, make use of historical-anthropological hypotheses,[8] which try to throw some light on the relationship between historical (*geschichtlich*) modes of experience and historical (*historisch*) epistemology. If I touch upon historical beginnings or the "origins" of certain methods, this genetic aspect is of secondary importance. My intentions are more systematic. I will try to track down the anthropological conditions of possible experiences and their methodological development. Since the anthropological presuppositions are themselves subject to a certain amount of historical change, even a systematically oriented approach is ultimately forced to address questions of diachrony.

Therefore, it would really be necessary to relate the so-called transformation of reality and the always corresponding change of epistemology to various theories of history which, whether openly or not, always already correlate these two terms to one another. But those theories themselves are subject to change over time—whether they are contained in a rational critique of mythology, in philosophical predispositions, in various theologies, philosophies of history, or even in explicit theories of history. In what follows, this theory of change, embracing both shifts in experience as well as methodological innovations, will not be discussed explicitly. Instead I will aim at certain formal features that might be common to all permutations of experience and all differentiations of method. The distinction between transformation of experience and methodological change, then, serves to clarify my argument by illuminating its historical-anthropological presuppositions. These presuppositions, perhaps, guarantee the unity of all history, which gives rise to individual histories.

III. Three Kinds of Acquisition of Experience

Because histories primarily come from the experiences of those who are involved or concerned, the possibility of their narration and thus also the possibility of narrating foreign experiences, the analysis of which is predominant in modern historiography, is presupposed. Directly or indirectly, then, every history is concerned with experiences, one's own or someone else's. Therefore, it can be assumed that the various ways of narrating histories or processing them methodologically can be related to the ways in which experiences are made, collected, or transformed. In order to grasp the threshold potential indicated by every acquisition or change of experience in its temporal and therefore historical dimension, we can distinguish between three kinds of experience.

The first kind of experience is always as unique as it is unrepeatable. It is the experience resulting from a surprise: "No one could have expected this!"[9] We could call this form of experience a primal experience, since without it no biography or history is possible. We have an experience in the sense that we are bound to be surprised. These experiences, once they happen or assert themselves, remain unique. Therefore, every experience contains its own history *in nuce*. Such a history is contained within the acquisition of experience, which, prompted by a surprise, resides in that minimal temporal difference between "before" and "after," or "too early" and "too late," retrospectively constituting the history of an experience. Facing it consciously or unconsciously, every individual lives through or undergoes this kind of experience anew. It is not that this type of experience is tied to a single person, since generally several or many people are affected by these surprises; however, surely this kind of acquisition of experience marks every individual in a particular way. Therefore it is reasonable to attribute the methodological practices of historians to their very own personal experiences that affected them at some point and without which their innovations, if innovations they are, could not be comprehended.

But experiences arise not only insofar as they are made but also insofar as they repeat themselves. This would be the second possibility of acquiring experience. Experiences are also collected; they are the result of a process of accumulation, insofar as they confirm or correct one another. As a saying goes: "If we don't experience it in a new way, then we experience it in the old way."[10] An experienced man will not be easily surprised, since he already knows beforehand, by experience, what to expect, or at least could expect. The minimal temporal span of the primary acquisition of experience is now stretched into periods that structure, reorient, or stabilize a life, and whose maximum length is the distance from birth until death: for no experience can be directly transmitted. If we focus on the group of people affected by such middle-range stabilizations of experience, it is obviously always those who have safeguarded such experiences within themselves. But we can suspect that greater spans of experience are specific to whole generations.

Generation-specific spans of experience result from the biological pre-givens that influence every individual life through the temporal difference between parents and children. A tension between education and emancipation, between the experience supplied by others and one's own experience, marks at least every individual history. Within the frame of their social units, these biologically determined and temporally graduated experiences—according to generation—gain a common profile. This profile endures and

changes as generations pass away and new ones grow up. Moreover, the accumulated experiences are refracted or intensified by political events, witnessed or acted in together. Depending on age or social group, a succession
of political experiences is naturally perceived and processed in different
ways. But successions of political experiences also evoke certain minimal features common to all age groups, which allows us to speak not only of biological or social generations, but political generational units as well. Their
common characteristics endure until the generation has finally died out. By
contrast to unique surprises, which could certainly also affect many people
simultaneously, confirmations and reinforcements of experiences are tied to
the similar experiences of one's contemporaries—otherwise they could
hardly have formed in the first place.

This is why there exist, beyond personal involvement, generation-
specific spans and thresholds of experience which, once they are instituted
or surpassed, create a common history. They encompass all people who live
together be they families; professional groups; inhabitants of a city; soldiers
of an army; members of states or social groups; believers or unbelievers
within or outside of churches; members of political formations of every sort,
be they parties, sects, factions, camarillas, staffs, localities, juries, communities. In short, every unit of action formed by way of life, chance, or organization partakes in the stabilization of given experiences. Considered temporally, one can speak of political and social generations whose commonalty
consists in making, collecting, and organizing unique or repeated experiences, or, for that matter, in undergoing common successions of experience.

Examples from political life can be readily supplied. Think of constitutional changes prompted or executed by civil or foreign wars, the Peloponnesian War, the transition from the Roman Republic to the Augustan
monarchy, the transpositions of the Roman Empire into its successor nations, the Reformation or the "classical" modern revolutions of the Dutch,
the British, the Americans, the French, or the Russians and the many nations of their continental empire.

The intersection of the respective generational experiences includes
both victors and vanquished, even if they are realized and processed in different ways, insofar as they can yet be processed. Even different biological
generations can be stabilized through relatively common experiences, which
can never be caught up with by succeeding generations, except in an analogous way. Therefore, from the inception of history, it remains methodolog-

ically necessary to rely on primary sources not only to track down unique but also generation-specific, collected experiences. Since Herodotus, this rule has been followed or implicitly assumed by historians who work with secondary material. We will come back to this.

Experiences, then, are unique—insofar as they are undergone; and also repeatable—insofar as they are collected. It follows that every history constituted by experience and capable of being derived from it has a double aspect. On the one hand, singular, that is to say, surprising events evoke experiences and bring about histories; on the other hand, accumulated histories help to structure histories of a middle range. There are generation-specific conditions and outcomes, which overlap with personal history but still refer to greater spans which create a common space of experience. Here the spirit of the age (*Zeitgeist*) is to be found. This is why Clarendon stressed that aspect of history reaching beyond personal history: it was, he said, "more useful to posterity to leave a character of the times, than of persons, or the narrative of the matter of fact, which cannot be so well understood, as by knowing the genius that prevailed when they were transacted."[11]

Our double temporal perspective on possible experiences allows us to draw a first interim conclusion. The change of experience, always unique in situ, nevertheless takes place on different temporal levels: namely, in the interaction between those events that generate new experiences situationally and spontaneously, or, more slowly, when experiences add up, confirm themselves, or react to changes in the relatively stable net of conditions within which events become possible. Insofar as experiences and their change generate histories, these histories are always tied to these pregivens: that human beings uniquely make experiences and also, that their experiences merge together according to different generations. To go beyond chronicling, it is, therefore, legitimate to organize histories according to the reigns of rulers or according to political events reflecting generation-specific thresholds. This is why every modern social history has to have recourse to concrete commonalties that temporally frame generation-specific units of experience.

But, thirdly, the transformation of experience can also take place over the long term, gradually or in phases, beyond all spontaneous effects and unexpected turns, and thus modify all generation-conditioned, continuous, and ritualized experiences: then, in a relatively short time, the previous framework of experience is entirely transformed in practice.

The destruction of the Roman Empire by the conquering Germanic nations and the simultaneous elimination and transformation of pagan cults through Christianization are two examples of this phenomenon that are often discussed. Despite all personal and generation-specific primary experiences, the whole societal system changed. This could only be experienced metaphorically as decline, or, in terms of salvation history, as the expectation of a future redemption. Another example is the evolution of the international economic system, which, extending from Europe, has changed the entire organization of state and societal constitution, affecting both domestic and international politics. By influencing or helping to cause every current conflict, such long-term processes remain present as a background experience, even if they are only realized through historical-methodological questions.

Generally speaking, one faces here a systemic change transcending persons and generations, which can only be captured retrospectively through historical reflection. In order to perceive this long-term change as such, the oral result, transmitted, as it were, from grandparents to grandchildren, is no longer sufficient. What we so far represented as the acquisition of experience and the change of experience was synchronous insofar as it remained tied to generations living together. The third case of long-term systemic change is strictly diachronous, layered in generation-spanning sequences that elude immediate experience.

This sort of foreign experience, which is mediated into personal experience, might today be called "historical" (*historisch*) in a delimited or specific sense. The distant past is adduced either to explain the character of the present or the specific alterity of earlier history. Anthropologically speaking, in both cases we are dealing with the incorporation of generation-spanning experiences of others into the framework of one's own experiences. A systemic change, formerly summed up in mythical images, can only be grasped through specific techniques of historical questioning. Our third form of transformation of experience, the long-term change, is not at all perceptible without historical methods. With this, we anticipate our next section. A generation-spanning transformation of experience, which refers to factors not accessible to individual experience, can only be treated by methods providing an analogue to experience. We could almost say, then, that we are dealing with a historical creation of experience (*Erfahrungsstiftung*) which provides the backdrop to all primary experiences.

Whether pagan histories are brought into a Christian perspective or

Christian histories are reinterpreted according to the standard of enlightened rationality, whether past experiences of others are caught up with one's own understanding, or whether the whole of history is interpreted as economically conditioned by way of an experiential analogy, historical science plays a constitutive role in integrating the long-term transformation of experience into individual experience.

It would be a mistake to believe that long-term systemic change has only been methodologically thematized since the modern period, that is, since the discovery of the Middle Ages, or since the accelerated change of experience brought about by industrialization. It is surely an attractive hypothesis to think that the retrospective discovery of a radically different past is the characteristic experience of our own hermeneutically or sociologically refined model of history. Certainly, through the organization of the whole of history into antiquity, the Middle Ages, and modernity since humanism, or through the modern classification based on criteria of production in which history runs from hunters and gatherers via agriculture and high civilization to the technical-industrial age, a generation-spanning space of experience is posited. It has slowly stabilized over hundreds and thousands of years and only changed in stages.

But if we look at the anthropological presuppositions of such long-term perspectives, we can argue that they have influenced history not just since the modern age but since the very beginning of history. Even if Herodotus had addressed the singular and generation-specific experiences of the conflict between Persians and Greeks as the still contemporaneous, grand theme of his *Histories*, his work stretched back two or three generations into a prehistory that could only be critically processed through the mediated experience of others. The very challenge, as far as it is rationally possible, to historicize myths and legends, required him to incorporate prior experiences by way of narration or interpretation.

In his introduction, Thucydides explicitly constructed a far-reaching structural change in Hellenic history, spanning many centuries, which finally, through the Athenians' accumulation of power, made possible the great and unique war.

Tacitus's genuine method of representing the terrors of the imperial age is based on his explicit reflection on its difference from the prior centuries of the Roman Republic.

Joachim of Fiore developed the doctrine of the three overlapping ages that necessarily implied long-term units of experience and equally long-term changes of experience. But enough examples from the premodern period.

If one accepts the three formalized modalities of experience as I have developed them here, it follows that the short, middle, and long-term spans of experience make possible histories on a commensurate scale.

The pressure of experience under which human beings exist and act is layered differently according to different time spans. We can assume that this has repercussions on historical methods since they have to correspond to the three above-mentioned ways of experience. For the methods a historian employs to transpose historical experience into narrative and scholarly discipline are always present and oriented toward present experience. They have to prove themselves in relation to this, even if the event in question is of the past. We will try to elucidate below how the temporal structure of experience correlates with various methods.

IV. The Writing of History: Recording, Continuing, Rewriting (Minimal Methodological Conditions)

If we fold the temporal structures of historical experience into the ways of their narration, their textual representation, and their methodological organization, we can—regardless of the question of genre—differentiate between three types: the recording (*aufschreiben*), the continuing (*fortschreiben*), and the rewriting (*umschreiben*) of history. Recording is a unique act; continuing accumulates temporal spans; rewriting corrects both, the recorded and the continued, in order to retrospectively arrive at a new history. In this way, the three types of historiography to be treated below can be correlated schematically with the three ways of acquiring experience. Let me mention right away, however, that such a tidy correlation does not do justice to the real intersections of all three temporal spans. Indeed, the unity of all history resides in the fact that all three modes of experience—short-, middle-, and long-range—are present, regardless of specific emphases, in all forms of historiography. It is the minimal methodological commonalties themselves that cannot do without the unique recording, the accumulated continuing, and the always required rewriting. Of course, the relations change over time and, consequently, so does their methodological correlation. But we are concerned with those anthropologically constant conditions that enable the very possibility of historical methods and characterize their formal compatibility.

The Recording of History

We might begin by saying that recording is the primary activity. Through a narrative or a record, a history is constituted and evidently includes the concrete experiences of the historian. This explains the prevalence of what is called "contemporary historiography" (*Zeitgeschichtsschreibung*) or, in the words of Fritz Ernst, the "chronicling of the present" (*Gegenwartschronistik*), something that could maintain an epistemological priority until the eighteenth century.[12] The novelty that distinguishes every historical event does not require a further reason for the historiographical comprehension of what is heretofore unexpected and surprising. It is no wonder, then, that since Herodotus and Thucydides, the uniqueness of reported events is especially emphasized, and that this topos is constantly and emphatically referred to. This is why historicism's axiom of uniqueness belongs to those primal experiences constituting all histories—if these histories are worth being remembered.

The distinctiveness of the unique experience calls directly for the writing of history. The glory or shamefulness of the people involved, their achievements and their sufferings, are recorded. The basic theme is the acquisition of experience worth remembering. Here resides the historical (*geschichtlich*) place of the historical (*historisch*) method in its most general sense. Experiences can also be spontaneously transposed into narratives, something that is generally the case in daily life. One can speak of methods only if specific questions propel the procedures of investigation in order to acquire knowledge that cannot otherwise be gained. Two questions have been posed—implicitly or explicitly—since classical history: What was the case? How did it happen?[13] Only in this way can the unique experience be translated into a knowledge that endures beyond its cause. To this end, minimal modes of research are required, which go beyond the mere acknowledgment of facts.

Regardless of the fact that new experiences are constantly brought into the purview of historiography, Herodotus and Thucydides opened up ways of research that have retained their power and validity up to today. Above all one should mention the method designated today as "oral history," without which no fact or matter of experience can be understood. Whether the testimonials remain juxtaposed, as in the case of Herodotus; whether they are measured according to their credibility; whether written records—or inscriptions, as was already the case with Herodotus and Thucydides—are adduced as a countermeasure; whether, in the eighteenth century, Robertson distributed questionnaires;[14] or whether, today, oral interview techniques elucidate certain generation-specific groups whose retrospective memories are confronted with extant diaries or letters, the methods generally remain the same: to translate experiences into knowledge. The question of facticity—what was the case?—aims at concrete uniqueness and thus makes use of general methods appropriate for capturing that uniqueness—whether Thucydides only wanted to tell how it was,[15] or whether Ranke asked "how it really happened" ("wie es eigentlich gewesen").[16]

The methodological, temporal layering, extending from the interviewing of direct eyewitnesses and the questioning of mediating earwitnesses to the countermeasure of written records, was as well developed in Herodotus as it was in Bede or present-day historians. There are anthropological pregivens for the possibility of gaining knowledge about events composed of personal experiences which, once discovered, cannot be relinquished. That is the distinction of methodology.

In order to recognize events in their uniqueness, a further step, of course, is necessary, namely the counterquestion of why it happened this and not some other way. That leads, in modern parlance, to the formation of hypotheses, which not only asks "how it really happened," but how it was possible in the first place. Behind every question of "How did it happen?" there is the question of "How could it happen?"

Thus Herodotus wondered how the Persian War would have ended if the Athenians had not taken part in it, and he concluded that their participation was decisive for the war's outcome. Methodologically speaking, it is the same argument that Montesquieu used when he asked why a single battle had decided a war. He traced it back to conditions that made it possible for a single battle to bring about such a turn of events.[17] The question of the conditions of possibility for a reality that is experienced as unique leads automatically to the difference between long-term reasons and situative causes allowing for the explanation of an event. Thucydides' whole oeuvre is marked by this double perspective. Not only does he describe the reasons and consequences of chains of events in their respective specificity, he also confronts the unique and always surprising events with their long-term, enduring presuppositions. He sees such presuppositions located in the pathology of human power, and they can explain why it happened this and not some other way.

Herodotus also employs this double perspective for other reasons. We find, for example, an analogous model of explanation when he reported from Egypt that Helen was not abducted to Troy but to the banks of the Nile.[18] "If Helen had been in Ilion, she would have been returned to the Greeks": this would have been rational. The Trojans, then, could not return Helen to avoid the war, but the Greeks did not believe them so that they could exact their revenge. The war was fought over a phantom. The true reason, prior to all causes, lay in the blindness of human beings whom the gods were punishing.

In whatever way historians transpose the fear or the happiness of surprising events into knowledge, they are compelled to adduce medium-range, long-term, or enduring causes for the explanation of unique experiences. The case analysis leads to the formation of hypotheses, and the formation of hypotheses leads to explanations that confront reality with its conditions of possibility. Thus the temporal difference between situative singularity and long-term causes enters into the argument, and without this, no history can be recognized. This difference survives every paradigm shift.

The temporal multilayeredness of modalities of experience developed above is thus mirrored in the methodological procedures. The unforeseeability of unique events can only be represented if one also considers the accumulated experiences of the medium, the long-term, or the quasi-permanent range. Only in this way can the questions "What happened?" and "How was it possible?" be methodologically answered. As we observed it in Herodotus and Thucydides, the difference between represented singular events and their long-term causes remains an anthropological constant in every method.

From the perspective of our formal historical anthropology, it does not matter whether the uniqueness of primary experiences is explained by causal reasoning along the succession of events, by long-term conditions, or by enduring pregiven meanings. In any event, the method that reconstructs a case and asks how it was possible in the first place, always relies on temporal multilayeredness, namely that experiences are uniquely made and yet accumulate. This is the minimum methodological condition without which the unique and surprising quality of all histories cannot be transposed into historical knowledge. This is why Herodotus saw an intrinsic justice in all his histories; this is why Thucydides interpreted the uniqueness of his description of the Peloponnesian War as revealing human nature, as *ktēma es aiei*; this is why unique histories can henceforth be invoked as exempla for the next case.

Method, then, is distinguished by the fact that it outlives the case for which it was developed. It can become autonomous, so to speak; one can abstract method from the motivating causes as well as formalize and generalize it. Concrete case analyses that employ interviews of witnesses and source interpretation, always have recourse to repeatable principles of experience in order to justify, comprehend, or even interpret the specific case.

This historical-anthropological precondition is variously redeemed according to the actually occurring change of experience in the course of history. This becomes especially clear when one considers the final causes that somehow have to be reconciled with what is unique and always surprising. What emerges simultaneously or in succession are authorities that help to secure the repeatability of experiences. Be they the gods or a still higher *fatum* (Herodotus, Polybius); be it man's inborn desire for power (Thucydides, Machiavelli, Acton); be it Fortune (Polybius, Tacitus, Otto of Freising, Machiavelli, Voltaire); be it the God of Christianity, to whom all the above-mentioned are subordinated for directing man's constantly self-reproducing mortality toward eternity[19] (Augustine, Bede, Otto of Freising); be it forces, ideas, or principles of long-term influence (Herder, Humboldt, Ranke), or enduring powers (Jacob Burckhardt); be it conditions of production, legal constants, economic or institutional determinants, or supra-human cyclical movements (Ferguson, Smith, Marx); or be it modern combinations and theoretical elaborations of experiential data that have accumulated over time: in every case, the methodological problem concerns correlating the primary experiences of unique surprises and novelties to their long-term conditions of possibility.

Notwithstanding the fact that those final causes have changed greatly over time, depending on whether Greeks, Romans, Christians, or modern "scientific" researchers are examined, the formal structure of the methodological processing of experience remains constant. It is based on the temporal refraction of every primary experience, which is, methodologically, and more or less consciously, differentiated, to correlate uniqueness and continuity. Here resides the minimal commonalty of all historical-methodological procedures, which also allows us to speak of the general unity of history, regardless of how concrete experiences have occurred, accumulated, changed, or refracted themselves.

The Continuing of History

With the diachronic course of history, the gains of experience naturally increase when viewed purely in terms of quantity. But it does not necessarily follow that this is also a growth of experience. Human beings are forgetful and prone to consider their own individual lives as the sole source of experience. In order to be able to speak about a growth of experience, a historical method is necessary that organizes the diachronic course systematically. A minimal presupposition is the elongation of temporal spans, retrospectively brought into view and thus ready for reflection.

The simplest case, of course, is the transcription and recording of previous histories, in order to add whatever has newly occurred. The writing of annals and, to some extent, chronicles, follows this principle, even if it has been called into question—and since the humanists, by increasingly systematic arguments. From more or less naive transcribing or recording, one can at least deduce that experimental knowledge has not fundamentally changed in regard to the recurring conditions of possibility of particular cases. This is also why it was logical to treat history (*Historie*) for one and a half millennia as an instance of rhetoric, as something based on the constant rules of truthful representation and narrative.[20] The subordination of history to rhetoric can certainly be seen as stabilizing historiographically processed experiences. Representable events themselves—once they are appropriately represented—do not really pose a problem. Even though the rules of representation are certainly as important as the methods of historical processing of experience, we will here shift our attention to those epistemological effects that came from, or better, were produced by, the continuation.

Whatever one thinks of Polybius's didactic tone, thanks to the Roman expansion he passed a threshold, namely to thematize the unity of geographically differentiated histories.[21] This growth of experience is explicitly called "acquisition of experience" by his generation, but it is he who knows how to use it methodologically. He inserts disparate spheres of action into a general framework that is, in principle, not accessible to individual experience. History is more highly aggregated, so to speak. Since

Polybius, it follows that geography is not only a presupposition of history but becomes its essential element. Once methodologically developed, this increase of knowledge can be repeatedly observed in historical studies. The transposition of Spittler's additive European national histories into the comprehensive history of the European state system and its colonial empires by Heeren comes to mind.

Since Polybius combined seemingly disparate histories with their specific and direct primary experiences, the increase of knowledge has been methodologically available. Today, this epistemological possibility belongs to the implicit presuppositions of countless individual histories which, since the eighteenth century, can increasingly only be adequately understood with respect to a global context. Many primary experiences of the short or middle range remain embedded—often without methodological reflection—in geographically remote conditions, such as the economy, without which many of our primary experiences would not be thinkable. Once it was introduced by Polybius and Poseidonius, the methodological principle that history can only be practiced as "world history" has become possible and, with the growing world-historical pressure of experience, imperative.[22]

Closely related to this geographical aspect of contextual thinking is the resultant drive toward synchronization. What Herodotus had already implicitly achieved in an unsophisticated way,[23] namely to correlate the various dates of dynasties, was for Polybius conscious method. With the accumulated experience of variously layered and interpreted spaces of history, the pressure grew for developing methodologically unified ways of dating—think of the later Dionysius Exiguus and Bede—until with Scaliger there was developed an astronomically secured, absolute, and natural chronology for all heterogeneous cultures on the globe together. Here, too, we can observe that the once-discovered situation of chronologically separated cultures was only transposed into historical knowledge after chronology was established and finally methodologically differentiated as an auxiliary discipline.

But we can name further methodologically framed insights that presuppose a minimum of already past histories able to be differentiated in parallel or successive fashion. Only then will it become possible to make comparisons that juxtapose one's own experience with someone else's.

Most common, and continuing up to today with surprising persistence, is the comparison of constitutions. Presented by Herodotus as a Sophistic dispute,[24] arguments already emerge here that can be traced via Plato and Aristotle to Polybius, and then remain available to all histories—for example, Roscher's[25]—which venture comparisons. We can even say that this is the classical case for the repeatability of single experiences of human self-organization and of certain regulated processes with differently evaluated consequences.

Our anthropological differentiation, that the always surprising novelty of all concrete histories can be methodologically transposed into knowledge only if it is correlated with medium- or long-term experiential data, finds here its world-historical application, valid until today. Minimal processes, which can be surveyed through the continuing of histories, enable points of comparison to be found, which otherwise could not be had. Once achieved —and this is a real increase of knowledge—the results can be applied to different cases. One may suspect that all modern typologies—such as Max Weber's heuristically quite useful doctrine of ideal types—can also be traced back to the same principle.

But not only the comparability and, consequently, the structural repeatability of similar or analogous histories is made possible by continuation: even purely diachronic rules of succession, corresponding to accumulated experience, belong to this context. The Aristotelian principle that small causes can have great effects—introduced to the field of history as an argument by Polybius and Tacitus[26]—was emphatically embraced in the eighteenth century (by Bayle, Voltaire, or Frederick the Great)[27] to explain middle-range cataracts of events. Irony thus became method.

I hesitate somewhat to enlist here the figurative interpretation of history from the Middle Ages, but it is tempting to assume that the multiple meaning of Scripture made it methodologically possible to read texts both in regard to their uniqueness and in regard to time-transcending contexts. First, it guaranteed the continuity of divine providence, which lent sense to particular cases. Later Condorcet could develop an analogous procedure to combine the multiplicity of concrete, singular, but heterogeneous progresses into one tableau of total history. The place given to God's chosen people was now occupied by a hypothetical people as epistemological construct: "Ici le tableau commence à s'appuyer en grande partie sur la suite des faits que l'histoire nous a transmis: mais il est nécessaire de les choisir dans celle de différents peuples, de les rapprocher, de les combiner, pour en tirer l'histoire hypothétique d'un peuple unique, et former le tableau de ses progrès."[28] In both cases, a procedure is employed that interprets the multiple scriptural meaning of a source in order to move the particular case into a larger context. Whether it involves the recognition of divine providence, the progressive interpretation of single actions, or today the social-historical comprehension of structural change, the experience is processed through analogous methods, which read the particular case against the backdrop of long-term contexts, without making the particular case disappear. On the contrary, it is through its double legibility that history is constituted.

In all these cases, with the empirical increase of time, methods were developed to do justice to the growing geographical interaction—from universal history to world history—and their temporal conjunction. The apparatus of research has made use of comparisons, analogies, and parallels with reference to possible repetitions, and it has also attempted to discover regularities in particular successions or in the entire course of history. Granted, such methods are tied very closely to philosophical, theological, or even historical-theoretical preconditions. But many of these methods have withstood the test of applicability and repeatability and thus proven to be valuable. They reflect a real increase in experience, which would disappear if it were not transferred into knowledge with a minimum of method and thus made durable. To be sure, there are never sufficient reasons to justify why a piece of historical knowledge came about at a certain time; but once it is articulated, it remains available for use. The insights of Thucydides cannot be surpassed, but they can be amplified. Herodotus's comparison of constitutions was differentiated and enriched over time, but it remained essentially the same. To this extent, we can speak of an epistemological progress, something that could not be registered without the repeated application of once-achieved insights. Progress in the methodological processing of historical experiences thus consists not in the so-called paradigm shift, but in the fact that precisely a paradigm shift tries to process new experiences yet has to rely on the repeated use of previously acquired procedures.

But history is not just written, recorded, or continued one time, complete with all the epistemological growth resulting from the refinement of methods. History is just as often rewritten, even newly constituted through critical retrospection. Thus the methodological burden of proof increases enormously, for without it, it cannot be shown why history, as heretofore reported or written down, was in reality so different from the way it was reported or written down.

The Rewriting of History

The rewriting of history is as unique as the very first time a history is written. It is certainly innovative because it moves in a conscious opposition to the previously reported or written history. It follows provisionally that this corresponds to a change of experience that amounts to a new experience. And in accordance with our three temporal spans of short-, medium-, and long-term acquisitions of experience (and the corresponding losses of experience), it can be expected that here, too, methodological procedures can be correlated with the three kinds of experience. The facts of the events and their causes have to be articulated anew, or at least differently; otherwise there is nothing but further recording or continuing of prior traditions.

Certainly no rewriting of history is thinkable or possible without also recording or continuing, without recourse to the stock of experience already captured. That is true not only for the medieval writing of annals and chronicles (whose detailed sources are today printed in small type), but it is also true for today's entire historiography. Not everything can be "revised." But if revision occurs, new methods must be employed, no matter how cogently theorized they are. Often they are hidden in new enunciations from which innovative methodological implications are derivable—as is the case with the symbolic historiography of the high Middle Ages. Or the recording is repudiated because the given report is based on books and not on the primary testimony of a direct participant or witness, or at least on the corresponding density of experience that alone allows the historian to pose the right questions.[29] Since antiquity the recourse to true or supposed primary experiences is a minimal part of the business of history in order to separate truth from error. But epistemologically speaking, this is not yet a rewriting, since the search for authentically transmitted primary experiences is still based on the final authority of direct reports by witnesses, which, when properly questioned, remain worthy of being recorded. In this methodological procedure, unchanged and valid until today, lies, then, the minimum continuity that since the time of Herodotus, historians cannot eschew without losing their credibility.

The rewriting of history, on the other hand, points toward a change of experience that would be lost to our current understanding without its methodological theorization. Even Thucydides testifies to the fact that all three temporally differentiated ways of experience are, or at least could be, affected by this. Whereas the wealth of particular histories reported by Herodotus from prehistory was still bound to an immanent religious horizon of meaning, Thucydides enacts a rigorous change of perspective. In his long-term archaeology, he poses—seemingly like Herodotus—a multiplicity of questions concerning economic, technical, demographic, political, archaeological, semantic, and comparative cultural matters, but only in order to structure, almost processually, the entire Hellenic prehistory (*Vorgeschichte*) until the Persian War. Thucydides no longer conceptualized distant history (*Vorvergangenheit*) in an additive fashion like Herodotus but as a diachronic unity in which the most diverse factors relate to each other. For Thucydides, the Greek "Enlightenment" reduced religious, mythologically mediated, pregiven meanings to a historical factor, one among others, which influenced the belief of the participants. Thus the whole of prehistory, still understood by Herodotus in religious terms, was now opened up, so to speak, to a hypothetical-argumentative reconstruction according to the new standard of Thucydides's own experience. His archaeology contains the newly discovered, long-term presuppositions which have made contemporary history (*Gegenwartsgeschichte*) possible.

But the mid-range accumulation of experience through which Thucydides could distinguish himself generationally from Herodotus, also testifies to his change of method. The Pentecontaetia (fifty-year-period between the Persian War and the Peloponnesian War) is interpreted through the poleis' internal oppositions to their constitutions, through the citizenry's differing modes of perception, and through the interplay of domestic and foreign policy in the city-states in order to elicit the true cause of war by an immanent teleology: the imperial accumulation of power by the Athenians, corresponded to an increasing fear on the part of the Spartans.[30]

Finally, Thucydides' very own, unique change of experience has to be taken into account. We will come back to his failure as a general. Strasburger pays particular attention to the specifically personal approach of Thucydides, who isolated the political, and only the political, from the innovative phase of that generation, heavily influenced by tradition.[31] This is the effect of Thucydides' radical strategy of disillusionment, which he pursues, at least on the plane of argument, against all traditional moral and legal norms in order to reveal a valid, historical truth for all historical events: that which is humanly possible.

We are dealing with that kind of realism which remains true to its name through today, reinforced by the translations of Valla and Hobbes as well as by their reception into the tradition of realpolitik since the early modern period. To give an example: the reinterpretation of the murder of the tyrant—the murderers have become heroes of a democratically legitimized memorial cult—testifies to the procedure of unmasking which Thucydides made into his own methodologically sound achievement. Herodotus had still dissected the overthrow of the tyrant into a variety of motives, including dreams, oracles, rites, blackmailings, and bribes. He paid particular attention to the role of the leading aristocratic families and the neighboring cities, without underscoring the role of Hipparchus's two murderers. But Thucydides goes a decisive step further insofar as he divests the murder of its publicly transmitted heroic function, which Herodotus had not touched. Thucydides depoliticizes the murder, tracing it back to the motives of homosexual jealousy. In modern parlance, politics manifests itself, between the extremes of natural preconditions and ideological illusions. Whoever concerns himself with politics must be capable of unmasking. Herodotus never went that far, playing "enlightenment" off against old experiences.[32] Not every testimony, wrote Thucydides, is equally worthy of being reported. He hierarchizes his sources in order to capture history's immanently demonstrable, naturally similar, partly tragic, and always self-concealing potential for conflict. Whatever direction our contemporary readings of Thucydides take,[33] he remains the classical case for the methodologically reflected rewriting of previously given historical reports, which could no longer be confirmed by his own experiences. Even if his reception happened in waves and phases and, moreover, was quite selective, his method of a systematically justified unmasking and demystification became a guide for rewriting.

Both retrospectively, in the diachronic structural analysis of his archaeology, and generation-specifically, in the theorization of the new multisubjective experiences of political power and their linguistic ramifications influencing the Pentecontaetia, as well as finally in the processing of very personal experiences of the Peloponnesian War, Thucydides rewrote previous history, and, insofar as he newly wrote it, it was written in a way different from everything prior.

We can go so far and state that even the ascertainment of the facts, for which he orally interrogated witnesses and checked written sources, aimed at a rewriting of everything that was previously said and written. He did this with methodological consciousness. For this reason, his work—not only because of the transposition of a particular experience into historically enduring knowledge—remains also methodologically a *ktēma es aiei.* That leads us to a further anthropological pregiven, which allows us to process methodologically the short-term and middle-range change of experience, just as the long-term perspectival shift.

For Thucydides has taught us why history can be rewritten in the first place. He demonstrated that the gathering of facts is not identical with what is said or written about them. Moreover, he showed that the question of why it happened this and not some other way, can only be answered from a dialogical perspective, inserted within the perspective of those involved. To put it differently: Thucydides was the first to recognize the contradiction between factual history and its linguistic description and interpretation, and interpreted this opposition as generally constitutive for the experience of history itself. This realization was his methodological contribution: he tied the factuality of events irrevocably to the facilitation of linguistic acts by the participants. This procedure, unsurpassable through today, is based on a processing of experience specific to Greek politics, which rationalized the fifth-century interaction and opposition, between religion and Sophistic enlightenment, the Persian Empire and the city-states, civic liberties and constitutional variety, colonial foundations and alliances, economic and moral power, law and pragmatism.[34] The methodological advantage Thucydides derived from this consisted in the enduring differentiation between saying and doing, between *logoi* and *erga.*[35]

The frequently stressed anthropological permanence of all historical premises, which Thucydides tried to elucidate, resides, as far as method is concerned, in the reflected tension between talk and action, between speech and intention, between language and reality, and constitutes history in this way and not another. In writing down the history of the Peloponnesian War, Thucydides has already "rewritten" it: its long-term conditions, its middle-term structures, and its short-term, unique events. He articulated the "primal experience" of anthropology, namely that there exists a rift between all the events that constitute a history and whatever is said about them when this history is constituted. Thucydides turned this rift into the methodological theme, so to speak, of his Peloponnesian War insofar as he confronted monological or dialogical speeches with annalistic events, without entirely deriving one from the other. Thanks to this method, he carved out an enduring anthropological method that explains why history can be rewritten at all. His text is open to other interpretations not only because he is sometimes partial, for instance, to the Athens of Pericles; rather, his innovative achievement consisted in the fact that he linguistically composed the difference between a sequence of events and the speeches that occurred before, during, and after as the presupposition of all history. With this, he demonstrated an essential condition of the possible rewriting of all history as the general presupposition of every historical processing of experience.

If one traces the history of methods over the course of time, methods could also be interpreted as a differentiation of the anthropological premises discussed in Thucydides, right down to the philological-historical method. Certainly since the eighteenth century, this has led to the renunciation of the so-called "invented speeches," without making it possible to dispense with the premise that even the most carefully edited and explicated textual source is never identical with the history that the historian tries to elucidate. The difference between language and history, once it was explained by Thucydides, who had explicitly thematized it in his speeches, cannot be bridged by any philological method. For the latter aims at textual criticism, textual reconstitution, explanation and interpretation of texts, without gaining criteria for how the history to be derived from it is itself constituted—a point well recognized by Niebuhr.[36]

The minimum of continuity that a historian has to preserve, insofar as he has recourse to direct linguistic testimonies of actions and events (or their representations), is never sufficient to guarantee the truth of the related history. Because of linguistic multivalency, it can always be read differently and it is always prone to being rewritten. Thucydides has shown us where words no longer hold, how they lost their meaning in civil wars, how arguments can both change and also miss a situation.[37] Polybius pondered why the true reasons for an event are not identical with the motives or the pretexts that humans adduce to explain the occurrence of events.[38] Tacitus strove methodologically to show us how much reality is constituted through the perceptions of those involved, that reality resides as much in the rumors and fears, in the contingent dispositions of those who act or are acted upon, as in the events that are thereby mediated. The Christian Enlightenment, because of its trust in God, could read pagan texts—whether myths, fables, or histories—in regard to their deception or self-deception, even more sarcastically than the pagan critics themselves. The difference between language and reality has an endless potential for processing new experiences methodologically. This is why Bodin could instruct the reader of historical texts to read them with respect to newly developed interests and the social conditions behind what the authors said.[39] This is why Niebuhr could interrogate all sources in regard to what they reveal, contrary to the narrative intention of the author, about the history of language or the history of institutions.

In short, whatever is central to modern ideology critique for rewriting also our own history, is contained in the anthropological pregiven that language and history, speech and action, are not entirely identical with each other. Every text says more and at the same time less, or at least something different, from what might really have been the case. This difference allows for a multiplicity of possible causes. This is why Thucydides could show—against Herodotus—that the writing of history is rewriting.

Of course, it would be absurd to trace all methodological consequences of textual criticism back to the unique accomplishment of Thucydides, especially because the dialogical structure of his processing of experience has been deemphasized now that fictional speeches have become taboo to the modern ideal of objectivity—something that should not be misunderstood as epistemological progress.[40] And it may be mentioned that Thucydides himself did not have a skeptical, relativistic attitude toward language; rather, in linguistic variety he wanted to uncover a common signature of man as an acting being who becomes mired in irresolvable aporias. But from the point of view of our interests here, we need not be concerned with the unique case of this unique historian, but with the anthropological conditions of possibility that allow for the reinterpretation of all histories. Thucydides has shown us a metahistorical presupposition insofar as he upholds the difference between speech and action as a methodological principle throughout his work.

With regard to the procedures of source criticism, three possibilities offer themselves for prompting a rewriting of history. First, new testimonies can surface that throw new light on the previous tradition. Even a historian who is simply recounting is thus forced to make choices, which lead *nolens volens* to rewriting. This is basically the genuine self-experience of the historian, which forces him to source criticism and which has become increasingly sophisticated and systematized since the humanists.

Second, new questions can help track down and find new testimonies. In that case, the heretofore uniformly recorded or continued tradition is seen from an altogether different perspective. When attention was redirected from the merely narrative sources toward charters, contracts, and inscriptions, all of which have been increasingly investigated by antiquarians and legal historians[41] since the humanists, a methodological increase of knowledge resulted that could no longer be ignored. It reinforces the already invoked criteria of authenticity. These are the progressive elements that transcend the liberal or nationalistic motifs of the German historical school and have helped pave the way toward a new mode of historical inquiry.

Third, all given testimonies can be newly read or interpreted, be it to rediscover what is thought to be the original sense, or be it to derive meanings from them that could never have been intended by their authors. We only need to bring to mind the discovery of so-called forgeries, a constant concern of historians since Valla for tracking down hidden intentions;[42] or the contradictions in the Bible, discussed by Richard Simon for the purpose of deriving from them the inevitability of clerical tradition and authority—which did not save him from being condemned for heresy by the Catholic Church or the Calvinists, the latter being where he looked in vain for refuge. The contradictoriness of the text itself, such as in the double story of the creation of the first humans, remained a stumbling block that could only be dissolved by way of extratextual explanations or later increase of experience. All modern primary experiences of economically conditioned social and political change can only be verified in prehistory when political or religious sources are read against the grain.

In contemporary practice, all three procedures for the use of textual sources are employed and combined simultaneously. But with respect to diachrony, we can suspect that this is a cumulative epistemological progress. Once Ranke expanded the investigation of sources and intensified their interpretation, insights were achieved that were not contradicted but rather expanded by Marx's new reading of different statistical and economic sources. Simply put, he methodologically processed different experiences than Ranke. Thus today we know more about and have a better methodological comprehension of our past than previous generations were able to have.

On the other hand, it cannot be denied that epistemological progress, once achieved, also entails loss. A prominent example already mentioned is the renunciation of the linguistically reflected, perspectivally differentiated history of experience handed down to us by Thucydides. The closest contemporary parallels might be found in novels, such as those by Faulkner or Christa Wolf, or in Alexander Kluge's "Description of a Battle" (*Schlachtbeschreibung*), all of which can easily be read as historical texts. The so-called history of mentalities may advance in a direction, in order to acquire experience, which, methodologically speaking, has already been taken by Thucydides or Tacitus. For mentalities, even if they include behavior patterns, can only be discovered through the specific, linguistically differentiated and linguistically conditioned experience of world and environment.

Based on the specific content of gained knowledge, it can be assumed that the above-mentioned three ways of using written testimonies correspond to specific changes of experience, which have elicited the discovery of new sources or new readings of old sources. I would like to illustrate this here by those epoch-spanning explanations that indicate a systemic change, namely epochal thresholds in the totality of accumulated experience. Once systemic change has been subsumed under a new concept, it follows that all of prehistory is also being rewritten, or, at least, could be rewritten to explain the conditions for the emergence of new forms of self-experience. Therefore, we will add analogously processed waves of experience in the course of history to Thucydides' retrospective change of perspective.

Because of the dogmatization of scriptural text, it became possible to synchronize also all the other, pagan histories (however "false" they might be) and to comprehend them as a unity. The theological compulsion toward homogenization reached beyond what the pagan authors were able to burden themselves with. Thus it became possible to newly interpret the heterogeneous and successive disintegration of the Roman Empire without having to relinquish the continuity of succeeding generations. For the latter stretched back to the unique story of Creation and the Fall from which the unity of the human race derived its meaning. This was based on a transpolitical, Christian experience thanks to the texts of revelation, which would also influence the theories of subsequent world histories, such as those of Voltaire and his followers.

Within the system of the Italian city-states and the European powers influencing them, another wave of experience led to the rediscovery of a genuinely political world, which inspired Machiavelli to make his large-scale and small-scale parallels and allowed him to read antiquity and modern history with regard to their common social presuppositions and possibilities for political action.

The disintegration of the universal church constituted another wave of experience that can be traced back to various readings of the Bible. It also led to mutually contradictory criticisms of the Bible and finally rendered those all too human texts legible as unique sources of historical revelation, if only to relativize the texts dogmatized by the church. Out of the heritage of theology and out of the heritage of the perennially conflictual history of law, came the birth of modern hermeneutics that finally helped to institutionalize philological methods. Since then, every retrospective reinterpretation of world history has access to all kinds of methods. Even with the specific ability of our hermeneutic procedures to open both the difference and the otherness of the past (which otherwise cannot be perceived at all), it remains necessary to translate this past into one's own language. To this extent, here, too, the anthropological condition—that all rewriting of the previous tradition is required to accommodate it to one's own hermeneutically reflected experience—is valid.

A new wave of experience revealed the differentiation of all units of action according to the interests that motivate them. First, it justified the autonomy of states against religious prohibitions, then the autonomy of citizens against feudal relations, and finally, it provided a lasting legitimization for colonial, industrial, and imperial expansion. All functional explanations that reduce the modern change of experience to the preservation of interests or the economic increase of needs, allow the whole of history henceforth to be reinterpreted retrospectively (like the archaeology of Thucydides) in order to discover the conditions of modern self-experience.

Regardless of what is adduced, especially in terms of statistical methods, the primary aim is still to discover long-term changes or lasting conditions in order to make comprehensible the uniqueness of individual surprises. The statistical columns of the eighteenth century were both evidence for an ongoing divine predetermination as well as the pragmatic planning instrument of state power.[43] Both aspects, the diachronic conditions eluding spontaneous self-experience and the attempt to influence events by way of the diagnosis of those conditions, are still common features of statistical methods.

Once they have become autonomous, statistical methods can be retrospectively applied to the entire past, something that no historian—with the exception, perhaps, of Thucydides—thought of before the seventeenth century. Where no statistical sources are extant, the existing sources are evaluated statistically in order to rewrite the previous past in accordance with experience. This did not fail to produce empirically verifiable results. Think of the prosopographical or the many demographic analyses that have led to new historical information, be it class-specific, regional, denominational, medical, or otherwise; or think of the reconstitution of families, not only of the aristocracy but now also of the lower classes; or of the lexical analyses that throw light upon long-term linguistic change beyond the hermeneutic investigation of single texts, and much more.

If one tries to derive a result from diachronically retrospective rewritings, two one-sided answers, as mentioned at the outset, offer themselves.[44] The entire history of the present and of the past could be reduced to the primary experiences of the living generational unity in question. Then, all history would be nothing else than history always retrospectively rewritten, insofar as it could be confirmed by one's own experience. This answer is not wrong, but insufficient. The result would be a radical relativism, which would surely vindicate a claim of totality for individual interpretations but would necessarily—by experience—be superseded.

The other answer would place the burden of proof on the immanent history of methods. Undoubtedly, once they are established, methods can be rationally checked, recalled, and corrected, so that, thanks to methodological innovations and differentiations, an accumulated epistemological progress can be measured. The alternatives of wrong and right have to be posed more radically, answered more exactly. This answer, too, is not wrong, but it is equally insufficient.

The present essay aims at an anthropological correlation, without necessarily achieving an exact fit between the history of methods and the history of experience. With their three temporal layers, the ways of human experience are formally prior to all specific acquisitions of experience. Only because of this can concrete experiences be undergone, collected, and changed. As soon as this procedure is consciously reflected, it can also lead to methods that allow these procedures to be rationally comprehended. The formalizable claim of all methods is most likely compatible with the formalizable ways of acquiring experience.

The continuation of history is based on the fact that experiences, once made, are potentially repeatable, not only because of their methodological reuse but because the modes of experience structurally repeat themselves—otherwise history would not be comprehensible. What really changes is far less than the subjectively unique surprises of participants lead us to suspect. It is the methods that enable us to reconstruct unique and repeatable experiences, and it is methodological change that allows us to process newly arrived experiences and make them, in turn, the basis for new applications.

Anthropologically speaking, then, enduring and long-term structures exist that contain the conditions of possibility for the emergence of singular histories. These conditions—the reasons why something happened in this and not some other way—have first to be defined theoretically and metahistorically, then be practiced methodologically; however, they belong as much to real history as do the unique surprises giving rise to specific, concrete histories. History always runs in different temporal rhythms, both repeating itself and slowly or spontaneously changing. This is why human experiences are preserved, changed, or differentiated according to their temporal gradation. The focus on the diachronic uniqueness of all events, which has overwhelmingly governed history, is understandable because all human beings make their own experiences for themselves—as unique as they are or seem to be as individual people. Why, then, are all events, analogous to individual experience, not unique? Herein lies a mistake that is just as obvious. Every history, incontestably unique, contains structures of its own conditions of possibility, the finitely delimited spaces for movement, which change with a speed other than that of the events themselves. If one focuses on this temporal multilayeredness, then history also proves to be the space for possible repeatability; it is never only diachronic, but, depending on how it is temporally perceived and experienced, is also synchronic. That is an insight of Thucydides worth recovering and developing with our differentiated methods. Therefore, in these last pages, I will endeavor to move in this direction. Many of the epochal waves of experience discussed so far that have necessitated the rewriting of previous history were first perceived and methodologically processed by the vanquished. This leads us to the assumption that we are facing a historical-anthropological constant here whose formal criterion consists in its—synchronic, so to speak—repeatability.

V. The History of the Victors—A History
of the Vanquished

The principle based on experience that history is made by the victors
in the short run, may be maintained over a middle-range span, but never
controlled for a long time, can easily be proven. Our last series of examples
involving long-term reinterpretations of the past can testify to this. The
structural change of Thucydides' archaeology; divine providence; Machiavellian patterns of behavior; interests, constants, or trends determined by
socioeconomic factors—acting human beings can react in some way to all
these long-term pregivens, but the pregivens themselves more or less elude
their control. It cannot be in the primary interest of the victors to thematize these. Their history has a short-term perspective and is focused on
those series of events that, through their own efforts, brought them victory.
And when they lay claim to long-term trends, such as divine providence,
or a teleological path to the nation-state, real socialism, or liberty, to legit-
imize their victory historically, this leads very easily to deformations of the
view of the past. Think of Guizot's history of civilization,[45] or Droysen's
Prussian history,[46] both of which are difficult to sustain even in the face of
a textually immanent ideology critique. The historian who is on the side of
the victor is prone to interpret short-term successes from the perspective of
a continuous, long-term teleology ex post facto.

This does not apply to the vanquished. Their first primary experience
is that everything happened differently from how it was planned or hoped.
If they reflect methodologically at all, they face a greater burden of proof
to explain why something happened in this and not the anticipated way.
From this, a search for middle- or long-range reasons might be initiated to
frame and perhaps explain the chance event of the unique surprise. It is
thus an attractive hypothesis that precisely from the unique gains in experience imposed upon them spring insights of lasting duration and, consequently, of greater explanatory power. If history is made in the short run by
the victors, historical gains in knowledge stem in the long run from the
vanquished.[47]

The hypothesis that far-reaching insights into history stem from the
vanquished, does not, of course, lead to the opposite conclusion that every
history written by the vanquished is therefore more insightful. After 1918,
the Germans were fixated on paragraph 231 of the Versailles treaty, incensed

over its fixing of guilt for the war on them. They unleashed a moralistic debate about innocence, which obstructed every insight into the deeper and longer-lasting reasons for the defeat. Compared to this, Hippolyte Taine's self-critical analysis of the French circumstances prior to their defeat in 1871 was much more sophisticated, precisely because of its long-term and psychological-anthropological thematics, namely, to look for *Les origines de la France contemporaine* in the Enlightenment and the revolution: "J'ai écrit comme si j'avais eu pour sujet les révolutions de Florence ou d'Athènes."[48] The antihistoric point of his potential comparison with other revolutions relates to our hypothesis. The experience of being vanquished contains an epistemological potential that transcends its cause, especially when the vanquished are required to rewrite general history in conjunction with their own. Many innovations in the field of new methodological interpretations of history, behind which stand very personal defeats and generation-specific waves of experience, can be explained in this way.

Herodotus's first political experience probably consisted in the banishment of his family by the tyrant Lygdamis from Halicarnassus. And the expansion of Athenian maritime power was also above all an experience imposed upon him, which drove him, perhaps in order to process it, to Athens, from where he moved to the Athenian colony of Thurii. To be sure, he does not count among those who were completely vanquished, but, as Christian Meier has shown,[49] within the accelerated change of experience in the classical fifth century, he certainly found himself among those who were in a precarious situation. The fact that once-great cities are now small, that previously small cities are now great, that fortune is generally inconstant—these maxims of experience that introduced the *Histories*, might also be read as a lasting principle derived from all individual histories.[50]

As commander, Thucydides came a few hours too late to liberate Amphipolis, which was allied with Athens. For this, he was banished for twenty years because he "was on both sides," as he added laconically.[51] After the unique surprise that things worked out differently than intended, a perspective was imposed which allowed him to reconstruct the war from a distance, from the standpoint of both parties. The minimal compulsion toward objectivity, which teaches to comprehend history solely from the experience of all participants, was used by Thucydides with the maximum methodological effect. From an enforced distance, Thucydides was able to recognize and represent the fact that every history contains more than what the individual participants might see in it, that history is undergirded by long-term forces. This was the consciously reflected distance of the vanquished and the banished. As an Athenian, he himself finally belonged among the losers. Because of his uniquely processed acquisition of experience, he can therefore still be read as a contemporary even today. There are simply histories that are resistant to every ideology critique and remain methodologically shielded because they have rendered primary experiences unmistakable and inexchangeable.

Polybius, taken to Rome as a hostage, had to first experience the absolute estrangement of the vanquished, before he learned to identify himself with the victor to such an extent that he was able to describe its ascent as a world power; but he did so necessarily from a perspective that was both internal and external, one which could never have been available to the victorious Romans.[52]

Certainly, empirically speaking, many strands lead to the notion that a historian would practice his history *apolis*, as Lucian demanded,[53] be they of a psychological, social, religious nature; or ones dependent on the obligatory voyages that equip him with the expertise for mediating proximity and distance, spatiality and temporality. But to be vanquished is a specific, genuinely historical experience, one which cannot be learned or substituted, and, as in the above-mentioned cases, one which enabled a method that guaranteed a continuous acquisition of experience.

This is also true for Roman historians. Sallust, the spiritual student of Thucydides, withdrew himself as soon as he was no longer, as a politician, able to treat the irresolvable conflicts of a century marked by civil wars, in order to inquire, as a historian, about the reasons for decay. In Tacitus we also find this primal experience of an open and shielded situation of civil war in a radicalized form. As a youthful witness of the year of the four emperors (68–69), and involved as a senator in the terroristic system of Domitian, Tacitus points to the boundaries of what is humanly possible, boundaries which can nevertheless always be extended and surpassed. How lies turn into corruption, fear and courage into crime, where perpetrator, spectator and bystander all work together to increase and perpetuate the terror: with his subtle method of representation, Tacitus transposed such experiences into generation-deep knowledge. "Reperies qui ob similitudinem morum aliena malefacta sibi objectari putent."[54] It was the knowledge gained by someone who was inextricably enveloped by circumstances, someone who was existentially vanquished.[55] This is why his acquired experience could be drawn upon in analogous situations without losing any of its applicability or, indeed, its truth. Thus Lipsius founded his political system on the *Annals* and *Histories* of Tacitus (which he structured in this way) in order to point toward possible exits from the turmoil of the religious civil wars, without quoting from the contested Bible. The mediated experience of Tacitus had in some way made the thresholds of surprise foreseeable, which were time and again a point of contestation for the fanatical denominations. Not only were new insights gained, but they became possible, because insights with long-term applicability were rediscovered. Rational, political answers became historically justifiable.

Finally, the Roman citizen Augustine belonged to the vanquished. When the stream of refugees poured into North Africa from Rome after its conquest by Alaric in 410, Augustine realized that the history of the successful Christianization of the Roman Empire could no longer continue to be written in the same way as in the past. The answer that Augustine found proved to be unique with respect to the situation, but enduring with respect to the history of its reception. Through his doctrine of the two worlds, he sought salvation from all history, and insofar as he relativized earthly attempts at self-organization eschatologically, he taught that they should be interpreted all the more austerely. He certainly processed the political experience of the catastrophe and its social consequences primarily in theological terms and only indirectly offered a historical exoneration. But his interpretation both contained the possibility of institutional solutions for the future—the twofold differentiation of *sacerdotium* and *imperium*—as well as taught that the entire past be read, in modern parlance, with regard to the structural limits of human power and societal bonds. If one no longer shares his method of scriptural exegesis, one can nevertheless adopt the principles of historical experience processed by it.

Also at the threshold of our modernity, there stand three vanquished men who taught how to write one's own time anew and how to rewrite the past with insights that have remained exemplary ever since. Up until the end of the nineteenth century, 123 editions of Commynes were recorded. He created the new genre of the memoir; it testifies to the uncanny experiences of a world that is politically autogenerative and transposed into enduring knowledge through situative reflections on the acquisition, enlargement, and—still God-given—limits of power. After he changed his alliance with Burgundy to one with Louis XI of France, he learned to judge "stereo-scopically"[56]—but he only wrote his memoirs after being banished from the French court. The same fate was suffered by both Machiavelli, driven from Florence in 1512 by the Medici, and Guicciardini, exiled and banned by the short-lived Florentine Republic in 1530. Both lost their leading positions in diplomacy, the military, and administration after they had unsuccessfully sought a moderately republican solution to the perennial crisis of their city-state. Both wrote their great works in exile and found causes that were not accessible to direct control. They thematize the interplay of social forms of conduct, mentalities, and constitutional forms, simultaneously embedded within the increasing interactions between domestic and foreign policy. The skeptical attitude that forced itself upon them became a method, and both became masters of modern politics and the political historiography that followed from it.[57]

Our specifically modern experience that not only events surpass one another but also the presuppositions of these events, the structures themselves, change—and this not just retrospectively, but already in the immediate perception—led to a temporally multilayered perspectivization of all of history, now reflected in a methodological consciousness. Not only the recurring changeability of all things, the *mutatio rerum*, but change itself became the great theme of history. Since then, a new type of the vanquished has existed: those who perceive themselves surpassed by history or progress, or who have set themselves the goal of catching up with or surpassing the development of things. Since then, not only has political localization been part of historical perception—this has more or less always been the case—but social or economic situation decides whether someone is left behind or thrust forward. This is "bourgeois" history, seen from the perspective of where progress and its negative consequences are first experienced. It is the distinction of the Scottish Enlightenment thinkers to have realized this and to be the first to have drawn the methodological consequences.

It is an attractive hypothesis to assume that the great methodological change brought about by the Scottish social historians was only possible within the vicinity of the English. For it was they who thought to explain the structural, long-term change that could be observed in the evolution of the English commercial nation toward industrialism. Compared with this, the Scots themselves still lived in an archaic clan system, the representatives of which were absorbed by the English Parliament in 1707, before and after the violently suppressed rebellion of the Stuarts in 1745–46 in a climate of anti-Jacobite suspicion. They were equipped with theologically and philo-sophically highly developed institutions, especially the universities, from where all these developments could be observed from the distance of those not directly involved.

Coming as they did from a country that had been left behind, En-gland's progress was the primary experience of Kames, Hume, Robertson, Ferguson, Smith, Millar, and Stewart, so much so as to elevate this tempo-ral differentiation to the methodological starting point for their new his-tory. Making the utmost of all the historical innovators of the past, ex-ploiting travel narratives old and new, the Scots looked for legal, economic, religious, moral, educational—in short, pregiven "social" conditions—so that they could derive from a minimum of natural constants a maximum of manifest change with their analysis. Since direct sources were difficult to find for such questions, which turned political history and its events into an epiphenomenon of structural change, the Scots consciously included hypotheses and conjectures in their arguments. The production of theory became an imperative of method. How else should "experiences," which were accessible to primary experience but neither in the past nor in the present, be verified if not through a theoretically presupposed "natural his-tory of bourgeois society"? The recourse to the "nature" of social and insti-tutional changes also made it possible to proceed in a systematic and com-parative fashion, so that empirical confirmation based on the sources could be left for future research. Since then, it has become possible to picture all of history with the help of economic, sociological, but also political, and, indeed, anthropological theories and analyses, moving gradually and to-ward an open future.[58]

I will only pose here the question whether the specifically method-ological insights of the German historical school may be seen as an enter-prise analogous to that of the Scots. It can be said that Niebuhr and Hum-boldt, the theoretical and empirical initiators of philologically reflected method, cannot be understood without the prior examples of the develop-ment of Britain and of the French Revolution. The politics and economy that were making their way from west to east imposed an intensified need for reflection on the entire German intellectual class. Whether the peculiar re-course to investigation of sources substantiated only by historico-linguistic analysis, a kind of knowledge that can be subjected to rational proof, can be sufficiently explained in this way is more than doubtful. Niebuhr, for one, saw himself as a member of the vanquished: he suffered the same fate "as Tacitus."[59] Both of them, Humboldt and Niebuhr, failed as statesmen—despite all their great administrative and political exploits. Accordingly, we might see their innovative works on history and the history of language, on constitutions, law, and economy as methodologically sound compensations for the renunciations imposed upon them.

The primary experience of French historiography, on the other hand, remains the Great Revolution itself, including its renewed enactments. All of French history after 1789 can be structured, to a slowly decreasing extent, according to who allied himself with which phase of the revolution and thus belonged among the vanquished or among the respective temporary victors. The most prominent figure is, of course, Tocqueville,[60] who, as an aristocrat, had fundamentally accepted the downfall of the ruling class. He remained one of the vanquished. He developed the first long-term interpretation of the revolution, the causes of which were only intensified by the revolutionary events, as the administrative control of society increased, a society that became proportionally more egalitarian. The revolution became the accelerator of prevailing tendencies, ones which were experienced as success by the temporary victors and as "history" by the vanquished.

Marx can be read from what is almost the opposite perspective. He interpreted the evolution of history as a pathway toward victory for the hitherto weaker class, while the temporary victors are always surpassed precisely by the class of proletarians. But notwithstanding all the historico-philosophical premises that guided his interpretations, in his specifically historical writings, on the Revolution of 1848–49 and the uprising of the Commune, he wrote *as* a person who was vanquished, if not *like* someone vanquished. He had to accept the situatively unique defeat as the intellectual spokesman of the proletariat, and from it, he sought to gain long-term explanations meant to guarantee future success. This is why he succeeded in developing methods of ideological critique that sought to correlate long-term economic processes with contemporary politics. The method he discovered has survived him, even if the actual development of history did not occur as he expected.

The question cannot be answered here whether Max Weber also belongs among the politically and existentially vanquished. It is a reasonable assumption that he was a vanquished person who could not catch up with actually experienced history and who—almost fatalistically—developed theories for it, which make possible at least a methodologically verifiable analysis of long-term structural changes that transcend all individual experiences.

Enough of examples. Every historian will be able to treat the historical innovators of the methodologically reflected comprehension of all historical experience as unique cases. Methodological innovations are either reconstructed in the texts themselves, or traced back to personal abilities, that is, social, psychological, or other dispositions. The present essay, too, cannot do without drawing upon such arguments, and this discussion of the vanquished is an attempt to provide an anthropological constant. The condition of being vanquished apparently contains an inexhaustible epistemological potential.

Historical change feeds upon the vanquished. Should they survive, they create the irreplaceable primary experience of all histories: that histories take another course than that intended by those involved. This always unique experience cannot be chosen and remains unrepeatable. Yet it can be processed through the search for causes, which last for a middle- or long-term period, and thus are repeatable. This is what distinguishes methods. They can be abstracted from the unique event; they can be applied elsewhere. Once experience has been methodologically transposed into knowledge by the vanquished—and which victor does not finally belong to them? —it remains accessible beyond all change of experience. This might offer some comfort, perhaps a gain. In practice, it would mean saving us from victories. Yet every experience speaks against it.

Translated by Jobst Welge

5

The Temporalization of Utopia

The dispute over the question of what a utopia is was newly rekindled in the last decade. Genre-historical definitions and conceptual-historical attempts at explanation scarcely agree. Philosophical interpretations attribute an anthropological function to utopia and social-historical exegeses historicize or ideologize these functions. In the following, all these questions will only be touched upon in passing.

The field of usage of "utopia" is certainly multivalent. Despite its positive valuation by Ernst Bloch, it is striking that writers of utopias only reluctantly call themselves "utopians" and that the term, despite its genealogy dating back to Thomas More, seldom appears in the titles of literary utopias. A good author of good utopias evidently has very little desire to be a utopian, in the same way that Machiavelli was no Machiavellian, or that Marx did not want to be a Marxist. This is also the case for both of the authors that I would like to use for developing my investigation. Although neither wrote a so-called utopia, seen in genre-historical terms they nevertheless did so. The first is Louis-Sébastien Mercier. In 1770 he composed a "dream," as he subtitled his work, whose main title was *The Year 2440.*[1] He wrote a futuristic novel, as we say today, and, furthermore, it was probably the first in world literature.

Our second witness is Carl Schmitt, the constitutional law expert. In 1918, he wrote *Die Buribunken,* and called his essay a *"historico-philosophical meditation."*[2] In genre-historical terms, it was a satire. Dressed in parodistic vestments, it was meant to be as funny as it was serious, while Mercier had taken his design of the future, in a naive sense, as bitterly serious.

My theme is thus the onset of the future in utopia, or stated differently: the metamorphosis of utopia into the philosophy of history, a term available in the strong sense of the word only since the second half of the eighteenth century—in short, the temporalization of utopia.

The year 1770, when Mercier's novel was first published, is a symbolic year. It was the start of a decade in which the state of the world began profoundly to change. In the east, the great powers began to partition Poland; on the other side of the Atlantic, the American colonies began to protest; and in France, the aggregate conditions of the Enlightenment began to change. It was the time in which the voices of *philosophes* lost their power; as Mercier provocatively stated in the dedication of his book: Enough of projects, enough of criticism—no more discussion, act!—so went the hidden message.[3]

Mercier himself was a writer, a prolific writer, "le premier livrier de la France," as he called himself,[4] imaginative, keen, and not without success. *The Year 2440* became a best-seller, and, in the editions that followed, he quadrupled the size of the book by enriching it with backdated prognoses, for instance regarding aviation, so as to remain up-to-date as an ex post facto prophet. His influence, extended by translations and imitations leading to the establishment of a new genre, can in no way be underestimated. Nevertheless, he remained a second-rate intellectual. Defamed as an ape of Rousseau or as a caricature of Diderot,[5] he tried, for a long time in vain, to procure a pension from an aristocratic patron. The style of his moral indignation over the corrupted ancien régime was correspondingly condescending, and in a note to *The Year 2440*, he surely made the sharpest and bloodiest prediction of revolution ever formulated prior to 1789.[6] But in 1788, when he was finally in the possession of a pension granted to him by Marie Antoinette,[7] he toned down his prognosis. Unrest could no longer deteriorate into insurrection—that had become morally impossible. The police were very careful, even minded their own business; affection for the court was widespread. With the foregoing avowal of the monarchical constitution, an ironic interpretation is out of the question since the great mass of unenlightened people would reject democratic regulations.[8]

Without doubt, even Mercier lived with the ambivalent conscience of all enlightened thinkers who, maneuvering and arguing between royalty and the people, had to dole out their moral compensations in varying amounts. Ivan Nagel gave Mercier the bitter appellation of "intellectual as scoundrel and martyr." But we will look at his work, which speaks for itself.

The genre-historical turning point that represents Mercier's real intellectual accomplishment can be precisely described. Mercier shows us Paris in the year 2440, as he experienced it in a dream. It is a precise utopia of the future.

To be sure, the "nowheres," the spatial counterworlds of traditional utopias, can also be read as potential visions of the future. Indeed, they always contain unrealities of all sorts whose critical programs of contrast may be calls for changing, reforming, or revolutionizing one's own world. But the space of experience of these traditional utopias was primarily spatial and so was its mode of representation. A traveler is driven onto a foreign, trans-European shore and discovers there all sorts of ideal states or prestate societies of the most varying orders. The discoverer returns home and tells how beautifully kept and pleasing the other world is. An unrealistic or even potential future for one's own world might then be derived from it. Although a great number of utopias related to the past already existed, what was fundamentally missing was the temporal dimension of the future as the site of utopia.

After Mercier, this changed, and one may add, not by chance either. In 1770, the year that his utopia was published, Cook had just explored the east coast of Australia, and the European voyages of discovery did not have very much left to reconnoiter in the eighteenth century. The finiteness of the surface of the earth left hardly a strip of coast between land and sea unexplored. Human beings have, as Rousseau once said, stretched themselves out across the globe with every fiber of their bodies, like polyps.[9] Therefore, the authors of "nowheres" had for some time already switched over to the moon or the stars or descended below the surface of the earth. Once recognized, the spatial possibilities for establishing a utopia on our earth's finite surface were exhausted. The utopian spaces had been surpassed by experience. The best solution for escaping this growing pressure of experience was simple, but it had to be found. If utopia was no longer to be discovered or established on our present-day earth nor in the divine world beyond, it had to be shifted into the future. Finally the additional space into which fantasies could stream in was available, and infinitely reproducible, like time itself. With Mercier, the futuristic novel was established. And with this, the status of utopia changed. Even though Mercier's utopia still contained many traditional elements when seen in genre-historical terms, two fundamental changes are worth mentioning.

The first concerns the function of the author. The role of the author of a utopian fiction shifts, seemingly subliminally, but definitely decisively. Authors no longer discover what they come across and find, that is to say, pretend to find. Rather the authors of a vision of the future become themselves, in an authentic sense, the producers of their utopia. What was contained in a spatial counterworld could previously be observed or registered, if only in the medium of fiction, in terms of the content of experience by someone who had traveled to faraway lands and might have presented his imagined discoveries at home as reality. His credibility grew, as it were, with spatial distance, which was not easily traversable. But the fiction itself lived off the fiction of its potential corroboration of what was to be found and what could be seen in space.

But with the utopia of the future, it was different: the future cannot be observed or checked; as the future, it cannot be captured by experience. In the repertoire of constructing fiction, the utopia of the future is, therefore, a genuine and pure achievement of the author's mind. Even the imagined support of spatial controls breaks free. In this way, the fictional status of a temporal utopia differentiates itself from a spatial utopia. The reality signals of the author's fiction no longer lie in the space existing today but rather in the mind of the author alone. He himself and no one else is the originator of the utopia that turns into a "*uchronia.*" The reality of the future exists only as the product of the writer while the controllable ground of the present is abandoned.

The Paris of the year 2440 is accommodating to this solipsistic, coerced stylization of its author, Mercier. For every citizen is actually a writer and vice versa. Herein lies the social-historical soil from which his vision takes nourishment. In the expanded edition of 1787, Mercier remarked about the contemporary situation, that the Crown and the citizens' freedoms balanced one another out. The missing Estates General and their tasks have long since been replaced or overtaken by the large number of citizens who speak and write; and speaking and writing eliminate all possibility of despotism.[10] In the year 2440, this has become the rule. Every citizen is an author. Since religion will be replaced by morality, there are also no longer the two outdated testaments. In their place are those testaments that the citizen-writers leave behind toward the end of their lives for posterity to read in order to guarantee the accumulation of accomplished moral achievements through testamentary means. Such a book is the soul of the deceased.[11] Thus the Paris of 2440 becomes a writer's paradise. By virtue of his authorship, every author is already an originator of authority. Indeed, it is a compensatory utopia of those enlightened literati who, prior to 1789, knew themselves to be just on the verge of a power that had for long not been theirs.

The citizen as writer and the writer as citizen: this is also the basic anthropological figure of the coming humanity that Mercier projected in the future from a perspective clearly prescribed by sociological terms. With this, I am coming to the second feature that differentiates the spatial counterworld from the utopia of the future.

Any utopia of the future has to assume temporal continuities regardless of whether they are openly thematized or not. The simple antithesis of a spatial counterworld, previously reachable by ship, must thus be temporally mediated. The argument from today to tomorrow, out of the present into the future, demands other criteria for credibility than the great leap across the water. Thus Mercier assumed the succession of generations; he confronts the old Paris with the new. The old streets are still there, only they are wider, more beautiful, and cleaner. The old carriages drive down the streets, only their passengers are different people: no more aristocrats, rather the elderly and the infirm, the poor or those citizens worthy of merit now ride, and they ride cautiously, unlike the aristocracy, so as not to besmirch, bother, or run over their fellow citizens.[12] The entire utopia of the future thus lived off points of connection not only in the realm of the fictive but in the empirically redeemable present.

In a word, what the future offers is compensation for the misery of the present: social, political, moral, and literary compensation—whatever the sentimental heart or enlightened rationality may desire. To put it differently: The imagined perfection of the formerly spatial counterworld is temporalized. Thus utopia moves directly in line with the objectives of enlightened philosophers.

Seen from a literary perspective, only a nuance distinguishes Mercier's utopia from the remaining projects, hopes, and intentions of the *sociétés de pensée*. Mercier did not show how the Paris of the future might be but rather how it will be. What is desired is presented as declarations about reality.

The constitutional monarchy still rules, but the estates have been replaced by an elite of merit. Monasteries have become obsolete, but the now married monks undertake, in the ascetic tradition, especially dangerous tasks for the benefit of humanity. The Bastille is destroyed; the monarch has left Versailles and is human just like everyone else. Mercier thus extracts in 1770 a rationally conceivable but not yet practically realizable horizon of planning. The argument of a better tomorrow emerging from an impoverished today is the model after which this utopia is constructed. Planning and optimization bind the present to the future. To this extent, Mercier's *The Year 2440* is more precisely classified as a progress philosopheme than a spatial counterworld. For his novel was more modern than the countless conventional utopias that flowed from the literati, especially after 1750.

This must be briefly explained.[13] Until the eighteenth century, the doctrine of *perfectio* offered a hierarchical classificatory model that was, in principle, conceived statically and spatially. Striving toward an earthly, relative perfection was the timeless imperative, so to speak. Whether it was utopia or political theory, moral philosophy or theology, in this respect, they fulfilled comparable tasks. Notwithstanding the history of utopia, the *perfectio* ideal became temporalized in the course of the early modern period. For this reason, St. Pierre and Turgot spoke of "perfectionnement," of the historical pathway to earthly perfection. The goal is included in the path that had to be covered in order to reach *perfectio*. Rousseau went even further with the neologism "perfectibilité." With perfectibility, with the capability of becoming perfect, the goal is completely temporalized and incorporated into the human agents themselves, without an end point. The setting of the goal becomes iterative. Perfectibility is a keyword of the new age. The static, quasi-spatial pregivens of the *perfectio* ideal are temporalized. As is well known, it was an open question for Rousseau whether advancement would necessarily lead to improvement. On the contrary, the process of civilization and creation of ownership, the formation of governments, the increasing division of labor and rising production all contain the danger that humans will be corrupted by these processes and degenerate morally. For Rousseau, perfectibility is, therefore, a dialectical concept, at once containing the chance of increasing dangers and growing benefits. In this respect, he is neutral toward progress, thematizing instead the temporalization of all social goals purely and simply.

Mercier, a disciple of Rousseau's, reinterpreted this optimistically. After 1789, he edited Rousseau and stylized him in accordance with constitutional history. Mercier no longer had the opportunity to take him seriously as a Jacobin because he had already landed in jail as a member of the Convention and narrowly escaped the guillotine. Mercier thus celebrated Rousseau as one of the "first authors of the revolution," as he called him.[14] It may remain open here whether he meant the writer or the originator of the revolution. Both senses are contained because the convergence of "writer" and "founder of authority" is the basic anthropological figure Mercier used to try to reposition his utopia as a political praxis.

With this, we have arrived at our first result: Mercier's utopia of the future is a variant of the philosophy of progress; its theoretical foundation is the temporalization of the *perfectio* ideal. The anticipation of the future was only redeemable as the cognitive achievement of the author and writer. The utopian narration of the future is but a particularly effectual literary configuration of what the philosophy of history of the time had to achieve as philosophy of the mind. The author is first of all no historian or chronicler but is foremost the producer of the coming time, executor of its aptitude for perfection. He is, so to speak, the incarnation of the utopian dimension that inheres within every philosophy of history. The literary means is the narration of a dream, namely Mercier's reverie of living in the Paris of 2440. As a wise man who is centuries old, he is, in a daydream, led through a city he hardly recognizes by a man who is just as wise and rational. He finds himself, as he says, on a rung of a progressive ladder of time, which will bring his Paris to still greater heights.[15]

The time produced in the mind of the author is the new, true sovereign. For this reason, Mercier dedicates his book not to a ruler but to the illustrious and sublime year 2440 itself. And he is quick to add that it is the writer's pen which alone bridges temporal distance and punishes or exonerates the rulers of this world. He could not be any clearer in characterizing the convergence of the historical future with its writerly production. The future no longer served, as it did earlier, to secure or increase posthumous fame or to dispense punishments by literary means; instead, the future is, as it were, historically anticipated through writing. Seen topologically, it is in this way that the role of historical prophets distinguishes itself from the traditional role of the judging historian.

As for the structural elements of this utopia of the future, let me make several remarks. These elements involve an anti-apocalypse. Eschatological elements are progressively reinterpreted. To be sure, initially the alternative is considered whether the future does not just end in ashes, rubble, and ruins. But despite this prophetic threat, in the end it is shown that only Versailles lies in ruins. The oppressor of the enslaved people, Louis XIV, is condemned to eternally lament his disgraceful deeds. Mercier visits him while aware of having-always-already-been-right—as he is bitten by a snake. With this etiological-theological point, the return to the lost paradise is apostrophized in the present of history.[16]

What, then, is history itself, which can be read from the distance of time? It is a question of the fulfillment of a moral demand. The violence of spirit and reason, a violence that eradicates all violence, is the thrust leading to the future. Thus we are dealing with a projection without and free from resistance, namely a linear model. Goodwill is already the guarantee of its fulfillment. When seen with respect to the contents of his utopia, one may speak of Mercier as a reformer; when seen with respect to his philosophy of history, he succumbed to the hypocrisy of the late Enlightenment. Individual examples, which can be easily adduced, testify to this.

As such, although censorship is not eliminated, censorship is not the issue for Mercier since it enforces morality. Scurrilous books, starting with Aristophanes or Petronius, are simply burned. Questionable works, for instance, by Voltaire or Montesquieu, are published in an abridged, expurgated form; only morally noble authors, such as Rousseau, are published in unabridged editions and simultaneously in paperback format so as to be generally accessible. Everything learned in school is to be based upon the *Encyclopédie*, the starting place in the future (chap. 28).

Yet censorship still functions much more subtly. For authors, the modus operandi is self-accusation. An indiscretion has to be atoned for over a period of two years; the author appears as "l'homme au masque," accompanied by virtuous citizens, until he has become acculturated once again to public morality (chap. 10). The symbol for resistance and the symbol for maintaining secrecy with respect to any censorship become reversed, turning into the testimony for moral coaching and its voluntary but compulsory enforcement.

The death penalty is hardly required anymore, and when it is, it is voluntarily accepted by those who are guilty. Since transgressions are not for social reasons, they will more likely concern murders out of passion or jealousy, and have to be atoned for due to their deficiency of reason. The enforcement is a moral festival of atonement and ends with the assurance of mutual goodwill upon the death of the repenter (chap. 16). Since the doctrine of reincarnation will have gained in credibility, death, too, is defused; in this way, Mercier opens a route to evade the aporia between death and progress (chap. 19, p. 186).

Marriage for love, anticipated in a prognostic fashion, is decreed by the state (chap. 38). Dowries are forbidden in order to prevent social differences from influencing the consummation of marriage. The ideal wife wears no makeup, and neither smokes nor drinks; she is not a woman of the salons nor a coquette. A woman remains who is reduced to her sexual characteristics and who seemingly naturally represents but a drained natural being. Mercier designed de facto the image of the intimate middle-class family, where the father rules in a patriarchal fashion, and the mother is sensitive and prepared to be subordinate. Mercier himself, as he writes, desired to get married shortly before his death so as to legalize his free love relationship.

Thus we have our second result: Mercier's temporal utopia is a naive projection of late Enlightenment demands, one which does not admit a historical factor of change. The result is the terror resulting from virtue unsuspectingly and unintentionally coming to power while trying to dispense with power. Therefore, virtuous terror sneaks in unchecked. In the foreground, utopia appears harmless and reformative, glazed over on the level of intentions and wishes by the dawn of a Rousseauian innocence; but utopia also supplies us with semantic background information which we, coming afterward, know to interpret.

But already contemporaries of Mercier had quickly recognized the explosive nature of his work. Wieland, who was later the first to predict the rise of the dictatorship of Napoleon, also immediately recognized what was really at stake here. Mercier's utopia, as he said, is "the Last Judgment of the present constitution of France."[17]

After 1789, Mercier proudly professed as much. He was to be the true prophet of the French Revolution. He announced and prepared for it. To be sure, he heralded and predicted quite a lot, surprisingly much; however, with the self-certainty of prophetic gesture, he doubtless aimed too high. For Mercier did not see what was concealed in his vision and what the revolution had brought to light without his noticing it: the terrorist implications of his virtuous wishes whose fulfillment he had projected as a writer into the future.

This is the subject of our second author.

As the Wilhelmine Kaiserreich collapsed, Carl Schmitt wrote his essay on the "Buribunks." It was published in the journal *SUMMA*, edited by Franz Blei and Jakob Hegner. In its subtitle, the essay is introduced as a "historico-philosophical meditation." Filled with a wealth of imagination and allusions, it is an extravagant parody of historicism and the belief in progress, as expressed in the agendas of the scientific and social organizations of the time. The content of this parody, or more accurately, this satire, can be characterized as a negative utopia. The implicit criticism was aimed at those utopian elements contained in the historical belief in facts and their historico-philosophical idealization. What was specifically utopian was the belief that humans, with their awareness, not only were able to grasp history, but that by virtue of their awareness, they could also execute and master history. This philosophy of the mind extended to all three temporal dimensions, mutually relativized and, at the same time, progressively interpreted. In this respect, Carl Schmitt's criticism aimed at the entire intellectual foundation of modernity, to the extent that it was designed and executed as historical progress.

The literary point is that the temporalization of self-propelling history is ironized as a mode of the performance of writing. Everybody is required to keep a diary. The interior is thus turned outward, making surveillance possible; surveillance is perfected and becomes a mode of the performance of perfected terror. Carl Schmitt presents the picture of a rising terror in the medium of writing, one which is legible as the unveiled reality of Mercier's utopia.

Let me briefly mention the content. The existence of the Buribunks is derived from the fact of a "Buribunkology." The discipline produces its own object, so that the convergence between Buribunkology and the actual "Buribunkdom" is generated in this way.

The authority of the Mercierian writer is taken at his word. The basic philosophical principle of this world's design is: "I think, therefore I am; I speak, therefore I am; I write, therefore I am; I publish, therefore I am."[18] In an increasing gradation of identities, all writers are forced, in logical conformity to the law, beyond themselves.

I write that I write myself. . . . What is the great engine that lifts me out of this complacent circle of egohood? History!—I am thus a letter on the typewriter of history. . . . But upon writing, the world spirit apprehends itself through me, so that I, apprehending myself, simultaneously apprehend the world spirit. . . . Meaning: I am not only the reader of world history, but also its writer.

In every second of world history, the letters on the typewriter keyboard leap, impelled by the nimble fingers of the world-I, onto the white paper and continue the historical narrative. Only in the second that a single letter, selected from the senseless and meaningless indifference of the keyboard, strikes the living fullness of the white paper, is a historical reality created. This is the moment of birth; that is to say, the birth of the past, for the present is but the midwife who delivers the lived historical past from the dark womb of the future. As long as it is not reached, the future lies there as mute and indifferent as the keyboard of a typewriter, like a dark rat hole from which one second after the other, like one rat after the other, emerges into the light of the past. (104)

In the ironizing light of this historical philosophy of identity, the individual stages of progressive development are illuminated. Of course, Buribunkdom has its historical precursors. They include the great practitioners of autobiography and diary writing from Marcus Aurelius, Augustine, and Pliny the Elder—who wrote when he was not reading, and read when he was not writing—up to Richard Wagner. The world spirit comes to terms with itself in human beings who write and reflect; from them, Carl Schmitt, with mostly invented (although some real) references, creates the context for the modernity of the Buribunk movement. The Buribunks are the diary-writing collective conscience of history.

Don Juan, whose amorous adventures were recorded in a register by Leporello, functions as the natural polar opposite to the historical reflection which finds its reality in diaries. By keeping a register of Don Juan's adventures, Leporello, the servant of his master, did not yet cross over from the empire of nature to that of history. He does not produce a biographical continuum of individual amorous adventures, nor does he refer to the social and political conditions of these adventures. Moreover, he does not discover any individuality in Don Juan who nonchalantly seduced 1,003 women; he does not yet know of any details that might explain the uniqueness of the specific case. Lastly, he also does not know of any group campaigns by Don Juan's victims united together against their seducer. He also does not give any statistical breakdown of the victims, nor does he refer to a social welfare organization of victims, as little as he thinks of women's suffrage as a way to escape Don Juan's domination. Finally, he does not know of any psychological backgrounds, or backgrounds in the history of mentality—in Lamprecht's sense—into which the development of a Don Juan and that of his victims could be embedded. For these reasons, *Don Juan* is still performed today as such, but "Leporello's Tales" have not become suitable for the stage.

Leporello remains the servant who has not yet climbed to the height of historical and scientific-methodological awareness. He was not yet in a position to transform, through historical reflection, his existence as a servant into an existence as a master; he had not yet autobiographically made himself into a hero "by presenting the impressive picture of a superior manager who, with his superior business knowledge and intelligence, pulls the strings of a colorful Don Juan marionette" (94). Leporello lived before Diderot's *Jacques le Fataliste*, before Hegel's chapter on the master-slave dialectic in the *Phenomenology of Spirit*, before the scientific patterns of interpretation of positivism, of relativism, of historicism, and other modes of reflection contained in social organizations. Buribunkdom only appeared when all these demands, which were still not fulfilled by Leporello, had been realized.

The transformation of scientific demands into historical time was carried out by the founder and leader of the Buribunkology movement, that is to say, the true Buribunkdom, a man by the name of Ferker. He was a man of the people, in the sense of the lower classes. He came from a humble background and, eager for concrete results, worked his way up, finally, in a checkered career, dying while a Professor of Marketing and Upward Mobility at the Institute of Commerce in Alexandria. With increasing experience and reflection, he arrived at the motto: "Be your own history!" (96). Rallying behind this motto there emerged a worldwide association that had already allowed more than four hundred thousand Buribunkological dissertations to be written. Their quality was assured by the International Buribunkology Institute for Ferker and Associated Research ("Ibuffuff"), which, for its part, was subordinate to a kind of central committee, the Buribunks and Ferker Research Commission ("Buffak"). "Precisely this tremendous reality is of impressive value as evidence" (90).

Upon his death, Ferker had asked that his body be cremated so that his ashes could be divided up among all the printing houses of the world and placed in their ink in order to procure for himself, in every piece of printed matter, earthly immortality in this world.

Of course, this great leader was only a harbinger of the progressively more noble Buribunks. For he had made two errors. He married his housekeeper shortly before his death without recording this in any diary entries. The lack of candor and publicity could only point to a neuro-psycho-pathological illness and to a second abnormality, namely that he finally had "given himself up to poisonous dreams of the atavistic fear of death" without repositioning them in light of productive creation. Despite his contributions, Ferker thus remained at the threshold of the true Buribunkdom. He had a secret love and feared death. Only when these naturally induced preconditions are overcome is the path to true progress unobstructed. To have opened up this path is the work of Schnekke. For him, "any particular singularity is missing. . . . His ego, working according to the most extreme rules of its own, is located within an unpronounced universality, within an indifferent colorlessness which is the result of the most sacrificial will to power" (100). As Ferker's successor, Schnekke becomes the new leader for the noble or original Buribunks, effortlessly realizing the identity of universality and ego.

How is this empire, founded by succeeding leaders, organized? It is an empire consisting of people just writing diaries who, with every second, record everything in order to become capable of being historicized. History comes true only while and to the extent that it is written down. The intensification first carried out by Schnekke leads to the fact that the writing of the diary itself becomes the only historically capable and historically consequential deed. Through a greatly structured organization, he developed an effective procedure for producing an obligatory collective diary of humanity. Copies of completed diaries are made available to any authority, and, through indices of subjects and persons, it becomes possible to exercise a general surveillance, beginning with districts and extending through central headquarters. Thus, for example, any psychopathologist can, at a given time, examine all the dreams of a particular class of Buribunks; simultaneously, the same work is, once again, registered in order to place the historian of psychopathology in a position, a few hours later, to already survey the motivational context in which the psychopathologist formulated his or her investigations. The historico-philosophical reflection, which keeps only to the facts and whose existence is its writtenness, is infinitely structured to secure an increasingly perfected surveillance through centralized authority. Films, photographs, readings, conferences, magazines, festivals, and much more of the same are produced for the purpose of preventing the permanent interest in the social tasks of surveyed self-reflection from slipping away. The supreme imperative of surveillance is "an unlimited . . . , never indignant tolerance and the highest respect for personal freedom" (102).

The offering of tolerance lowers all thresholds of inhibition so as to set free people's innermost psychological stirrings, and thereby becomes a prerequisite for effective surveillance. In the diaries, this reveals itself as the compulsion toward voluntary self-disclosure. In order to prevent anti-Buribunkic rebellions, everyone who opposes the writing of diaries is still required to continue keeping and disclosing a diary. The Buribunk organization has been perfected to such a degree that all changes can be absorbed over the course of time and progressively redirected. Thus there is "a respected assembly whose task it is to buribunkically document anti-Buribunkdom" (102). Should neo-Buribunkic forces nevertheless begin to emerge, they are tempted by rewards to make written self-disclosures so that change can be controlled and connected back to the centralized leadership authority.

Should one dare to entirely neglect one's diary, a natural selection of the fittest moves in. For whoever does not face up to the intellectual challenge of keeping a diary remains behind in terms of personal development. He is extinguished. "The iron law takes no mercy on the unworthy who have made pariahs of themselves" (103).

While the true Buribunks are distinguished by a racial feature, namely that they are more broad-mouthed than everyone else, a class stratum also enters in by virtue of this selection. The winnowing out of those who are not fit to write a diary leads to their being relegated to a lower class. They have to create superfine paper by hand, providing the leading diary writers with the best material for the world spirit to come to them while writing. Through all these security measures, any opposition that many a revolutionary imagines to incite disappears. Opponents are contained, progressives are controlled, and only those who are unfit to write a diary, and are thus uncontrollable, are expelled. They turn into nonentities. Such techniques of negation lead to the Buribunks' outwitting the cunning of world history itself.

Schmitt's meditation certainly concerns a rigorously temporalized utopia whose driving power is the modern philosophy of the mind. With respect to the past, everything is relative. But to take historical relativism ab-

solutely seriously would mean to raise the Buribunks to the level of an om-
nipotent spirit able to unlock the future. Such a spirit works on the previously unheard of ennoblement of itself. Infinite higher development leads
to means of communication that will in the future already enable fetuses to
exchange their intrauterine sexual experiences with one another for the purpose of supplying "the necessary and factual basis for a refined sexual ethics"
(103). The fear of death itself will have disappeared since true life—as with
Mercier—only persists in its written rendition. "We are, therefore, restor-
ing to our heads the right direction to the real, seeking immortality where
it really is: behind us, not in front of us" (105). Thus the Buribunks march
"triumphantly into the red dawn of their historicity" (103).

The classical obstacles to a traditional utopia—individual death and
private love—are surmounted in order to become absorbed into the pure
awareness of general self-determination. Concealed behind this, of course,
is absolute servitude in the name of science and tolerance.

Carl Schmitt calls upon a wealth of silent testimonies, often only able
to be gleaned from allusions, to ground his negative utopia in the appearance of scientificity: Certainly belonging to it are the likes of Descartes,
Adam Smith, Hegel and Marx, Richard Wagner and Nietzsche, Lamprecht,
Haeckel or Ostwald; perhaps even Lenin and the Communist party, perhaps even Wilson and the American capitalist system. Altogether, they enter into a symbiosis in the doctrine of the Buribunkdom, of modern humanity. Self-blindness and terror offer the inner and outer aspect of its
consciously controlled organization.

Through this negative utopia, readers are situated before an alternative that they are scarcely capable of perceiving in the tradition of the historical and progressive view of the world. Death and love remain the only
counterauthorities that could have prevented progress from ending in a
racially legitimized two-class state where the ruling class is composed of
writing-conscious ideologues and the other class is drowned in the nothingness of intellectual oblivion.

One could easily see a replica of Mercier in Carl Schmitt's Buribunkology, something that could be expected after a century of experienced progress in 1918. But Carl Schmitt probably did not know of Mercier. Moreover,
he pointed just as much toward 1984 as he referred back to 1770.

Out of the naive utopia of the future came a negative temporal utopia.
The sociological common denominator of both utopias is the activity of

writing, the social medium, as it were, of transcendental philosophy of history. It would be senseless to try to deny the constitutive role and task of consciousness for the course of history—on the contrary. But we should learn from both utopias that historical times run differently than how we are retrospectively and anticipatively generally forced to interpret them. Actual history is always simultaneously more and less, and seen ex post facto, it is also always different than we are capable of imagining. For this reason, there are utopias, and also for this reason, they are condemned to be wrong. And their success may more likely lean toward unhappiness than toward the happiness they promise. But we must not forget the prognostic content, proven true by later history, of both of our utopias. Mercier's utopia fulfilled itself, only in a way that was opposite to what he thought. Carl Schmitt's utopia was likewise fulfilled—despite its admonitory function—and, indeed, in a way that was even worse than what he parodied.

Translated by Todd Presner

6

Time and History

Today is January 24. For us, it would be an arbitrary date if it were not a Wednesday, on which this series of lectures by different speakers is regularly taking place. This date is only accidentally connected to history, because it is *today* and not on another Wednesday that I am supposed to speak about the topic "Time and History." In my youth, things were different. Back then, knowing that the birthday of Frederick the Great was on January 24 was an established part of the general education of a Prussian bourgeois family, and among the nobility it would have been the same. One was able to remember this date—January 24, 1712—thanks to a foppish school education, even if the date was not celebrated any longer. At the most, the day was publicly commemorated every fifty or hundred years. Today, huge exhibitions are organized for these occasions, as is well known. But two hundred years ago, when "der Alte Fritz" [Frederick the Great] was still alive, the day was actually celebrated. At least he was remembered in thanksgiving and rogation services in all Prussian churches. The life of the king and supreme sovereign not only had a symbolic or historical meaning in the everyday lives of his subjects, it was part of the world of political experience, of the school, the tax burden, military service, the courts, all of which were derived from and legalized by the monarch. For this reason, the date had a political-ritual and cultic meaning that became lost with the death of the king. Since then it has been a historical date, long forgotten today.

That is not surprising. So many things have happened during the two hundred years that separate us from the death of "der Alte Fritz": the French Revolution, the dissolution of the old Reich, the founding of a German Confederation, of a new, so-called Second Reich, followed by the Republic, the so-called Third Reich, the division of Germany—we must remember that the Federal Republic existed for longer than the eventful years of Weimar and Hitler's Germany taken together. If one considers the economic and social changes conditioned by the technical-industrial development that have reshaped our life-world, then the world of two hundred years ago appears to be a different world, to which we are not connected by any recollection but only by the historical research that tells of it.

Our reflections on today's date and today's occasion have already deeply engaged us in the question of time and history. We have spoken of two dates in our Christian chronology, two dates that, depending on how we ask a question, mean something completely different; and we have sketched out two centuries during which there were at least six different constitutions—if we add in the Confederation of the Rhine, the constitution of the 1848 Revolution, and the constitution of the GDR, then there were nine. We were thus speaking of relatively long-lasting, more or less stable constitutional modes, which provided the political organization of what can roughly be called "Germany." The beginning and the ending dates of these constitutions can also be named, but what lies between these dates can obviously not be conceived as the sum of certain selective dates that can be strung together. One generally speaks of a constitution as existing *within* a certain time period, for instance, from 1871 to 1918. I am thus indicating milestone dates, which are supplied by historical chronology. When faced with the question of the relationship between time and history, however, one thinks spontaneously of more than a mere series of dates, about which Plötz, for instance, amply instructs us. Is there anything like a specifically historical time that differs from natural time, on which chronology is based? Or are there several historical times, just as there are numerous distinguishable units of action in history? Do those units of action have their own temporal courses and rhythms? Or does historical time in the singular and in the plural constitute itself only through the mutual interaction of such units of action? Assuming that there are such genuinely historical times, how do they relate to chronology? These issues raise questions that will occupy us in what follows.

To talk about history and time is difficult for a reason that has to do with more than "history." Time cannot be intuited (*ist anschauungslos*). If a historian brings past events back to mind through his language, then the listener or reader will perhaps associate an intuition with them as well. But does he thereby have an intuition of past *time*? Hardly so, or only in a metaphorical use of language, for instance, in the sense in which one speaks of the time of the French Revolution without thereby making visible anything specifically temporal.

When one seeks to form an intuition of time as such, one is referred to spatial indications, to the hand of the clock or the leaves of a calendar that one pulls off every day. And when one tries to guide one's intuition in a historical direction, one perhaps pays attention to the wrinkles of an aged human being or the scars in which a life's past fate is present. Or one calls to mind the juxtaposition of ruins and new buildings or, today, looks at obvious changes in style that lend temporal depth to a spatial row of houses. Or one looks at the various levels—side by side, below, and above one another—of differently modernized means of transportation, ranging from the sled to the supersonic aircraft. Entire ages meet within them—namely, the last Ice Age or, rather, the Paleolithic Age as part of it and our century. Finally, above all one thinks of the succession of generations within one's own family or professional world; within them, different spaces of experience overlap and different perspectives on the future intersect, including all the conflicts that they contain as seeds. All the examples that are intended to render historical time visible to us refer us to the space in which humans live and to the nature within which they are embedded, be it the system of planets by which clocks and calendars are regulated, or the succession of biological generations as it is expressed in the social and political realm.

With this, I arrive at my first aspect, the prerequisites of natural time for human history and its historiography.

In order to be able to live and work, humans depend on time limits that are pregiven by nature. They remain dependent on such limits even when they increasingly learn to manipulate these times more and more through technology or medicine. Let me recall a well-known joke from the Soviet Union—"Sleep faster, comrade!"—to indicate a natural limit that cannot be transcended by any planning.

The times of the day and the seasons were guiding forces for the first self-organization of human societies. The habits of deer for hunting cultures; location, climate, and weather conditions for farming cultures; all this embedded within the seasons, shaped everyday life and induced magical and religious attitudes, plus the modes of behavior oriented by them. This is still valid today, although decreasingly so, corresponding to the decline in the food-producing sector, which now amounts to fewer than 10 percent of the employees within our society. In other words, the natural time prerequisites of our lives can never be eliminated; rather, they have their own history. This will be outlined briefly following several instances of time measurement.

Ethnologists report how deeply earlier measurements of time remained embedded within the context of human action. In Madagascar, for instance, there still exists the temporal unit of "the time it takes to cook rice" or of the moment that is necessary "to roast a locust." Temporal measure and course of action are still completely convergent. Such expressions are even more concrete than, for instance, the "blink of an eye" (*Augenblick*) in our language, which is likewise a natural unit of time.

Even the elementary chronometers of advanced civilizations, which indicate the course of time via a decrease in matter—sand or water—were still adapted to the enactment of concrete actions: they measured the length of a sermon or determined the hour of mass, or, like Cicero's water clock, of an address to the jury in court. These elementary chronometers were supplemented by sundials, which, depending on the season or geographical location, announced different times, since these indications were based in nature itself. Even mechanical clocks were able to adjust to this condition. As late as the nineteenth century, the Japanese used clocks of a particularly artful design: the way the hand and face indicated the hours was kept variable so that, depending on the season, the hour of the day was in reverse relation to the hour of the night, that is, longer during the summer and shorter during the winter. By way of these clocks, the seasonal difference between the hours of the day and those of the night entered directly into the rhythm of work from which they received their purpose.

Yet the introduction of the mechanical clock in the thirteenth century already effected a new organization of the human division of time over the long term. Following some precursors in antiquity, it led to quantifying the day by means of twenty-four equal hours. Le Goff speaks of commercial time, the time of businesspeople, which entered into competition with the liturgical time of the church and pushed it more and more into the background. The mechanical clock, once it had been invented, descended from the church tower to town and city halls, then moved into the living rooms of the wealthy and the bourgeoisie, and finally found its way into watch pockets. Since the sixteenth century, this clock has been able to indicate minutes and, since the seventeenth century, seconds; it indicated, but also stimulated, a disciplining and rationalizing of the world of human work and its latitude for action. In the first half of the nineteenth century, numerous industrial workers in England already carried their own watches—as status symbols, but also so as to check on their supervisors' watches. With the emergence of the railroad traffic system and its standardized schedule, standard times were finally introduced—in Prussia, before the Revolution of 1848—which completely differed from the respective local time and the position of the sun. Henry Ford began his career as an industrialist by producing clocks that were able to indicate standard time and local time simultaneously on two faces: a final indication of the development of units of time made necessary by technology, which became separated from naturebound, traditional rhythms of time. Day and night seemed to become more alike, just as tracks made it possible for railroads to run at night. This corresponded to the introduction of night work in the large companies of the last century so as to increase production.

What does this retrospective look at the history of chronometry in everyday life mean? We are dealing with a long-term process of increasing acts of abstraction designed to remove humans from what was naturally pregiven to them. First, chronometry was inserted into the human context of action. Second, the sundial made it possible to, as it were, objectify natural time. Third, the mechanical clock and, later, the pendulum clock initiated a reshaping of everyday life through quantified, uniform units of time, which pervaded and causally affected social organization and economic production. One can also call this a denaturalization of the division of time and of the experience of time included in it. In the course of mechanization (*Technifizierung*), physical instruments of measurement have increasingly contributed to divesting the course of everyday life of its natural preconditions, a process that has been interpreted as both a relief and a burden.

Our retrospective look also tells us about other things. We have traced the history of chronometry in social changes in everyday life. Here the interpretation of a denaturalization takes on meaning, though with the reservation that, to this day, all forms of chronometry mentioned have remained dependent upon our planetary system, on the revolution of the earth around the sun, on that of the moon around the earth (though less so), and on the turning of the globe around its axis. In other words, regardless of the social function of the respective form of chronometry, any form of chronometry remains embedded in scientifically verifiable and, in this sense, objective data. These data of the solar system were already calculated with great precision by astronomers of advanced civilizations in the second millennium B.C. or by the Maya; they are valid regardless of history, regardless of the historical situation in which they were first ascertained. Not without reason is chronology called an *auxiliary* science of history. It answers questions of dating by referring the numerous calendars and chronologies that have been used in the course of our history back to a common time of our planetary system, which is calculated in a physical-astronomical manner.

With the inception of overseas land acquisition, the number of calendars competing in Europe around 1600 (Julian, Gregorian, Byzantine, and also Muslim) was increased by several chronologies. Employing different sequences of numbers, they all referred to objectively equal dates of the same natural time. Scaliger, for instance, defined January 1, 4713 B.C., as day "one," from which every day and every year was to receive its natural identity, to which all calendars could be referred.

This brings me to the second part of our question, the natural prerequisites of our history, namely, historio*graphy*.

I cannot here address the difficulties that result from the conversion of cultic calendar dates into a natural chronology. Let me just call to mind that the year zero is lacking; accordingly, Christ was born on December 25 of the year one B.C. Or let me call to mind the difficulty that our months no longer correspond to the revolutions of the moon around the earth, or that the days comprise neither the year nor the month without remainder; the conversions of the different calendars presuppose a science of their own. Or let me call to mind the replacement of Julian years by Gregorian years, whose introduction was delayed over a period of centuries from country to country in Europe; according to our calendar, which was introduced in Russia in 1923, the October Revolution of 1917 took place thirteen days later, that is, actually in November.

By addressing all the difficulties of chronology, I want to emphasize the following: our entire chronometry, in minutes and hours, in units of years and centuries, which we create artificially, is based on the regularity and cyclical return of naturally pregiven dates. For historical chronology, at least, time is measurable only because of its natural recurrence.

To be sure, all chronologies are products of certain cultures and are, in this respect, relative. This is also true for the Christian chronology, which has been largely universalized. Since the sixth century, it has started counting from the birth of Christ. Only since the seventeenth century has it counted the years before Christ backward: *ante Christum natum*. This became indispensable, first, because the discovered world also included Chinese calendars extending even before the date of the world's creation, which required coordination; second, because geology was slowly opening up periods of time in the face of which biblical chronology dwindled. The roughly five thousand years of biblical world time became a phase in the history of our cultural development. Finally, once the infinity of space in the universe was hypostasized, time became expandable to infinity, into the past and into the future. But apart from the context of the history of this change in scholarship during the Enlightenment, there remains the prerequisite that, for purposes of chronology, our time measurements are tied to the recurrence of natural time. Every historically relative chronology is based in a time that is pregiven by nature.

This finding is a tacit yet fundamental prerequisite for our research. Because history itself remains embedded in time periods that are pregiven by nature, historiography is likewise unable to dispense with them. To make meaningful statements, we need to tie each of our relative chronologies back to a chronology that is as "absolute" as possible and independent of history. For prehistory before writing or for early history, obviously paleontological findings become meaningful only when they can be geologically classified, which today is made easier by the carbon 14 test. But exact, objectifiable dating is also required for the kind of history that is based on written sources and human monuments. Only in this way can a before and after be ascertained, without which no event can be thought and interpreted. Any succession that provides a history with meaning is linear, but it can only be dated on the basis of the cyclical return of natural time. Let me give you an example.

It is certainly of world-historical importance that at the Diet of Speyer in 1529 the Protestant Estates came together in a protestation that gave them their name and that set the course, within imperial law, for modern Protestantism. The protestation was directed against a Diet proposal that

Charles V had issued. The emperor himself was in Madrid at the time. It would be wrong to suppose that Charles, through his proposal to postpone the Reformation until a general council, drove the Protestant Estates to their protest, that is, drove them to refer to their free moral decision. The emperor wanted to be accommodating, because he was still at war with France and wished to damp down conflicts within the empire. The Diet proposal that was actually presented came from his brother Ferdinand, however, the emperor's viceroy in Germany. He presented the harsh regulations, issued as imperial regulations, that evoked the protest. The reason for these wrongly attributed harsh proposals can now be determined in a chronologically definite form—something that was only discovered in the twentieth century. Because of the war with France, the emperor's accommodating propositions had to be sent by sea, across the Mediterranean and then to Vienna. They arrived too late to be presented on time to the Diet of Speyer. Therefore Ferdinand acted on his own authority, and he did so with consequences that had a world-historical effect. He passed his own, uncompromising proposals off as the emperor's.

Only an exact chronology of "earlier than" and "later than" informs us—ex post facto—about true occurrences and allows us to give an interpretation that is adequate to real events.

Admittedly, no historian will reduce his interpretation of Protestantism to the events of the Diet of Speyer in 1529, at which the Protestant minority assembled for the first time according to imperial law. But already the question of how the protest came about *in actu* and concretely, the question about what role Charles V played in it and what role his brother Ferdinand played, can only be answered if the exact chronology, in this case that of the path that the documents took, is reconstructed and safeguarded. The evaluation of statesmen's actions depends on such procedures.

A historian will, of course, stop at such evaluations, which involve the motives of agents and the ways in which these motives influenced the network of actions, so as finally to issue in a chain of events. He will, for example, ask about the general conditions that made it possible for such actions as the one at the Diet of Speyer to happen at all. He might surmise that general conditions during the time of the Reformation would have given rise to a protest of the Protestant Estates, if not in 1529, then perhaps one or two years later. The conflict that had erupted about the church constitution of the German empire had longer-term causes than those that led, in a single act at a Diet, to the protest that made the schism irreparable. Even an interpretation of the Reformation in terms of social or religious history will already give less weight to this, or perhaps not even mention it at all.

But our mental operations, which are familiar to every historian, make clear the following: they lead further and further away from the history of events that take place along a chronological order. This procedure is necessary, but it cannot be infinitely continued.

Each individual event is embedded in a chronological series of dates that is to be naturally presupposed, and its uniqueness remains unparalleled. No matter how I research and represent the history of the Reformation—in economic terms, in those of the sociology of religion, of constitutional history, of the history of ideas, or of politics alone—no general statement can get past the fact of an unalterable before and after of events that are actually past. What happened once cannot be undone, it can only be forgotten. Individual dates are pregiven; they have to be presupposed and are often no longer known. In their unalterable succession, they form a chronological grid, and any interpretation that goes beyond this must be capable of being brought into accord with it.

To stay with our example of how Protestantism is explained and comprehended historically—as a movement of religious internalization, as bourgeois emancipation, as the revolution of the rulers, as a superstructure of early capitalism, as the severance of the German people from Roman rule, as a German uprising, just to name a few familiar interpretations from the last one hundred years—no interpretation is able to bypass the irrevocable act of a solemn protestation at Speyer in 1529.

I just stated that, chronologically, generalizations cannot be extended to infinity. Let us continue to pursue this thought for a moment. Even longer-term statements about the Reformation as a unit of events remain tied to milestone dates, before and after which it does not make any sense to speak of the Reformation as a historical period at all. Among these are, on the one hand, backdating the beginning to the late Middle Ages with its popular religious movements, or preconditions pertaining to the history of ideas, which one can find in the entire history of the Christian Church; and on the other, continuations of the Reformation as a factor with effects right into the modern age. Any such procedures—which are completely legitimate in historical terms—remain, finally, tied to a unique succession of events.

We can take our historiographical thought experiment one step further and bring into play seemingly extratemporal factors. Thus one might start out from human nature and interpret the Reformation in psychological or even psychoanalytical terms: as a case of the detachment from external authority that allegedly led to the establishment of an internal authority (namely, conscience), which then could be engaged in different ways. In purely theoretical terms, it is also possible to use an anthropological model of enduring applicability that is intended to rise above any historically unique situation. We would then be on a level of proof of supertemporal achronic permanence, as it were, this being the condition for any possible history. Such explanatory patterns have occurred again and again, in different attire. Thus it is possible to quote a proverb for any history—many dogs are the death of the hare, or pride goes before a fall—in order to reduce a lost war to general human and, as it were, antehistorical regularities.

I do not want to underestimate or downplay the influence of such pieces of wisdom, which can also be translated into the statements of an anthropologically based academic discipline. But on closer view, even these explanations always contain the inescapable indicator of a before and an after, without which a piece of epigrammatic wisdom or a psychological or sociological model of explanation become meaningless. Neither the reorientation of a need for authority nor the pride that goes before a fall can do without temporal indications. When they are applied to history, even seemingly general patterns of explanation inevitably refer to chronological succession, without which every history would be not only meaningless but impossible.

Chronology borrowed from natural time is thus indispensable for a historical reality that is to be redeemed empirically, whether approximation to the absolute exactness of data establishes meaning, or whether the cogency of the relative before and after, which is unalterable in itself, is the prerequisite for a meaningful reconstruction of historical events.

We thus arrive at a result that appears to be banal but is really fundamental: natural time, with its recurrence and its time limits, is a permanent premise both of history and of its interpretation as an academic discipline.

Everything we have dealt with so far can be defined as the objectifiable core of the calculation and determination of time. Now that it has been discovered and recognized, there can be no more dispute about the chronological order of the file that did not reach the Diet of Speyer on time. No matter which interpretation of the Reformation one subscribes to, the above-mentioned milestone date within the chronology remains within rational control and generally acceptable. But do we sufficiently understand what can, as a result, be called historical time or historical times? Certainly not. I thus arrive at the second part of my lecture.

The singular form of a single historical time, which is supposed to distinguish itself from measurable natural time, is already open to doubt. Historical time, if the term is to have a meaning, is tied to social and political units of action, to particular acting and suffering human beings, and to their institutions and organizations. They all have certain inherent modes of performance, each of which has its own temporal rhythm. Let us, to remain in the world of the everyday, think of the different festival calendars that structure social life, of changes in work times and their duration, which have determined and continue to determine the succession of life on a daily basis.

We might speak, not of one historical time, but of many that overlie one another. Even here, measures of time that derive from the mathematical-physical understanding of nature are needed: the dates or length of a life or of an institution, the nodal points or turning points of political or military series of events, the speed of means of transportation and its increase, the acceleration—or retardation—of a production line, the velocity of weapons systems. All these, to give just a few examples, can be historically evaluated only when calculated or dated with reference to the natural measurement of time.

But an interpretation of the interrelations that result already leads beyond natural, physically or astronomically processed determinations of time. Political constraints on decisions made under the pressure of deadlines, the repercussions upon the economy or military actions of the time spans required by means of travel and communication, the permanence or mobility of social modes of behavior in the field of temporally limited political or economic requirements—all this, plus other things, in their mutual interaction or dependence finally forces us to adopt social and political determinations of time that, although they are naturally caused, must be defined as specifically historical.

In contrast to the objective determinations of time outlined so far, one could call them "subjective," if this is not associated with an epistemological devaluation.

The uncovering or discovery of such subjective historical times is itself a product of modernity. In Germany, Herder was the first to define this, in his metacritique of Kant's *Critique of Pure Reason*. Instead of seeing time only as a formal, a priori condition of all phenomena, a condition of inner intuition, Herder pointed toward the plurality of concrete carriers of action. "Properly speaking, any changeable object contains the measure of its time within itself; it exists even if there were no other one; no two things in the world share the same measure of time. . . . At one time, there exist (one can say it truly and boldly) countlessly many times in the universe."

Has anything been gained from such a historical-anthropological premise for the recognition of history in its relation to time or, rather, its times? Historical research that becomes involved in factual questions does not explicitly have to pose the question of historical time. In addition, the sources "from" a certain time rarely provide any direct information "about" this time.

We must therefore clarify our question theoretically in order to make it operational for research. I will attempt to do this in conclusion, again with examples, which will—as before—engage first history, then historiography.

Historical times can be identified if we direct our view to where time itself occurs or is subjectively enacted in humans as historical beings: in the relationship between past and future, which always constitutes an elusive present. The compulsion to coordinate past and future so as to be able to live at all is inherent in any human being. Put more concretely, on the one hand, every human being and every human community has a space of experience out of which one acts, in which past things are present or can be remembered, and, on the other, one always acts with reference to specific horizons of expectation. I propose investigating this relationship between past and future or, more precisely, the relationship of specific experiences and expectations, so as to get a grasp on historical time. That historical time occurs within the difference between these two temporal dimensions can already be shown by the fact that the difference between experience and expectation itself changes—that is, it is specifically historical. Let me explain.

Until the early modern period, it was a general principle derived from experience that the future could bring nothing fundamentally new. Until the expected end of the world, sinful human beings (as seen from a Christian perspective) would not change; until then, the nature of man (as seen from a humanist perspective) would remain the same. For that reason it was possible to issue prognoses, because the factors of human action or the naturally possible forms of government (as seen from an Aristotelian viewpoint) remained fundamentally the same. Whatever was to be expected could be sufficiently justified by previous experience. The Solomonic wisdom of *nil novum sub sole* was equally valid in the world of peasants and of politics, even though individual cases might bring surprises. Using such an inference from experience to expectation, Frederick the Great, for instance, whose date of birth was our point of departure, made an astonishingly clear prognosis of the French Revolution. He arrived at his prediction by confronting his collected historical-political experience with the discreet expectations of a French philosopher, Holbach. The prognosis is found in a review of Holbach's *Système de la Nature*: "For the fantastic ideas of our philosophers to be fulfilled, the forms of government of all the states in Europe would first need to be transformed"—which undoubtedly interpreted Holbach's secret expectation correctly. Yet Frederick went further in his conclusions, for he mobilized the expectations of a political history that was two thousand years old. "It would be necessary for the dethroned generations of rulers to be completely exterminated, or the seed of civil wars will arise, in which party leaders put themselves at the head of factions in order to disrupt the state." Then, it would no longer be possible to stop revolts and revolutions, and the misery to come would be a thousand times greater than that caused by all foreign wars being waged at the time.

Roughly speaking, the events of the French Revolution verified Frederick's prognosis. He undoubtedly saw the misery to come and the drawbacks of the Revolution more clearly than those who placed their hopes in a coming radical change of the constitution. This is authentically a prognosis that draws conclusions from previous experience for the future. Seen from a structural perspective, the difference between past and future history is zero, even if individual concrete events as such cannot be foreseen.

In the same time period, the difference between experience and expectation has also been drawn out in a completely different way. For this, Kant can be called as our witness. For him, a prognosis that in principle expects the same as what has always been possible so far is no real prognosis at all. Kant assumes that the future will be different from the past because it is supposed to be different. For him, the moral requirement of establishing a republican constitution receives a political thrust that is supposed to change the history to come as well. He is concerned to surpass all previous experience and open up a new future—for instance, to establish a league of nations, which had thus far been unprecedented in history.

His is authentically a prediction ruled by willpower, in which past and future are coordinated in a completely new way. If Frederick is right, so is Kant, in his way. For Kant addresses a specifically historical time, one that it is possible to experience only in our *Neuzeit*, in contrast to earlier ages. For in our modern age (*Moderne*), as it is shaped by science, technology, and industry, the future in fact implies different and new things, which cannot be entirely derived from previous experience. Precisely the impossibility of foreseeing technical inventions has become a principle derived from experience, and permanently keeps open the difference between past and future.

I do not need to explain further the far-reaching way in which the structure of society and its modes of organization have changed since technological progress set in. The enormous acceleration in communication and rates of production is the most conspicuous criterion for a changed time, which is also constantly changing our everyday world and its habits. As Goethe noted shrewdly: "It is bad enough that now one can no longer learn anything for one's whole life. Our ancestors stuck to the lessons they received in their youth; we, however, have to relearn things every five years if we do not want to fall out of fashion completely."

Here Goethe articulates shortened temporal rhythms and time limits that cannot be derived any more from natural time and the succession of biological generations. And—to speak in more abstract terms—he also illustrates the differential experience of past and future. The shortening of the time spans necessary for gaining new experiences that the technical-industrial world forces upon us can be described as a historical acceleration. It provides evidence of a history in which time continually seems to overtake itself, as it were, and it is thus conceived of as *Neuzeit* in an emphatic sense.

In Frederick, Kant, and Goethe we have called three witnesses; each of them has been right and has continued to be right in his own way. Frederick uses an anthropological–historically based time structure as it has been known since Thucydides. It refers to sequences that, as it were, appear on their own out of a certain pregiven situation—a revolution, for instance. History, too, has its recurring possibilities. For that reason, his prognosis came true. Kant assumes that there is a moral demand for a difference between past and future, so as to open up a horizon of planning, from which the present situation can be changed. This has an effect on history. These reasons underlie his demand for a league of nations, which was realized in the long term. Goethe, finally, observes the shortening of the spans of experience as they are forced upon modern man by the emerging industrial world. There is a limit to inferences for the future that can be drawn from convention. In this respect, the future is as unknown as it is open—not only in individual cases, but in principle.

We have thus made three differential determinations, all of which, located at three different temporal levels, represent accurate aspects of historical reality. Our supposition that it is only meaningful to speak of historical times in the plural has thus been confirmed. In addition, our differential determination of past and future has shown that this difference has its own history and is thus suited to thematizing historical time.

Thus we have all of a sudden arrived at the final question: How can the times of history themselves be historically recognized and described? The question of which temporal level needs to be thematized in each case is a question of historical perspective. Using our example, I can cut out the historical sphere that Frederick, Kant, or Goethe has illuminated, and I can attempt to combine them. But any perspective that I choose has itself a temporal content, because the temporal difference between my position *today* and the past histories (*Geschichten*) investigated enters into my recognition. To have recognized this finding is also an achievement of our *Neuzeit*. As Goethe once said: "One will, in the same city, hear an important event narrated differently in the morning and in the evening." With his usual casualness, Goethe has recorded an apt observation, which reveals more than the long-known fact that people talk about the same thing in different and contradictory ways. It is a historical time that he is referring to, and the pressure to perspectivalism he reveals was first conceptualized in the epistemology of the Enlightenment, at a time when the plurality of historical times was made conscious for the first time.

It may therefore be that at other times one will speak differently about historical times than we have done this afternoon.

Translated by Kerstin Behnke

7

Concepts of Historical Time and Social History

During the last thirty years, roughly since the Second World War, there have been significant changes on the scene of historical scholarship. One of these concerns a field of history that has been fashionably termed "social history." This term can be likened to a rubber band, that is to say it is flexible enough to embrace several more or less heterogeneous areas. But the term "social history" seems to exclude, wrongly, I think, that kind of history which limits itself strictly to factual events and which is, again wrongly, linked with political history. It is only for reasons of scholarly polemics that the history of events or political history is presumed not to be part of social history, as are for instance the long-term changes in the relations between different strata and classes.

A second change on the historical scene is the fact that theoretical debates are exerting a significant and growing influence on the discipline. The subject of theory is rejected by the determined advocates of the history of events as an imposition and aberration, but is welcomed by social historians. In this context, we have to single out those theories of the social sciences that have had a general influence on the science of history and that have stimulated many ideas and questions. I am referring to those theories that originated in economics, sociology, the political sciences, anthropology, linguistics, and other research areas in the humanities and that have extended into the diachronic optics of our discipline.

Another strand of the theoretical debate has remained, at least in Germany, relatively ineffective. I am referring to those epistemological problems that are being discussed by Anglo-Saxon philosophers and that since Hempel and Popper have developed a lively existence of their own. Their influence on practical research has been limited, unlike the theories of the social sciences that have strongly influenced our particular field. The reason for this seems clear: the empirical examples that are examined by an analytically and linguistically inspired philosophy have been dissected very cleverly, it is true, but mostly they are of such simplicity that they have no immediate methodological value for the practicing historian. This is not to say that they are of no epistemological interest. But, as we well know, the theory of knowledge does not necessarily have an effect on the practical research to which it refers. The situation is different for those materially and sociologically based theories that originated in economics, mathematics, the political sciences, sociology, and so forth, and that have inspired a great many models and hypotheses found in modern historical research.

So, under the heading of social history, the subject area of historical research has greatly expanded. Today there is nothing that does not fit somehow into the historical sciences. The history of wages and prices, the economic climate, productivity, economic development in general belong to the best established research areas that after a period of isolation, are increasingly being reabsorbed into social history. But this is not the end of the story, considering all the subjects that have been added since: demography, the history of family relationships, of childhood, even the history of death which, as we know, is beyond human experience; or the history of diseases, of modes of behavior, customs, rites and legends, as well as of transportation, the press and communication networks, the history of verbal and nonverbal relationships, of mentalities and unconscious behavior, not to mention the particular history of the various sciences.

All this can be more or less covered by the umbrella of social history, although it has—under a different name—had quite a long tradition in our field, going back to Herodotus. We can say that there is hardly a relic from the past that is not considered worth preserving (thanks to the technical acceleration of our living conditions) and that has not been declared a subject for research. The boundary with archeology, too, is becoming less well defined since even the unwritten and silent sources of tradition have become a theme for social historians who are concerning themselves with everything without exception.

So we are faced with two facts, first historical research, which is becoming increasingly theoretical, and second, an enormous extension of empirical questions. Both facts are closely related, of course. The more use is made of them in differing and numerous ways, the more confusing are the results. Small wonder that the theorists have come to the fore to establish boundaries, fit together subject areas, or make them comparable. Theorems, models, and hypotheses accompany and order the surge of curiosity. On the other hand, it should be borne in mind that the enormous extension of historical fields of interest calls for theoretical clarification so that they do not lapse into the antiquarian or the anecdotal.

Extension of research and a need for theory are thus obviously connected and seem to be complementary phenomena of our discipline. It is against this background that the catchword of social history has come to play a key role. Its concepts have been frequently described by Braudel, Hobsbawm, or Kocka among others, so that I do not have to list them all. In any case, the boundaries are not strictly defined: at one end, there is the so-called nonpolitical history of human relationships involving groups, communities, or specific societies, and at the other, the history of politically organized societies that is virtually claiming to interpret social history as the totality of history. Social history can for instance mean the history of individual classes or individual areas as well as the history of all mankind. Nothing is gained by this.

Before I begin to ask questions about historical time in relation to social-historical models, I would like to raise two methodological cautions. The first is aimed at the concept of a total history and the second at the use of the term "social" history.

Anyone who attempts to integrate the sum total of individual histories into one single total history is bound to fail. This can only be attempted if and when a theory has been developed that would make a total history possible. This would in turn reveal that any total history would always be the product of a necessary perspective. It would have to be established for instance whether it is the relations of production or the market conditions that play a primary role. The same applies to power and social stratification, or to religious attitudes and expectations in a social context, which for instance remain open for discussion in relation to the Reformation period. In developing such a model, we would be joining in the controversies over possible theories. All this is happening in the area of empirical research, however abundant the empirical results may be that emerge from the various theoretical premises.

The second warning concerns the casual use of the word "social." Social history as a subject of discourse obviously dates from the nineteenth and twentieth centuries. This expression reveals a modern problem whose implications cannot necessarily claim validity for earlier centuries. Before the French Revolution, every society was always a "societas civilis et politica." The economics of trading companies or of the territorial states remained integral parts of the estates that were characterized by the fact that economic, social, and political definitions converged. Only since the development of world trade and the rise of national economic systems has it become possible to define economics as a separate area alongside the state, society, culture, or religion. And only since then has it been possible, from the point of view of historical development, to distinguish empirically between political rule, social constitutions, and economic structure—differentiations that were not possible for people living in a feudal world.

It is permissible, of course, to take such modern distinctions and apply them analytically to an earlier past, but always remembering that they were not meant for the dimensions of human experience of that time. As I said, an estate could be defined politically, socially, and economically at the same time whereas a class of the nineteenth century could be defined differently from any of these angles. Nevertheless, these modern categories can be projected onto the past so that, in analyzing it, results may be obtained, something that could not be done by those who were alive then.

After these two caveats regarding the naive notion of a total history and against the uncritical use of "social," I would like to propose three items for discussion. First, I would like to say something on the origin of an awareness of a specifically historical time. Secondly, I would like to speak on the various dimensions of time that are part of events and structures, and thirdly and lastly, I would like to make a proposal as to how, in the area of political and social semantics, something like historical time can be investigated.

I. Development of an Understanding of Specifically Historical Time

It is a truism that history has always to do with time. But it took a long time until something like historical time came to be explicitly defined.

Its discovery probably occurred, I suspect, during the Enlightenment. Before then, the historical time-plan was divided up according to mythical or theological categories and had a beginning, a middle, and an end. We also know of the doctrine of eons into which individual historical events were made to fit. Everyday chronology was based on the natural measurements of the solar and lunar orbits, just as it is today. In cases where this chronology was historically enriched, we find the recurrent rites of seasonal calendars or the biological ages of ruling dynasties and their representatives. All these definitions of time placed the many histories existing then into a certain order, but they did not attempt to deduce the criteria of time from the course of history itself.

The invention of the Middle Ages was a first step toward building out of historical events something like a historically immanent construction that did not have to justify itself by referring to persons, nature, or mythology. But three to four centuries went by until the eighteenth century when the Middle Ages had gradually become accepted as a specific name for a period. The notion of Renaissance became a general historical name for a period only in the nineteenth century. During those centuries that enabled history to be rearranged ex post facto only, the notion of modern time became established just as slowly. My thesis would be that only this notion of modern time has gained a genuinely historical meaning, distinct from mythical, theological, or natural chronological origins. As Kant put it: so far history had followed chronology: and now it was necessary that chronology should follow history. That was the program of the Enlightenment: to subject historical time to criteria which could only be derived from an understanding of history itself. Then and only then did people begin to organize history according to generalized aspects of politics, and later of economics, or of a history of societies relating to the churches or peoples, or according to aspects of the history of scientific discovery, or to ask about cultural achievements that were supposed to provide a criterion for a historically immanent structure. In the eighteenth century, the fruit was picked that had grown since its rebirth in the Renaissance.

For the new position to be developed further, reflection on criteria of historical time became necessary. This reflection took place through the medium of the philosophy of history, which is a product of the eighteenth century, even if its subject matter had been described in earlier periods. But the level of reflection can be deduced from the use of two central notions of time: that of modern time and that of progress. Modern time differs from earlier "age" theories in that it is experienced, not ex post facto but directly. This is one of the novelties of this particular new notion. It is less of a retrospective notion because it has arisen from the present, which is opening out toward the future. The future of modern time is thought to be open and without boundaries. The vision of last things or the theory of the return of all things has been radically pushed aside by the venture of opening up a new future: a future which, in the emphatic sense of the notion, is totally different from all that has passed before.

Through this experience of historical time as modern time, many conclusions became possible. I would like to mention a few. Modern time was identified with progress, since it was progress that conceptualized the difference between the past so far and the coming future. This meant that time gained a new historical quality which, within the horizon of sameness and recurrence of the exemplary, it did not possess before. One could also say that progress is the first genuinely historical definition of time that has not derived its meaning from other areas of experience such as theology or mythical foreknowledge. Progress could be discovered only when people began to reflect on historical time itself. It is a reflexive notion. In practice this means that progress can only occur, if people want it and plan for it. That the future should be a horizon of planning, not only of days, weeks, or even years, but of the long-term kind in terms of changes, is one of the features of a historical time that is seen as progressive.

Furthermore, to name another criterion related to the discovery of progress, there is the discovery of the historical world. The historical and the progressive views of the world have a common origin. They complement one another like the faces of Janus. If the new time is offering something new all the time, the different past has to be discovered and recognized, that is to say, its strangeness which increases with the passing of years.

History became a modern science at the point where the break in tradition qualitatively separates the past from the future. Since then it has been necessary to develop special methods that teach us to recognize the different character of the past. Since then it has been possible that the truth of history changes with changing time, or to be more exact, that historical truth can become outdated. Since then historical method has also meant having to define a point of view from which conclusions can be drawn. Since then an eyewitness is no longer the authentic principal witness of an event; he will be questioned in the light of changing and advanced perspectives that are applied to the past.

Finally, it is only since then that the axiom of the uniqueness of all history and its individuality has become conceivable. This was a countermove against previous historical experience which, in the sense both of antiquity and Christianity, had not expected anything fundamentally new, but something similar or analogous in the future.

With Lovejoy one could call these processes that I have briefly described "the temporalization of history."

So far I have only talked about methodological criteria that have served to expose historical time, particularly within our discipline. This means, of course, that we are dealing with implications involving factual history. The consequences for the concepts of social history are clear. If we, the historians, want to develop a genuine theory that is to be distinct from the theories of the social sciences in general, it obviously has to be a theory that makes it possible to accommodate the changes in temporal experience.

The discovery of temporalization, to use this ex post facto expression, was certainly at first an idea of the intellectual elite. But with it, new modes of behavior emerged that reached beyond the world of the estates, that is to say the ancien régime. We see an acceleration in the changes which, since the advent of technology and industry, have provoked an additional and specific experience of time. The transition from the stagecoach, by way of trains and motor cars to jet planes has fundamentally changed all time-space relations and with them our working conditions, social mobility, war technology, global communication networks—all of them factors that constitute the history of our world as it proceeds on this finite planet of ours. Temporalization and acceleration constitute the temporal framework that will probably have to be applied to all concepts of modern social history. This framework makes possible diachronic and synchronic comparisons, and provokes one central question, the question of what has changed (in the sense of historical times) when time has remained the same (in a chronological sense). I am thinking of the classic work by Barrington Moore.

Or to mention an example from Prussian history: after the French Revolution, Prussia was faced with the challenge of reforming its social system of estates, a challenge that was taken up with the intention to introduce a written constitution. Although the latter was promised several times, it was introduced as late as 1848 and only by force. Let us look at this process from a temporal perspective.

During the reform period after 1807, the first task was to liberalize the economy in order to create a free market in property and labor. It was necessary to create the economic conditions for the establishment of a functioning liberal constitution in which the estates would be represented, not because of birthright, but because of education and property. So there was a practical priority for economic reforms, if a liberal constitution was to be implemented. In temporal terms: first the economic reforms and then the political consequences. Hardenberg clearly saw the alternative. If, under the ruling powers as they existed at the beginning of the reform era, he had immediately convened a parliamentary chamber, the result for the economic reforms would have been disastrous. The nobility were the first to insist on a constitution, and they would have been sufficiently powerful to act against the weak bourgeoisie and the politically ignorant peasantry and reject any legislation for economic reform. In short, the economic conditions for liberalization would have been made impossible. It was too early in 1815 to introduce a written constitution. Paradoxically, the result of this was that at any time after that it was always too late. The more successful the reforms were, the easier it became for the nobility to pull the leading bourgeois classes over to their side. Around 1848, nearly half of the estates of the nobility were in bourgeois hands, but with the result that the nobility became a modernized propertied class as well as financially secure. Important sections of the bourgeoisie had been absorbed, a prerequisite for the failure of the 1848 Revolution and the liberal hopes placed in it.

In one sentence, one could say that the economic modernization based on the principles of Adam Smith prevented a political modernization in the sense of a Western constitutional system. The economic dimension of time and the political dimension of time led to contradictory results, if they are measured against the initial planning data. The outcome was the so-called specifically Prussian solution in which the traditional estates, who were politically reactionary, provided the resources for an economic modernization. The transformation of an old society of estates into a class society must therefore be measured with different time scales in order to explain the specifically Prussian implications against the horizon of European industrialization. This would be a rough outline of how temporalization can be utilized for social-historical questions. I am not assuming that the temporal priorities of economic reforms that I have described, and their political consequences, namely that the constitutional opportunities were missed in this way, provide an adequate explanatory model for the long-term social changes in Prussia. However, it seems to me that the question of the temporal structures is a *conditio sine qua non* of social-historical knowledge.

II. Relations of Events to Social Structures

I now come to the second part of my talk. I shall speak about the relationship of events to so-called structures, but allow me first to comment on something before I proceed. It is a false simplification to regard historical time as either linear or circular. This approach has dominated historical thought for too long, until Braudel made (and implemented) an important proposal, namely to analyze historical time on several levels. The antonyms "event" and "structure" are suitable for throwing light on these levels.

"Progress," too, and "modern time," which I described earlier, contain simplifications that were understandable in the eighteenth century because the discovery of modern time also conceptualized modern experience. In the case of our own discipline, however, this category of the forever modern time, in which we are supposedly living, does not fit. Progress, which can only be thought of as a linear time process, conceals the broad foundation of all those structures that have survived and which, in temporal terms, are based on repetition.

Events and structures are of course interlocked in historical reality. It is the historian's task to take them apart methodologically on the assumption that he cannot discuss both of them at the same time. One could compare this process to a photographic lens that cannot at the same time take a close-up and a long-distance shot.

What, then, is the temporal structure of an event? Events can be perceived by those affected as interconnected or as a unit of meaning. This was the reason for the methodological priority of eyewitnesses whose accounts were considered as particularly reliable up to the eighteenth century. This fact also accounts for the high reliability of traditional stories that tell of countless events. The first framework in which a number of incidents combine into an event is natural chronology. Only a minimum of before-and-after constitutes a unit of meaning that makes an event out of single incidents. The inner coherence of an event, its before-and-after, may be extended, but its consistency remains linked to the progression of natural time. We only need to think back to the events at the outbreak of war in 1914 or 1939. What really happened, the interdependence of actions and omissions, became clear only in the subsequent hour, the next day, and so on.

The transposition, too, of past actions and experiences into historical knowledge remains inseparable from the chronologically measurable sequence. The before-and-after constitutes the semantic horizon of a story that can hardly be briefer than Caesar's brief story, "veni, vidi, vici." Every event has to conform to the inevitable progression of time. It is in this sense that Schiller's dictum—that world history is at once the trial and judgment of the world—should be read. What is lost in one minute, eternity will not replace. As we know, sequences of events are not incidental. Events, too, have their diachronic structures. The before-and-after or the too early and too late prescribe the inevitable sequences of things that could be called diachronic structures. Only in this way is it possible to compare the sequence of revolutions, of wars, or of constitutions on a specific level of abstraction or of typology.

Apart from these diachronic structures of events there are longer-term structures whose temporal characteristic is repetition. Whereas in the case of events, the before-and-after is virtually constitutive, the exactness of chronological definitions seems less important when describing the state of something or a long-term process. All events are based on preexistent structures that become a part of the events concerned, but that existed before the events in a different way from the chronological sense of the before. Let me mention some structures in this connection. Consider constitutional forms and modes of power which are based on the repetition of well-known rules. Or take productive forces and the relations of production, which change slowly, with sudden bursts at intervals. Their effect derives from the repetition of certain procedures and from the rational constancy of general market conditions. I could also mention the given geographical and spatial factors which in the long-term stabilize everyday life or which may also provoke political conflict situations which in the course of history are similar to and repeat one another. Furthermore there are conscious and even more subconscious modes of behavior that may be determined by institutions or that can in turn shape their own institutions, and whose characteristic is their *longue durée*. They include customs and legal systems whose strength tends to arrange and outlive individual events. Finally, I would like to mention procreative behavior, which despite all love affairs or love tragedies, implies supraindividual continuities or long-term changes. This list could easily be continued, but enough is enough. The temporal characteristic of such structures lies in the repetition of the same thing, even if that thing changes cumulatively in the long or medium term.

Events and structures thus seem to have within the movement of history different temporal dimensions that should be studied separately by historical scholarship. Usually the account of structures tends to become a description, and that of events a narrative. But it would mean setting the wrong priorities to define history exclusively in one way or another. Both levels, of events and of structures, remain interdependent.

My proposition would be that events can never be fully explained by assumed structures, just as structures cannot only be explained by events. There is an epistemological aporia involving the two levels so that one can never entirely deduce one thing from another.

The before and after of an event gives it its own temporal quality that can never be entirely reduced to its longer-term conditions. Every event is more and at the same time less than what is indicated in such conditions: hence its always surprising novelty.

Let me give you an example. The structural prerequisites for the battle of Leuthen cannot adequately explain why Frederick the Great won the battle in the way he did. There were certainly preexistent structures for this event: the Prussian army regulations, its recruitment system, and the fact that it was firmly rooted in the social and agrarian constitution of the territories east of the Elbe, as well as the tax system and war fund based on that constitution. All these factors made the victory at Leuthen possible, but December 5, 1757, remains a unique event in its chronologically immanent sequence.

I will give you another example: a court case involving labor law may be a dramatic event for the person concerned. But at the same time, it may be an indicator of social, legal, and economic conditions of long standing. Depending on how the questions are asked, the emphasis of the described event is shifted, just as the way in which it is told changes. The account is then looked at from different temporal angles. Either the exciting before and after of the incident, the trial, and its outcome are discussed, including all the consequences, or the event is taken apart into its elements, giving indicators of those social conditions that provide an insight into the structure of the event and into how it happened. In that case the description of such structures can sometimes be more dramatic than the account of the court proceedings themselves.

So we could say that history can only be investigated if the various temporal dimensions are kept separate. I want to repeat my proposition: events and structures are interlocked with one another, but one can never be reduced to the other.

Two conclusions may be drawn for the practice of social history. In keeping apart the different temporal levels, the conditions and limitations of possible prognosis are revealed. Single events are difficult to forecast since they are unique in themselves. But the prerequisites for what is possible in the future can be predicted insofar as certain possibilities keep repeating themselves within the structural frame. So we can forecast the conditions of possible events, for which there is ample evidence in the history of prognostication.

Secondly, I would like to draw attention to the peculiar feature of modern social history. It seems to be characterized by the fact that since the French Revolution and the Industrial Revolution, structures themselves have changed more rapidly than they did before. Structural changes have taken on the quality of an event, so to speak. But this statement does not apply to all structures, and the investigation of their different temporal dimensions will remain a subject for research.

III. How Historical Time Could Be Examined within the Life Cycles of the Various Generations

I am now coming to my third and final part, and at this stage I would like to make some suggestions as to how historical time could be examined within the life cycles of the various generations. As we all know, historical time is a difficult thing to convey; it lives on spatial background connotations and can be expressed in metaphorical terms only. But there is a way of analyzing sources with respect to historical time. This purpose is served by two anthropological categories that are suited for deducing from written sources the notion of time contained in them. I am speaking of the categories of the space of experience and the horizon of expectation. There is no historical act that is not based on the experiences and expectations of those involved. To this extent we have a pair of metahistorical categories that set out the condition of potential history. And both these categories are excellently suited for discussing historical time, for the past and the future are joined together in the presence of both experience and expectation. These categories are suited also for discovering historical time in empirical research, since, through their content, they guide concrete agents in their actions relating to social and political movement. I will give you a simple example: the experience of the execution of Charles I opened up Turgot's horizon of expectation when he insisted that Louis XVI should introduce reforms so that he might be spared the same fate. Turgot warned his king, but to no avail. However, a temporal connection between the past English and the coming French Revolution could now be experienced and explored, and this connection pointed beyond mere chronology. Through the medium of certain experiences and certain expectations concrete history is produced.

Unfortunately, I cannot analyze in detail the interplay of experience and expectation on this occasion. But let me say this much, that both temporal extensions are dependent on one another in very different ways. In experience, historical knowledge is stored that cannot be transformed into expectation without a break. If this were possible, history would always repeat itself. Just like memory and hope, these dimensions have a different status. This is highlighted by a political joke from Russia: "On the horizon, we can see communism," Khrushchev remarked in a speech. Someone interrupted and asked, "Comrade Khrushchev, what is a horizon?" "Look it up in the dictionary," he replied. Back home, the inquisitive fellow found the following definition: "Horizon: an imaginary line that separates the earth from the sky and that moves away when being approached."

That which is expected in the future is apparently limited in a different way from that which has been experienced in the past. Expectations that one may be entertaining can be superseded, but experiences one has had are being collected. The space of experience and the horizon of expectation cannot therefore be related to one another in a static way. They constitute a temporal difference within the here and now, by joining together the past and the future in an asymmetric manner. All this means that we have found a characteristic of historical time which at the same time demonstrates its variability.

My historical thesis would be that in modern time, the difference between experience and expectation has steadily increased. To be more exact, modern time has only been conceived as such since expectations have moved away from all previous experiences. In the beginning, I explained how the expression "progress" conceptualized this difference for the first time. At this point, I would like to add that since the eighteenth century, the entire political and social vocabulary has completely changed. Political and social concepts have a temporal internal structure which tells us that since the eighteenth century the weight of experience and the weight of expectation have shifted in favor of the latter.

It has been a consistent finding from Aristotle to the Enlightenment that the concepts of political language have primarily served to collect experiences and develop them theoretically. The notions obtained from this, such as monarchy, aristocracy, democracy, and their degenerate varieties, were sufficient for conclusions to be drawn for the future from past experiences processed in this way. And this is true despite changing social structures. What could be expected from the future could be derived directly from previous experience. Since the Enlightenment this has changed radically. Let us look at the old general term "res publica," under which the specific forms of rule were listed. During the Enlightenment, all types of constitution were forced into an alternative choice. There was only *the* Republic: everything else was despotism. The decisive aspect of these antonyms is their temporalization. All constitutions were given a temporal indicator. The path of history led away from the tyranny of the past—toward the republic of the future. The notion of "republic" which was filled out with experiences became a concept of expectation.

It was a change of perspective that can be demonstrated by taking Kant, for example. The republic was for him a historical objective that could be deduced from practical reason. In anticipation of this future, he used the new expression "republicanism." Republicanism indicated a principle of historical movement, the promoting of which was a moral and political imperative.

Republicanism meant a concept of movement that achieved for political action what progress promised to achieve for history in general. It served to anticipate the forthcoming historical movement in theory and to influence it in practice. The temporal difference between the forms of rule previously experienced and the constitution to be expected and intended, was conceptualized by this term.

I have now defined the temporal structure of a concept that recurs in numerous subsequent concepts, and the projections based on it have been superseding and outdoing one another. Republicanism was followed by democratism, liberalism, socialism, communism, and fascism. Considered from a temporal angle, all of them have something in common. At the time when these concepts were created, they had no content in terms of experience. Whereas the Aristotelian notions of forms of government were directed at the finite possibilities of political organization so that one could be deduced from another, the new concepts of movement were meant to open up a new future. The lower their content in terms of experience, the greater were the expectations they created—this would be a short formula for the new type of political and historical concepts.

Our anthropological premise can thus be verified semantically. Modern time is characterized by the fact that the difference between experience and expectation has increased. Of course, the elements of experience and of expectation change positions to the extent that the projected systems are being realized. But the temporal tension that was once created has left its mark on our political and social language to this day. The new concepts of movement served the purpose of reorganizing the masses, released from the system of estates, under the banner of new slogans. In this respect they also had a slogan-forming effect that could be instrumental in creating parties.

Political and social concepts become the navigational instruments of the changing movement of history. They do not only indicate or record given facts. They themselves become factors in the formation of consciousness and the control of behavior. This brings us to the point where linguistic analysis of experiences of time merges into social history. Properly speaking, the latter would require some differentiation in terms of the specific level involved and pragmatism of language. But in view of our initial theme, the above will suffice. The linguistic reflection of the changing experiences of time is probably one of the specifically historical contributions to the concepts of social history, regardless of the extent to which they are otherwise controlled by systematic considerations.

I have attempted, in three steps, to formulate the challenge that arises out of the question of historical time and that has a bearing on social history.

I have tried to show historiographically that temporalization was at the beginning of the modern history that today is being studied from a social-historical angle with regard to general change.

Secondly, I have tried, by using the antonyms of "event" and "structure," to show theoretically that we depend on the distinction between different time levels in order to be able to work within social history.

Thirdly, I have employed the metahistorical categories of experience and expectation in order to show how the change of historical time itself can be made empirically transparent.

Translated by Adelheis Baker

The Unknown Future and the Art of Prognosis

"Can one recognize that which is past if one does not even understand that which is present? And who can conceptually appraise what the present is without knowing what is to come in the future? What is to come determines what is present, and this determines what is past." These words are those of Johann Georg Hamann. For every reader who metaphorically construes time as a line that runs from the past through the fictive point of the present into the open future, Hamann's statement is nonsensical. For intellectual historians, it is readily apparent that Hamann's words draw on the expectation of salvation history which is accessible through revelation and offers a knowledge of the future, affecting not only every individual personally but also world history in its entirety. For political or social historians professionally occupied with the past and who, for instance, investigate it by seeking out causal chains leading into the present, the future remains systematically left out. Such historians might concede on psychological or epistemological grounds that their own expectations might influence the kind of questions they pose and that these questions might stimulate the so-called cognitive interests (*Erkenntnisinteresse*) that they pursue. They can, after all, entertain a few thoughts about the future without compromising their professional integrity. More is required, nowadays, of the specialized disciplines of political science, economics, and sociology, insofar as they project structures (as opposed to individual cases) in order to deduce future trends from them.

Future predictions of every ilk abound in historical sources. We do not need to live in the year 1984 to think of the legion of temporal utopias—more dystopic than utopic—that recent times have projected, or to use Hamann's formulation, to diagnose the present from the perspective of the future. But the round dance continues: think, for instance, of how electoral prognoses influence actual elections, be it through the agreement or the dissent that they arouse; or of how projected numbers and figures for a production line depend on market analyses to deduce possibilities to be realized in the future; or of how computers stored alternatives for all thinkable decisions for a planned atomic war; or of the predictions of the Club of Rome, which have in the meantime been reinforced by the environmentally conscious Green party endeavoring to transpose its fear into a political rationality of the future; or of the customary business of any diplomacy that could not exist without calculating future actions. Our examples extend to the everyday, in which the financial consequences of a child's birth must be carefully considered, all the more so because the possible loss of one's job or a pay cut has also to be figured into what is to come. Finally, let us not forget the dream, to which prophetic power was already attributed in its canonization by Artemidorus, and which also enters into diagnoses of present-day analyses, ranging from the therapeutic to the prognostic. Examples could be multiplied endlessly. They stretch from the everyday life of individuals to the broad realm of the political, and, moreover, they reach into a space of uncontrollable processes, even if their framing conditions are changeable. I am reminded of how long-term data forecasting the correlation between energy reserves and the demographic curve of the earth's population increasingly came to affect middle- and short-term planning data in politics and economics. In general terms, Hamann's point about what is to come in the future affecting the present can hardly be disputed.

The status of what is to come surely does not correspond completely to that which is past. Past events are contained in our experience and are empirically verifiable. What is to come is fundamentally beyond our experience and, as such, is not empirically verifiable. This notwithstanding, there are predictions that can be transposed, with more or less plausibility, from experience into expectation. In this case, as a keen intellectual rival of Hamann indicated, it is a question of the faculty of foreseeing (*praevisio*). "To possess this faculty," says Kant, is of greater interest than anything else because it is the condition of all possible practice and all possible purposes to which man relates the use of his powers. All desire contains (doubtful or certain) anticipation of what is possible through foresight. Recalling the past (remembering) occurs only with the intention of making it possible to foresee the future; we look about us from the standpoint of the present in order to determine something, or to be prepared for something.[1]

Kant traces historical time dimensions back to their anthropological core. In contrast to Augustine's reduction of time dimensions to something within humans, but already similarly to Chladenius's historical hermeneutics, the emphasis on the human agent makes available anthropological and, to this extent, metahistorical categories that define the conditions of possibility for history. Of the three time dimensions, Kant unequivocally granted the greatest weight to the future and its attendant faculty of foresight.

The finding is clear. Desires, as Kant says, but also anxieties and hopes, wishes and apprehensions, rational plans and calculations, and especially predictions, are all types of expectations belonging to our experience, or better put, corresponding with our experience. Humans, as cosmopolitan beings, necessarily conduct their lives, simply to exist, by remaining future-oriented. In order to even act, one must take into account and plan for the empirical inexperience of the future. Whether it makes sense or not, one must foresee the future. It is with this paradox that we come to the core of our investigation and can pose the following questions.

What do humans foresee, what can they foresee? The coming reality, or only possibilities? One possibility, several, or many? Is foresight guided by fear or by reason, or, as Hobbes would say, by both at the same time? Is foresight commanded by the belief in a prophecy, or safeguarded through recourse to a historically and philosophically grounded necessity, or perhaps fed from criticism and skepticism? Is it tied to omens of oracular or mantic nature, or to a sign system of historical interpretations, or to attempts at scientific analysis?

The historical answers can be delimited if one subsumes predictions under a few basic types that in the course of history can be found to both overtake and overlap one another. Moreover, the answers can be reduced if we investigate only the preconditions of when and why certain prognoses came true and why others did not. In what follows, I will concern myself with the latter question, and, in so doing, will not be able to dispense with a crude typology.

Given the abundance of prognoses that have come true and the equally large, perhaps even larger, number that did not or have not come true and are hence forgotten, we should think of an alternative line of inquiry. Either it is a question of the play of pure luck or chance that one prognosis turns out to be true and another does not, or there are criteria to be found as to why one prognosis is more likely to be fulfilled than another, why one will become historically verifiable and another will not. I will try to develop some criteria below by drawing on a series of examples from political prognoses.

If we leave aside every historical experience, it can be said that either the future is completely unknown and, consequently, every prognosis is just chance, a roll of the dice, or there are gradations of greater or lesser probability with which future reality can be predicted. Historical experience seems to specify the latter. There are clusters of possibilities that individually or collectively indicate various chances for their realization. Accordingly, there must be an art of prognosis that contains at least minimal rules for its success.

In purely formal terms, the following rule could be postulated: the scope of future predictions ranges from absolutely certain prognoses to those that contain the highest level of improbability. Thus it must be considered absolutely certain that our earth could survive the catastrophe that would be brought about for the whole of humanity by an atomic war. Significantly more difficult to predict, however, is whether such a catastrophe would be caused by chance, by mistake, or on purpose, or whether it will turn out to be entirely prevented in the first place. That is to say, the further we distance ourselves from long-term data of what is naturally pregiven and concentrate our predictions on situations involving political decision making, the more difficult the art of prognosis becomes. The tentative light-ray of a searching prognosis oscillates between dependable and certain framework conditions and those that procedurally change and are comparatively uncertain in the field of political action. But in every case, prognostics draws its evidence from previous experience that is treated scientifically. To this extent, forecasting the future is an art of combining data from diverse experiences.

As historians, we are in the position to ask the following question: of the prognoses that did, in fact, come true, how come these and not others were fulfilled? And, as historians, we also know that in history there always happens more or less than what is contained in pregiven data. In this respect, history is always new and replete with surprise. Nevertheless, if there are predictions that turn out to be true, it follows that history is never entirely new, that there are evidently longer-term conditions or even enduring conditions within which what is new appears. We experience every single story (*Geschichte*)[2] that we are enmeshed in as unique, yet the very circumstances under which this uniqueness presents itself are themselves in no way new. There are structures that endure and there are processes that persist: both necessitate and outlast the respective individual events in which history itself takes place. In other words, there are different velocities of change.

Geographical conditions do not change at all, or, if they do change, it is only by way of technological mastery over precisely these geographical presuppositions of human activities. Juridical and institutional conditions likewise change more slowly than the political actions making use of them. And similarly, behavior patterns and mentalities change more slowly than the art of transforming these patterns and mentalities in terms of the ideology or propaganda that formed them. Likewise, political power constellations appear to barely change over the longer term, particularly when compared with their real transformation during wars or revolutions when accelerated processes of change are rendered visible.

Even if concrete history remains unique in each case, there are different layers of the tempos of change that we must theoretically distinguish in order to be able to measure uniqueness and persistence with regard to each other. But if we are going to talk about the persistence of geographical, institutional, and juridical conditions, or of conditions involving mentalities (*mentalitätsgebundene*), we are forced to attribute the characteristic of repetition to them within the concrete completion of diachronic flows of time. For instance, the letter I receive in the mail at nine o'clock in the morning may contain joyful or sad news that profoundly affects and absorbs me. Regardless, the postal delivery is still carried out from day to day at nine o'clock in the morning. Behind the postal delivery service stands an organization whose stability is contained in the repetition of established rules, and whose financial reserves are furnished through continual fiscal projections of collected postal revenue. This example could be extended to all aspects of human life.

To state my thesis more precisely: prognoses are only possible because there are formal structures in history that are themselves repeated, even while their concrete content is unique in each case and remains surprising to those most involved and affected. Without constants in the different levels of permanence within the multitude of factors contributing to the formation of events to come, it would be impossible to predict anything at all.

Let me examine a series of examples from the field of modern revolutions.

1. Of the historical-theoretical concepts that we could name, perhaps the best concept for us to illustrate the interplay between singularity and repetition is that of revolution. Certainly every revolution that occurs is entirely unique for those involved in and affected by it, either ushering in disaster or leading to happiness. But also contained within the concept of revolution are the notions of repetition, return, and even cyclical movement. This meaning is in no way just an incidental residuum from the borrowed Latin word, *revolutio.* On the contrary, the concept contains a structural statement about revolutions pure and simple, as we see again and again in the numerous variants across the world. The doctrine of recurrence, theoretically contained in the concept of revolution, implies both diachronic course constraints, which analogously repeat themselves, and acts by definite agents that can occur side by side. Thus the concept includes the exercise of extralegal violence, which, in the case of its success, involves a change in practices of governing or constitutional forms, a turnover of elites (but most of the time only partial), and a change in property ownership brought about by insurrection, expropriation, and redistribution of gains. Even further, the concept contains familiar behavior patterns: cravenness, courage, fear, hope, the use of terror out of anxiety or out of contempt, the formation of parties and of factions within them, rivalry between leaders, the capability of the masses for acclamation, as well as their own need for acclamation. In short, every revolution contains synchronic factors that analogously repeat themselves as well as chains of effects that exhibit diachronic relationships. They are unique in their individual occurrences, but their formal structures always betray recurring elements. To put it differently, history does not just run in a unique, diachronic succession but always already contains repetitions—metaphorically speaking, revolutions—in which unique changes and the recurrence of the same or similar (or at least comparable) phenomena occur together.

The course of the French Revolution from 1787 through 1815 resembles in many respects—not only in the trial of the king, which led to his execution—the order of events in the English Revolution of 1640 to 1660–88. Thus, it cannot be too surprising that predictions of the French Revolution time and again fell back upon the example of the English Revolution, and that the diagnoses during the course of the French Revolution were time and again given substance by analogy with the English parallel—in order to be credible. Cromwell was the dictatorial figure that Robespierre wanted to avoid becoming, who would then be outdone by Napoleon.

2. With regard to the conclusions drawn from the argument that ideas about the future rest upon a structural repeatability derived from the past, I will mention three instances of increasing concreteness with which the rise of Napoleon's dictatorship was predicted.

In 1764, d'Argenson was one of the first who excellently predicted the coming events in France when he defined the combination of monarchy and democracy as a probable and momentous event to come to pass in the near future.[3] For him, the aristocracy, as in the Aristotelian topology, was the real hindrance to a forthcoming balance that must lead, sooner or later, to a change in the constitution. A social-historical and procedural interpretation of the Aristotelian categories of government made it possible for d'Argenson to predict the cooperation of the monarch with the rising bourgeois strata (*bürgerliche Schichten*), so as to prognosticate the revolution in the case that their cooperation was prevented. The destruction of the nobility and the *démocratie royale* corresponded to one another. The prognosis rested on a new, temporalized combination of conventional concepts and discernment. The fruitfulness of the historical prediction was contingent upon various historical strata as well as upon vertical temporal gradations that were transposed from historical experience onto statements about the future. To ask which layer (*Schicht*) of experience is called upon each time, it may be helpful to bear in mind the spatial metaphorics contained in our word for "history" (*Geschichte*).[4] This becomes much clearer in the second prediction, from 1780. It comes from Diderot and reads as follows:

Under the rule of despotism, the people, embittered by their lengthy sorrows, will miss no opportunity to take back their rights. But since they have neither a goal nor a plan, one moment of slavery lapses in another moment back into anarchy. In the midst of this general confusion, a single cry rings out: Freedom. But how can this valuable good be secured? No one knows. And already, the people are divided into various factions, roused up by conflicting interests. . . . In little time, there are only two factions within the state; they are distinguished by two names: "Royalists" and "Antiroyalists," behind which everyone hides. This is the moment of great convulsion, the moment of plotting and conspiracy. . . . In this, Royalism serves as a pretext as much as Antiroyalism. Both are masks for ambition and avarice. The nation is now only a mass being held together by a band of criminals and corrupt persons. In this situation only one man and a suitable moment are needed for an entirely unexpected result to emerge. If the moment comes, the great man will have also already risen. . . . He speaks to the people, who up until this time still believed themselves to be everything: You are nothing. And they speak: We are nothing. And he speaks to them: I am the Lord. And they speak with one voice: You are the Lord. And he speaks to them: Here are the conditions under which I am ready to subject you. And they speak: We accept them. . . . How will the revolution turn out? No one knows.[5]

Diderot's prognosis was smuggled anonymously (in accordance with Enlightenment tactics) into Raynal's work on European colonial expansion. His prognosis, which in terms of its broad outline turned out to be entirely true, belongs among the most astonishing predictions of the middle-term course of the coming revolution. It was far more concrete than a similarly astute prognosis made by Frederick the Great.[6] The latter had predicted the coming civil war in France as the result of the Enlightenment; however, Diderot went still a step farther as an "Enlightener of the Enlightenment" when he converted the dialectic between master and slave into a structural political statement that had the result of a voluntarily accepted dictatorship.

Numerous layers of historical experience entered into Diderot's prediction. For one, the contemporaneous Swedish revolution of Gustav III, culminating in 1772 with a supraparliamentary monarchy, offered Diderot a point of entry for his own analysis by modeling a result that he projected as a possible parallel in France's future.

Yet historically, deeper layers formed the basis of his prediction: more structurally repeatable elements entered into its formulation. These concern figures of argumentation that Diderot derived from Roman history, specifically from Tacitus and his analysis of the civil war in the year of the three emperors. That the wish for freedom, like a catchword, could entirely change into a yearning for voluntary subjugation was not something derivable from the enlightened assumptions that Diderot shared. Behind it stood experiences that could, instead, be traced back to the Roman civil wars and to the civil wars during the imperial period. An additional force behind his prediction was Polybius's cyclical model of history. Polybius's model, derived from that recorded in the Sophist tradition by Herodotus,[7] made the path to a monarchy readable as an inevitability. Thus the accuracy of Diderot's prognosis rested on a vertical historical (*geschichtliche*) gradation into which both fully conceptualized historical (*historische*) experiences and their theoretical processings entered. Although Diderot conceded that he did not know how the revolution would turn out, the perspicacity of his analysis can be attributed to the repeatability of historical principles derived from experience.

The same can be said for a prediction of Wieland's. Bound by the concrete, short-term context of events that constituted the French Revolution, Wieland prognosticated that Napoleon Bonaparte would seize power and become the dictator of France. He made this prediction one and a half years before the actual coup d'état and added that it would be the best solution that the French civil war could find. For his prediction, Wieland found himself in no little trouble because he was living in Weimar where he was denounced as a Jacobin and as a Bonapartist (if the word was even coined yet).

The certainty of his prognosis (a prognosis that was, of course, confirmed) rested not only on political instinct or the play of chance but first and foremost on the significant parallel that he drew, once again, with the English Revolution. More than this, his prognosis grew out of his own classical training, predisposing him to see constitutional changes in terms of Polybius's doctrine of cycles as well as to draw on his knowledge of the Roman civil war. The upshot of the Roman civil war was, of course, the rise of the dictatorship of Julius Caesar. Thus what distinguishes Wieland's concrete prognosis is that it rests on the theoretical premise that it is possible to derive even an individual case, namely the coming to power of the dictator Napoleon himself, because determinable sequences will repeat themselves in the course of a revolution.[8]

We are now in the fortunate position of being able to cite another prognosis made by Wieland, but, this time, one that did not come true. After the convening of the Assembly of Notables in 1787, Wieland predicted that the coming revolution in France would be mild, charitable, and guided by reason, peaceful and displaying goodwill. His exact words read as follows:

In these important matters, which are also essential for the good fortune of peoples, the present situation in Europe appears (if we are not deceived by our trustfulness) to be moving toward a benevolent revolution; a revolution that will not be carried out by wild rebellions and civil wars but through a peaceful, unshakably steadfast persistence, by dutiful resistance—not through a corrupt wrestling of passions against passions, violence against violence, but through the gentle, persuasive, and finally irresistible omnipotence of reason: in short, a revolution in which Europe is not flooded in blood and consumed by fire and flames. This revolution will be the mere beneficent work of human teachings about their true interests, their rights and duties, and the purpose of their existence, and it is the only means by which this purpose can be surely and infallibly achieved.[9]

In terms of our investigation, one thing becomes immediately clear: Wieland's gentle and trusting prediction rested on the fact that he believed himself to be capable of countermanding all previous experience by way of the self-certain guardianship of the Enlightenment. Inspired by optimistic Enlightenment hopefulness, Wieland predicted a revolution that would be different from all previous revolutions because it would be executed without civil war. In favor of the singularity of historical progression, Wieland, trusting his own trustfulness, refrained from any argument by analogy that he could have made from previous history—a line of argumentation that he would pursue ten years later. It was precisely this historical singularity alongside the linear projecting of enlightened optimism that allowed him to formulate a prediction which would be controverted soon enough by political events.

The first criterion that we have examined is thus contained in the test question of whether a prognosis refers back to possibilities of historical repetition or whether it supposes an absolute uniqueness of historical progression. In instances where Wieland drew on experience to make arguments by analogy, he turned out to be right; in instances where he defined history as incomparably new, he proved to be wrong.

We can posit the following as our first interim result: as more temporal layers of a possible repetition entered into the prognosis, the more likely the prediction was to turn out to be correct. The more a prediction referred to and relied upon the incomparability and uniqueness of the coming revolution, the less likely it was to be fulfilled. There is scarcely a revolution that was so often and so accurately predicted in its actual occurrence as the French Revolution. Yet just as frequently, the information about what course its future would take proved to be illusory. The *belle révolution* that Voltaire never grew tired of longing for and extolling comes to mind. He saw nothing other than the enforcement of moral righteousness in the longed-for revolution, something that he, as a philosopher, polemically demanded and never gave up. Only rarely have predictions been so exactly and precisely formulated as those of Frederick the Great, Diderot, or Rousseau, all of whom relativized linear progress into uniqueness. Thus a share of historical experience entered into their respective prognoses in varying amounts. In instances where the chances of historical repetition were denied, the predictions fell into a web of great desirability; in instances where the repeatability of historical possibilities was taken seriously, the prognoses had a greater chance of coming true. The ability to judge the prospects of success for a given prediction thus depends on the temporal multilayeredness of historical experience out of which predictions are composed.

As clarification, another series of examples may be examined that belongs to our own past and points toward the outbreak of World War II. With these examples, I will present three types which explain our thesis that a vertical historical gradation is the prerequisite of successful prognoses.

On November 16, 1937, Edvard Beneš, then president of Czechoslovakia, wrote: "I stalwartly believe that we will preserve freedom. I do not believe that a war in Europe is possible within the foreseeable future. On the contrary, I am of the hope that it will not come." We need only to prepare ourselves for defense. "I do not fear a thing for Czechoslovakia."[10] One year later, Beneš found himself in exile in London.

Here, it is a question of a wishful prognosis, admittedly fed by optimism, and the expression of an opinion that can only evoke astonishment at a politician in such a position and at such a time. It is certainly part of every prediction that one's own attitude toward the future enters as a factor in the prognosis. But the chances of fulfillment of a self-fashioned prognosis will only increase when there is power great enough to realize it.

At that time, Hitler was in precisely this position. Seven days after Beneš's optimistic remarks, Hitler declared at a local branch of the Nazi party in Augsburg: "It is truly something wonderful when destiny has chosen human beings to be able to champion the cause of our people. Today, new tasks are in store for us. For the lebensraum of our people is too cramped. One day, the world will have to consider our demands. I do not doubt for a second that, just as it was possible for us to galvanize the nation from within, we will also obtain for ourselves the same external rights to life that other peoples have gained."[11]

Without calling the possibly ensuing war by name, Hitler announces in this speech his scarcely even veiled program of expansion. In this respect, it is also a question of a desired prognosis. However, Hitler's prediction of the future was different from Beneš's because it was composed of elements that were more multilayered.

Hitler swore, as he always did, that domestic political advancement was also a pledge of future success in the field of foreign politics. His declaration represents a typical case of a middle-term linear projection from the past onto the future (not unlike the sort we have already seen with Wieland), where no newly appearing factors of world politics in Europe are named, even though Hitler might have considered them as a politician. It was here that the striking power of Hitler's initial successes was to be found, but it was, at the same time, also where the deeply rooted source of error, which helped to bring about his own destruction and with him the downfall of the old Germany, was concealed. The linear projection was but one layer deep (*einschichtig*). In addition, there is the appeal to destiny, an ideological stripe with deep roots in the history of the German mind (*Geistesgeschichte*), the very destiny that Hitler never doubted for a second and instead autosuggestively affirmed. The structure of this prognosis thus reveals itself as an ultimatum-like, compulsory prognosis. Again and again, Hitler set it up for himself. It corresponds with the sort of linear projection that does not permit any alternatives, and instead excludes them. Its compulsoriness is summed up in the single-mindedness through which Hitler tried to self-suggestively substantiate his sense of his own chosenness. His prognosis approached the structure of prophetic foretellings of the future.

We can confront the wishful prognosis of Beneš and the ultimatum-like, compulsory prognosis of Hitler with a third type. On November 27, 1932, Churchill announced in the House of Commons:[12] "It would be in our better interest to newly revisit the Danzig question and that of the Polish Corridor in a cool and deliberate atmosphere, despite how delicate and tricky these questions are, while the victorious powers still hold onto their wide superiority, instead of watching and waiting, little by little and step by step, until a great confrontation mounts, in which we are, once again, pushed up against one another, poised on the brink of war."

Of course, wishes also enter into this prognosis and an ultimatum-like compulsion to act is also contained within it, but with the goal of averting a second world war. Churchill's prognosis has to do with an alternative conditional prognosis that contains instructions for acting. What distinguishes this prognosis is the clear formulation of two possibilities, one of which goes back to the enduring experience of World War I and the other of which takes into account the uniqueness of the changing postwar situation. Its structure is multilayered (*vielschichtig*). The diagnosis rests on the continuous experience of the catastrophe of 1914, in order to formulate, in 1932, an alternative while the latitude for action was dwindling. The warning of the return to world war evokes an instruction to prevent this possibility.

One might reduce the simple alternative to the suggestive power of Churchill's rhetoric—he certainly would have had further possibilities in the back of his head. The catastrophe that Churchill tried to avoid politically came true in line with his prediction. The experience of the outbreak of war in 1914 together with the argument from analogy derived from it did not mislead him. Yet for Churchill, it was not a question of a linear projection of an inescapable future; rather this projection posited a condition of possible repetition, precisely in order to fight against it in actuality. The correctness of his prognosis was thus based on the employment of instructions for acting in several vertical historical dimensions, whose combination brought about such accuracy.

Our investigation of historical layers of time (*geschichtliche Zeitschichten*) makes it possible for us to bring prognostics out of the frame of reference of pure anthropology or even beyond the psychology of particular agents. Neither the touching optimism of a Beneš, nor the autosuggestion of Hitler, nor the imaginative sobriety of Churchill gives us the key to unlock the accuracy or wrongness of their predictions. The objectivizable criteria are contained in the vertical temporal gradation that was invoked as an argument for the prognosis.

It is not only the formal repeatability of possible history that guarantees a minimum amount of prognostic certainty, but success also depends on taking into account the multilayeredness of historical courses of time.

Therefore, in a second stage of our investigation, I would like to state more precisely our question regarding the various layers of time. Theoretically, three different temporal planes can be distinguished; they are retrievable in different ways in order to make prognoses possible.

First, there is the short-term succession of the before and after characterizing the constraints of our everyday actions. Always bound situationally, the prerequisites for the agents involved change in terms of the temporal spans that are experienced either sooner or later—whether in years, months, weeks, hours, or even from minute to minute. In this context, it is especially difficult to make exact prognoses, not least because all of the actions and reactions can never be grasped at the same time, or even be recognized. It is like a game of chess in which only after a certain number of moves does the situation become sufficiently clear so that prognoses can be made with greater, and finally even absolute, accuracy.

Second, there is the plane of middle-term trends deriving from the course of events, into which there enter an enormous number of factors beyond the control of acting subjects. Here, the many transpersonal conditions exert an influence on what is happening, but the conditions themselves only change in turn at a slower speed than that of the actions of the agents themselves. In this sphere, we find, for example, economic crises, or the courses of a war or a civil war, or the longer-term changes caused by the introduction of new techniques of production, or those processes viewed by the people affected as a decline in moral standards or the corruption of a group of political agents. It is always a matter of figures of progression influenced by transpersonal framework conditions that can finally reach so far as to even transform these conditions themselves. It is a question of processual progressions which, despite all kinds of innovation, still permit many arguments by analogy, as our series of examples of revolutionary prognoses has demonstrated.

Third, there is a plane of metahistorical duration, so to speak, which is nevertheless still not timeless. On this plane, one can hypothetically establish certain anthropological constants such that they, more than all other factors, elude the historical pressure of change. A wealth of principles derived from experience stem from this sphere. They repeat themselves by definition and are applicable over and over again. They are thus principles derived from experience that *eo ipso* possess a prognostic truth.

The simple form of proverbs belongs here. Proverbs often provide conflicting practical instructions, but nonetheless always remain applicable. "Pride goeth before a fall." "You can't take on city hall." "Too many cooks spoil the broth." Of course, the applicability depends on whether one is on the side of city hall, the cooks, or the broth! However, the significance of such seemingly banal words of wisdom cannot be underestimated. They even appear in the most densely formulated treatises. And even if one concedes that the course of history is not directed by our moral judgments and proverbial pearls of wisdom, pride still remains a predictable and occasionally tamable factor in the play of powers. Finally, there are such pithy maxims whose prognostic truth remains irrefutable. Thus Seneca warned Nero in vain that he could beat to death everyone except his successor. Here, it is a matter of a formal statement about the future whose content can be realized at any time. Such statements are seemingly timeless and are always situatively applicable. Stalin suspected it when he had Trotsky murdered. Regardless, he could not prevent the work of de-Stalinization by his successors.

Seen in a more highly condensed state, it is a question of metahistorical statements in which the conditions of possible histories and thus of possible futures are reflected. I am referring here to the speeches of Thucydides or to the themes of Tacitus, who described less the actuality of events than the manner in which they were experienced as contradictory. The analyses of civil war by both authors are not only structured in terms of the courses taken but are also semantically reflected and interrogated with respect to their content of experience; the analyses lead to doctrines of history that not only can be repeated rhetorically but can actually be applied. The overcoming of the religious civil wars in the early modern period might have happened successfully without the authors from antiquity; however, they actually provided doctrines with direct instructions for action. These doctrines contained a prognostic potential that emptied new experiences of their surprising effects. Religious intolerance became calculable, politically predictable, and therefore capable of being tamed.

We can move to the present and make an assumption. We do not know what sort of arguments Dubček heard in the Kremlin in 1968 before he submitted to the conditions of the Soviets. But the basic structure of the argumentation can be found in Thucydides' famous dialogue between the Athenians and the citizens of Melos.[13] The Melian Dialogue consists of argumentation divided between two participants. It can be formulated in modern terms as leading to an alternative conditional prognosis with the goal of bringing about instructions for action. In just one sentence, Thucydides defines the attitude of the Melians as a wishful prognosis: from pure wish, they take the veiled future already to be present and, for this reason, are mistaken. The Athenians, by contrast, appeal to the law of power, a law that they did not invent but rather have only adopted in order to apply it. After the exchange of arguments in which hope faces off against experience—with regard to the content, the Melians' sense of justice versus the Athenians' desired abuse of power—Thucydides reports in just three lines how the Melians, following their subjugation, were put to death and their wives and children enslaved. Prague was spared the analogous fate in 1968. The Czechs acquiesced to power.

It would be senseless to try to construct a linear reception history of Thucydides. There are, rather, historical structures of experience that, once formulated, are not lost but continue to persist even under the entirely different conditions of the modern exercise of power or under new conceptions of legality. They possess a prognostic power of metahistorical duration that can be used at any time to render political projections.

I am approaching my conclusion. The theoretical distinction between our three temporal courses (short-term actions, middle-term procedural constraints, and long-term, or rather, permanently repeatable possibilities) reveals to us that their relationship to each other has changed fundamentally in the course of recent history.

Today, short-term prognoses are more difficult to render because the number of factors that must enter into them has multiplied. Certainly, elements of metahistorical duration enter into these prognoses, but the variety of universal framework conditions for each individual action has increased; in other words, their complexity is more difficult to master. Short-term prognoses were easier to make in the early modern period when the number of active agents remained manageable, when the life span of rulers as human beings in their finite limitedness remained politically calculable. The calculation of constellations of inheritance for the next war belonged to the permanent work of early modern prognostics. The closer we draw to our own time, the more difficult the art of making short-term prognoses becomes because even the longer-lasting framing conditions for short-term theaters of action have multiplied and changed.

But also the transpersonal constants, which, as conditions, determined the middle-term course of events, have also changed with increasing speed in the last two hundred years. Technology and industry have reduced the spans of experience, and they could only be stabilized when their presuppositions remained the same. The presuppositions of the courses of our lives change more quickly today than they did in the past, and even structures become events because they change still faster. The good old saw, "We don't learn for the sake of school but for the sake of life," has lost its force. We only learn how we can relearn. And even this we have not yet learned. In view of our model of three layers of time, it can be said that formerly long-lasting constants, those which kept the framework conditions of middle-term courses and the interconnected short-term actions stable, have themselves come under increased pressure of change. There are ever more variables, and it becomes more and more difficult to project and relate them to one another today. For this reason, seen in terms of historical disciplines, sociology has developed out of and differentiated itself from the profession of history. The question of how the short, middle, and long terms relate to each other forces sociologists to make prognoses, whether they want to or not. Allow me, then, a last word from a historical perspective: prognostic certainty ought to increase again if it becomes possible to incorporate more delaying effects into the future, delaying effects that become calculable as soon as the economic and institutional framework conditions of our actions become more stable. But this is probably only a utopia, one which cannot even be derived from previous history.

Translated by Todd Presner

Remarks on the Revolutionary Calendar and *Neue Zeit*

As a historical concept, *Neue Zeit* (new time) or *Neuzeit* (modern age or modernity) contains a contradiction. On the one hand, time is always new, insofar as every present differentiates itself from every past and every future; it is unique and therefore new. We are speaking, in this case, of an iterative expression of time that can always be subjectively enriched by new experiences. In this sense, every time that is experienced is a new time. It enters into the everyday experiences of everyone.

Or, on the other hand, "time" indicates the same manner of repetition always embodied in the natural course of the heavenly bodies or in the rotation of the earth. We are speaking, in this case, of objectivizable modes of experience that, with the help of calendrical calculations, can be generally and universally mediated. This sort of reckoning of time (*Zeitrechnung*) does not allow for any new time to arise, unless the particular beginning of such a natural calculation of time (*Zeitberechnung*) was innovative as a cultural achievement and could, in this respect, also be secondarily felt as modern or as relating to a new time (*neuzeitlich*). In this sense, every calendar reform is an event relating to a new time.

However, that there should be a special time which is differentiated from all other times and, as such, emphatically distinguished as *Neue Zeit*, is a historical formation of consciousness or a political-historical form of knowledge that stands in only a loose connection with both of the subjective and objective expressions of time that were mentioned above.

That an entirely new time could begin is difficult to derive from the expressions of time themselves. New events may emerge or new behavior patterns may develop, but to what extent such changes also indicate a genuinely new time is hard to know.

As the construction of a historical consciousness or as political-social forms of knowledge, two possible experiences of time may be distinguished from one another. First, we can point to experiences of time that can be derived on an hourly, daily, weekly, or monthly basis from events and patterns of behavior as well as from factors that cause these very patterns of behavior and events. The new experience of time is set, then, into the realm of the everyday and always repeats itself corresponding to the natural expressions of time. One can call this a social-anthropologically sustained time which—analogous to natural time (*Naturzeit*)—is dependent on the recurrence of its conditions.

Secondly, as a form of historical consciousness, new time can be projected onto the sequence of years: it is, then, a question of a unique manner of counting that also remains unique within the succession of years, thanks to their numeration. This manner of counting, in contrast to days, hours, weeks, and months, does not repeat itself but instead refers to a historically and philosophically impregnated experience of time.

Remaining tied to natural and biological prerequisites, the subjective and objective ways of experiencing time are contained in social and historical reformulations of the interpretation of time. How they can be related to one another is a constant problem of human history that is always posed anew. Without doubt, new experiences of time can be registered directly on the plane of the social everyday, provided that events and patterns of behavior come under an increased pressure of time and, to this extent, fundamentally change. If there is talk about *Neuzeit* today, this phenomenon must, without doubt, be brought into view empirically.

In the same way, the counting of years in terms of their succession is always a historical interpretation of their entire course, be it that such an interpretation takes places only enumeratively, or be it that such an interpretation is projected, in terms of content, onto specific ages (*Zeitalter*).

Michael Meinzer's paper[1] leads us directly into these complex ambivalences of the concept of time by showing how the French revolutionaries attempted to cope with it. They evidently dealt with the difficulties that arose with the introduction of a new calendar in very different ways.

On the one hand, the new calendar was to open up and announce a new time—that is to say, inaugurate a historical *Neuzeit*. On the other hand, the calendar is necessarily tied back to the natural cycles of return underlying the continuous course of repetition in the paths of the stars and the rotation of the earth. Even if decimalization, scheduling systems, rhythms, and periodicities must be understood as social creations, at least days, months, and years appear to be pregiven from nature.

But the point of these social creations, which have emerged from political planning, is that they are a matter of regularities that, when maintained, mean precisely not innovation or anything new but rather stability and routine both in the everyday and in the modes of organization of a political society. Packed into this new order of time is something that may be like the beginnings of a new consciousness of time. But through repetition, precisely that which is new in it turns into the everyday and loses its meaning as a new time. The new time may, for example, become completely absorbed into administrative routines or into the increasing freedom of choice with regard to marriage outside of societal customs. Of course, whether these experiences of innovation are already sufficient for living with the consciousness of a new time may be justifiably doubted. In comparison with an analysis of the metropolis, the rural everyday will be less fertile for the experiences of innovation contained in the new sequences of time.

First of all, we must ask about the rhythms of everyday life upon which the system of *décades* was imposed. Work performed at a desk or in the ivory tower lends itself more quickly to decimalization than the kind of work whose time constraints are set by the craft of working at a carpenter's bench or with a farmer's plow. It could be that the social-anthropological component of the new revolutionary calendar only becomes visible with the negation of this calendar.

The question that Michael Meinzer keeps open may now turn out to be answerable: Were the new time schedules in the wake of the *décade* system also suited for coordinating the interdependencies of the various administrative branches, that is to say, for achieving what the time of day (*Uhrzeit*) and the Christian week-based time (*Wochenzeit*) had made possible independently of the decimal system?

Since all the innovations that occurred with the decimal system played out in a preindustrial period, doubt may be raised as to whether enough scheduling pressure had already been exerted on the everyday so that the new *décade* rhythms could be felt as provocation, assistance, or relief—in short, as modes of a new time. There is precisely one specific characteristic of modern (*neuzeitlich*) experience—acceleration—that seems to have been in no way caused or influenced by the calendar reform.

The other aspect of Michael Meinzer's interpretation seems to me to be more important: that the calendar reform concerned ideological attempts at control, primarily directed against the church, which could claim for themselves a general, unquestioned justification. The new calendar should not just enumeratively initiate a new era but should establish and stabilize this new era day by day.

But if one inquires into the historico-philosophical ideology behind the revolutionary calendar, one immediately encounters a critical ambivalence: that, of all things, an appeal to a rationalized nature should ring in a new epoch of history. Here, the critical contradictions become so striking that they are impossible to overlook. Why the equinox (a random date with respect to the introduction of the calendar) should be a symbol for political or social equality may be justifiably regarded as the revolutionary rhetoric of the moment. However, behind this natural metaphor stands a fundamental problem of the entire revolutionary metaphoric insofar as it refers back to nature and, at the same time, wants to thereby initiate a new age (*Zeitalter*). This contradiction becomes particularly glaring with regard to the political justifications for the introduction of the calendar. The same sun uniformly illuminates both the earth's poles and, successively, all the earth; half the earth will always be covered in darkness. The natural metaphor compromises itself as soon as it is referred to the new time in which everything is to be entirely different and new. Robespierre succumbed to the same contradiction when he explained the progress of the revolution: half the earth was already bathed in light and, in so being, had already been revolutionized; the other half would follow suit in the near future.[2] The metaphor breaks down at the point where darkness must be evoked.

Of course, one of the fundamental difficulties is to design historical symbols that fully divest themselves of their natural origins. The calendar reform in particular has demonstrated this impossibility. Again and again, one proceeds from the notion of return within which reason is said to be contained—be it in the recurrence of diurnal and nocturnal rhythms or monthly and yearly rhythms. In themselves, they are unable to represent a new time symbolically. Something similar holds true for the metaphors of rebirth conjured up by the prefix "re-" in the concept of revolution. The aspiration to a just order is always already pregiven as that which is to be reborn. To realize a just order thus means to reestablish it. In the horizon of our experience of time in a technological-industrial age, it is easy to overlook how strong the metaphorics of return really were in the French concept of revolution.

Calendar reform itself is not suited to open up a new historical period, especially if the calendar only organizes the regularity of the everyday. Only the reckoning of years (*Jahresrechnung*), whose counting is open toward the future, offers the permanent possibility for innovation. Therefore, it must be given special consideration. Only as an anti-Christian reckoning of time (*Zeitrechnung*) does the reckoning of years have symbolic meaning for an interpretation of the mental time line that enumeratively mediates between the past and the future on a new numerical scale. It is the new historical date, the founding of the republic, which is to be commemorated and thereby rendered perennial by the calendar reform. This commemoration can be interpreted as a pledge of constant innovation, even if it does not necessarily result from the new form of dating.

In any case, the introduction of a new reckoning of years (*Jahresrechnung*) was actually an innovation to the extent that it laid claim to opening up a new world era, analogous to the birth of Christ, with consequences for all of humanity and the entire world. It is likely that this thought only held sway within the horizon of Christian expectation which, of course, is newly occupied with finding analogous means—such as with the help of saints, new regulations for holidays, and the like.

But in contrast to the Christian calendar (*Zeitrechnung*), which was only introduced several centuries after the birth of Christ, the founding of a new calendar (*Kalender*) parallel to this one is something new in itself. What is really new about it is not a different manner of counting, or the supposedly greater naturalness and metaphorics of names, or a higher rationality. What is really new about it is the idea of being able to begin history anew by accounting for it in terms of a calendar. It is this work of reflection which commits one's own action to innovation and which may be recognized as that which is specifically modern (*das spezifisch Neuzeitliche*) about it. To what extent this work of reflection has actually transformed the practice of the everyday may be measured more by the intention than by the success. For the remainder of the new everyday rhythms moves completely within the orbits of analogy or the transfer of experience: the planning of the everyday continues to be tied back to the pregivens of nature, something that no calendar can finally and fully dispense with.

Translated by Todd Presner

The Eighteenth Century as the Beginning of Modernity

There is always something awkward about the organization of epochs. Numerous inconsistencies must simply be accepted because the individually proposed divisions cannot be brought into agreement with all the historical findings. For this reason, difficulties surface that seem to reinforce each other according to shifts in the way questions are posed. The first one lies in the lack of sharpness in chronologically determining which years characterize epochal breaks. Thus well-known dates in the history of events are offered to indicate caesuras. We need only to bring to mind years like 1917, 1789, 1640, 1517, 1492, or 800, 410, 375. It is obvious that such numbers can only be key dates for a vertical temporal determination whose symbolic value is attributable to the entire period of time. Even someone who does not undervalue the history of events will still have a hard time trying to define entire centuries, with respect to their content, from one date to another date.

Indeed, up until the eighteenth century, such key dates or turning points were satisfying because they seemed sufficiently well-defined for isolating periods out of the course of events. Periods were to stretch from one such date to the next. It was in this sense that the word "epoch" was used until the eighteenth century: an epoch indicated a cut, bringing one proposed period of time to an end and allowing another to begin without paying any heed to the following or preceding periods themselves. It was only linguistic usage in the period of German Idealism that established a concept of epoch which signified longer-term coherences both emerging from and referring to one another. Such epochs in the sense of periods could be less precisely dated because they had, so to speak, both a shifting beginning and a shifting ending from which they could be grasped as relative units.

In this already differentiated approach, the second major difficulty lies concealed. The greater the envisaged coherences were, the more difficult it became to make exact demarcations. The demarcation between so-called antiquity and the so-called Middle Ages has already fluctuated by centuries since the very invention of the concept of the Middle Ages, and it still does today. Similarly, our concept of modernity (*Neuzeit*) is also enormously elastic. An early modern period has been distinguished from modernity in a strict sense, corresponding to the French usage of *histoire moderne* and *histoire contemporaine*, respectively. According to their political tradition, the French locate the caesura between these two periods at the time of the French Revolution. While in Russia, the year 1917 (instead of 1789) was considered the separating date to divide recent history from the most recent, or rather, contemporary history. In Germany, the term *Zeitgeschichte* (contemporary history) has come to vaguely thematize the era of National Socialism and everything that has followed since then. Obviously, such dates derived from national histories are poorly suited to serve as caesuras in attempts at structuration applicable to universal history and graduated over several centuries.

In order to find a compromise between key chronological dates and deep structural determinants, the concept "epochal threshold" (*Epochen-schwelle*) has arisen in Germany. This concept makes it easier to grasp long-term processes that are definable as transitional periods so as to be able to establish, under specifically indicated criteria, the minimal conditions for a "beforehand not yet" or an "afterward no longer." Admittedly, it is very difficult to derive content-related criteria for determining this historically and theoretically fruitful concept.

All of these difficulties—projecting onto the concept of epochs chronological dates of events and long-term coherences spanning across dates—have only arisen since something like *neue Zeit* (new time) or *Neuzeit* (modernity) was conceived as a historical, periodizing concept. It was only in the eighteenth century that the problems surfaced with which we are still grappling today. They belong among the characteristic features of our age that can still be indisputably termed modern (*Neuzeit*). Whether it will stay this way remains to be seen. I would first like to take a quick look at generally well-known attempts at marking temporal boundaries in order to then turn from the present-day problematic back to the Enlightenment, a period whose new questions still confront us as historians today.

I

The difficulties connected with any formation of epochs and periods can be easily perceived in the organization of textbooks, schoolbooks, and reference books. Let me mention a few examples for the so-called period of modernity (*Neuzeit*). Whether the epochal threshold of modernity is to be positioned at 1500 or 1800 is today disputed, and not just since Troeltsch vehemently opted for the eighteenth century. Ranke had already fought the division between the Middle Ages and recent history, without, of course, being able to dispense with either concept.

There are still compelling arguments today for a threshold time situated more or less around 1500: the discovery of America and, with it, the European exploitation of the world; the tentative beginning of worldwide economic interdependence on the basis of the slave trade and slave economy (which was perhaps worse than it ever was in Greek and Roman antiquity); the interrelationship between work on American plantations and in silver mines and the East Asian trade conducted from Iberia; the invention of the printing press, which transformed the entire system of communication and spoken languages themselves; the development of gunpowder weapons, which affected the entire social constitution via the transformation of the military, having profound structural changes as a consequence; finally, the scientific revolution in the wake of Copernicus and Galileo— all of this must be cited, not to mention the religious schism, which was understood by its contemporaries as the first indicator of a new, that is, of a final world epoch.

Yet counterarguments can be quickly made. The dualism of the corporative state, institutionalized to a varying extent in different European countries since the high Middle Ages, exerted a formative influence on constitutions up until the French Revolution and even beyond it. Economic history points to a cycle between 1450 and 1650, one that did not lead to a lasting breakthrough: the marginal increase in productivity remained connected to a corresponding deterioration in general living conditions, rooting the cyclical model in earlier times. According to Marx, there were still no machines that could have made a breakthrough possible to increase productivity.

But even if one leaves aside those findings from structural history that erase a threshold at the year 1500, similar difficulties still surface on the plane of the history of events. Here, too, caesuras can be moved backwards or forwards, depending on the weight accorded to the thrust of events. The Peasant War was an ambivalent revolution, whose backward-facing side becomes all the more striking when it is confronted with "modern," early capitalistic constraints, to which the peasants' revolt, among other things, had also reacted. In any case, the revolution failed, despite having positive long-term consequences for the position of peasants in the Holy Roman Empire.

As the first successful revolution on the way toward a constitution safeguarded by commercial capitalism, one might point to the Dutch independence movement. But then the question arises as to what guiding role commercial and financial capitalism played in the northern Italian city-states, whose heyday was certainly to be found before 1500.

Finally, the English Revolution may be interpreted as the first successful breakthrough, as Zukov for instance interpreted it, when he dated the beginning of modernity (*Neuzeit*) as 1640. But if the weight is instead shifted to the Industrial Revolution, the prolonged beginning of modernity (*Moderne*) accordingly shifts into the eighteenth and nineteenth centuries.

One result of this sketch (which probably looks more like a caricature) becomes clear: depending on the way in which questions are asked, various types of events carrying the heading of a "beforehand not yet" can be included and excluded in order to distinguish modernity from the so-called Middle Ages. In this, all my examples cited remain Eurocentrically oriented, without claiming to be generalizable on the level of universal history. One may presume that from a twenty-first-century Chinese perspective, many things would look very different.

But considering 1800 as the threshold time also has its pros and cons. The repercussions of the Industrial Revolution only gain an expansive power in the nineteenth century, affecting from then on all the continents, from the developing European countries to the colonies. And social history research done by the *Annales* school has directed new questions at French history and transformed the image of the French Revolution. The simple

sequence model of events, as if feudalism, represented by the two upper estates, was supplanted by the class of the bourgeois and a capitalist system,
has been strongly criticized. Even despite a new social mobility in the course
of the revolution, the continuity and homogeneity of the French ruling
classes can hardly be questioned. The role of lawyers, as well as the role of
the nobility and the bourgeois, was as decisive and leading at the beginning
of the revolution as it proved to be after the revolution. The schema of three
estates was already strongly undermined before 1789; professional forces derived from the government hierarchy continued to structure French society
even after 1815. Similarly, continuities in the distribution of property ownership, despite changes in the groups of proprietors, remained amazingly
constant through the period around 1800. Above all, what changed was the
legal system, more than social conditions. But both are comparatively insignificant when measured against the continuity of the work of the French
administration, which had already rendered the boundaries of the ruling
noble class porous prior to the revolution and had reduced the weight of the
feudal burden as well. And finally, history subsequent to the French Revolution in particular shows that, in comparison with modernizing industrial
capitalism, finance capitalism held out far more strongly in France than it
did, for example, in Germany, where the achievements of the French Revolution were only accepted to a limited extent. When viewed in the light of
long-term structures, then, the French Revolution loses much of the weight
attributed to it by participants and their descendants.

Similarly crucial is the question of whether the Prussian response to
the French Revolution may be regarded in any respect as an epochal break.
Without doubt, economic conditions changed profoundly through the
deregulation of ownership rights and competition as well as through the
abolition of feudalistic compulsory labor. The conditions of both ownership and work were rigorously liberalized, but the social structure changed
only very slightly in the countryside as a result. The class of lords adapted
to capitalist market conditions, but without having to give up their political leadership roles as a consequence. A far-reaching modernization of the
agrarian regime—and that went for both eastern and western Germany—
was only carried out slowly—and then not decisively—until after 1945. In
the nineteenth century, the increase in productivity was made possible
through a combination of chemical developments and manual labor that
was generally displaced by mechanical means of production only in the

twentieth century. Only since then has agriculture been functionally and significantly integrated into the economic system of capitalism or—in the GDR—socialism, as well as brought up to the standards of a modern industrial society in terms of the internal structures of business operations and working conditions. Depending on whether one places the emphasis on the legal liberalization of economic conditions or on the employment of new production techniques, one can ask: Since when may the social conditions in the countryside be characterized as modern?

Thus the same goes for the threshold time of 1800 as for the threshold time of 1500: Depending on the way questions are asked, a very different organization of time—in terms of specific strata, regions, nations, continents, or the world as a whole—can be found for defining an epochal boundary that marks the commencement of something like "modernity" (*Neuzeit*). Examples, of course, can be endlessly multiplied according to what grid of questions is used to establish which historical findings.

Despite the diachronic distortions we have described so far, no one would doubt that there are always also synchronic units to be found that bind together all differences from generation to generation, marking coherences that confer a distinctive profile, regardless of all differences, to a particular period of time. It is easy to infer a particular *Zeitgeist* whose specificity and whose change can be registered throughout all strata and all regions almost from year to year (certainly from decade to decade) by examining speech patterns, dress and fashion, modes of building construction and memorials, ways of thinking and expressions of ideas, and, finally, types of political and social conflicts and their resolutions.

But even if one constructs such synchronic units, which appear to connect culture and politics, economics and religion, a renewed difficulty turns up: such synchronized epochal units can hardly be universalized for grounding general epochal divisions in the history of humanity. The nonsimultaneity of the simultaneous (*Ungleichzeitigkeit des Gleichzeitigen*) immediately imposes itself. One could think, for instance, of the enormous precedent of scientific, economic, and technical developments which, coming from England, spread to the United States and to many, but not all, European countries and finally to Japan. Measured against such precursors or trailblazers, all the remaining countries and peoples fall into their wake and have to catch up. They appear to be lagging behind, as developing countries (something that may be completely unjustified culturally).

Thus every epochal division that reckons with scientific and technological forces of production leads to decelerations and accelerations, to overlappings and temporal shifts specific to individual countries. This is what makes every general statement on the structuring of epochs enormously difficult to make. What is new about a particular time cannot obviously be stated universally. The natural chronology derived from the solar cycle places a wealth of data at our disposal that can be interpreted as turning points or key dates, depending on a change in perspective. And even if one inquires into long-term structural transformations, there are still variable stretches of time from area to area and from country to country that cannot be universally reduced to a common denominator.

My thesis, then, is this: with respect to the state of present-day research, the problematic outlined above became clear for the first time in the eighteenth century. The beginning of modernity (*Neuzeit*), with all the difficulties that arise out of this concept, was manifested for the first time in the Enlightenment, which had identified itself as the standard-bearer of a new time (*neue Zeit*). Behind the following historical interpretation thus stands our own present-day systematic way of formulating the questions—because the problems arising out of the concept of *Neuzeit* have become evident.

II

The concept of modernity, or of new history or new time, arose unexpectedly out of the formation of the concept of a "Middle Ages." If, dealing in terms of individuals, one declares Petrarch to be the founder of the concept of the Middle Ages in a limited humanistic context, it still took around three centuries before the new time (*die neue Zeit*), as the connecting concept to the Middle Ages, began to gain acceptance as a general historical concept. The new concept gained acceptance in scholarly circles only very slowly and first spread out among specific social strata after around 1700, just as slowly. The following will be my thesis: the concept of modernity (*Neuzeit*) and the experience gained with it differ structurally from the concepts of antiquity and the Middle Ages.

Up until the seventeenth century, time was still reckoned in terms of large, theologically pregiven periods behind which a number of ancient mythologemes could be discerned: such as Golden, Silver, and Bronze ages, conceived as correlating Paradise and the Fall; or the three theological periods of the age before the law, the age under the law, and the age of grace structuring the course of history; or the four monarchies in Daniel opening up perspectives of universal history. Without doubt, problems of long-term, temporal structures lay hidden in these prescientific doctrines of ages, and Joachim of Fiore had already presented a bold speculation of ages overlapping one another.

Within this long-term, pregiven structure, it became possible to register individual events chronologically, which in turn enabled a precise organization of historical time. The dates of Olympiads, the tenure of Roman consuls, emperors, and popes, the regnal years of rulers, and the rulers' succeeding generations (in France, the official guideline for structuring national history up to the nineteenth century) were all common dating grids used in order to be able to chronologically project forward the succession of events. What is significant for our study is that well into the seventeenth century, it was theoretically and generally assumed that nothing fundamentally new could occur until the end of the world. Within the Christian doctrine of ages, all chronological datings belonged to the last epoch of world history.

Within the horizon of this, so to speak, static experience of the world, there was certainly also the linguistic usage of a new time. In the fourteenth century, for instance, there is mention of histories that extend from the creation of humanity "usque ad moderna tempora" (up to modern times). This usage signifies the time of the writer in question, thought of as necessarily following upon the time preceding it. To be sure, every single day brings something new, but the new is not fundamentally different from what has already happened before it or what has been heralded. Each modern (*moderne*) time or such expression opens up an additive, annalistic, or chronologically structured linear time within whose sequence individual histories (*Historien*) can be registered.

It was Chladenius who, at the end of this experience of time—the middle of the eighteenth century—provided an epistemological justification for treating history as a science. He recognized only three time dimensions and suggested that on the basis of these, history in its entirety is organized from the subjectivity of the respective living historians. First, there are the ancient histories, whose content includes everything that can no longer be determined through the testimony of eyes and ears. Next, there are the cases of new history, which cover everything that living generations experience and do. And, finally, there is the future history in which one looks ahead. As such, as generations pass away and new generations open up a new history for themselves, ancient history grows accordingly.

This epistemologically enduring position is the reflected result of that additive experience of time predominant up into the eighteenth century, and it still cannot be renounced today. What was modern (*Modern*) about Chladenius was that he dispensed with any doctrine of ages with a pre-structured content in order to epistemologically articulate the perspectival position of historians. With this, we already find ourselves in the vicinity of that problematic brought about by modern (*neuzeitlich*) experiences.

In contrast to that particular modernity (*Modernität*) of a purely additive chronology, the formation of the concept new time (*neue Zeit*) or "modernity" (*Neuzeit*)—a word first coined in the nineteenth century—aims, roughly speaking, at something really new, at something that had never been there before. Formulated more precisely, *Neuzeit* seeks to conceptually grasp what previously was not at all *possible*. To this extent, *Neuzeit* ushers in something absolutely new; measured against all prior history, it is unique. It is only this emphatic use of our concept which aims at a shift in experience that we may still associate today with the concept of modernity.

How did the concept gain acceptance? The question cannot be answered without taking a look at the concept it logically presupposes, namely the Middle Ages, and the two connecting concepts of the Renaissance and the Reformation. The latter form the temporal hinges, so to speak, prior to the conceptualization of *Neuzeit* itself. All three concepts—Middle Ages, Renaissance, and Reformation—can be distinguished by the fact that they historically and theoretically exclude both additive chronology and vertical theological gradations of the succession of time in order to develop factual, or as it were, historically immanent criteria. The exclusion of a dark Middle Ages in favor of a Renaissance was first a matter that concerned scholars and humanistically educated writers. The new epochal concept was strictly factual and sectoral. It referred to available sources and literary evidence; it was a concept used by textual exegetes, critics, and editors. Its content was primarily literary and aesthetic without reference to general history, such as to questions of politics or economics. It took several centuries before the concept of Middle Ages rose to the status of a general category of universal history—for the first time in Germany in 1601 and for the first time in France in 1640. It was only in the eighteenth century that the term, primarily still in its pejorative sense, was generally accepted but without, of course, being able to lay claims to an interpretative monopoly for itself.

The history of how the two terms "Renaissance" and "Reformation" gained acceptance ran similarly, connecting somewhat later to the concept of Middle Ages. As it is well known, these terms aimed at a restoration of a past state of affairs in the domains of art and literature, humanistic studies, and religious doctrine and ecclesiastical institutions. Despite their emphasis, the words did not initially contain any claim to designating historical periods. The standard of reference for renewal did not lie in the future but rather in the past, in the Bible and in the works and texts of classical antiquity. The noun "Renaissance" did not even appear until the middle of the sixteenth century, after the rebirth metaphorics denoted by the term had already been used for two centuries. Even in the Enlightenment, the term "Renaissance" still referred primarily to the fields of literature and aesthetics. It was only with Michelet and Jacob Burckhardt that the term became a concept of universal history, signifying a self-contained period inserted, as it were, between the Middle Ages and modernity (*Neuzeit*).

Something similar goes for the concept of Reformation, which at first had a theologically or institutionally limited meaning. It was only in the middle of the seventeenth century that people began to speak of the "saeculum reformationis" as concluded and henceforth a part of the past. Thus, after a little more than two hundred years, a retrospective and general periodizing concept, one which only became completely established with Ranke, emerged from the particular epochal break.

The expression "modern history" (*neue Geschichte*) or "new time" (*neue Zeit*) gained acceptance as a periodizing concept with similar delay. Notwithstanding the point that there always was and will continue to be the additive linguistic usage of present-day histories, the concept of a new time was only slowly established in the second half of the seventeenth century as a general periodizing concept. Leibniz was familiar with the universal-historical triad ancient history/Middle Ages/modern history, and, as a schoolbook author, Cellarius accepted it in 1696, as seen in the numerous editions during the following century. The new historical period was then retrospectively fixed with respect to key dates that were biographically connected with the names of Columbus, Luther, or Charles V.

Two points should be made, the first of which seems to be self-evident and the second of which demands particular attention. First, the periodizing concepts in question are still formed and coined retrospectively. Only after the lapse of certain spans of experience—of about two hundred years —was it possible to retroactively define the above-mentioned temporal units that seemed to exhibit common universal-historical structures. Obviously, a minimal amount of time was required before even the new time (*neue Zeit*) could be understood as an independent period.

Secondly, it is striking that the new way of designating attempts at universal-historical and, at the same time, factual structuration, has gained acceptance and been consolidated in shorter and shorter spans of time. When the concept was coined, the Middle Ages extended over seven hundred to eight hundred years, while in comparison, the Reformation and the Renaissance were not only much more quickly accepted as periodizing concepts, but they also indicated correspondingly shorter temporal units. This shortening of temporal stages may be interpreted as perspectival illusion; however, there is every reason to believe that more and more new experiences had actually accumulated in shorter and shorter amounts of time, so that with such shortened as well as more quickly established determinations of periods, a new experience of time seems also to have announced itself. This new experience of time already belongs to the signature of what comes under our concept of modernity (*Neuzeit*).

The same finding results from the criteria that structure history from the standpoint of the economic system. It was only in the eighteenth century that the concept of feudalism was retrospectively coined. It embraced the previous thousand years and, as a concept of universal history, coincided to a large degree with the concept of the dark Middle Ages. Under the new perspective that criticized existing constitutional arrangements, the feudal Middle Ages extended even up to the then contemporaneous system of estates.

The concept of capitalism, following upon and corresponding to the concept of feudalism, was only coined in the second half of the nineteenth century so that the new experiences that had amassed since the Industrial Revolution could be much more quickly conceptualized than the comparatively contourless, long-lasting stretch of so-called feudalism. Here, a similar rhythm of the shortening of time can be found again in the determination of periods, as we have observed with the employment of the other concepts in the span from the sixteenth through the eighteenth centuries.

Finally, we also find an analogous temporal perspective in contemporary linguistic usage directed at three newly defined epochs of universal history: the long warming-up time to the Neolithic period; developing out of it, the "advanced civilizations" whose structural duration is conceived of as repeatable and comparable until the Industrial Revolution; and since the eighteenth century, the thenceforth constantly accelerating shift in experience.

With each of these retrospective formations of periods sustained by shorter and shorter time spans the closer they come to the present, we have already found a general criterion to distinguish so-called modernity (*Neuzeit*): *acceleration*. In concluding, let me mention several other criteria, whose common ground was first discovered in the eighteenth century.

III

Since the second half of the eighteenth century, circumstantial evidence pointing toward the concept of a new time in the strong sense has accrued. Time does not just remain the form in which all histories take place, but time itself gains a historical quality. Consequently, history no longer takes place in time, but rather through time. Time is metaphorically dynamicized into a force of history itself.

Besides acceleration, the second criterion to be mentioned is the development of an *open future*. The emphatic use of the expression "new time" was not only sustained by previous inventions, innovations, and discoveries that, on looking back, would have conferred an entirely new shape to the world, but this concept was likewise directed at the future in which new things would continue to come about. We need only refer to the two accompanying concepts of progress and development, both conceived for the first time as categories of universal history at the end of the eighteenth century. Both concepts (*Begriffe*) also contain anticipations (*Vorgriffe*) of a changeable future. Moreover, within historiography, it is significant that since the last third of the eighteenth century, the term "newest time" (*neueste Zeit*) begins to distinguish itself from new time: With the French revolutionary calendar, then, the attempt to let a new era of time already begin with that caesura was officially sanctioned and celebrated as a revolution. The "newest time" is thus not only one's own time, but it is more: the beginning of a new epoch.

A third criterion is to be found in the linguistic use of the term *sae-cula*, or *Jahrhunderte* (centuries), as it became possible to call them in German from the seventeenth century onward. These terms gain a historical meaning of their own. At first, the *saecula* were just chronological-additive classificatory aids (for instance, until Flacius Illyricus), used to diachronically arrange multifarious and simultaneous domains. But from the seventeenth century on, they gain an increasing claim of their own. Centuries are thought of as cohering units loaded with meaning. Here we see an epochal organization that not only retrospectively structures history but that also allows such structuring to take place as new during one's own century. The century of Enlightenment is already reflected as such by its contemporaries, and with an awareness, as for instance by Voltaire, that it is qualitatively different from all preceding centuries. Since then, the character of the ancients as model, having rested on the structural similarity of all possible past and future histories, has been bid farewell. The singularity, that is to say, the absolute newness of events, gradually fills out the space of experience. Here, we can see the theoretical common ground between historicism and the faith in progress, both still regarded in the eighteenth century as allies before they become divisible from one another from the nineteenth century on.

A fourth criterion is to be found in the theorem, replete with experience, of the *nonsimultaneity* of diverse but, in a chronological sense, *simultaneous histories*. With the opening up of the world, the most different but coexisting cultural levels were brought into view spatially and, by way of synchronic comparison, were diachronically classified. World history became for the first time empirically redeemable; however, it was only interpretable to the extent that the most differentiated levels of development, decelerations and accelerations of temporal courses in various countries, social strata, classes, or areas were at the same time necessarily reduced to a common denominator. The French Encyclopédie project lives tacitly off a theory of pluralistic historical times that indicate varying levels of the development of humanity according to geographical location and social class. As such, the question still remained open as to whether one should expect an improvement toward perfection in the future or, perhaps, a setback with coming catastrophes.

Fifth, in connection with the experience of multifarious temporal rhythms, the doctrine of subjective position, of *historical perspective* gained cogency. Chladenius was a pathbreaker in this respect as well. Along with and since Chladenius, the Enlightenment thinkers gained the confidence to see the positionality of historical statements not as an objection to but rather as the only possible prerequisite of their discipline. Since then, all historical representations have become contingent upon the conscious selection that authors make and have to make because they are always moving within pre-given social, religious, and political bounds. Since then, it has become acceptable that different representations of the same events could be equally true. But even more than this, the notion of perspective gained a temporal dimension. For Gatterer was convinced that the truth of history did not remain the same once and for all. An experience-founding quality that teaches a retrospective recognition of the past as new was extended to the course of historical time. Since then, the reception history of past events has belonged to the stock of events themselves. For many things are only recognizable ex post facto, after they have exerted the requisite influence, which can only be perceived in its "true" significance by posterity.

History becomes temporalized in the sense that, by virtue of the passing of time, it changes at each given present, and with growing distance, it also changes in the past, or better said: history unveils itself in the truth of its day. As Goethe summarized this temporal shift in experience at the end of the century, "Surely there is no doubt remaining in our day that world history has to be rewritten from time to time."[1]

Once new experiences, supposedly never had by anyone up until then, were registered in one's own history, it was also possible to conceive of the past in its fundamental otherness. In Humboldt's words: "In the history of all times, the eighteenth century occupies the most favorable position for investigating and appreciating its own character."[2] The specificity and difference between antiquity and the Middle Ages, then, could only now be recognized by its effects because it became possible to distinguish one's own period from previous ones through conscious reflection on this distant past. It was only now that the discipline of history (*Geschichtswissenschaft*) outgrew the mere employment of its methods that it had already been developing and improving for centuries. And it was only now that the discipline of history developed a theory of its own—under the new concept of the philosophy of history.

As the sixth and last criterion, the experience of *transition* can be mentioned. It marks the new epochal consciousness developed toward the end of the eighteenth century in which one's own time was not only experienced simultaneously as an end and a beginning but also as a period of transition. There are two specifically temporal determinations, already mentioned in another context, that characterize this new experience of transition: first, the expected otherness of the future; and, second, connected with it, the experience, at once disturbing and widely gaining acceptance, of acceleration by means of which one's own time is distinguished from the preceding time. Humboldt explicitly emphasized this in his analysis of the eighteenth century (shortly after the end of the Jacobin rule): "Our age appears to carry us out of one period, which is just passing by, and into a new, quite different one." The criterion for this change is to be found in a historical time that seems to generate ever shorter and shorter intervals between events and experiences. For "whoever even superficially compares the present state of affairs with that of fifteen or twenty years ago cannot deny that a greater dissimilarity prevails today than in a period twice as long at the beginning of this century."[3]

To summarize, the concept of modernity (*Neuzeit*) can be characterized by the fact that it is not only intended to be a formal concept following upon earlier periodizing determinations. It contains criteria that are hypothetically also applicable to the earlier histories of previous ages. Conceptualized in the eighteenth century, they have, however, given rise to all those questions for which it is first a task of *Neuzeit* to provide answers: the dynamization and temporalization of the experiential world; the task of trying to plan for the open future without being able to foresee the paths of history; the simultaneity of the nonsimultaneous, which pluralistically differentiates events in our world; arising out of it, the perspectival diversity within which historical knowledge must be gained and evaluated; furthermore, the knowledge that one is living in a period of transition in which it becomes harder and harder to reconcile established traditions with necessary innovations; and, finally, the feeling of acceleration by which processes of economic or political change appear to be taking place.

All of these criteria were individually developed and thought through in the time span between the sixteenth and eighteenth centuries. But it was only in the eighteenth century, with its awareness of historical theory, that they were coordinated with one another in various ways. It is a question of the conscious achievement and processing of experiences by a small group of literary figures, authors, critics, and *philosophes*, who gave the names "Enlightenment" and "Critique" to their century. Without doubt, we are dealing with ideas in the realm of historical theory that were developed in the space preceding the technological and industrial transformations. Only the shock of the French Revolution led to the fact that possibilities of experience, at first formulated in an anticipatory way, could be condensed into a new content of experience. For this reason, it is not possible to immediately apply the relation between base and superstructure, for instance, to the new stock of knowledge and experience described and to its socio-economic conditions. Nonetheless, it may be said with certainty that since the eighteenth century, the criteria for a new time (*eine neue Zeit*) that were mentioned above have characterized ever more strongly the everyday life of all humans inhabiting our world today.

What can be deduced from this for our academic linguistic use? The concept of *Neuzeit* contains a multitude of temporal indicators. For one, *Neuzeit* can be retrospectively understood as a period. At the same time, however, it refers to political thrusts of events understood in shortened intervals as far-reaching, new, and epochal. Finally, in the longer term, *Neuzeit* proves to be a period of transition. We may reflect and work on its tempo and duration, its economic, political, social, and cultural conditions, but its end continues to remain open. As such, our concept contains chronologically selective, structural and processual moments that it binds together in an unsorted, catalogue-like way. At the same time, the concept is formal enough to allow for the most varied interpretations and possibilities for application. Precisely because of its formality, it may be well suited to serve the theoretical mediation of different points of view.

Translated by Todd Presner

On the Anthropological and Semantic Structure
of *Bildung*

Bildung is neither formal education (*Ausbildung*) nor imagination (*Einbildung*). The present-day use of the concept draws clear boundaries here. *Bildung* can neither be reduced to its institutional presuppositions—the mere result of formal education; nor can *Bildung* be dissolved into the terms of a psychological or ideological critique—the mere imagination of those who take themselves for educated (*Gebildeten*). The linguistic usage of the concept of *Bildung* betrays a peculiar resistance. Anyone who functionalizes *Bildung* as formal education or exposes it as imaginary qualifies as educated (*gebildet*) within this critical perspective itself. A productive tension, stabilized over and over again through self-critical use, obviously inheres within the concept *Bildung*. Otherwise, its continuous usage for over two hundred years and its constant reestablishment in spite of numerous frictions could not be explained.

This finding represented a challenge for the Research Group for Modern Social History when it turned to the phenomenon of the educated bourgeoisie (*Bildungsbürgertum*). Among social historians, a general, although vague, consensus exists that modern *Bildung* gained acceptance together with the formation that can be characterized as the "bourgeoisie" (*Bürgertum*). "From where did the most beautiful *Bildung* come / if not from the middle class (*Bürger*)?"—Goethe's rhetorical question[1] was also, in a traditionally educated fashion (*gutbildungsbürgerlich*), the question posed by the research group. Only the answer is no longer as clear as it was two hundred years ago. Methodologically aware, the research group undertook this challenge and documented its conclusions in a four-volume series on *Bildungsbürgertum*.[2]

Within the compound concept of *Bildungsbürgertum*, all of the methodological difficulties that call for clarification are already contained for marking out the field of investigation. It was out of the question to explain the *Bildungsbürgertum* only by way of its *Bildung*, as it was vice versa, only to trace *Bildung* back to the bourgeois way of life (*Bürgerlichkeit*): Both efforts would have led to circular arguments or tautological statements. It is already empirically evident that *Bildung* is not limited to the bourgeois social strata (*bürgerliche Schichten*). The nobility and the nonbourgeois strata were or are also bearers of *Bildung* and have participated in it in various ways. On the other side, any definition of the bourgeoisie also remains extremely complex. In social, political, or economic respects, various classifications can intersect which range from the bourgeois nation-state, through features specific to classes and estates, to community life and informal sociability. As such, *Bildung* can in no way act as a dominant feature; at the most, it functions as one feature among others. To specifically clarify what the *Bildungsbürgertum* was, how it arose, and to what extent it still exists, thus requires the analytic separation of the compound concept. The precarious amalgamation of two heterogeneous features—the coinage of "*Bildungsbürgertum*" only arose retrospectively, at the latest in the 1920s[3]—must thus be loosened so as to theoretically justify and historically (*historisch*) explain their respective relationship. As historical (*geschichtliche*) phenomena, *Bildung* and *Bürgertum* are not congruent.

The task before us in the second volume is to investigate the concept of *Bildung* itself. The kind of questions posed are organized both temporally and by subject matter. Diachronically, we want to ask how the concept of *Bildung* came about, how the concept was employed, and how the concept provoked specific forms of self-critique. In terms of subject matter, we want to ask how the concept of *Bildung* was articulated in philosophy, in theology and religion, in Judaism, in history, in the natural sciences, in literature, the arts, music, and last but not least, in pedagogy. Without any claim to completeness, definite fields of experience have thus to be explored in an exemplary fashion, fields whose contents have been understood as cultural knowledge (*Bildungswissen*) and cultural heritage (*Bildungsgüter*). Beyond all these diverse approaches, formal common grounds emerge that distinguish the concept of *Bildung* as a guiding concept of our modern age (*Neuzeit*). With respect to the sociohistorical questions posed by the research group, we tried to elucidate the connectability of the concept *Bildung* in order to be able to trace an institutional, political, or social relation to the bourgeoisie (*Bürgertum*).

In the first volume, those processes that had institutionalized *Bildung* as formal education (*Ausbildung*) were investigated and compared internationally. That volume dealt with the process of professionalization that regulated the career paths of the traditional academic faculties and those of the new natural sciences. By way of the state-secured, autonomous control of the examination process through experts, by way of the self-governing bodies of the universities and associations, the proprietors of educational monopolies (*Bildungspatente*) created career paths and career organizations through which *Bildung* was converted into formal education to such an extent that class-specific privileges or those of new corporate groups could be derived from it. Whatever has become of the bourgeoisie of the nineteenth century, in view of the organization of civil society (*bürgerliche Gesellschaft*) as a whole, the career-specific functions of "privileges" have remained in effect. Examinations and career chances are not only regulated by the free market; they demarcate individual functional elites from other functional agents of society.

The third volume will thematize the internal forms of socialization by virtue of which the bourgeoisie (*Bürgertum*)—in marriage, in the family, in social life, and in clubs—secured a specific identity for itself that cannot be understood without a minimal shared reference to *Bildung*.

The last volume will investigate the political tasks and the social functions of that bourgeoisie able to implicitly and explicitly call upon its *Bildung*—in contrast, for instance, to the economic bourgeoisie (*Wirtschaftsbürgertum*) or the so-called petty bourgeoisie (*Kleinbürgertum*), both of whom might have shared in cultural knowledge and the cultural heritage but did not define themselves in terms of their cultural knowledge.

To begin with, *Bildung*—like Enlightenment or religion—is not primarily a social concept. Those who frequently use the word *Bildung* may be described as a social group, but a person who is cultured (*ein Gebildeter*) will scarcely define himself or herself in such a way. An entrepreneur or cobbler, a member of the liberal professions, a priest, worker, or state-employed civil servant can accept these socially and economically enclosed designations—they say nothing about the person's *Bildung*. Yet *Bildung* only gains its historical profile when it is seen in terms of its social or political functions. Without its functional context in society, *Bildung* could neither be acquired nor preserved. From this, however, it does not follow that *Bildung* is reducible to concrete interest groups and units of action. *Bildung* forms; it is itself a genuine historical factor. Like Enlightenment or religion, *Bildung* is more than just an epiphenomenon of social forces. To be sure, *Bildung* can also be defined as "property" (*Besitz*), but property cannot be defined as *Bildung*.

Bildung is a peculiar, self-inducing pattern of behavior and form of knowledge that remains reliant on economic presuppositions and political conditions in order to flourish; but this does not mean that *Bildung* can be causally and sufficiently derived from these conditions. If causal determinations are brought into play, it could then be maintained with the same plausibility that *Bildung*, certainly in nineteenth-century Germany, had a great influence on economic and political history. The analytical separation of *Bildung* and *Bürger* thus serves to prevent simplistic explanations and causal arguments by making possible functional relationships among heterogeneous factors.

I. Preliminary Conceptual-Historical Clarification

Bildung is a specifically German coinage for which it is extraordinarily difficult to find equivalents in other languages. For this reason, literal renderings or awkward descriptions are necessary in neighboring languages in order to clarify what *Bildung* is. If *Bildung* is translated as "education" in English or French, the aspect of formal education (*Ausbildung*) which is precisely excluded by the concept of *Bildung*, in the sense of self-formation (*Selbstbildung*), is given too much weight. "Self-education" remains a concocted word and approaches the sense of autodidacticism. "Self-formation," a word coined by Shaftesbury which strongly influenced the German concept of *Bildung* in the eighteenth century, perhaps comes closest to our meaning. In his autobiographical novel, Disraeli also spoke of his "individual experience of self-formation",[4] translating back, as it were, Goethe's concept of *Bildung*. By contrast, Bruford's translation "self-cultivation"[5] sounds like sublime irony. If *Bildung* is translated in English or French as "civilization," certainly the aspect of agency is well expressed: namely, that

Bildung does not refer to a condition but to an active behavior and marks out fields of social activity. But contained within the Western conceptual field of "civilization" is an old European meaning stemming from the *civitas civilis*, from civil society (*bürgerliche Gesellschaft*), to which a new political edge has been added since the eighteenth century. This sense of "civilization" only intermittently belongs to the German concept of *Bildung*, and it certainly does not constitute its central axis of meaning. Richard Wagner could even employ *Bildung* and *Zivilisation* (civilization)—after Königgrätz, directed against Paris—as opposing concepts.[6] On the other hand, if *Bildung* is translated in the languages of our neighbors as "culture," the fields of meaning indeed overlap; however, as in German, culture refers to the sum of common activities and their productions, first physical then intellectual, in contradistinction to the concept of nature. When translated as "culture," the specific differentiating criterion in German linguistic usage—the fact that *Bildung* is attributable to natural aptitudes, but above all that it represents an individual achievement only attainable through self-reflection—is lost.

It is characteristic of the German concept of *Bildung* that it recasts the sense of an upbringing offered from the outside (which still belongs to the concept during the eighteenth century) into the autonomous claim for a person to transform the world: in this respect, *Bildung* is fundamentally different from "education." Secondly, it is characteristic of the German concept of *Bildung* that it no longer refers the social circle of communication back to the politically conceived *societas civilis*, but rather, and above all, back to a society which understands itself primarily in terms of its manifold self-formation (*Eigenbildung*): in this respect, the concept of *Bildung* is different from "civility" or "civilization." Finally, it is characteristic of the German concept of *Bildung* that it relates common cultural achievements, to which it also naturally refers, back to a personal, internal reflection, without which a social culture might not be possible.

These general distinctions, which can differentiate German linguistic usage from Western linguistic usage since around 1800, testify through today to a provocative fact. The conversion of the originally Europe-wide Latin languages of the later so-called intellectual (*gebildet*) world takes place in entirely different rhythms according to country. In the Romance languages, the basic Latin concepts remain preserved, even though they were adopted into vernacular languages. Because of early Norman influence, England shares in this continuous process in the same way. That goes for all the equivalents mentioned above: *culture, civilization, education,* but also for *formation* or *instruction,* concepts from which the German idea of *Bildung* clearly demarcated itself in the nineteenth century. Whereas this conversion took place smoothly in the national languages grounded in Latin, *Kultur,* just like *Zivilisation,* first had to be Germanized (by Leibniz and Pufendorf) in order to be able to be used as a central concept. In the West, "civility" and "civilization" almost always referred to the *civis,* to the political citizen (*Bürger*) of a *civitas,* whereas in German, "*Bildung*" did not refer back to the German *Bürger* in the same way. To manufacture such a relationship is all the more artificial because in German *Bürger* first of all meant a member of a privileged estate, a *Stadtbürger,* who had little to do with *Bildung* and absolutely nothing to do with the French *citoyen.* From the Enlightenment on, "civilization" had the undertone of *Verbürgerlichung* ("making or becoming bourgeois") in the West—so that here, the concept of an educated bourgeoisie (*Bildungsbürgertum*) was not at all necessary or possible.

The differentiation of the common European Latin language into reflexively conscious national languages capable of theoretical thought thus took place along completely different paths. Whereas in the West it was a question of easily recoining what was pregiven in the linguistic stocks beholden to Latin, in Germany it was a question of importing foreign words or conceptually jazzing up genuinely German words in order to make them capable of theoretical and reflexive conceptualizations. *Bildung* is one of those specifically German concepts whose content and scope of meaning is not matched by Western concepts, as little as the other fundamental German concept *Geschichte* was congruent around 1800 with the Western concepts of *histoire* or "history." *Bildung* and *Geschichte* are two mutually illuminating fundamental concepts of the German language which, in the last third of the eighteenth century, had become so alienated from the shared European language context that they could be considered to be a genuine contribution to the linguistic process of coming to terms with experience in revolutionary Europe. Both concepts concern a collective singular in which reflection, as the condition of possible actions, was embraced by the same concept as the ways of acting themselves. *Geschichte* is the performance space of real actions as well as their historical (*historisch*) reflection. *Bildung* is not a pregiven form waiting to be fulfilled but rather a processual state that constantly and actively changes through reflexivity. *Bildung* is both the process of producing as well as the result of having been produced.[7]

As concepts impregnated with a transcendental and philosophical dimension, or better put, as concepts that set in motion a transcendental-philosophical reflection, *Bildung* and *Geschichte*—just like *Geist*—have acquired a particular status. Both have increasingly explained and reinforced one another over the course of the nineteenth century. Since Herder, *Geschichte* without *Bildung*, *Bildung* without *Geschichte*, is incomprehensible. *Bildung* can only substantiate itself—actively and reflexively at the same time—in the medium of diachronic change; *Bildung* is historical. And history, as the diachronic space of action, only takes place in the medium of reflexively self-determining, always newly forming (*sich bildend*), conscious units of action. In terms of their linguistic self-expression, both concepts are not specifically bourgeois (*bürgerlich*)—in the sense of the German bourgeoisie, to the extent that it articulated itself politically or socially. In the German language, neither *Bildung* nor *Geschichte* attain—as little as *Geist*—the degree of social and political tangibility of "civilization," or the direct character of appeal to articulate and carry out specifically middle-class demands of *révolution* or *république* in French.

A historical survey of the history of the German concept of *Bildung* substantiates this finding.[8] The German concept of *Bildung* is precisely distinguished by the fact that it was not conceived specifically in terms of the bourgeoisie (*bürgerlich*) or politics but primarily in terms of theology. One may interpret this finding by means of a critique of ideology. It speaks first of all for itself. The German word *bilden* contains an active meaning, namely of creating and forming, which is discernible in "molding" (*Bildnerei*), for example that of a potter; this meaning also became applicable to spiritual creation. However, since the fourteenth century, the term also refers, in theological context, to a more passive, certainly reception-oriented meaning that comes from creation theology. "God created human beings in his image (*Bilde*)."[9] From this followed the possibility of *imitatio Christi* or the *imago Dei* doctrine, or the requirement of Neoplatonism that the copy (*Abbild*) approach the original (*Urbild*). The language of mysticism evoked a wealth of locutions, still primarily verbal ones: *Entbilden* (to deform), *einbilden* (to imagine), and *überbilden* (to transfigure) are steps in the dissolution from earthly reality in order to fuse together God and the soul. *Bildung* turns into *deificatio*.[10] Transformation and rebirth are the enduring meanings that belonged to the religious concept of *Bildung*. With Luther, *verbilden* (to transform) and *verklären* (to apotheosize) become contaminated.[11] In the language of mysticism, the field of usage of *bilden* gains a power and intensity that in the Latin equivalents presumably waned. To imagine (*einbilden*) God in oneself, to reform (*umbilden*) oneself through Christ in order to share in God while a human being, even more, to transform God into a living human being—such semantic discharges have nothing to do with the bourgeoisie (*Bürger*) of either the Middle Ages or modern times (*Neuzeit*). According to Scheler, this *Bildung* is part of the knowledge of redemption and the sharing in God's grace. As Gottfried Arnold interpreted the receiving sense: "Grace thus forms humans" ("Also bildet . . . die Gnade den Menschen").[12]

And if Herder, someone who helped the humanistic concept of *Bildung* achieve its breakthrough in its historico-philosophical and cosmological dimension, could still write, "Every man has an image (*ein Bild*) of himself, of what he shall be and become; as long as he is not yet that, in his bones he is still unsatisfied",[13] then the religious definition clearly and audibly rings through. Even the young Humboldt, who resolutely liberated himself from every foreign, authoritarian definition of religion in order to advocate spiritual and moral self-determination, did not escape a Christian-Neoplatonic stereotype: "For all *Bildung* has its origin in the interior of the soul alone, and can only be induced by outer events, never produced." The moral man forms himself (*bildet sich*) "in the image (*im Bilde*) of divinity through the intuition of the highest idealistic perfection."[14]

Research has traced the history of the concept of *Bildung* and, in so doing, demonstrated both the ways in which the word was employed in baroque mysticism and the theosophical, Neoplatonic, or pietistic influences on the word's usage. In his essay, Timm establishes the theological connection between past conceptual history and present-day linguistic usage.[15] In sum, it may be said that the theological underpinning still comes into view, sometimes to a greater and sometimes to a lesser extent, through the semantics of the modern concept of *Bildung*.

Roughly sketched, the conceptual history of *Bildung* can be structured in three stages: one which is theologically dominated, one which is enlightened and pedagogic, and one which is modern and primarily defined self-reflexively. But such a way of seeing things fails to recognize that the first, theological stage is also contained in the second, enlightened stage and that both of the foregoing phases also contributed to the modern concept of *Bildung*. There is a semantically long-term, diachronic thrust of the history of the concept that enters into each of the unique ways of speaking.

The language of the Enlightenment also remained theologically impregnated in Germany, something which helps to explain the radicalism of the late German Enlightenment, as embodied by the young Hegelians. Thereafter, the hope of redemption and the educational mission (*Erziehungsanspruch*) converge in *Bildung*. In the eighteenth century, that variant of meaning emerges, bringing *Bildung* and Enlightenment close to one another. The educational mission of those who consider themselves enlightened set the concept of *Bildung* on a pedagogic track. Thus, for Wieland, *Bildung* was identical with instruction, formal education, developing, and unfolding. Or as Moses Mendelssohn put it: "I consider the *Bildung* of humans to include the endeavor to arrange both convictions and actions such that they are in consonance with happiness; to rear and govern human beings."[16] *Bildung* is understood actively as a forming that is supposed to direct humans toward pregiven goals. Whether natural capabilities unfold, or whether social or political tasks are supposed to be fulfilled through an upbringing specific to a particular social group, it is this meaning of "formal education" (*Ausbildung*) which is still retrievable today. Even Humboldt, certainly the most influential representative of a self-actuated individual *Bildung* (*Eigenbildung*) prior to all social bonds, inevitably made use of the enlightened-pedagogic variant. In 1809, when he petitioned to have a university established in Berlin, he appealed to its future task of ensuring "national upbringing and *Bildung*." "Everyone in Germany who is interested in *Bildung* and Enlightenment" was to find a sanctuary here.[17]

As Max Scheler said, besides knowledge necessary to salvation, practical knowledge also thus inheres within the concept of *Bildung*.[18] And out of both, a proper claim to knowledge about ruling follows, for knowledge was power; the university education (*Universitätsbildung*) opened the door beyond the traditional order of estates for seeking and gaining political influence. In contrast to Max Scheler's categorical separation, it may thus be said with regard to the German concept of *Bildung* as it developed around 1800 that it joined together, in various amounts, both knowledge necessary to salvation and practical knowledge as well as knowledge about ruling. Nevertheless, the concept cannot be reduced to these three determinants.

What, then, are the specific meanings that could be called upon or evoked over and over again since the turn to our modern age?

II. Ideal-typical Outline of *Bildung*

Bildung, a fundamental modern concept, is the result of the Enlightenment and, at the same time, an answer to it. The Enlightenment was chiefly understood in historical-philosophical terms, as a period able to be diachronically organized but whose agenda raised a supratemporal, systematic claim. Enlightenment implies more than its epochal definition; it is lasting and repeatable. For this reason, Enlightenment can be recognized in the Greek Sophists as much as it could become the emancipatory banner of the student movement. It is, so to speak, an anthropologically derivable mission of self-determination, undertaken in accordance with reason and with ethically, socially, or politically redeemable norms.

Analogously, *Bildung* can be described as a historically given challenge that constantly provokes new answers and, therefore, can both be found again in the past, for instance that of the Greeks, as well as repeated in the future. Even though the eighteenth century was named an age of Enlightenment, and even though the nineteenth century can be named a century of *Bildung*, both concepts are more than just historical designations.

When "Enlightenment" was conceptualized, this process of conceptualization occurred by looking back at the time that had already elapsed since its increasing realization in the eighteenth century. The modern concept of *Bildung* emerged at the same time, in the last third of that century, but with a view toward a constantly innovative future. According to the unending flood of didactic, educational, and instructive writings circulated by state, literary, theological, pedagogic, and economic authorities in the name of Enlightenment, there was—as Kant insisted—only one way out: by taking Enlightenment itself in one's hand. The new slogan for so doing was *Bildung*. The path of vulgar Enlightenment, from above down or from outside in, should be, as it were, turned around: from inside out, in order to produce the conditions in which the self might realize its potential in society through self-actualization and precisely through *Bildung*. The concept of *Bildung* was more modern and more open to surprising experiences and new points of view, more "interesting," and, above all, free in terms of its multifaceted range of definition. While the Enlightenment had primarily appealed to reason, by which humans should allow themselves to be guided, and to nature, knowledge of which would provide permanent rules and laws for all spheres of experience, and while both of these tasks simultaneously established social, economic, political, and collectively historical goals, *Bildung* challenged a large multitude of human possibilities. The world was brought under a host of perspectives, and for the formation of personal character (*die Bildung der Persönlichkeit*)—the central assignment—countless pathways stood open for finding oneself. The Kantian demand of self-determination, a morally general obligation, was pluralized, historically reproduced, and individualized, without, however, loosening the tether to the Enlightenment. Kant's demand: "Have the courage to use your own understanding!"[19]—this motto of the Enlightenment was directed at the whole person and his self-formation (*Selbstbildung*). "*Bildung* of the mind without *Bildung* of the heart and of taste results just in Enlightenment."[20] With this, Enlightenment was not bid farewell, as little as upbringing (*Erziehung*) was separated from the means of formal education (*Ausbildung*). Rather, both were integrated into a communicative process which, in religious-sociological terms, the Protestant lay priests championed in order to induce personal self-formation. The aim was the *Bildung* of the whole human being as his own purpose.

1. 'Bildung' as Personal Self-Determination

Regardless of what the cult of the genius achieved as the midwife of the concept of *Bildung*, regardless of what the discovery of personal character contributed to it, the concept of *Bildung* primarily referred to the individual human being. He must form himself (*sich bilden*), irrespective of the circumstances exerting themselves on him. Without working through these circumstances, he cannot form himself. Countless diaries combined all the relationships between interior and exterior into the personal process of *Bildung*. They belong to the signature of the educated (*Gebildeten*).

The self-reflexive concept of *Bildung* was transferred to other units of action: to the people, the nation, the community, the society, children, youth (and other gradations of age), to a class or the state, and finally, to nature and history. All these units of action or subjects capable of *Bildung* turned into derivatives of self-formation (*Selbstbildung*). They live off the primary meaning that all *Bildung* is the self-formation of an individual. At first, *Bild* metaphorics were eluded in normal linguistic usage.

The many conformities that could be sociologically ascribed to an ideal of *Bildung* did not prevent the fundamental definition of all *Bildung* from referring to the individual. When Rotteck considered the state's mission of *Bildung*, he defined its true purpose as follows: "namely the guarantee of personal freedom, thus the free self-formation of all."[21] Moreover, it was self-evident for him that this self-formation of everyone, beyond any class distinctions, referred to the "self-formation of all the citizens."[22] In contrast to the Western catalogues of constitutional rights, this involved a definition that entered into the second article of the Basic Law in a similar form. Even if such a definition can be called into question in sociological or psychological terms, or in terms of critique of ideology—and rightly so, in terms of scientific theory—the concept of *Bildung* raises an indispensable claim that cannot be ignored as an anthropological possibility: that man can only be and become himself through his individuation. As Hegel said: "Man is what he ought to be only through *Bildung*."[23]

The integration of self-unfolding within socioeconomic, political, or spiritual conditions (the only conditions under which it can take place) belonged to the reflexive processing which at the same time socially obliged all *Bildung*. "In contrast to *Bildung* in itself, every actual *Bildung* is, therefore, a social *Bildung*."[24] The often extolled or ridiculed "inwardness" of German *Bildung* is certainly a simplification. Personal self-formation (*personale Selbstbildung*) leads rather to active and guiding behavior patterns that have to include the social presuppositions of their own process of *Bildung*. *Bildung* does not lead to contemplative passivity but instead always necessitates communicative achievements, leading to the *vita activa*. *Bildung* shapes a lifestyle that goes beyond the Enlightenment and that was particularly effectual and influential during the nineteenth century. This leads to a further definition.

2. 'Bildung' as the Conduct of Life

The basic anthropological pattern of *Bildung* aimed at the entire human being. From this, a constantly reflected relationship between reason and sensibility followed. Not that both of these spheres would have been summoned alternatively to a final justification, as in Enlightenment philosophies; rather, body and heart, soul, all the senses, and the mind belonged to the field of tension, always thought anew in psychological terms, within which *Bildung* would take place. Such a demand for self-discovery had to rely upon interhuman relationships from the onset, and not just in the obvious sense that the human being is an *animal social.* Rather, both individually distinctive as well as group-specific sociability belongs constitutively to *Bildung.* "For sociability," writes Friedrich Schlegel in 1799, "is the true element for all *Bildung* that aims at the entire human being."[25]

It is often enough underscored that self-formation (*Selbstbildung*) through sociability had an emancipatory function because it was directed against all authorities, because it constituted itself outside the state, and because it openly positioned itself against differences of social estate and prevailing ecclesiastical precepts. For this reason, *Bildung* was the legitimate place where Jews and women shared in equal rights and, even more so, was where they could take initiative. The Berlin salon culture produced *Bildung* at the same time as it generated the new emancipatory concept of *Bildung.* Thus a model was established that could be invoked again and again under different circumstances and in different times.

Something analogous goes for the new space of experience opened up for love. Sexuality was liberated from its socially and theologically subordinate role and gained a morally integrative power. "Sexual love," a term newly conceptualized at this time, brought spirit and sensuality into a mutual relationship between the sexes in order to allow a common process of *Bildung* to emerge from it.[26] This love, in which husband and wife mutually form each other, bade farewell to the traditional concept of love that had primarily aimed at reproduction and familial self-preservation. The liberation of sensuality from moral-theological dictates and those related to a person's social estate became a ferment of mutual self-formation (*Selbstbildung*) and was discovered as such. "Sensuality used to be, if I may put it this way," wrote Henriette Herz, "infused with a kind of purifying principle which one was afraid of violating, and, to a certain extent, *Lucinde* emerged from the idea of this association."[27] The determination of the difference between love and marriage was reflected with clarity by that generation, especially by women, thereby exposing the unconscious tendency through which an anthropological model was also established here. Psychoanalysis rests upon this newly discovered, individualized sexual love. That all self-discovery could both presuppose and bring about love between the sexes belongs just as much to the labile as to the provocative elements that promoted the process of *Bildung* ever anew, even at the cost of marriage. A marriage without love became—according to Bluntschli—liable to dissolution. With this, an epoch was inaugurated whose social power of transformation was only reached in the twentieth century.

We can add other aspects of the cultivated (*gebildet*) lifestyle whose self-reflection involves the mutual reflection of the participants. These aspects testify to the Pietist heritage. The wealth of autobiographies, often as straightforward as they are masterful, is not only a continuation of diaries but also a continuation of the highly developed art of letter writing: namely, to let descendants, too, share in self-enlightenment, in the self-critical conduct of life, something which would not have been possible without written communication. The intensive exchange of letters between men, between the sexes, and between women had mutual participation as its goal, and without it, lasting autobiographical reflection also could not have taken place. Everyone's life was always real and literary at the same time, precisely mediated by *Bildung*. And autobiographies show how little the self-descriptions remained restricted to the circles of the so-called cultivated (*Gebildeten*) in the narrow sense, such as those which Nettelbeck or Carl Schurz or Werner von Siemens dedicated to their own lives. Trade, economy, science, technology, and politics were linked together in the communicative process of self-formation (*Selbstbildung*).

The same thing can be said of the diverse and overlapping circles of friends that regularly met to cultivate sociability and which were expanded through countless journeys throughout Germany and abroad. *Bildung* was the guiding concept that reflexively tied together this manifold of mutually induced life experience. Even though this lifestyle did not persist uninterrupted in the wake of technologically accelerated conditions of communication, a model of the cultivated (*gebildet*) lifestyle became established that still subtly shapes our modern behavior patterns. Land and air tourism thirsty for nature and eager for culture; shared music, museum, theater, film, and television interests, and even sports, produce circles of communication not specifically bound by profession or class. And all the cultural criticism connected to these behavior patterns today attests to the traditional claim of *Bildung* associated with them.

That life has to be conducted and not just tolerated or suffered thus characterized the style that was shaped—reflexively or communicatively—by *Bildung*. This lifestyle opened countless points of connection from which public functions could be realized in social, political, economic, literary, artistic, or other terms. Despite all individual variations, *Bildung* has common essential features.

3. Common Essential Features of 'Bildung'

No definitive knowledge and no single discipline, no political stance or social pregiven, no denominational affiliation and no religious tie, no ideological option or philosophical preference, not to mention any specific aesthetic inclination in art and literature, is sufficient to characterize *Bildung*. With respect to all concrete exemplifications in its life-world (*Lebenswelt*), *Bildung* is a metaconcept that constantly adapts to the empirical conditions of its own possibility. *Bildung* cannot be sufficiently defined by a particular cultural heritage (*Bildungsgüter*) or cultural knowledge (*Bildungswissen*). If there are nevertheless common, ideal-typical essential features, they are contained in that conduct of life which is always moving on the path of self-discovery.

The following essential features are not purely ideal-typical constructions in Max Weber's sense. Rather, they are based upon semantic self-interpretations by the educated (*Gebildeten*), self-interpretations that implicitly or explicitly continue to persist—but no single definition of *Bildung* could have expressed those meanings. Thus, linguistically, scarcely varied structures become evident which condition all change and delimit all individual contexts. The essential features, attested to semantically, are thus ensconced between ideal-typical and real-typical determinations and are empirically controllable.

(a) The first feature to be mentioned here is *religiosity*, and it was not by chance that this was newly conceptualized around 1800. Despite its increasing connotations of the pedagogy of the Enlightenment, *Bildung* never lost its religious content. Directed against theological orthodoxy and rational Enlightenment, the Pietist cult of personal involvement and individual self-obligation had a lasting effect here. On the other hand, the eighteenth-century historical critique of religion, specifically of Protestant theology, contributed to transforming religion into religiosity, that is, to converting it into a style of educated (*gebildet*) piety. Dogmatic beliefs could be transformed back into myths through historical Enlightenment while Christianity remained preserved "for private use."[28] The Christian message became absorbed into the process of *Bildung* as a religious experience. "At the most, religion is only a supplement or even a surrogate of *Bildung*, and nothing is religious in the strong sense of the word that is not a product of freedom. One can say: the freer, the more religious; and the more *Bildung*, the less religion."[29] The formation of conscience (*Gewissensbildung*) and self-awareness bade farewell to all dogmatism, and ethical praxis opened a diversity of behavior patterns that still remained true to their religiosity. Not only could this religiosity assimilate Christian doctrines, but it could also entertain naturalistic or materialistic worldviews. Above all, the devout consciousness of *Bildung* was adaptable to all knowledge from the natural sciences; however, Christian dogmas became even more debilitated by it, as these dogmas had already been called into question by their historicization. "Whoever possesses science and art; / also has religion; / Whoever does not possess either of these, / gets to have religion."[30] Cultural knowledge (*Bildungswissen*) and aesthetic ability are by their own nature religious; whoever does not share in them sees himself turned back to the traditional, outwardly defined, and still theologically administered religion.

The new religiosity of *Bildung* (*Bildungsreligiosität*) is thus characterized by the fact that it can forgo both church and dogmatism without therefore having to give up a Christian self-interpretation or charitable, that is to say, social reforming, praxis. In this respect, the German religiosity of *Bildung* differentiates itself from the French anticlerical laicism that had developed in a strict opposition to the Catholic church. But through this, the rift separating the invisible church of the educated (*Kirche der Gebildeten*) from the devoutly active members of the Catholic church was simultaneously deepened. How carefully the Catholic church on its part monitored and looked after the rift is revealed by the work of Klöcker and Weber. Surpassing the Protestant self-censorship by far, the clerical taboo sounded like this in the voice of the Catholic people: "Goethe, Schiller, Heine—these are the greatest swine." Even though the modern documents of *Bildung* were not unknown and were read (*Catholica non leguntur*) in the Catholic world of the educated (*Gebildeten*), the ferment of secular piety was missing, as it was cultivated by the apostles of *Bildung*.

Modern piety was secular to the extent that the Christian doctrine of sin which referred to divine grace (in whatever way it was mediated by the church) now gave way to a feeling of inner turmoil, a reflected awareness of self-alienation that was assured of itself as *"Bildung."* Hegel traced and conceptualized this process as the result of prior history. Religion appeared, then, "as the faith of the world of *Bildung*," as "unhappy consciousness."[31]

Theologically, it is the doctrine of the two worlds; philosophically, the Cartesian separation of *res cogitans* from *res extensa*; politically, the conflict between state and economy; morally and intellectually, the tension between individuality and the general public, which, put boldly, drove forward the world of *Bildung* as "the world of the self-alienated spirit." "The spirit of self-alienation has its existence in the world of *Bildung*," and it is the task of precisely this *Bildung* to perceive and alleviate alienation in order to mediate reality and self-awareness. How much "reality and power" an individual gets thus depends on his *Bildung*.[32] What is only presented here from Hegel in a piecemeal fashion nevertheless throws light on that *Bildung* which over and over again sought to dispose of its religious surplus through an act of consciousness—all the way to Du Bois-Reymond's "ignorabimus"[33] or to emphatic agnosticism.

When Humboldt declared against the perfect world of the Greeks, "We have made a double human being out of ourselves through reflection",[34] he coined a short formula that laid out a constant task for mediation. Or, as Friedrich Ast, the humanistic philologist, formulated it while searching for Greek archetypes (*Urbilder*): "The goal of our *Bildung* is this: to return to the paradise humans had to escape to arrive at self-knowledge."[35] Whether attainable or not, *Bildung* is in any case the knowledge of self-alienation and, at the same time, the way to escape it. "The revolutionary wish of realizing the kingdom of God is the elastic point of progressive *Bildung* and the start of modern history."[36]

The adaptable religiosity of *Bildung* contained an activist potential for changing the world. Countless political, social, and ideological (*weltanschaulich*) movements strove to fulfill it, and it was expressed in just as many political party programs. Even if a secular claim of redemption is not directly derivable from the concept of *Bildung*, the concept set free the disposition for it.

Thus worldviews (*Weltanschauungen*)—this concept was also coined around 1800—belong to the secondary features of *Bildung*, to the extent that *Bildung* strove to secure its subjective piety by way of general programs for interpreting the world. "Our intuitions of the world have become great, irrefutably internal concerns."[37] From this, it can be explained—this is the topic of Gründer's essay[38]—why the academic philosophers were not nearly as effective as the great project designs that came from the cloth of educated (*gebildet*) people who found themselves, for the most part, on the margins of the university. Without saying anything about their varying status, one may argue that Schopenhauer and Eduard von Hartmann, David Friedrich Strauss and Feuerbach, Bruno Bauer, Marx, Stirner, and Engels, Richard Wagner and de Lagarde, the "appropriated" Darwin and Haeckel, Nietzsche and Freud, had an effect that stabilized an ideologically (*weltanschaulich*) self-reassuring religious consciousness of *Bildung* as a secular faith. The list of representatives can easily be extended if we also count the many professional natural scientists, as Engelhardt shows.[39] The openness to differently realized worldviews belongs to the signature of the religiously impregnated concept of *Bildung*.

(b) *The Political and Social Openness of Bildung.* Moreover, *Bildung* cannot be politically and socially fixed; it is open and connectable in many directions. As such, *Bildung* has neither the ability nor the requirement to make alliances, as was the case with the churches after the French Revolution in order for them to be able to act politically. *Bildung* is not an institution even though its bearers associate it with many institutions: the family, school, and university; colleges, clubs, parties, alliances, and associations; cultural arrangements of every sort as well as in the Protestant church.

 Bildung is foremost—and this testifies to its religious origin—a political metaconcept. For this reason, any political party could call upon its *Bildung*, from the revolutionary to the conservative romantics, members of student dueling societies as well as the officials who tracked them, liberals from all decades and of all stripes as well as conservatives and leaders of social democracy, even workers themselves with their insatiable thirst for *Bildung*. Treitschke keenly observed that in 1859. The middle class, "in possession of higher education (*höhere Bildung*)" and economically active, would seek to open class boundaries upward and downward. But "with regard to *Bildung* alone, it will be difficult to conceptualize it (the middle class) as a whole." From its "mobility, a specific political conviction of the middle class, for instance of liberalism, in no way follows; on the contrary, what follows is its capacity to splinter into all kinds of different political parties."[40] The so-called educated bourgeoisie (*Bildungsbürger*) occupied seats in every parliamentary faction in 1848; it was their *Bildung*, their common language, which manufactured that minimal consensus extending through the founding of the Reich and beyond. In this way, as Virchow put it most succinctly in 1849, *Bildung* could quickly enter into directly political functions: "Freedom without *Bildung* brings anarchy; *Bildung* without freedom, revolution."[41] Thus, although *Bildung* is primarily suprapolitical, it can be called upon politically, which is why in German the additional modifier "political" *Bildung* is necessary. To this extent, Thomas Mann's strongly felt assertion was correct, albeit a half-truth: " . . . the political element is actually missing in the German concept of *Bildung*."[42] The concept of *Bildung* was politically transferable and, for this reason, could never be restricted to a single party line. And, therefore, the attempt to found a "party of intellectuals (*Gebildeten*)" as a "new party," as Grabowsky tried to do with conservative aims in 1911, was condemned to fail from the start.[43]

The suprasocial concept of *Bildung* appears to be much more difficult to define than the suprapolitical concept. For there are countless instances that point to a self-understanding of the educated (*Gebildeten*) in terms of class as a modern elite or as a traditional aristocracy. Since the French Revolution, the social dichotomy between the educated and the uneducated has been a constant in descriptions of civil society (*bürgerliche Gesellschaft*). The categories of "*Bildung*" or "*Unbildung*" are assigned, not without empirical justification, to estates or classes, strata or occupational groups. The diachronically organized work of Ulrich Engelhardt provides the supporting evidence.[44] Nevertheless, it has to be held that the concept of *Bildung* precludes, by definition, a primarily social description, or even one that is specific to a social class or estate. As self-formation (*Selbstbildung*) and the communicative conduct of life, *Bildung* is socially open and connectable to all strata.

"Only that kind of *Bildung* which strives toward a goal and dares to render itself universal and embrace all human beings without difference is an actual component of life and is certain of itself."[45] Even if Fichte raises here a revolutionary claim that evangelizes for democracy, *Bildung* can in no way be considered other than that which every human being demands and remains open to. Moreover, by contrast to political rule and economic dependence or exploitation, the sphere of *Bildung* directly presupposes and makes possible freedom and equality. So Lorenz von Stein argued,[46] and he proposed that the spread of *Bildung* would benefit everyone. It would be "nothing but" the educating (*bildende*) work of the individual, work which "makes the recipients rich in intellectual goods and yet does not make the givers any poorer, and . . . the fulfillment of the one through the intellectual life of the other does not arouse the deep contradiction which lies in all rule by humans over humans."[47]

Not only can an emancipatory result be derived from the concept of *Bildung* but, from the beginning, so can a legislated claim to reflexive autonomy and self-realization. This claim demands the extension of the concept to all strata of the population, as the Brockhaus encyclopedia definitively demanded in 1820 and as Eichendorff believed could be critically seen in 1847: the rule of outstanding individual minds would now be over. "In its natural heaviness, the *Bildung* invented by those [minds] gradually broadened; from many hidden sources came torrents, washing away all high land and violently opening up new paths, which no amount of human foresight can fix any longer." "*Bildung*-fever" would inaugurate "the age of the masses."[48] Whether Meyer's *Groschenbibliothek für deutsche Classiker* (*Penny Library of German Classics*) was sold under the motto "Bildung macht frei" ("*Bildung* sets you free") from 1826 on, or whether the early socialist Karl Grün spoke in 1844 "about true *Bildung* for the benefit of the poor spinners around Ravensberg";[49] whether Virchow initiated a "society for the dissemination of *Bildung* among the people (*Volksbildung*)," or Wilhelm Liebknecht opened the Educational School for Workers (*Arbeiterbildungsschule*) in Berlin in 1891 with the slogan "Uniformity of *Bildung* is a cultural necessity";[50] or whether Wilhelm Wundt turned with touching hopefulness to the Adult Education Centers (*Volkshochschulen*) after a lost war, writing that "The most significant sign of this reversal is surely the striving for the general dissemination and deepening of intellectual *Bildung* which has galvanized all levels and classes of the population":[51] in each case, *Bildung* remains a concept which—like religion—refuses to be restricted to social definitions; instead, it always demands their transgression. That still applies today when, for instance, Dahrendorf affirmatively takes up Jacob Burckhardt's skeptical remark that the newest thing in the world might be "the desire for *Bildung* as a human right."[52]

This evidence can be interpreted in a social-historical manner, and a corresponding number of quotations can be supplied which substantiate the defense mechanisms of the so-called educated middle class (*gebildete Bürger*) against all democratic or socialist claims of *Bildung*. Formally, *Bildung* is universal but in terms of content, it is an elite manifestation. In its concrete social context, *Bildung* remains communicable only for those who share in the presupposed cultural knowledge (*Bildungswissen*) and who evidently possess the ability to judge cultural heritage (*Bildungsgüter*). Whoever does not, may be granted moral integrity, having a *Bildung* of the heart or soul, without therefore being brought into the circle of the cultivated (*Gebildeten*). But such empirically effectual dividing lines could not generate the universal concept of *Bildung*. For this reason, Diesterweg appealed to such a concept when he wanted to see "the necessity of the *Bildung* of the German middle class" recognized in the same way as "old-fashioned *Bildung*." Especially in the Latin language, he saw—from a democratic perspective—a "general means of *Bildung*" for those who "wanted to rise above the lower strata of society."[53] *Bildung* would not rule out different and new means of *Bildung*. It was quite the opposite, but what Diesterweg demands is the awakening of "autonomy" by a teacher, "united with the religion of progress in every respect."[54] No evidence can be produced for fixing the fundamental anthropological definition as a purely political or social category. And if that is attempted, it is easy to put forward an ideology critique, immanent in the nature of the argument, of such a functionalized use of the concept.

The opposition between *Bildung* and *Halbbildung* (semi- or superficial education) or *Unbildung* (lack of education) is not primarily a social but a self-critical definition that actually constitutes the concept of *Bildung*. That *Bildung* cannot be restricted to a known content; that the danger of *Überbildung* (overeducation) or *Verbildung* (miseducation) would lurk here; that the form of knowledge is more important than knowledge itself; that *Bildung* must always be on guard against the false appearance of itself, against *Scheinbildung* (spurious *Bildung*): this self-criticism accompanied the conceptual history of *Bildung* like its shadow from 1800 up until Adorno's "Theorie der Halbbildung" ("Theory of Semi-Education").[55] The trivial remark that the proof of *Bildung* cannot be its sheer universality beyond all specialization belongs here; rather it is the awareness of its limits and the capability of recognizing them in order to extend and surpass them. In the words of Rahel Varnhagen: "An educated (*gebildet*) person is not one whom nature has treated generously; an educated person is one who treats the gifts that he has kindly, wisely, properly, and with the highest regard. He who takes this seriously, he who can bear to look with resolute eyes at his own shortcomings and admit them: this is, in my opinion, a duty and no gift; and it constitutes for me, all by itself, an educated person."[56] "An educated person knows," to quote Hegel, "the limit of his competence to judge."[57] The self-criticism which helps to explain the awareness of self-alienation is, spoken with and against Marx, not class-specific. And for this reason, Hoffmann, the statistician, had to classify *Bildung* in his 1844 work as purely social, running up against heterogeneous, overlapping categories: there are educated people (*Gebildete*) who are gainfully employed and there are educated people who are not gainfully employed, just as there are uneducated (*ungebildete*) proprietors and uneducated people who are propertyless.[58] *Bildung* is socially conditioned but not socially reducible.

Jacob Burckhardt and Friedrich Nietzsche, the most radical critics of the German *Bildung* industry, also testify to this. Their criticism aimed at the social result of a rampant philistinism of *Bildung*;[59] however, the standard of measurement for their criticism remained tied to that type of *Bildung* passed down to them in the idealist, classical, and romantic tradition. Burckhardt despised "this damned universal *Bildung*" because it only bred mediocrities who perceived every "opportunity for *Bildung*" as an opportunity to boast about it. One could consider "oneself educated (*gebildet*), patch together a 'Weltanschauung,' and start preaching to one's fellow men." But "that a man could educate himself purely on his own initiative has been out of the question for a long time." The self-formation (*Selbstbildung*) of individuals, their mutual influence and recognition, remained, despite all the nostalgia, the challenge to actual *Bildung*.

The young Nietzsche argued similarly, indeed more bitingly. He diagnosed "symptoms of a perishing of *Bildung* everywhere, of a complete eradication."[60] The fact that *Bildung* has become dependent on the state, that it is tied to position or property, that it has become a scientific factor of production primarily oriented toward profit, all this will lead to barbarism. The external penchant for success would correspond to that "characteristic inwardness"[61] which, with the renunciation of any form, will transform the educated (*Gebildete*) into "walking encyclopedias." "And thus the entire modern *Bildung* is essentially directed inward: the bookbinder imprinted something outwardly on it like 'Manual of Internal *Bildung* for External Barbarians.'" Our modern *Bildung*, externally related to the state and the production of science and internally a formless mass of accumulating, historically mediated knowledge, "is in no way an actual *Bildung* but only a kind of knowledge about *Bildung*." For this reason, Nietzsche rejects any association with the "educated" so that he can save or recover that actual *Bildung* which, in its essential features, remained entirely compatible with Humboldt and likewise, as Löwith indicated,[62] with the criticism of *Bildung* by Herder, Fichte, and Goethe.

The ideal type persists, even where vocational education (*Berufsbil-*

dung) has to be professionally included by educationalists in the definition of the concept. As such, Friedrich Paulsen, holder of the Berlin Chair [of Pedagogy], counted "the ability to function as a participating member in the historical life of the social whole"[63] as specific to vocational education. But for him, the mutual harmony of body and spirit, mind and reason, will and disposition, remains central for generating or liberating the autonomy of the person. Paulsen, a pedagogic beacon in Wilhelminian society, fought for the independence of the educational apparatus (*Bildungswesen*) from state supervision; he championed for the separation of educational opportunities (*Bildungschancen*) from social constraints; he supported the equality of different paths of formal education, such as the natural sciences and the humanities; he warned of the "overextension of nationalism" and of the "deification of one's own people and state"[64]—and defined *Bildung* in unbroken continuity. *Bildung* could "not be made from the outside, it grows from the inside out. . . . *Bildung* does not consist in the possession of knowledge but in the possession of living powers of cognition and efficacy with which the inner form of life occupies itself." One could be an educated person (*ein gebildeter Mensch*) without even having orthographic knowledge; so-called universal *Bildung* might be nothing but *Halbbildung* (superficial *Bildung*).[65] The suprapolitical and suprasocial concepts of *Bildung* appear to be, quite consistently, newly stabilized thanks not least to Nietzsche's critique, against all the classifications of the so-called educated bourgeoisie (*Bildungsbürger*) established by the criticism of ideology. This view is espoused—likewise compatibly with Nietzsche's critique—by Ulrich Herrmann in our volume.[66] When it does not seek other explanations, for instance of the political or social-psychological sort, even the social-historical criticism of the deteriorating forms of *Bildung* continues to live off that ideal concept of *Bildung* that is always already constituted through self-criticism.

(c) A further criterion, the contamination of the concept of *Bildung* with *work* (*Arbeit*), testifies to how little the concept is suited to being reduced to socially dichotomous definitions. Hegel also had a formative effect here when he discerned that work forms (*bildet*) and liberates, but the origin of this observation has been long forgotten and developed into a typology of *Bildung*. Hegel eschewed the Aristotelian opposition between a free person's activity in leisure and the useful work of simpletons and serfs. On the contrary, every activity is work to the extent that it satisfies the needs that it generates. *Bildung* is not defined by the line between manual work and intellectual work but rather any work forms (*bildet*). "Work" refers to an occupation that mediates between particular abilities and tasks and the demands of the general public. In his *Philosophical Propaedeutic*, Hegel treats theoretical and practical, moral and intellectual *Bildung* under the precept of "duties toward oneself."[67] There, complex relationships between self-restraint and ability, between immediacy and forbearance, between the diversity of knowledge and its definitiveness are analyzed. Learning to control these is called "forming oneself" (*sich bilden*). This anthropological foundation for any *Bildung* then appears in paragraphs 196 to 198 of the *Philosophy of Right* as "The Nature of Work," and it allows the reciprocal determination of work and *Bildung* to enter into the canon of the multiple definitions of *Bildung* since then.

The substantiation of work through *Bildung* and vice versa can be classified in terms of critique of ideology. This is especially the case in an age of growing conflicts, instigated economically or sociopolitically, between manual and intellectual activities. However, it was precisely Hegel's achievement to see *Bildung* emerge from work and work from *Bildung*; here the potential was to be found for criticizing any circumstances that privileged *Bildung* at the expense of factory work, something which Marx made use of as well as Virchow—the latter expecting (with Hegel) machines to provide relief for workers. Technology became the symbol—or the vehicle—of equalization for Virchow because theoretical and practical work always converge here, something not possible without shared scientific *Bildung*.[68] In bringing *Bildung* and work together, Hegel recognized that specialization and overarching competence are interdependent. Thus he found a concept of *Bildung* that was dependable and effective beyond boundaries specific to social classes and estates.

The line of division separating the clergy or the estate of lawyers from the laity in the Aristotelian tradition[69] opened up and became porous through *Bildung*'s conception of work. If *Bildung*, in the words of Lorenz von Stein, turned "into the working deed," then it can also "no longer [be described] as an individual, fixed concept exhausted by its definition."[70] *Bildung* turns into a "living process," compelled to constantly coordinate equality and freedom, theory and praxis anew in the modern world of work. An additional legacy of the Hegelian definition of the concept is that it also underpins and outlasts the already established, empirically unruly antithesis between the natural sciences and the human sciences, that is to say, the *Bildungswissenschaften*. Modern *Bildung* does not exist without science; however, it cannot be reduced to any individual science. *Bildung* alone produces those ties between heterogeneous factors, and without them, our world based on the division of labor could not exist.

Alfred Weber stated that empathetically in 1922 when the Verein für Socialpolitik placed the rapidly dwindling economic base for the "intellectual worker" on its agenda. The "educated class" ("*Bildungsschicht*"), he argued, "is not something socially enclosed," above all it "is not identical . . . to the class of the academically educated (*akademisch Gebildete*)." Rather, it ran through the whole of society "in an invisible way," and Alfred Weber tried to redefine this class "now that its background in pension support has disappeared."[71] He named it the *Arbeitsintellektuellentum* ("working intelligentsia"), the inheritors of the dying *Bildungsbürger* (educated bourgeoisie). Redundant as always, Weber invented a complex designation for renaming the continuous task of *Bildung*, even if its economic presuppositions broke apart. Without being able to prescribe specific professions to the newly defined intelligentsia (something which he tentatively attempted to do), Weber considered concrete work—seemingly banal—as the minimum common denominator: as the indispensable prerequisite for life, for intellectual activity, and for political engagement.

Typified by its essential semantic features, modern *Bildung* thus distinguishes itself through the fact that it recasts religious pregivens into challenges for the personal conduct of life, that generating the autonomy of individuality, it is open and connectable to all concrete situations in life, and that understood as work, it is the integrating element of the world based on the division of labor.

III. Cultural Heritage and Cultural Knowledge

The essential features delineated so far are structural characteristics of *Bildung*. From the end of the eighteenth century, they appear regularly; they repeat themselves irrespective of the particular individual concepts of *Bildung* that were formulated and maintained in connection with personal, situative, and historical contexts. Certainly *Bildung* can logically be historicized and dissected into the composite parts from which it was individually and variously composed. Or, in terms of social history, more highly aggregated groups can be joined together, for instance the neo-humanistically educated secondary school and university graduates whose diachronic change can be tracked. Or, beyond thresholds of political events, alternating functional definitions of *Bildung* can be pinpointed. In the political-social milieu, *Bildung* was up until the 1848 revolution, directed against the privileged estates and, to this extent, had an aggressive purpose. After the 1848 revolution, a stabilizing function can be detected with regard to the bourgeoisie (*Bürgertum*). With the decline of the Wilhelminian Reich, such a function may have finally made way for defensive, status-preserving definitions. Counter to this tendency, it is observable that *Bildung* released innovative forces again and again with its self-critical potential: "youth" movements, the avant-garde, and forerunners of reform or revolution. Or it can be argued that without *Bildung*, the successful separation and differentiation of the natural sciences (whose original place was the faculty of arts) cannot be explained. The parity gained by the technical universities (*Technische Hochschulen*) and the initiation of the Kaiser-Wilhelm-Gesellschaft by the theologian Harnack symbolically vouch for this.

So long as any such historicization thematizes *Bildung* in the first place, it lives off those structural pregivens which, in a recurring manner, belong to the common signature of our modern age (*Neuzeit*). The same thing also applies to cultural heritage and cultural knowledge, the two spheres according to which our volume is organized.[72] This methodologically necessary segmentation points toward commonalities that tie all the arts and all the sciences—*Kunst und Wissenschaft*—back to the task of *Bildung* belonging to them. *Bildung* could, then, be defined as the reflexive and communicative force field that has attempted to integrate all the heritage of life and of the arts as well as all the specific knowledge. One may discern a utopia in it, like one of those utopias brought forth by modernity with its open future. However, such a criterion would already be carried over, from the outside and ex post facto, to *Bildung* by ideology critique. In the context of our argument, we first have to outline the empirically separable cultural heritage and specifications of knowledge as elements of a prevailing *Bildung*.

1. First of all, it can be said that cultural heritage (*Bildungsgüter*) and spheres of knowledge permit *no hierarchy* with regard to their educational function (*Bildungsfunktion*). All modern experiences impacting art, litera-

ture, or science acquire a mutually illuminating and stabilizing context of reference here. Every individual field of knowledge that differentiates and establishes itself must contain explanations for other fields of knowledge within itself. The test case for a specialized method is still whether it is compatible with related fields of knowledge or whether it has a transforming effect on all neighboring fields. Thus a new context, a common style, emerges; the demand placed on *Bildung*, which always already embraces the natural sciences, social sciences, and humanities, is to manufacture it —even if in practice *Bildung* often enough toils at this in vain. The methodological independence of the increasingly "positive" sciences makes it difficult to simply integrate their specifications and procedures into a canon of *Bildung*. This is true for the technological and natural sciences, for jurisprudence as well as sociology, but above all for economics. Corresponding to this is the fact that the textually bound, historical sciences, which increasingly consider themselves as "positive," are forced into a supposedly traditional refuge of so-called *Bildungswissenschaften*. Resentments can be derived from this finding, but no hierarchy.

The regeneration of disciplines happens over and over again. The historical sciences responded to the new situation through their interdisciplinary criticism of historicism (see Muhlack's essay),[73] which extended to all the related disciplines; and highly educated natural scientists are always in a position to convey their pathbreaking discoveries to the public. The popular writings of Planck—including his stance of piety—or of Heisenberg on the fundamental shift in the natural sciences testify to this. *Bildung* continues to mediate the allegedly separate cultures; however, it does not hierarchize them.

Despite subjective preferences, even the arts or literary genres can no longer be hierarchically structured nor restricted to carrying out tasks. The utopia of a "progressive universal poetry"[74] or the "total work of art"[75] is only a confirmation of this result. And "life experience" (*Erlebnis*), Dilthey's central interpretative category, brings together all imaginable occasions to serve *Bildung*—including the so-called "war experience," something which Erich Weniger still wanted to treat as *Bildung* in the 1920s.[76]

2. The next criterion for the integrative power of *Bildung* is the *individual activity* of those who involve themselves with or call upon it. Art, music, and literature are actively received, that is, reproduced by the edu-

cated (*Gebildete*), a behavior that rapidly leads to one's own creative production. In view of specializations in the sciences and in view of masterful achievements in the arts, a conscious and accomplished dilettantism belongs to *Bildung*. This dilettantism creates a protective zone of autonomy that is always claimed for art and science. Not only do artists become autonomous figures who, despite lasting support from royal courts, increasingly live from the market; their products are also, to a large extent, no longer determined by state or ecclesiastical functions. But art does not turn into *l'art pour l'art* as a result; rather it remains—beyond its active reception—the medium of *Bildung* (see Dahlhaus's essay).[77] The fundamental aesthetic experience that always mediates spirit and sense (see Büttner's essay)[78]—in the formation of judgment (*Urteilsbildung*) and during the process of creation—thus constitutes, anthropologically speaking, *Bildung*. It is an active mode of the consummation of the cultivated (*gebildet*) life.

Music, whose public performances are accompanied by the study of scores, is reproduced at home as chamber music or sung in semipublic choirs or choral societies. Poetry, too, is privately cultivated in family circles of readers or private theater performances, not to mention the numerous poetic outpourings of varying quality exchanged between intellectuals (*Gebildeten*). Likewise, drawing or painting belongs to private *Bildung*, including self-portraits, the correlate to autobiography. Not anyone can produce anything, but sociability does induce a creative autonomy and vice versa, without which *Bildung* would not exist. Moreover, photomechanical and electronic technologies of reproduction have raised the criteria of quality in a way that lessens the integrative power of *Bildung*. This has led to a division between artistic specialists and intellectual criticism; to be sure, they condition one another, like a vanishing point of *Bildung* that cannot be escaped.

3. A further characteristic through which all the arts and sciences are integrated into *Bildung* is its *historical reflexivity*. Within the concept of *Bildung*, a temporal factor of change is always already contained; when seen biographically or in general historical terms, it is variable in different ways. Traditions are no longer passed down but are retrospectively established; any future is newly opened up without the knowledge of historical *Bildung*—of the individual as well as of the society—being lost as a continuous process. The fact that the arts and literature continually reestablish

their difference from classical antiquity does not constitute neo-humanistic "cultural knowledge" ("*Bildungswissen*"). Rather the enduring quarrel between yesterday and today generates the shared *Bildung* process of artistic activity and its criticism. Literary genres, now regularly accompanied by the history of literature, are newly constituted by constantly refracting and always referring to the formerly canonized classics of antiquity, of neighboring European peoples and those of Asia (which are increasingly being made available through new translations). To the degree that Weimar Classicism from 1770 to 1830 is canonized, it provokes new stylistic tendencies that in turn transform the canon, for instance, integrating Kleist, E. T. A. Hoffmann, Hölderlin, or Büchner, as well as Heine. The Bildungsroman is a representative medium in which author and reader are related to one another through historical reflection on person and environment and design their own life histories. The telos of this *Bildung* is logically temporalized and pulled into the process of self-formation (*Selbstbildung*).

A classical canon has also been retrospectively established in music. Any composition with intentions of entering into the repertoire of the new classics that are gaining acceptance must signify an irreversible step toward a new "creation." The constant expectation of *Bildung* in music is the achievement of composition as well as of historically reflected reception that helps set the standards of innovation. Composers, too, are involved in this business, in the same way that Wagner plunged his work—analogous to the Bildungsroman—into the historical perspectives of the entire past and its desired future his whole life long.

In the plastic arts (*bildende Kunst*), a term that can itself be read as a historical reflection, the artist's commentary is part of productivity[79] in the same way that a provocative tension between possible prior models and individual achievement is maintained through the institution of the museum. Since then, any art can be historical, innovative, or both at the same time. In particular, historicizing architecture (one need only think of Schinkel) was a highly reflected accomplishment of art that could render present the otherness of the past as such and convert it into formally harmonious new buildings.

The value of citing the past, something associated with all the arts, is thus changed. Formerly the witness to biblical presence or the humanistic continuity of knowledge, citation turns into sign. It can deteriorate into the sign of a flaunted *Bildung* (see Frühwald's essay),[80] but first and foremost, it is a sign in and for the process of *Bildung* itself. Whenever it is ironically alienating or preserves continuity, citation is a historical achievement of art which, by virtue of its *Bildung* function, extends from all the arts into the everyday.

Thus any aesthetic production and reception remains bound to its historical reflection; only from this can the uniqueness and distinctiveness of a work be derived. The historicity of genres, of styles, of forms, and of their combinations was the common denominator that could not exist without historical reflection as the driving force of *Bildung*. It would be a methodological short circuit to link *Bildung* back to its unique, originary situation around 1800 in order to definitively circumscribe *Bildung* to its neo-humanistic, classical, or romantic knowledge contents, modes of thought, and artistic products. Those ephemeral perspectives of imitation and decadence then emerge; their inventions and experiences are themselves nothing other than witnesses to a historically reflected, continually engendering *Bildung*.

In the first decade of the twentieth century, the explosion (as in physics) that tore apart all historical pregivens, all prior formations of music, art, and literature, may be characterized in retrospect as post-historical. But they can still be described as the logical products of self-formation (*Selbstbildung*): *Jugendstil*, Expressionism, Cubism, abstract art, Dada, Bauhaus, atonal music, and other such terms. More than before, the development of any of these movements still lives off the modern pretext of historical reflection, something which was never restricted to the safeguarding of tradition. And for this reason, it is not surprising when historically legible signs reappear today in all the art movements—metacitations, so to speak, of historical *Bildung*.

4. Finally, the German concept of *Bildung* is characterized by the fact that individual spheres of life, corresponding to so-called cultural heritage (*Bildungsgüter*) and cultural knowledge (*Bildungswissen*), are always newly semantically folded into one another. Religion, work, history, language, music, art, and science refer to and mutually justify one another in the medium of *Bildung*. The intellectual-historical affiliations cannot be traced here; however, the semantic system of cross-referencing is the performance and the result of a *Bildung*, which understands itself as that mode of performance and as an always provisional result.

Reflection through and on *language* is an originary and constant feature of *Bildung*. For Herder, language is grounded in reflection, something that is anthropologically logical and audible; it is grounded in "consciousness" and "deliberation," as he says,[81] in a reflection which is co-original with "*Bildung* through language."[82] Language itself, to quote Humboldt,[83] precedes every "division" between the so-called educated and uneducated "classes." Every language contains "a totality corresponding to the size of the unbounded human capability for *Bildung*."[84] Since Herder, it has acquired the power of a posttheological revelation that frees itself from the text of the Bible and expresses itself across all languages in a way that constantly improves. "If language is the means of *human Bildung* for our species, then writing is the means of *learned Bildung*."[85] As Nietzsche later said, "the scientific person and the educated (*gebildete*) person are members of two different spheres. . . . *Bildung*, however, begins with the correct use of language."[86] If all the specialized disciplines of language and literature and all the arts are, then, supposed to bear witness to or generate *Bildung*, they are referred back again and again to the reflexivity contained in language.

Analogous to Herder's interpretation of language, *history* also acquires the quality of revelation. Hegel's *Phenomenology of Mind* can be read both as the process of *Bildung* and as revelation, and that had an effect on all the hermeneutical sciences, even where they developed into the positivistic history of ideas. Or, in Schleiermacher's analysis of the subjective piety of the educated (*Gebildeten*) who "no longer require a mediator," such piety must in any case fall back upon history, on the history which "in the most actual sense [is the] richest source for religion—but not, for example, to accelerate and govern the advancement of humanity in its development, rather only to observe it as the most universal and greatest revelation of the innermost and the holiest."[87] The historically (*historisch*) unique revelation that was assured up until now by biblical texts is simply extended or traced back to history (*Geschichte*), the presupposition of that historical *Bildung* from which the historical school emerges. Then, taking up the Hegelian definition, historical *Bildung* can also be understood as work. In Droysen's words, we have *Bildung* "not until we have acquired it through our own work; not until we have recognized it as what it is, as the result of the unremitting work of those who came before us."[88] Although trivialized, such equations show up everywhere, for instance with the Munich history painters in 1876: "We have to paint history; history is the religion of our time. Only history is contemporary."[89]

The concept of *Kunstreligion* ("religion of art"), coined by the romantics and developed by Hegel in terms of his philosophy of history, also contains a semantic charge that still enters into the theoretical justifications of nonrepresentational art. Kandinsky called upon the "evangelical talent" of the artist: "he has no right to live irresponsibly; he has difficult work to perform." The artist's duties are "precise, great, and holy," aim at a "rearing of the soul" and, by mediating between art and its reception, look forward "to the empire of tomorrow."[90]

Once the terms merged, *"Bildungsreligion"* had an effect most persistently in music. Not only did it invent the "church concert," not only did it evoke silent prayer or demand contemplation, raising and carrying away souls;[91] but, as art, music created a second world, at once transcending and penetrating this world. Both worlds are mediated by one another in the process of creation (*Bildungsprozeß*) and reception of a composition. "Music is actually a direct objectivation and reflection of the entire will, as is the world itself, as indeed are ideas, whose duplicated appearance constitutes the world of individual things." Therefore, according to Schopenhauer,[92] music's effect is much stronger and more impressive than that of the other arts; music brings the lost world of the beyond into this world. "One could say," the aged Richard Wagner concluded, "that where religion is artificial, it is the privilege of art to save the essence of religion,"[93] a principle which still presupposes the unhappy consciousness of *Bildung*, regardless of its tremendous musical innovations. It oscillates between destruction and redemption.

In his commentary to the second part of *Faust*, Eichendorff sarcastically traced—as a Catholic—this contamination between *Bildung*, art, and religion. For Faust would appear "as a knight of the divine court, full of vitality," "impressing" both God and the devil "with his eminent conception of the world (*Weltbildung*)—an operatic canonization of this *Bildung* which makes an impression on the uninitiated, like a noble description of the trivial vernacular text, 'lived joyously and died blissfully.'" Goethe had reached the pinnacle, unparalleled and unsurpassable; this is what "poetry could achieve by itself, once it turned its back on positive Christianity: the perfected self-idolization of both the emancipated subject and veiled earthly beauty."[94]

Whatever our shifts in perspective from Herder through Eichendorff to Kandinsky mixed together with respect to their different views on language, religion, music, art, science, and history, behind all diachronic change and behind nearly infinite variations, there are common semantic features, minimal, though not displaceable, structures of self-interpretation, which anthropologically can only be understood as *Bildung*. The essential features of *Bildung* sketched above—secular piety, openness to all political and social challenges, as well as work—are reencountered when the individual cultural inheritances (*Bildungsgüter*) of the arts and the individual contents of the forms of knowledge and the sciences are considered. Consciously reflected language, i.e. linguistics, consciously reflected history, i.e. historicity, consciously reflected religion, i.e. religiosity, consciously reflected art, i.e. aesthetics—these are the shorthand catchwords whose common denominator is *Bildung*.

IV. Outlook

Once they were brought together in Protestant-dominated, German-speaking regions, the semantically stable and, in this respect, structural features of *Bildung* persisted from the late eighteenth century until the First World War. Seen in real historical terms, that is, not primarily tied to linguistic self-reflection, this *Bildung* remains embedded within a wealth of social conditions and political challenges. The educated (*Gebildeten*) have reacted to, shared in, and not least, helped to evoke them in their bourgeois social formation. Nevertheless, nation building (*Nationsbildung*) and class formation (*Klassenbildung*), dominant processes of this time, do not directly correlate with the German concept of *Bildung*. Here, economic and societal factors had an effect that can neither be derived from *Bildung* nor traced back to it. That which characterizes *Bildung* in the long term can be as rarely forced into a diachronically constructed straitjacket as "Enlightenment." The concept has no diachronically homogeneous history. For this reason, the question posed is this: After the idea of *Bildung* was conceptualized, which of its essential features made possible or even survived the catastrophes of our century?

It is certainly a methodological fallacy to causally derive the relative failure of liberalism and extreme nationalism from the kind of *Bildung* by which a part of the bourgeoisie defined itself. First, these vast European movements betray similar courses throughout neighboring countries; they have to thus be derivable from more general conditions. Second, the fact that the membership of educated circles overlapped in a shifting way with that of liberal political parties, and with that of national or nationalistic movements, does not constitute their identity. And even where agreement between these heterogeneous group classifications can be manufactured, it still does not follow that *Bildung* can be considered the most effective factor behind political courses of action.

More likely, *Bildung* functionally, not causally, occupied a central position within the context of the social system of the Wilhelminian Reich. *Bildung* did not change anything from this position precisely because it was not primarily political. However, it could be connected in many directions, certainly connected with ambivalent policies in regard to culture, with successful ones in regard to science and scholarship, as well as with political parties, associations, and Protestant churches. The occasionally justified pride over what was called "German culture" or "German science and scholarship," led again and again to an arrogance that understood itself culturally but not politically—the symptom of a misunderstood, depraved *Bildung* that also repeatedly provoked criticism in the Wilhelminian Reich.

Institutionally, the educated strata remained, to a large extent, reliant on the state they supported but without directly influencing its politics. Whether an earlier constitutional parliamentarianism, that is, direct political responsibility involving the so-called intellectuals (*Gebildeten*), could have prevented the catastrophe of the First World War can be justifiably doubted. In that case, war probably would have broken out even earlier. Yet precisely in its prepolitical formation, *Bildung* plays a role in German history that is difficult to estimate and can hardly be underestimated: it did not help create any genuinely political culture that might have met the challenges of industrialized society. This silent function of *Bildung* gained an eminent significance when the traditional state disintegrated in 1918. *Bildung* lost its free space which was, up until then, secured by the state and the economic system. *Bildung*, too, had to become directly political, that is, demands were made of the educated (*Gebildeten*) to become politically involved through the parties and the parliament. With this, the political status of *Bildung* changed. Now it became clear that the economic crisis which took away countless intellectuals' pension support, and the constitutional crisis which forced intellectuals to take sides, was also a crisis of *Bildung* itself. In other words, the self-stabilizing concept of *Bildung* no longer appeared to be viable in the long term; the crisis of *Bildung* could no longer be mastered through self-criticism. Three texts by Spranger, C. H. Becker, and Freyer from the years 1929 to 1931 testify to this.

In 1929, Spranger brought the German ideal of *Bildung* into a historico-philosophical light, invoking world history in its entirety, weighing everything against everything, in order to rescue the debilitated ideal of *Bildung* from the crisis of the time. He expresses his longing for secular piety over and over again as the dominant feature of the concept of *Bildung* and declares it to be mediated by labor. "Thus our ideal of *Bildung* culminates in the most general formula: The work's permeation by the soul, the soul's enthusiasm for work (*Durchseelung des Werkes, Werkfreudigkeit der Seele*)."[95] The political diagnosis is clear. Had ethical ideals not degenerated into the "calculation" of interests, parliamentary democracy would have outlived itself. Thus the goal of German *Bildung* is to regenerate the state: "Here, too, as the formula for the new ideal of *Bildung*, one can posit the dual claim: the soul's permeation of the state and the state's permeation of the soul."[96] But that cannot exist without the "formation of a leader (*Führerbildung*)." "The spiritual forces that define the time must be alive almost demonically in the true leader."[97] While Spranger, using the most up-to-date wording, tried to rescue traditional *Bildung*, he had unknowingly already bidden it farewell.

It was different with C. H. Becker, who in 1930 clearly and unambiguously posed the "problem of *Bildung* in the cultural crisis of the present." He, too, demands secular piety: "One must have the courage and strength to believe in the meaning of life." He registers a tendency in this direction: "In the past, the educated (*Gebildeten*) were associated with knowledge and the uneducated (*Ungebildeten*) with faith; today, however, the belief in knowledge is almost a sign of miseducation (*Unbildung*) and the stamp of *Bildung* is a new religious faith."[98] Moreover, the program of *Bildung* developed by Becker moves—critically reflected—along the pathways of the already formed tradition of *Bildung*. He tries only to set this *Bildung* on new pedagogic tracks—"perhaps someday our age will be called the pedagogic age"[99]—and sociopolitically redeem it. "We are not striving for knowledge," which will always remain incomplete, "but for achievement."[100] Not a single word about *Volk* or race or Germanness comes up. Granted—in terms of the youth movement—*Gefolgschaft* (allegiance) and *Führer* (leader) appear; however, the goal is unshakably the *Bildung* of character: socially bound, capable of organizing and shaping the "masses," and committed to humanity through "the belief in the sanctity or divinity of humans."[101]

"What we need is a humanistic *Bildung* in a new sense, one which does not depend upon humanistic subject matter but upon the spirit of true human- ity, not the learned but the lived *humanitas*."[102] Becker fought courageously for this simultaneously new and old humanistic *Bildung* so as to make it part of the young republic. And he tried to establish sociology as a sort of ersatz science of *Bildung*. If he failed, despite great successes, then it was foremost because the republic as a whole failed. The majority of intellectu- als admittedly shared in it by negation because they were no longer prepared to uphold, in view of "Versailles," the minimal consensus regarding *Bildung* as a political program applied to humans and humanity.

Freyer bears witness to this in 1931. "The problem of *Bildung* is not current"; with this change of perspective, he initiated his analysis of "the present-day crisis of *Bildung*"[103] in terms of intellectual history and sociol- ogy. Freyer argued that the classic concept of *Bildung* would be surpassed; the claim to autonomy and self-formation (*Selbstbildung*) of character is no longer redeemable; *Bildung* is no longer an authority precisely because—in its formerly idealistic form—it has become unpolitical. The industrial soci- ety created by science demands completely new responses. The form and function of *Bildung* need, therefore, to be redefined, even if traditional cri- teria remain in force. Thus, as with Humboldt, *Bildung* is assumed to be possible in any situation. Precisely industrial society will carry its own con- tent of *Bildung* within itself; the issue will only be that of recognizing and receiving it. There is talk neither of religiosity nor of leaders; on the con- trary, the linking of all strata back to their respective interests is to be ac- knowledged in order to derive proper and functional claims to *Bildung* from it. He has great confidence in "public education" ("*Volksbildung*"), no longer intended as instruction for upbringing but rather in the sense of an active self-endeavor of the public, without calling it democratic. And as a sociolo- gist, he is opposed to any cultural criticism (*Kulturkritik*): "we all are . . . the masses."[104] *Bildung* will "not [have] the mission to stop radicalization at any cost." Rather, any diagnosis consciously adopting a "position" will require the incorporation of the "compulsion to decide" as a "constitutive factor" into the seemingly peaceful and distant question of *Bildung*.[105]

Thus the politicization of *Bildung* is newly conceptualized at the ex- pense of the liberal relics that Spranger had fitted into his ubiquitous world- view (*Weltbild*), but likewise at the expense of Becker's strong republican- humanistic feeling—something that had cost him his office—in favor of a vague, radical right-wing democracy. Freyer certainly possessed greater analytic power and perspicuity, but his diagnosis of the crisis of *Bildung* also remained entangled in it. Freyer consciously accepted that and was, for this reason, not in a position to derive a content-defined theory of political *Bildung* from the German tradition of *Bildung*. He did not go beyond the metapolitical necessity of decision.

Two years later, in 1933, things had moved so far that Richard Benz, certainly "educated" (*gebildet*) and no national socialist, could condemn the "de-Germanization through *Bildung*" because it would have bred *Unvolksmäßigkeit* ("Un-Germanness"): "One may rightfully lament the general, present-day shunning of intellect—yet one should not bemoan the collapse of German *Bildung* which is occurring with it."[106] Ignoring the hysterical nonsense produced here, semantically we are reading an authentic testimony of the self-surrender of *Bildung*. Neither the traditional structures of *Bildung* nor their implicit self-criticism is called upon, as was always the case until then, to prevent the abdication of *Bildung*.

Bildung could survive the time when it was openly disdained, if at all, only in political refuge, and that meant more and more in the political underground. Only here could autonomy, the constant feature of *Bildung*, be preserved. And if *Bildung* survived, then certainly it did so enriched by the experience that it could no longer exist without the creation of a political consciousness (*politische Bewußtseinsbildung*) and without the ability to level political criticism in modern society. The old political and social openness no longer leads to a subjective field of arbitrariness. Today, the task of *Bildung* is to continually reflect upon its political or social function in order to attune agency and action to it.

And if one inquires about the additional structural feature, secular piety, it continues to smolder, but has, by and large, migrated over into mass movements or sects which siphoned off, so to speak, the share of salvation knowledge from the canon of *Bildung*. With the rapid disappearance of faith in dogmas, its *Bildung*-religious opposition dissipated too. In addition, the denominational opposition is flattened to such an extent that it no longer arranges the presently exchanged cultural heritage (*Bildungsgüter*) or even cultural knowledge (*Bildungswissen*) in antithetical terms.

Thus there remains the specific combination of knowledge regarding achievement and knowledge regarding government that blends *Bildung* with work (our third criterion). Here, this combination is indispensable for encountering the challenges of the world based on the division of labor and for being continuously realized anew with the succession of generations. As little as *Bildung* could at one time be traced back to the bourgeoisie, so too today its chances remain as great for outliving the transformations of civil society (*bürgerliche Gesellschaft*). There are structures of *Bildung*, once conceptualized, which remain effective and stretch across epochs. And if the outmoded-sounding *Persönlichkeitsbildung* ("building of character")—the demand to also conduct one's life in society in a responsible way, that is, the demand that at one time initiated the concept of *Bildung*—is today called into question by critique of ideology or social diagnosis, then it is to be remembered that behind such criticism lurks the self-surrender of the critic.

Translated by Todd Presner

Three *bürgerliche* Worlds?

PRELIMINARY THEORETICAL-HISTORICAL REMARKS
ON THE COMPARATIVE SEMANTICS OF CIVIL SOCIETY
IN GERMANY, ENGLAND, AND FRANCE

Whoever uses the term "bourgeoisie" (*Bürgertum*), is thinking of a modern social formation whose origin seems to be clearly in the French and the Industrial revolutions.[1] Whoever speaks of "civil society" (*bürgerliche Gesellschaft*) may come to the same finding but proceeds on the shaky ground of a millennial tradition. For *bürgerliche Gesellschaft, société civile,* or civil society are etymologically translations from the Latin. They refer to the Roman *societas civilis* which, for its part, had its terminological model in the *koinōnia politikē* of the Greeks. Purely etymologically, we are thus facing a finding of astounding continuity, and what Aristotle or Cicero said about "civil society" is, then, in no way entirely outdated. For contained in the etymology are the earlier conceptions of a free political self-organization that cannot be erased from the European experience. Thus, as a recallable meaning, the idea that citizens (*die Bürger*) can or should rule over themselves was at no time eliminated from the concept of "civil society." In the theoretical definition of the *cives* of a *societas civilis,* the political self-definition of those who exercise power as free citizens was always emphasized, be it over themselves, over others, or in an alternating fashion, as in the case of democracy, such that ruler and ruled theoretically overlap. Even though they have been enriched or contested over and over again, there are normative elements that continue to endure, at least in the theoretical history of civil society in Europe, regardless of changing political and social situations. That a citizen could only be someone who held political responsibility (be it in a community or city, in an estate, in a territory or state, or as the prince) and that a citizen could only be someone who exerted power (be it over oneself or over others or alternately with others): in this formal generality, the meaning—derived from constitution of the Greek polis—of a *politēs*, a *civis*, a citizen, a *citoyen*, or indeed a *Bürger* is never lost. To this extent, *bürgerliche Gesellschaft* (civil society) and its equivalents are as traditional as they are modern.

Whoever speaks of modern civil society and simply calls it "civil society," seemingly tied to the present day, cannot dispense with the traditional meanings of this concept. Thus the so-called rule of law or the sociologically high assessment of the stabilizing roles played by the middle strata (*Mittelschichten*) for a social existence belongs to Aristotle's principles. They surface again and again behind all historical transformations in characterizing a civil society. Something similar goes for the conserving function of the moderately rich, or the mediating task of the nobility between the people and the ruler, or the similar mediating task of the middle estates between the nobility and the lower strata (*Unterschichten*): such determinations of position could always call upon Aristotle.

However, the concepts of *Bürger* and *bürgerliche Gesellschaft* are not just characterized by the fact that they preserved their normative content over the long term and kept it constantly available; on the contrary, the constructions of the concept also referred over and over again to unique situations. These situations concerned the ways in which concrete understandings were comprehended linguistically by the particular concept. In conformity with his experience, Aristotle always let his *koinōnia politikē* rest upon slaves and metics who were, by nature, not entitled to civil rights. Work was not a qualifying criterion for participation in political power, quite in contrast to modernity, or more precisely, to modernity at least since Locke defined work as a prerequisite of property and property as a prerequisite of political rights.

Three epochal stages can be cited which transformed and enriched the concept of civil society beyond the initial local community, or even dissolved its specifically urban-bourgeois (*stadtbürgerliche*) components. From the first century B.C., Roman rights of citizenship were increasingly expanded, finally extending—in 212 A.D.—to all the free inhabitants of Imperial Rome. Thus a double citizenship became possible, that of the regional community and that of the general political formation, something which, seen structurally, could always repeat itself thereafter. Against this background, Stoic teachings gained a wider sense, embracing not only all the citizens but all human beings as members of a *societas humana*.[2]

A new, epochal shift in meaning brought about by the Augustinian doctrine of two *civitates* was not possible without the influence of Stoic teachings on a narrower civil society and a broader human society. The citizenry of the *civitas dei* was to include every human being, irrespective of gender, age, race, or social and political status. Participation in the theocracy conferred spiritual qualities of citizenship on Christians without regard to their earthly or worldly situation. Still contained within the concept of the educated German bourgeoisie (*deutsche Bildungsbürger*) or the intelligentsia are elements of this nonpolitical, intellectual, or spiritual tradition.

A similarly profound epochal shift also took place in the early modern period. It helped spur our present-day meaning of the term "civil society." Up through the eighteenth century, it was evident in the common European Latin linguistic tradition that a *civis* could only be one who exercised power. Any head of household who, with regard to internal matters, could be in charge of house and home, spouse, children, and servants, was capable of exercising political power externally: as a participant in the judicature or administration of a municipality, as a member of or representative in the estates, finally and above all, as ruling lord of a territory. In the sense of this traditional, conformist theory based on the experience of a society of estates, free peasants, citizens, or members of the lower or upper nobility were always *cives* of the *societas civilis*. Since the high Middle Ages, an indicator of this estate-based ruling order was that it was always simultaneously defined in political, social, and legal terms—spheres that could not be empirically separated. That changed gradually, although profoundly, during the course of early modern times.

Politically, the ruling estates lost ground in the same measure as the royal sovereign took all political power of decision upon himself. Prior to the French Revolution, this was never entirely successful because the estates still had their say in what happened, but by and large, only legal privileges and positions of social leadership remained for the old estates. Apart from England, where sovereignty remained with the king in Parliament, the political power of decision migrated to the jurisdiction of the monarch and his court. In view of the sovereignty of royalty, but only in this respect, all the "citizens" became transformed into an association of subjects (*Untertanen-*

verband). As Zedler reflected, a citizen becomes both subjected and subject (*Untertan* and *Subjekt*): And as such, citizens no longer have any ruling rights. "Here, 'republic' is understood as civil society, a composite of rulers and subjects who have merged together with one another to preserve and promote the common welfare."[3] Thus, slowly arising from the association of subjects there emerged a civil society (*Bürgergesellschaft*) still directed at the common good but apolitical in the sense of exercising power—in a variation of Schlözer's definition of the concept: a *societas civilis sine imperio*.[4] With this, a previously unimaginable result is tentatively conceptualized, namely that there could be a civil society without domination, or, at the very least, that this is thinkable.

The traditional estate society not only changed politically but also *legally* in its graduated organization. The privileged estates, particularly the nobility and the clergy, abruptly lost all their privileges in the French Revolution, and the same thing happened gradually in other European countries. Any supremacy secured up until then by the birthright of the nobility and the bourgeoisie was subjected to the civil-juridical principle of equality. After the French Revolution, rule could no longer be a personal, legal entitlement. This became a norm which, of course, first acquired weight with the revolutions of 1830 and 1848. Old ruling rights persisted only in the House of Lords and the Upper Chamber. All rule was theoretically depersonalized in favor of the sovereignty of the state, which could be represented by a ruler or a parliament, or by both at once.

Seen only in *social* terms, the former ruling estates still remained in the leadership positions that they had always occupied within the framework of the *societas civilis* envisaged by Aristotle. Their reputation, their relationships, their familial cohesion, their assets, and above all, their ownership of land and access to royal courts secured continued influence for the old estates, above all the nobility, on the political decisions of the authorities of the states to which they belonged. Even though they were no longer politically influential in the same way as they had been under the old order of civil society, and even though they were also no longer legally influential as they had been under the old order of privileges, the old estates remained socially (*sozial*) powerful—that is, since the nineteenth century, effectively shaping society in the field of foreign policy.

Here, we already find ourselves within the sphere of pure "society" (*Gesellschaft*), of modern civil society. In exaggerated terms, its citizens were not concerned with exercising political rule but rather with procuring participation in the authority of the state in order to secure their economic interests. On the grounds of legal equality—political power delegated to the state or bound up with its particular constitution—these citizens moved within a space of living conditions that were secured but not prescribed by the state. It was no longer the space of legal but of social inequality, the space of working and economically active citizens in which the individual principle of achievement predominated. This involved satisfying increasing needs on a daily basis, engendering a mutual and growing economic dependence of everyone on everyone.

As the Brockhaus encyclopedia matter-of-factly put it around the middle of the century:

More recent linguistic usage occasionally differentiates between "state" and "society" or "civil society." The latter term refers to the common life of human beings and the developing relationships emerging automatically from it, without the involvement of the authority of the state, for example relationships between different estates and professional classes, or between opposites like employers and workers, producers and consumers.[5]

It is that civil society which Hegel defined as a sphere reliant upon the state but economically independent, the civil society that inserted itself unpolitically, as it were, with its respective individual interests, between the family and the state and that did not exist before the nineteenth century. Or, it is the civil society that is definable for Marx only by its economic presuppositions and its social class differences; with respect to these, all politics still remain only superstructure or epiphenomena. According to the polemical definition by a French Republican in 1841, civil society involved the rule of the bourgeoisie. What is a bourgeois, he asked: yesterday a slave, a servant—today, a master. "Un maître d'aujourd'hui. Qu'est ce que la Bourgeoisie? La réunion des maîtres qui font travailler, au profit de qui travaillent, les prolétaires. Où commence la Bourgeoisie? Où finit le prolétariat?"[6] Ruling is no longer defined politically but rather economically, above all by the exploitation that precipitated its social and revolutionary consequences. And the intention of our author (Duclerc) was to provoke precisely these.

A conceptual-historical reference needs to be added to clarify the epochal shift from the old-style politically determined civil society *eo ipso*, to the modern, economically determined civil society. It concerns the dissemination of the concept of the economy (*Ökonomie*), which only became theoretically capable of opening up new experiences from the eighteenth century onward. From the Greeks up until the eighteenth century, the idea of the *oikos* dealt with household economy (*Hauswirtschaft*) and domestic rule over a household. This concrete, experience-saturated, and restricted concept of the economy widened in the eighteenth century, dogmatized, as it were, by Adam Smith. The economy moved out of the Aristotelian triad of ethics, economics, and politics and differentiated itself as an independent sphere of a purely interest-driven civil society henceforth designated as modern. Since then, "economy" refers to large-scale territorial, state, national, and, finally, worldwide networks of constantly growing needs: It is the sphere of industrial society stretching across nations, dependent upon capitalism, and driven forward by science and technology that is henceforth understood as "civil." Its dynamics encompass the entire world since then, and today, for the first time, it has come to be threatened by outside, noneconomic factors, namely ecological ones.

Our theoretical-historical retrospective has come so far as to require a considerable modification. However much the economically determined emergence of a civil society was the product of our recent history, the ancient meaning conceptualized by Aristotle of the *koinōnia politikē* as a self-ruling community of citizens was never lost. The opposite was the case. This model—that the earlier citizenry (*Bürgerschaft*) of the polis or the Roman Republic was such a community of free citizens—not only guided the French revolutionaries and the German idealists but even the Scottish moral philosophers. Moreover, the Stoic public ethic (*Bürgerethik*) and the Christian spiritual principle of the equality of all citizens in a theocracy remained present as a legacy. They were merely transformed and merged to become inner-worldly. These constitutional designs already take shape and gain in penetrating power prior to the social repercussions of industrialization, that is, in the age of the Enlightenment, vindicating all human beings who, as citizens, participate in political power and general self-determination. Thus our semantics, conducted up until now in terms of a conceptual history, move into concrete contexts of action. Several social-historical references are, therefore, allowed.

It was always concrete, delimitable groups of actors that made use of the *Bürger* terminology to register entirely pragmatic demands or to assert themselves within the contested sphere of politics. The battle for political power, for influence on "the state authorities," and even for political rule went still further under the conditions of a liberalized competitive society. For even the economic bourgeoisie (*Wirtschaftsbürger*) sought to suit and submit their interests to the state. Thus the individual states in Europe became targets for those groups who defined themselves as *Bürger*, as *citoyens*, or as the middle classes. And if these groups are to be characterized as the core of modern civil society—moving out of the theoretical concept of a politically organized society as a whole—then it appears that the influence of this society, in the narrow sense, was variously strong from nation to nation and that it was nowhere dominant before the last third of the nineteenth century. If we take Germany, England, and France as the three nations in which the *Bürgertum*, the middle classes, and the *bourgeoisie*, respectively, are supposed to have gained acceptance, then such a conclusion can only be rendered with significant reservations. In all three nations, there were electoral systems based on restricted suffrage and indirect elections, which pragmatically limited the say of the so-called bourgeois middle strata (*bürgerliche Mittelschichten*). The ownership of land remained politically dominant: "Hors de la propriété foncière point de salut."[7] Entrenched behind the land-ownership clauses, a throwback to the *ancien régime*, the nobility knew to preserve a position of leadership for themselves that did not contradict middle-class (*bürgerliche*) (Civil Law) equality. It was that way in Great Britain, where the nobility, with all its familial connections with the *bürgerliche* strata, was always concerned with keeping the "middle classes" middle-class: Because they were not presentable at court, they had de facto only restricted access to Parliament. The social hierarchy remained strictly preserved; wealth alone brought no prestige and, therefore, only limited political influence. It was that way in Germany, where the princes and court nobility remained socially dominant and where the *Bürgertum* could only move into positions of political leadership by finding jobs in the civil service or as attendants to the nobility. The estate-based and parliamentary channels of influence remained rigidly delimited. It was that way in France where the old, prerevolutionary nobility and the new Napoleonic nobility set high suffrage qualifications until 1848 and, moreover, as landowners, comprised a considerable part of those notables who stood out against the bourgeois and petit bourgeois population until far into the Third Republic.

To be radical in England, to be a Republican in France, or simply to be bourgeois in Germany, was still not a sufficient criterion to be accepted by the old leadership strata. Without forfeiting indirect influence or socially inscribed power, the nobility thus receded slowly into the background (in France, somewhat more quickly than in the rest of Europe). Only in the last third of the nineteenth century did the balance shift when the working lower strata not only learned to become articulate but also gradually began to influence political decisions. As such, in all three nations, the so-called *Bürgertum* came under increasing pressure by those segments of society that did not count as "civil society" in the sense of everyday language.

These social-historical indications only point to the fact that the structures of prerevolutionary ruling orders changed very slowly. The liberal model of order, the attempt to economically stratify society by achievement, wealth, and personal income, continued to be politically structured by landowning leadership groups. At the same time, the new challenges of the growing wage-dependent lower strata already undermined the claim to leadership of the so-called bourgeoisie. The civil society of the nineteenth century could thus be characterized from the beginning as a transitional society whose estate-based past and whose democratic future held it under the constant pressure of change.

Our theoretical-historical retrospective and our social-historical references have moved on a high level of generality in order to render visible epochal thrusts diachronically and Europe-wide challenges synchronically. The political semantics testify to how dubious or provisional such a procedure is. Should one place in a direct context the concrete linguistic acts that helped formulate the social and political claims of a newly conceptualized civil society, then our overview would require still further, more considerable modifications. For each of our three languages of comparison, German, English, and French, treated their various social presuppositions in their own ways, and they correspondingly stylized their politically articulated demands in different ways. Very divergent experiences were condensed into strictly different concepts, according to the language. In precise terms, the new civil society existed only to the extent that it could linguistically assure itself. Everything else implied about it is historical exegesis, ex post facto.

The common European theoretical tradition regarding the *societas civilis* was broken apart increasingly along national-linguistic lines in the early modern period. Not only was the praxis differentiated, as it had always been, but since then, the theory also developed separately. The common tradition took on national peculiarities, suggesting the hypothesis that, empirically, there were three different *bürgerliche* worlds which developed from the Enlightenment onward in Germany, England, and France. A quick look at the semantics of the concept *Bürger* already testifies to this in the case of all three nations.

In France, a dualistic conceptuality stemming from the Enlightenment prevailed that permitted rhetorical rigor and impact but stood in the way of all pragmatic solutions. A *grand bourgeois* could be distinguished from a *petit bourgeois* but not a high *citoyen* from a petty *citoyen*. Semantically, no lasting compromise was possible between the interests of the economic bourgeoisie and the general civil rights that the French Revolution granted to everyone. The revolutions of 1830 and 1848 and the Paris Commune rebellion of 1871 were linguistically preprogrammed, so to speak.

In Germany, because there was only one concept—namely *Bürger*—which gathered together so many different privilege-oriented and estate-based, state, and regional connotations, it was not well suited for producing a homogeneous revolutionary thrust within concrete situations involving action. Just as in 1848, there was barely a geographic center where the revolution could have condensed so there was barely a semantic core around which the demands of the new *Bürger* could have crystallized. The German *Bürger*-concept always remained multivalent and could only develop a comparatively weak political impact.

Finally, in Great Britain, the term "citizen," a concept of expectation connoting democratic and natural rights, played—perhaps surprisingly to continental Europeans—an entirely marginal role. Rather, until far into the nineteenth century, concrete, individual, and corporate concepts of legality from the Middle Ages competed here with an experience-saturated vocabulary of social description that could better justify the claims of the middle classes—for instance, in situations of parliamentary conflict. One after another, however, the advocates for the middle classes were compelled to make semantic compromises in order to both thwart conflicts and allow for measured changes.

Given these findings, a comparative analysis of European *Bürgertümer* runs into considerable difficulties unless one is content with a descriptive inventory of usages.

The investigation of all societal conditions and their transformations remains dependent upon linguistic sources that can bear witness to them.

Thus any comparison must proceed along two avenues. The linguistic witnesses have to be translated in order to be semantically comparable. But at the same time, the social, economic, and political processes deduced from them must be made, for their part, comparable—something not possible without the linguistic pregivens and their translations. To this extent, any comparison depends upon the translatability of diverse, linguistically stored experiences which, as experiences, remain connected to the uniqueness of the language concerned. Methodologically, we are thus faced with an aporetic situation.

Not all conceptualized experiences can be reproduced in other languages by their seemingly corresponding concepts. Any descriptive translation loses the content of experience of the concrete concept. A comparative analysis of the facts relating to the concept can thus only be methodologically verifiable when unintegratable linguistic differentiations are also reflected. Thus, in addition to a social-historical metatheory that enables international comparisons, there also really needs to be a metalanguage that mediates the differences. But there is no such metalanguage. The *Gesellschaft der Bürger* in the nineteenth century was not only a society in transition; it can also only be analyzed and recognized when it is translated interlinguistically and diachronically.

Translated by Todd Presner

13

"Progress" and "Decline"

AN APPENDIX TO THE HISTORY OF TWO CONCEPTS

"Progress" and "Decline"

The following incident is said to have taken place in the 1880s in the small town of Frenke, located on the Weser river. The second to last son of an artisan family had been confirmed. Upon returning home, he received a resounding slap for the last time and was, as a result, allowed to eat dinner sitting at the adults' table. Previously, like all the children, he had to eat while standing up. That was the custom. And now, there took place the incident, which was told to me by the actual person himself who experienced it.[1] He was the youngest member of the family, not yet confirmed, and he, too, was allowed to sit at the adults' table just like his confirmed brother, without incident. When the mother astonishingly asked what this meant, the father said: "That comes from progress."

In vain, the youngster kept his ears open for what that could be, progress? At that time, the town consisted of five owners of full peasant holdings (*Vollmeyerhöfen*), two owners of half-holdings (*Halbmeyerhöfen*), seven artisans, and seven cottagers. However, nobody here knew that answer. And still this word circulated: it may have been a catchword that came from reading books or living in the city; it intersected with the new facts at hand. An old custom was disintegrating. We do not know how the mother characterized the event. If she had had a command of nostalgic, educated language—as was not the case—perhaps she would have employed the concept of "decay" or "decline" to describe, quite differently, the same facts at hand.

Here, we will refrain from suggesting that our story is symptomatic of the long-term process by which the old Europe transformed itself and is still transforming the world of modern industrial societies. We want to ask, first of all, about the employment of the word, about what the usage of the word achieves here.

Obviously, the characterization "that comes from progress" suddenly intervenes in the traditional social structure of an artisan household by moving it into a temporal perspective. Previously, confirmation was treated not only as a religious ritual but also as a social ritual of initiation: now that was changing. The graduation to the adults' table was uncoupled from ecclesiastical tradition. In the past things were done in one way, today in another—that is the minimum relation which our chief witness established with the employment of the word progress. And the overtone that the new behavior is better than the old resounds as well.

But something else was also emphasized: it was not the father's very own deed to fetch the youngest son to the table, but "that comes from progress." Thus the artisan only carried out what was time. The empirical agent of action is exonerated; he consummates a deed whose origin and sense is attributed to progress. The individual deed unveils itself as an event that extends straight through to the agents.

Thus we have gained two criteria for characterizing our linguistic action from the everyday world of around 1890. The first concerns a temporal concept of perspective, and the second is that this concept indicates a transpersonal subject of action. "That comes from progress."

With this, we are already at the center of our investigation. For both conditions—the temporal perspective and the employment of progress as a suprapersonal organ of performance of events—find themselves, once again, on the level of colloquial language as well as on the level of political and scientific language.

In what follows, I will trace the origin and modes of employment of the concept of progress in three stages and, in particular, ask how the concept of decline stood in opposition to it. To anticipate my thesis: in contrast to decline, progress is a modern category whose content of experience and whose surplus of expectation was not available before the eighteenth century. Decline or decay correspondingly change their topological relation in modern times (*Neuzeit*).

It may be indisputably presupposed that progress is a concept specifically calibrated to cope with modern experiences, namely that traditional experiences are surpassed by new ones with astonishing speed. One need only bring to mind the change from the stagecoach to the railway and from the automobile to the jet airplane: through acceleration, the spatial pre-givens in nature have been completely reconfigured anew within the span of one and a half centuries. And with the new forms of movement for human beings, their everyday world has certainly changed, altering their working world and altering their expectations.

But behind the characterization of this technological-social process as "progress" (because of its problematic consequences the term is increasingly employed skeptically), stands a problem of our language concerning political, social, and historical transformations and processes.

"Progress" and "decline" are both terms that are meant to conceptualize transformations of historical time. But considered linguistically, it is always an enormous abstraction when time itself is supposed to be described, for time eludes intuition. Certainly the past can be intuited: wrinkles in the face refer to age and the intensity of work. The height of trees, or the style of buildings, or the kind of cars allows us to recognize past times, beginnings, growth or duration, and decay in a glance. The past can be shown. But already the folding together of the future, the past, and the present, which is pregiven in humans, can no longer be made evident, let alone the future by itself.

This anthropological finding results in the employment of historical terms that are supposed to thematize time. Almost all such terms have to fall back upon natural and spatial background meanings to become comprehensible. "Movement" (*Bewegung*) contains the "way" (*Weg*) laid out, while "progress" (*Fortschritt*) marks the act of spatially stepping forward (*Fortschreiten*) from here to there; in "decay" or "decline," a downward path is indicated; even "revolution" initially had its spatial meaning in the circular orbit of the stars before the term was applied to social and political trends.

As such, the ways of speaking about history, specifically historical time, derive their terminology from the nature of humans and their surroundings. Numerous borrowings come from the spheres of experience prevailing during a given time—from mythology, from the political life of constitutional states, from the church and theology, from technology and the natural sciences—in order to describe historical phenomena. At first, genuinely historical concepts, ones which have to do with historical time, do not exist. It is always a question of metaphors. In the following, we will thus have to pay attention to the metaphorical content of our concepts in order to be able to evaluate the power of their historical expressiveness.

At the start, I simply presupposed that progress is a modern (*neuzeitlich*) concept. My specifically conceptual-historical thesis is now as follows. Progress became a modern concept when it shed or forgot its natural background meaning of stepping through space. The figurative reference faded. Since around 1800, progress has turned into a genuinely historical concept while "decline" and "decay" have not been able to shed their natural and biological background meaning in the same way.

To demonstrate this, we shall first take a look back to antiquity and the Middle Ages.

I

It is trivial to maintain that whenever humans are involved in histories, experiences of transformation or change are to be found, for better or worse, for those affected in a given time. In this sense, there are numerous references from the Greeks and Romans that can characterize a relative progression (*Fortschreiten*) in particular spheres of fact and experience: *prokopē, epidōsis, progressus, profectus*—as well as the opposing indicators of *metabolē* with the trend towards decay, *tarakhē kai kinēsis* in the sense of confusion and destruction, or metaphors of sickness to describe political disintegration.[2]

One need only bring to mind the notion of constitutional cycles with whose help the ups and downs of human self-organization can be described. In this way Polybius, for instance, summarizing Hellenic arguments, described the emergence of three pure forms of government and their subsequent decay over a period of three generations. In this respect, ascension and decline are here two concepts in which one results from the other. Within the same political community of action, we are speaking of *concepts of succession*. And, if two different political communities of action are to be compared, for instance Greece and Rome, then the decline of one can be tied to or contrasted with the rise of the other. Seemingly seldom employed in antiquity, this involved, then, *oppositional concepts* of equal rank. Constitutions always remained in the vicinity of finite, pregiven possibilities stemming from human nature which themselves could not be exceeded (*überschritten*). The only action that appears to be capable of break-

ing through the cycle is the politically admissible mixing of different constitutional elements in order to effect a greater stability. Such mixing prevents standard decline, so to speak; however, it in no way opens up a process of progress leading to a better future. This is something we should
keep in mind when we describe the modern concept of progress later.

Let us proceed with a second reference to classical linguistic usage. In
those places where progress was registered in antiquity, it always concerned
a look back, not an opening up of new horizons. In his famous introduction
to the history of the Peloponnesian wars, Thucydides demonstrates the extent to which the Greeks, thanks to their legal system and to their technological and militaristic expansion of power, distinguished themselves from
the barbarians. Earlier, even the Greeks had lived like the barbarians—carrying weapons during times of peace, raping women, and following more
of the same barbarian customs. Now, in the fifth century, the Greeks had
left these behaviors far behind them. But precisely because of their polis
constitutions, their expanded trade, and their increased potential for power,
they became henceforth capable of waging a civil war against each other,
one whose cruelty and whose expenditure of instruments of power was not
to be outdone by any earlier wars.

From both past history and the comparison with contemporaneously
living barbarians, we thus find, formulated in modern terms, a relative
model of progress that recognizes the uniqueness and singularity of the
level of civilization reached by the Hellenes. But the path does not lead to
the future. The result, namely the civil war, can only be described in the
medical categories of sickness, far removed from a further progress (*Pro-
greß*) opening up into the future. A general, overarching concept is, then,
lacking in Thucydides as well, a concept that might have encapsulated earlier Greek history as a process of progress.

One further reference: in other instances where cases of progress were
noted during antiquity, for instance in science or in the peace achieved by
the Pax Romana throughout the region of the Mediterranean Sea, it was always and only of a partial nature. Progress did not refer to an entire social
process, as we associate it today with technological practices and industrialization, for instance. What eternal Rome's world domination could promise was duration and security but no progress leading to a better future. Indeed, on the contrary, the frequent programs of historical interpretation
during the age of the Caesars measured it in relation to the model of the

past republic. The duration of the empire and its decadence complemented one another so as to betray centuries of experience. That the world was in a state of old age is a late-antique self-interpretation that was conceptualized over and over again by one term: that of the *senectus*.[3] "Decline" was thus better suited to describe an entire societal course, even one of cosmological dimensions, than the variants of a partial advancement.

That went for pagans as well as for Christians. For pious Christians, a new horizon of the future was opened up, namely the expectation of divine Jerusalem; however, this involved a kingdom that would only be realized after the end of history. In this world, they might cling to Rome's duration, or rather that of the Roman Empire, especially since Christianity had become the religion of the empire, and in this, Christians could discern a certain progress in comparison with the time of their persecution. But all that suggested nothing against the actual expectation that the entire world would change with Christ's Second Coming, and that with the Last Judgment, an end would be drawn to previous existence. Thus, also according to the Christian teaching of the interim time between creation and the end of the world, people found themselves, since the coming of Christ, in principle within the last time period, within the last *aetas*, namely the *senectus*, within which nothing else fundamentally new could occur. The biological metaphor of *senectus* could then be understood both in pagan terms—namely, the expectation of a new youth that reopened the cycle everywhere—and as the portent of the end of the world itself and the resurrection of the dead.

In places where theologians spoke of *profectus*, less often of *progressus*, this progress (*Fortschritt*) referred to the soul's salvation.[4] In this way, Augustine, using a biological metaphor, compared the people of God to a human being reared by God. From age to age, the people of God would advance over time—and upon this the metaphor turns—rising from the ephemeral to the experience of the eternal, ascending from the visible to the invisible.[5] This manner of progressing is described again and again by the Church Fathers and Scholastics in such terms as *profectus hominis donum Dei est*,[6] or as Bernard of Clairvaux once preached: *in via vitae non progredi, retrogredi est*. Whoever does not advance, falls back, or: "no one is perfect who does not keep striving for perfection."[7]

Here, we already find that asymmetric relationship prevailing between progress and regression that opposes the eternal alternation of earthly existence to a directed, goal-oriented movement (an opposition that can appear to be a modern one in another context). However, this progress—*profectus* in the direction of *perfectio*—referred to God's kingdom and must not be confused with the temporal kingdom of this world. The way to perfection cannot be counted in years but only in the soul: *perfectio non in annis, sed in animis.*[8]

Quite frequently in linguistic usage during the Middle Ages, it is a question of *correlational concepts*, whose meaning could be derived from the doctrine of two worlds. The doctrine of the two kingdoms, the kingdom of God and that of the world, underwent many metamorphoses over the course of the Middle Ages; however, these metamorphoses only seldom reached so far as to identify progress as an inner-worldly law. On the contrary, for example with Otto of Freising, the aging world falls into ever greater misery—*defectus*—in the same measure as the faithful become certain of their proximity to the coming kingdom of eternal freedom—*perfectio.* With respect to this world, the ascension to perfection and decline, mostly described verbally, were correlational concepts for Otto of Freising: the more misery there is in this world, the nearer the salvation of the elect. However, the future is not the dimension of progress but rather that of the end of the world; signs of it were repeatedly sought and were repeatedly found anew.[9]

To be sure, there were also unique or occasional cases of progress within this world during the Middle Ages as in antiquity: in the sciences or in imperial doctrine regarding the route from East to West, in architecture, in ecclesiastical law, and seen in social terms, briefly in times of peace, too. However, such examples of secular progress did not in any way contradict the fundamental experience that the world as a whole was aging and rushing toward its end. Spiritual progress and the decline of the world were to this extent correlational concepts that obstructed the interpretation of the earthly future in progressive terms.

II

Forgive me for treating two millennia with such freedom here, but it was only with the purpose of allowing that new stage to appear in relief against the background of a different past and of helping bring the modern concept of progress into view. My overview differentiated the modern concept of progress from its original religious meanings, transforming the constant expectation of the end of the world into an open future. In terms of nomenclature, spiritual *profectus* was displaced by or detached from a worldly *progressus.* This process extended throughout early modern times. Although the Renaissance did evoke the consciousness of a new time, this consciousness was not yet that of the progression to a better future as long as the Middle Ages appeared as a dark interim period beyond which antiquity was considered the model. Only the growth of knowledge about nature, by way of which the authority of antiquity was displaced through the autonomous use of reason, opened up—at first only partially—a progressive interpretation of the future. Nature itself would remain the same, but the discovery of it would be methodically driven forward, and thus, so would its increasing domination. Farther-reaching inner-worldly goals, such as a general improvement of life, followed from it, allowing the doctrine of Last Things to be displaced by the gamble of an open future. Since then, past and future differentiate themselves qualitatively from one another and, to this extent, a genuinely historical time is discovered that is finally encapsulated in the term "progress."

If I am now going to trace this formation of the modern concept of progress, I will have to refrain from proceeding from the subjects covered by it, the concept's content of experience. The invention of the printing press; the spread of literacy and reading; the inventions of the compass, telescope, and microscope; the development of the experimental sciences; the discovery of the globe; overseas colonization and the comparison with savages; the conflict of modern art with the old; the rise of the middle class; the development of capitalism and industry; the unleashing of natural forces through technology—all this belongs to the experiences or facts that are always conjured up and tied to the concept of progress and, more than that, to the progression toward something better.

Here, I only want to reconstruct the linguistic formation of the concept, of that concept which finally brought together all these phenomena under a single term—in other words, the experience of a new time condensed into a word.

1. The employment of our term testifies first of all to a *denaturalization of age metaphors.* The increasing age of the world lost its biological-moral sense of decay. The association of a decline dissipated and, with this dissipation, a boundless progress was opened up.

The slow process of becoming conscious of the future can be directly measured by the change in metaphors of growth. Taken literally, every metaphor of natural growth contains the inevitability of eventual decay. Thus whoever takes the category of nature seriously must also—as in antiquity—allow decay to follow from progress. In this respect, the course from youth to old age always excludes the sense of progress to an open future.

At best, a doctrine of rebirth could be connected to the natural metaphorics of youth and old age. Therefore, the cyclical doctrines of antiquity and the Christian teachings about the aging world that remained fixed to the eschatological horizon of expectation could both make use (although in different ways) of comparisons involving age. There are numerous witnesses in the sixteenth and seventeenth centuries who attest to the fact that scholars found themselves searching for an expression of time that broke from the tether of natural meanings. Bacon, for instance, famously denied the authorities of old their standing claim to truth; rather truth itself was a daughter of time. *Veritas filia temporis.*[10] Generally formulated, truth was only recognized and acknowledged to the extent that it entered into the temporal performance of human knowledge—and thus it also became surpassable.

Already widespread in the high Middle Ages, Christian striving for the kingdom of eternal truth crossed into a process of progressing knowledge in this world. This becomes especially clear with Pascal in his tractate on empty space, the *Traité du vide*. In contrast to animals, man, Pascal writes, is always perfecting himself, a being destined to infinity. He is created for infinity, but now already in an ambiguous sense. For infinity is no longer to be considered beyond the realm of human affairs; instead, individual humans learn and, gradually, all humans learn together. They advance more and more in science from day to day such that humanity finds itself entirely within a continuous progress from its youth onwards—in the same measure as the world itself ages. "Tous les hommes ensemble y font un continuel progrez à mesure que l'univers vieillit."[11] From the formerly divine upbringing of the faithful came the self-rearing of all rationally gifted human beings. Infinite progress opened up a future that shirked the natural metaphors of aging. Although the world as nature may age in the course of time, this no longer involves the decline of all of humanity.

Quite openly in 1688, Fontenelle finally repudiated the age comparison because it was no longer suitable for describing progress. Everything in the world pointed to the fact that reason constantly perfected itself. Therefore, reason shares the advantages of youth with the advantages of mature, sensible humans: that is to say, leaving the allegory behind, humans never degenerate.[12]

Leibniz went a step farther and also bypassed the metaphors of aging from the cosmos. For him, continuous progress was not only a product of the human spirit, but it also related to the universe. Happiness, he said, demanded a constant advancement (*Fortgang*) toward ever newer wishes and perfections. For this reason, the universe could never reach a last degree of maturity. As a whole, the universe neither slipped backwards nor aged, *nunquam etiam regreditur aut senescit.*[13] Thus not only humans, but also the entire world, constantly improved, and if there was a regression, then it was only to advance again twice as fast and twice as far after it. In a word: The world is, therefore, the best of all worlds because it is constantly improving: *progressus est in infinitum perfectionis.*[14]

Without wanting to restrict Leibniz in all his multiplicity to this one central thought, it can certainly be said that he anticipated all the positions available in the eighteenth century in order to interpret the newly discovered historical world. During the eighteenth century and in the time since then, it has become a widespread belief that progress is general and constant while every regression, decline, or decay occurs only partially and temporarily. In other words, decline or regression is no longer a pure oppositional concept to advancement or progress. This can be corroborated from numerous authors. One need only mention Turgot, Condorcet, Iselin, Wieland, or Kant, or in the nineteenth century, Engels, Haeckel, or Eduard von Hartmann. With these authors, the asymmetry between progress and decline is no longer related to the next world, on the one hand, and this world, on the other, as in the Christian Middle Ages, but rather progress has become a world historical category whose tendency is to interpret all regressions as temporary and finally even as the stimulus for new progress.

2. In order to characterize the emergence of the new concept more precisely, a second point of view will be introduced: *temporalization*, in a sense that I will have to explain.

Until well into the eighteenth century, people spoke less of "progress" or *"Fortschritte"* than of *perfectio*, or of perfection as the goal to be striven for in the arts, the sciences, and, finally, in all of society. To discover the eternal laws of nature meant to steer toward a finite goal on the basis of which one became capable of mastering nature. Or, to unlock the laws of morality, for instance with mathematical methods, likewise meant reaching a goal on the basis of which human society could then be justly organized. These goals became temporalized in the eighteenth century; that is to say, they became part of the performance of human history. It is evident that here Leibniz's metaphysics had a further effect on many lines of inquiry.

In terms of etymology, it can be shown that "perfection" was slowly displaced and detached from the new concept of *perfectionnement,* for the first time in 1725 by St. Pierre. From "perfection" to *perfectionnement*: from the expression of a goal came a processual category of movement. The emulation of unique perfection was placed in the iterative. As such, Turgot first spoke about the mass of the entire human race marching incessantly toward its completion (*Vollendung*). Then, he corrected himself and spoke of the human race as on its way and hurrying toward a *greater and greater* perfection (*Perfection*), through fortune and despair, tranquillity and disquiet.[15] Anticipating Hegel, Condorcet could finally resolve the logical contradiction, the inconsistency by way of a new concept: the *perfectionnement* of the human race is, at once, the goal (*terme*) and unlimited (*indéfini*). The expression of the goal is included in the process of constant improvement itself. As Condorcet also said: the limits of various forms of progress are themselves only forms of progress.[16] Thus we could describe that temporalization which, in the eighteenth century, encompassed more and more spheres of human experience and expectation. Out of the system of nature comes a history of nature, out of the laws of political order come the laws for their constant improvement. In the words of Lessing: "I believe that the creator had to make everything that he created capable of becoming perfect, if it is supposed to remain in the state of perfection in which he created it."[17] The Christian dictum from the Middle Ages comes to mind: no one is perfect who does not strive for further perfection. This principle, first involving the individual soul, is now transformed. It aims at the earthly future and, while tied back to human consciousness, bestows a direction on history. It is, so to speak, the progress of progress which surpasses any regression. "Progress" becomes a processual concept of reflection.

To use a cliché, one can say that historical time was dynamicized, as it were, when it was discovered as a process. Or, as Kant said: "Creation is never completed. It certainly began on a particular day, but it will never cease."[18] No previous experience could force expectations that were not coming to pass. The experience of the past and the expectation of the future moved apart; they were progressively dismantled, and this difference was finally conceptualized by a common word, "progress."

3. What was previously described as temporalization and as the unlocking of an open horizon of the future was the genesis of a new concept. Perhaps it will be surprising to hear that the word *der Fortschritt* (progress) was only coined in German toward the end of the eighteenth century. We have only used the word here in order to discuss the prehistory of our concept. As we have already seen, the Latin terms *profectus, progressio, progressus,* and other similar variants had existed for a long time. In French, *le progrès* was seldom used in the singular. One mostly spoke of *les progrès* in the plural, of cases of progress in individual sectors. Even Condorcet spoke only of the sum of individual instances of progress, not of *progrès* as such, as its own subject. In English as well, "progress" was used almost exclusively in the plural, like "improvement" or "advancement." Similarly, German usage was very multifarious. With a stronger dependence upon spatial meaning, one still spoke of *Fortgang* (advancement), of *Fortschreiten* or *Fortschreitung* (progression), or one spoke more in the biological metaphorics of *Wachstum* (growth), *Anwachs* (increase), *Zuwachs* (accretion), or more often in a moral meaning, of *Verbesserung* (improvement) or, generally, of *Vervollkommnung* (perfection). However, in all of these cases, a central term is missing that could have brought the various interpretations and nuances of usage under a common concept. Progress (*der Fortschritt*), a term first put forth by Kant, was now a word that neatly and deftly brought the manifold of scientific, technological, and industrial meanings of progress, and finally also those meanings involving social morality and even the totality of history, under a common concept.

"Progress itself" is a *collective singular*. It ties together numerous experiences into a single term. It is one of those collective singulars (they abruptly increased toward the end of the eighteenth century) that condense ever more complex experiences on a higher level of abstraction. In terms of etymology, this involved a process corresponding to the French Revolution in politics and to world commerce and the Industrial Revolution in economics in a way that still has to be investigated.

How progress emerged as a collective singular and since then became a guiding historical concept can be described in formal terms. It came about in three overlapping phases. First of all, the subject of progress was universalized. It no longer referred to a delimitable sphere, such as science, technology, art, etc., any of which were formerly the concrete substratum of particular progressions. Instead, the subject of progress was expanded to become an agent of the highest generality, or one with a forced claim to generality: it was a question of the progress of humanity. At first, "humanity" was not meant as the acting but rather the referential subject, for instance in the sense of those "hypothetical people" to which Condorcet subordinates all individual instances of progress as an intellectually constructed subject. The chosen people of the Judeo-Christian heritage become the hypostasis of progress. Soon one can also speak of the "progress of time" and much later, of "the progress of history."

Thus, out of the histories of individual cases of progress comes the progress of history. This is the second phase. For in the course of the universalization of our concept, subject and object switch their roles. The subjective genitive turns into the objective genitive: In the expression "the progress of time" or "the progress of history," progress assumes the leading role. Progress itself becomes the historical agent. We might recall our opening example, "That comes from progress." Now we can say: the temporal modality shifts to the function of the agent.

Finally, in a third phase, this expression came to stand alone: progress became "progress purely and simply," a subject of itself. While previously one could only speak of the progress of art, of technology, and finally of time or of history, it became common and customary in the nineteenth century to call upon progress by itself. With this, the term turned into a political catchword, a catchword that first had an effect on the formation of political parties and awareness, but that was eventually claimed more and more by all factions. Thus, since the nineteenth century, it has become difficult to gain political legitimacy without being progressive at the same time.

This can be seen, for example, in a Catholic pamphlet from Paderborn in 1877: "The Catholic church is the social-conservative power *par excellence* as well as the creator of freedom and of progress."[19] But I want to forgo pursuing the history of the catchword in the nineteenth century since it had already faded toward the end of the century and in many places fallen into discredit. Rather, in concluding, I want to direct our attention to what actually happened in the conceptual field of decline, of decadence, of decay or of regression.

4. We became acquainted with progress and decline as successive con-

cepts in antiquity and as complementary concepts relating, in uneven ways, to the kingdom of God and to this world during the Middle Ages. In early modern times, regression or decline was obviously mediatized and every set-back was credited to the account of progress. Progress and decline fell into an asymmetric relationship of tension, something that permitted Enlightenment intellectuals to interpret any decay and any detour as a step that would be followed by even more rapid progress. As it is well known, this scheme of thought is still employed today when political ideologies prescribe a linear progress that allows for interruptions but creates political legitimacy through its inexorability. Admittedly, things have not always stuck to this schema. Thus we need only ask—I am thinking of Oswald Spengler's *The Decline of the West*—where every concept of decline, decadence, or even destruction remained.

Decline surfaces again and again as the aporia of progress or as the reproduction of decline through progress itself.

First of all, it must be remembered that many kinds of progress did belong to the experience of the eighteenth century; however, progress itself was in no way the exclusive, overarching concept from which history was understood.

Diderot published his encyclopedia in order to accelerate general enlightenment, but, at the same time, he saw a catastrophe, analogous to the cycles of antiquity, threatening on the horizon. Having organized all knowledge, his encyclopedia was supposed to be a Noah's Ark of *raison* that might salvage all prior knowledge for the coming age.

Even Voltaire, who again and again sought to stimulate the progress of individuals through his sharp criticism of injustices, remained entirely reserved with respect to any optimism. The panorama of history offered him constant ups and downs. In terms of historiography, he granted only four high points to culture—Athens, Augustan Rome, the Renaissance, and the age of Louis XIV—high points that were always followed by decline. His *Candide* completely demolishes any progressive-mindedness like that offered by Leibniz's metaphysics.

Neither Diderot nor Voltaire were dogmatists of a linear progress, nor were they even dogmatists of a discontinuous progress. Too many opposing experiences, not to mention their classical education through which they processed their experiences, stood in their way.

Rousseau's achievement was to bring progress and decline under a new complementary formula suited to grasp many phenomena of our modernity (*Neuzeit*). In both of his *Discourses*, he thematized the contradictions which for him seemed to prevail between the progressive development of art and science on the one side and morals and their decay on the other side, or the correlation between the progress of civilization on the one side and growing political inequality on the other. To explain this tension, Rousseau coined a new term, *perfectibilité*, clumsily translated into German as *Vervollkommnungsfähigkeit* or as *Vervollkommlichkeit*, or simply Germanized as *Perfektibilität*. As Novalis said: "Humans are differentiated from all other creatures of nature by (rapid) progression (*Progressivität*) or perfectibility (*Perfektibilität*)."[20]

The ability to perfect oneself, perfectibility, was for Rousseau the criterion that differentiated individual human beings as well as the entire *genus humanum* from animals. This perfectibility was not an empirical-historical determination but rather an anthropological, that is to say, meta-historical category. It specified the basic definition of a human as a historical being, the condition of all possible history. Humans are condemned to progress, to direct all their energies at mastering the powers of nature, to bring the pillars of civilization into their everyday life, to organize themselves politically in order to be able to live, and to develop their industry through the growing employment of reason. But this summation of progress is only one side of the balance sheet. The other side reads: loss of natural innocence, decay of morals, instrumentalization of language at the cost of the unity of feeling and reason. Progress thus produces decadence. But it is not my purpose here to work through the culture-critical or neurotic components of Jean-Jacques Rousseau.

What should become clear is that perfectibility (*Perfektibilität*) is a temporal compensatory concept. With their perfectibility (*Vervollkommnungsfähigkeit*), human beings are constantly capable of, even condemned to producing, steady decay, corruption, and crime. Moreover, if progress is already irreversible, something which Rousseau had accepted, then a gap opens up over time. The more humans are required to perfect themselves in civilization, the greater their chances of losing their integrity.[21]

Thus Rousseau set up a consciously hypothetical cognitive model, one which is certainly suitable for understanding the many experiences of modernity in our own time. It was precisely progress that reproduced the phenomena of decay that are part and parcel of it. And the more violent the progress—one need only to think of atomic energy and the atomic bomb, of gas and gassing—the greater the human capability to realize catastrophes.

Kant, too, took this into account when he considered progress a moral task and derived from it the idea that humanity will progress for the better because it is supposed to progress. The thesis of continuous decline, that the world is speeding toward its end in an accelerating descent, is not, according to Kant, to be substantiated because in that case, we would have long since been destroyed. Quite the opposite: the infinite view into the future is unhindered by any obstructions. However, with this, the view of *an infinite succession of evil* presents itself, something that Kant never conceals from himself.[22] To this extent, Kant also remains indebted to Rousseau.

Rousseau's quixotic nature qualified him as the first to recognize the aporia of progress. Precisely because and so long as progress is unfinished, the chances of decay increase—admittedly, no longer read in natural metaphorics but rather in the sense of catastrophes that human beings have become capable of bringing about for themselves with the technological powers at their disposal.

It was another outsider, namely Nietzsche, who probed the aporetic structure of progress as originally and provocatively as did Rousseau. "Progress" and "regression" served as diagnostic categories for Nietzsche. At the same time, he unmasked them as historical and perspectival illusions if only "to implant into that which is degenerate and desires to die a longing for the end."[23] But we will break off at this point[24] and take a look back.

The concept of progress brought about its historically unique achievement. For in it is contained the idea that following industrialization and the growth of technology, the conditions of our prior experience will never suffice to predict coming surprises and innovations. Since the eighteenth century, progress produces a necessity for planning but its goals must be constantly redefined as a result of the steady influx of new factors. The concept of progress encompasses precisely that experience of our own modernity: again and again, it has yielded unforeseeable innovations that are incomparable when measured against anything in the past. Taking this into account has itself become an element of the concept of progress so that it has already gained a stabilizing, conservative field of meaning within modernity. The faith in progress as always leading onward became, so to speak, outmoded, without thereby becoming completely unjustified.

Of course, the concept distinguished itself foremost by thematizing the uniqueness of change. The transformation of the agrarian dominated world of the estates with its recurring famines into a modern, technologically shaped industrial society was unique when seen with respect to all previous history. With increasing speed, new spaces were opened up, not only across the globe but above all in the mobility between places and in the social improvement of the masses, in the increase in consumption and comfort for almost everyone. Finally, life expectancy increased on average nearly threefold from that of the Middle Ages.

But staggered spatially and temporally, all this applies in different ways. The phenomena of indisputable progress that were mentioned above remain unequally distributed in terms of class and, up until now, remain limited to the areas along the Atlantic, to Europe and North America, and occasionally additional territories such as Japan and other regions within the remaining continents. The greater part of the world is scarcely affected, or only negatively, by this progress.

In terms of power politics, an opposing account can be quickly proposed. The relations between political units of action in our world can hardly be understood linearly on the scale of a singular progression. The shrinkage of the formerly centralized European power base has allowed stark disproportions to emerge between civilizing progress and political potency. Here, a discrepancy emerged, diagnosed in 1919 by Paul Valéry with extraordinary clarity. Formerly the model and forerunner of all progress, Europe has seen its position of leadership deteriorate. And the question arises as to whether the imperial self-destruction of the European great powers will not repeat itself on a global scale so that here, too, the conditions of possible progression will simultaneously also prove to be their obstruction.

If one leaves aside the spatially staggered gradient of heretofore differing rates of progress, the immanent opposing account first proposed by Rousseau always still remains. The possibilities of effecting mass death through technology have risen alongside the civilizing gains—and have been already realized, regardless of the further threat of ABC weapons.

Thus we still have the chance to look back at the experiences of earlier times in order to historically relativize progress from the perspective that we have learned. The knowledge that for identical units of action a decline follows every rise is already an unsurpassed formulation of antiquity; furthermore, with different units of action, the rise of one implies the decline of the other. But even the Christian interpretation of *profectus*—exchanging all the chaos of the world for mental composure and poise—cannot be refuted for the people involved.

Hence, the following conclusion is unavoidable. The progress of modernity, despite its universal claim, reflects only a partial, self-consistent experience and, instead, masks or obscures other modes of experience for understandable reasons. Obviously, there are long-term structures that persist across human history without being affected by technologically and industrially determined progress at all.

This can already be demonstrated from the discussions among progressives (*Progressisten*) since the seventeenth century. In particular, as soon as our category was filled with meaning, a discrepancy was already discovered to exist between the technological progress of civilization and the moral stance of humans. It was noticed again and again that morality hobbled along behind technology and its development. Hobbes took this as his starting point when he directed all of his efforts at finding rules, even for the state, which would be as certain as geometry. Kant took it as his starting point that civilization had already progressed to excess, while humans, as moral beings, could only reduce this lead with great effort and that they must do so quickly if they wanted to adapt morality to the status of technical knowledge. Even in the nineteenth century, it was customary to assert that technology and industry were rushing forward at a geometrical rate but that morality was only hobbling along at an arithmetical rate. It is this difference, evidently belonging to progress right from the beginning, which constitutes the following aporia: progress itself cannot catch up with what it has triggered; or in other words, the planning of progress can never keep to that direction in which "progress itself" is carried out over the heads of those involved.

Translated by Todd Presner

Some Questions Regarding the Conceptual History of "Crisis"

Whoever opens the newspaper today comes across the term "crisis." The concept indicates insecurity, misfortune, and test, and refers to an unknown future whose conditions cannot be sufficiently elucidated. A French lexicon pointed this out in 1840.[1] Even today, the situation is no different. Its inflationary usage covers almost all aspects of life: domestic politics and foreign policy, culture, economics, theology, and religion, all the humanities and social sciences, as well as the natural sciences, technology, and industry, provided these are understood as parts of our political and social system, as indispensable elements of our life-world (*Lebenswelt*). If this ever-accumulating word usage is an adequate sign for an actual crisis, then we must live in an all-embracing crisis. However, this conclusion attests more to a diffuse manner of speaking than it contributes to the diagnosis of our situation.

In the following discussion, I will try to separate out several structural features of the term in the medium of conceptual history. This may contribute to strengthening the power of arguments by making them more precise. In so doing, I will first give an overview of the history of the concept; secondly, I will sketch a semantic model for focusing the modern use of the word; and, thirdly, I would like to newly pose several questions that arise out of the relationship between Christian tradition and the modern language of concepts.

I. Conceptual-Historical Overview

"Crisis" belongs among the fundamental concepts, that is to say, ir-replaceable concepts, of the Greek language. Derived from *krinō*, to cut, to select, to decide, to judge; by extension, to measure, to quarrel, to fight—"crisis" aimed at a definitive, irrevocable decision. The concept implied strict alternatives that permitted no further revision: success or failure, right or wrong, life or death, and finally, salvation or damnation.

In the field of power politics, the concept implied—according to Thucydides—decisive battles determining the outcome of war, four of which would have decided the great Persian War. In so arguing, Thucydides already places the battles (as Montesquieu later does) into the general background conditions which first made it possible that four battles could become decisive for the outcome of war.

For the Hippocratic school, the concept involved the critical phase of a sickness in which the battle between life and death was definitively settled, in which the decision was due but not yet made.

In the sphere of politics—according to Aristotle—it had to do with the enforcement of law or the legal findings that all citizens were called to be involved in, but it also concerned political decisions that ought to pre-condition all required legal judgment.

In theology, specifically since the New Testament, *krisis* and *judicium* both gain a new and, to a certain extent, unsurpassable meaning taken up from legal language: the judgment before God. This might be that *crisis* meant the Last Judgment at the end of time, or the judgment that appeared with Christ's Second Coming through the light that he brought to this world, something that would already be present to all believers during their lifetimes.

Thus the concept potentially registered all the decision situations of inner and outer life, of individual humans and their communities. It was always a question of definitive alternatives about which an appropriate judgment had to be passed and whose alternative consummation was also determined by and in connection with the particular issues themselves.

It was a concept that always posited a temporal dimension, which, parsed in modern terms, actually implied a theory of time. Be it that the right point in time must be met for successful action, be it that the ruling order was stabilized through legal preservation or legal finding, or be it that medical judgment—according to Galen—had to diagnose the correct temporal phase of the progression of a sickness in order to be able to risk making a prognosis. Or be it in theology that God's message is accepted in order to—according to John—*hic et nunc* escape damnation, despite the still pending Last Judgment toward which the cosmos moved and whose arrival still remained veiled in darkness.

"Crisis" pointed toward the pressure of time, so to speak, which constituted the understanding of the sense of the concept. The knowledge of uncertainty and the compulsion toward foresight were part of almost every mention of crisis in order to prevent disaster or to search for salvation. In so doing, the particular temporal spans were delimited in varying ways according to the spheres of life thematized.

From antiquity to early modern times, word and concept endured in the Latin language: *crisis* in medical fields, *judicium* or *judicium maximum* in theology. Thomas Aquinas differentiated, for example, in his *Compendium Theologiae* (c. 242) three temporal phases of judgment practiced by the Son of God: the judgment exerted over human beings during the course of their lives; judgment at the hour of their death; and, lastly, the final judgment after the Second Coming of Christ. The conceptual history of "crisis" took place in terms of the language of institutions, so to speak, bound to the church or various university faculties. Since the adoption of the Greek word into European vernaculars—toward the end of the Middle Ages—its gradual and increasing dissemination can be registered. The concept encompasses more and more spheres of life: politics, psychology, the evolving economy, and, finally, newly discovered history. One can venture that the concept of "crisis" even contributed to establishing these fields as autonomous disciplines.

The medical usage of the word first acted as the influence behind its spread. The use of figures of speech drawn from the body for the life of states may have fostered the medical metaphor. It served to diagnose sickness or health and predict life or death.

In the eighteenth century, the concept certainly became freestanding. The reference to the medical sense was now consciously apostrophized as a metaphor, as with Rousseau. In Germany, for instance, there was talk about the crisis of the German Reich system, in which the federal structure of the constitution was criticized because its internal rules no longer sufficed to stabilize the Reich. Therefore, a special Fürstenbund was to be established from which the formulations of the 1785 preamble stemmed.

To this extent, "crisis" followed a career similar to that of "revolution" or "progress." Both of the latter turned into temporal concepts, and their initial spatial or natural meaning dissipated with the Enlightenment as they became primarily historical concepts. This can be shown, for example, with Leibniz who saw a new world constellation of power beckoning with the rise of the Russian Empire during the Northern War: "Momenta temporum pretiosissima sunt in transitu rerum. Et l'Europe est maintenant dans un état de changement et dans une crise où elle n'a jamais été depuis l'Empire de Charlemagne."[2] The concept moved toward a historico-philosophical dimension, and even more than this, it opened up this dimension and occupied it to an ever greater extent in the course of the eighteenth century. "Crisis" becomes a fundamental historico-philosophical concept on the basis of which the claim is made that the entire course of history can be interpreted out of its diagnosis of time. Since then, it is always one's own particular time that is experienced as crisis. And reflection upon the particular temporal situation disposes one to both a knowledge of the entire past and a prognosis of the future.

At least since the French Revolution, "crisis" turned into a central *interpretament* for both political and social history. The same goes for the long-term Industrial Revolution, which was accompanied and influenced by a scientifically differentiated doctrine of crises and economic activity.

It is certainly striking that no explicit theory of crisis was developed for the overall historical conceptualizations, as opposed to the economic system, of the nineteenth century. Jacob Burckhardt is the sole exception. And even Marx, who tried to connect his economic theory to a philosophy of history, became mired in developing a theory of crisis, something which Schumpeter—in reference to this concept—expressly renounced. Even in the twentieth century, theories of crisis are restricted to specialized scientific spheres like psychiatry or political science. Global theories of crisis, like those on which the philosophy of history in the eighteenth and nineteenth centuries was implicitly based, quickly come to be regarded as dubious nowadays because they cannot be sufficiently confirmed or empirically substantiated. With this, we will now turn toward the semantics of crisis as a fundamental historical concept.

II. Three Semantic Models

While the medical meaning of "crisis" originally shaped the political deployment of the word, numerous theological elements now began to feed into this fundamental historical concept. This was already the case with the language of the English Civil War from 1640 to 1660. It was likewise the case with the historically and philosophically reflected linguistic usage that became generally accepted since the late Enlightenment. The associative power of both God's judgment and the Apocalypse constantly contributed to the use of the word such that no doubt can be raised as to the theological origin of the new form of the concept. Not least of all, this is proven by the fact that historico-philosophical diagnoses of crises often operate within rigid compulsory alternatives which preclude a differentiated diagnosis but which appear to be all the more effective and plausible because of their prophetic associations.

The following outline of three semantic models accepts the risk of inappropriately simplifying the historical facts concerning the usage of the concept. The three semantic options can be stated as follows.

First, history can be interpreted as a permanent crisis. World history is the judgment of the world. It is, then, a question of a concept of trial (*Prozeßbegriff*).

Secondly, "crisis" can characterize a singular, accelerating process in which many conflicts, bursting the system apart, accumulate so as to bring about a new situation after the crisis has passed. "Crisis," then, indicates the crossing of an epochal threshold, a process that can repeat itself *mutatis mutandis*. Even if history always remains unique in individual cases, this concept attests to the possibility that the thrusts of change can take place in analogous forms. Therefore, I will suggest characterizing it as an iterative periodizing concept.

Thirdly, "crisis" can mean purely and simply the final crisis of all history that precedes it, where proclamations of the Last Judgment are everywhere employed, but only metaphorically. When measured with respect to the prior course of our history, it can no longer be excluded that this model, necessarily characterized as utopian, has every chance of being realized in light of present-day means of self-destruction. In contrast to the others, this concept of crisis is a purely future-oriented one and aims at a final decision.

These models do not actually appear in philosophical-historical or theoretical-historical language in a pure form but rather support one another and become mixed together in different proportions. Despite their theological impregnation, what is common to all three models is that they make the claim to offer historically immanent patterns of interpretation for crises that are theoretically able to do without the intervention of God.

Let me follow up with some clarification of the three fundamental semantic positions.

1. "World history is the judgment of the world" is a dictum of Schiller's[3] and was promoted as a motto, so to speak, for modernity (*Neuzeit*). Seemingly by chance, the phrase came up in a love poem where Schiller laments a missed opportunity. "What one has missed in one minute / No eternity gives back."[4] Formally, this concerns the temporalization of the Last Judgment which is always and constantly enforced. It has a pronounced anti-Christian thrust because all guilt mercilessly enters into the personal life of the individual, into the history of political communities, into world history in its entirety. This model is compatible with fate, which in Herodotus appears behind all individual histories and which can be read again and again as the consummation of a world-immanent justice. However, Schiller's dictum raises a greater claim. An inherent justice, one which acquires almost a magical air, is not only required of individual histories but of all world history in toto. Logically, every injustice, every incommensurability, every unatoned crime, every senselessness and uselessness is apodictically excluded. Thus the burden of proof for the meaning of this history increases enormously. It is no longer historians who, because of their better knowledge, believe themselves to be able to morally judge the past ex post facto, but rather it is assumed that history, as an acting subject, enforces justice. Hegel took it upon himself to settle the moral discrepancies and shortcomings resulting from this dictum. His world history remains the judgment of the world because the world spirit or the thoughts of God are realized in it in order to achieve their identity. Seen theologically, it is a question of the last imaginable heresy which wants to fully reckon with a Christian interpretation of history.

But Schiller's dictum could be henceforth easily applied, provided history was interpreted as a world-immanent trial. Because liberals could derive a moral legitimacy for their action from it, they never became tired of appealing to this interpretation. But even Darwinian and imperialistic philosophies of history could easily take up this interpretation because success, survival of the fittest, redeemed the claim to historical legitimacy—up until Hitler's sentimental repudiation of self-pity: those who drown, in all fairness, deserve it.

There are semantic options whose consequences can in no way be attributed to their authors. Whoever tries to trace Hitler back to Hegel or Schiller succumbs to a claim to be able to chart influences through history, one that proceeds in a selective manner. World history as the judgment of the world implies foremost and above all the statement that every situation is marked by the same urgent sense of decision.

In this sense, Schiller's dictum was also theologically adaptable, for instance when Richard Rothe proclaimed in 1837: "All of Christian history is a great and continual crisis of humankind";[5] or when Karl Barth stripped this perpetual crisis of all final or teleological overtones in order to interpret it existentially: "So-called 'salvation history' is but the ongoing crisis of all of history, not a history in or next to history."[6] Here, as a concept, "crisis" lost its apocalyptic or transitional meaning—it turns into a structural category of Christianly understood history pure and simple; eschatology is, so to speak, historically monopolized.

2. Theoretically less demanding is an understanding of "crisis" as an iterative periodizing concept. It asks about the conditions of possible courses of history in order to be able to work out commonalities and differences based on their comparability. The semantic model does not make the claim to interpret history as a whole or permanently. Jacob Burckhardt, for example, was able to isolate anthropological constants that made possible varying courses of crises in their particular historical articulations. He defined the period of the barbarian invasions as a historically unique crisis which, not least of all, furthered the emergence of a church with universal claims. Next to this, he only allowed modernity (*Neuzeit*) to be considered as a permanent crisis with an open end. Ultimately, behind all other crises, he discovered more continuities than those involved at a particular time perceived and were ready to admit.

Here the economic concept of crisis can also be mentioned. Economic models of crisis are based on the equilibrium metaphorics of the eighteenth century which, empirically, can never be completely confirmed. Roughly said, crises always surface when the balance between supply and demand, between production and consumption, between the circulation of money and the circulation of goods is disturbed to such an extent that recessions and deterioration become visible everywhere. At the same time, however, previous experience teaches us that a general increase in productivity always follows a crisis. The paradox of this doctrine of crisis seems to consist in the fact that a balance can only be preserved or regained when productivity increases steadily and does not, for instance, stagnate: for, at such times, regression would appear to be inevitable. In this respect, this model hitherto requires progress, without which it would not be empirically provable. As Molinari, an economic theorist of the nineteenth century, said: "Every small or large progress possesses its crisis."[7] That crises are the generators of progress seems to me to be a semantic model that has been confirmed up until now only in the spheres of economics, natural sciences, technology, and industry. I will spare myself citations illustrating the application of the model to the whole history of humanity. Their number is enormous. Instead, one reference may stand for them all: "Out of every crisis mankind rises with some greater share of knowledge, higher decency, purer purpose."[8] These words were spoken by Franklin D. Roosevelt shortly before his death. Proceeding from the semantic option, the question must be posed as to whether "progress" is the guiding concept for "crisis" or whether the iterative periodizing concept of "crisis" is the true guiding concept under which "progress" is also subsumed. If, as an iterative periodizing concept, "crisis" may make claims to a greater explanatory power, then "progress"—which undoubtedly exists—could be admitted in its relative right.

3. *Crisis as a final decision.* That the crisis in which one currently finds oneself could be the last, great, and unique decision, after which history would look entirely different in the future—this semantic option is taken up more and more frequently the less the absolute end of history is believed to be approaching with the Last Judgment. To this extent, it is a question of recasting a theological principle of belief. It is expected of world-immanent history itself. Several witnesses can be cited. Robespierre saw himself as the enforcer of a moral justice whose final breakthrough would be obtained by violence, not will. In regard to the crisis of the American and French revolutions, Thomas Paine believed that the future harbored an absolute turning point. Even initial partisans of the French Revolution who became embittered opponents of its Bonapartist consequences could maintain this

semantic option. One need only name Friedrich Schlegel, Fichte, or Ernst Moritz Arndt from the German-speaking lands. The absolute nadir of history guarantees the change toward salvation. In France, the birth of sociology out of the spirit of the revolution (not just the Restoration) can be mentioned. St. Simon or Auguste Comte saw themselves as living during the "grande crise finale": through scientific planning and an increase in industrial productivity, it would be possible to pass through and overcome it. Lorenz von Stein can also be mentioned here. He saw the last chance to save Europe from slipping back into barbarism in the balance between capital and labor. Here, Karl Marx is stuck, so to speak, in an in-between position. On the one hand, he was completely convinced that the final crisis of capitalism would bring about the withering away of the state and the eradication of class differences in the future; on the other hand, he did not see himself in a position to interpret the crises of capitalism as necessitating the inevitable scuttling—as opposed to the conserving—of the system.

On the one side, he operated with a concept of crisis immanent to the system while he expounded the iterative structure of economic crises. On the other side, he knew of a concept of crisis destroying the system which he derived from other premises, making it possible to see world history drifting toward a last great crisis. The supposedly final struggle between the proletariat and the bourgeoisie is, without doubt, consummated for Marx in the dimensions of a Last Judgment, which he did not succeed in defining on purely economic grounds. With this, I come to my conclusion.

III. "Crisis" as a Question Posed to the Christian Tradition

The assumption that every crisis is a final decision is easily revealed as a perspectival illusion. It is part of human mortality to view our own particular situation as more important and to take it more seriously than all preceding situations have ever been. However, one should be on the guard against dismissing this hyperbolic self-estimation—especially in light of the doctrine of the Last Judgment—as only a perspectival fallacy. Precisely when safeguarding survival is at stake, it could be that many decisions prove to be final decisions. As in the Greek sense of a compulsion to judge and act under the pressure of time, "crisis" remains a necessary concept even under the complex conditions of modern society. I would like to explain this with a historical thought experiment.

In Christian teaching, before the end of the world arrives, God is said to make time pass by more quickly. Behind this teaching stands the cosmological idea that God, as master of times, could bring about the planned end of the world earlier than scheduled and, in fact, would do so for the sake of the elect whose suffering would be alleviated (Mark 13:20, Matthew 24:22). Of course, one might psychologize or ideologize this mythological language of apocalyptic expectation. Within this belief in the imminent foreshortening of time, it is not difficult to see the wish of the suffering and the oppressed to exchange misery as fast as possible for paradise. However, if one observes the topos of the eschatological foreshortening of time in terms of its historical interpretations, one arrives at the astonishing finding that from the initially suprahistorical foreshortening of time came a gradual acceleration of history itself. Luther, for example, strongly believed that God would foreshorten time before the unknown end of the world. But he no longer believed years would turn into months, months into weeks, and weeks into days before the eternal light would negate the difference between day and night; instead, he already interpreted the foreshortening of time historically: events themselves, with the disintegration of the church rapidly rushing onward, were for him a harbinger of the coming end of the world. The burden of proof for the engulfing Last Judgment was no longer summed up in the mythological imagination that time itself is able to be foreshortened, but rather it was expected from empirically observable historical events as such. From an entirely different perspective, the history of discoveries in the natural sciences was analogously interpreted. For Bacon, it was still a principle of expectation and hope that inventions would occur at shorter and shorter intervals so as to be able to better and better master nature. From this, the cognoscenti of early modern times, for instance Leibniz, concluded that world-immanent progress was accelerating faster and faster and would lead to a better world order. From the apocalyptic foreshortening of time came the acceleration of historical progress. The contents of the interpretative pattern were completely interchanged. The attainability of paradise only after the end of the world and its attainability already in this world logically excluded one another.

Yet the cosmic foreshortening of time, which formerly was supposed to precede the Last Judgment, did not rob the concept of crisis of its sense. Even the acceleration of the modern world, the reality of which is not to be doubted, can be comprehended as crisis. Obviously, decisions are due, scientific or not, wanted or unwanted, which will determine whether and how survival on this earth is possible or not. The cosmic foreshortening of time, which was formerly supposed to precede the Last Judgment in mythic language, can today be empirically verified as the acceleration of historical sequences of events. In Jacob Burckhardt's words: "The process of the world (*Weltprozeß*) suddenly assumes a dreadful rapidity; developments that used to require centuries appear in months and weeks, passing by like fleeting phantoms and, with their passing, vanish."[9] The generic concept for the apocalyptic foreshortening of time that precedes the Last Judgment, and for historical acceleration, is "crisis." Should that only be a linguistic accident? In Christian and in non-Christian usage, "crisis" indicates in every case a growing pressure of time that appears inescapable to humanity on this earth.

Therefore, in concluding, a temporal hypothesis can be offered that is not new at all. Considered from the standpoint of today, the previous history of humanity can be represented by three exponential time curves. Measured with respect to five billion years, the time that it took for the earth to be covered with a solid crust, one billion years of organic life is a short time span. But still much shorter is the time span of ten million years during which there have presumably been humanoid creatures, and only for the past two million years can artificial tools be shown to have been used.

The second exponential time curve can be drawn within the two million years during which humans distinguish themselves by using artificial tools. The first record of genuine art, so to speak, is thirty thousand years ago, the origin of agriculture and the breeding of livestock is around ten thousand years ago. And measured with respect to the two million years of self-productivity, the approximately six thousand years of urban high culture with written communication symbols is a short time span. And philosophy, poetry, and the writing of history have only taken place in an even shorter span.

The third exponential time curve begins to emerge when one proceeds from the organization of state-like high cultures that came into existence only six thousand years ago. Measured with respect to their comparatively continuous history, modern industrial society grounded in science and technology has only unfolded in the last three hundred years. The acceleration curve can be demonstrated by three series of data. The transmission of news has accelerated in a way that has practically led to the identity of the event and news of it. Transportation has also accelerated tenfold: natural means such as wind, water, and animals have been displaced by technical devices like steam engines, electric motors, and internal combustion engines. The acceleration of the means of communication has made the earth shrink to the size of a spaceship. At the same time, the increase in the population has resulted in an analogous exponential time curve: at about a half billion in the seventeenth century, the population of the world has grown, despite all mass annihilations, to 2.5 billion human beings in the middle of our century, and already approaches eight billion at the end of the twentieth century.

The three exponential time curves might be dismissed as mere number play. However, a limit obviously begins to emerge that can no longer be overstepped by technological and scientific progress. Moreover, there is the fact that in the same exponential time curve, the power for the self-destruction of autonomous humanity has multiplied.

So, the question can be raised as to whether our semantic model of crisis as final decision has gained more chances of realization than it has ever had before. If this is the case, everything would depend upon directing all our powers toward deterring destruction. The catechon is also a theological answer to crisis.

The three exponential time curves can be read as an amplifier for acceleration, rendering it completely impossible to venture projections into the future. Perhaps the answer to crisis consists in looking out for stabilizers which can be derived from the long duration of prior human history. It could be that this question allows itself to be formulated not only historically and politically but also theologically.

Translated by Todd Presner

15

The Limits of Emancipation

A CONCEPTUAL-HISTORICAL SKETCH

> You know how servants are: without a master
> They have no will to labor, or excel.
> For Zeus who views the wide world takes away
> Half the manhood of a man, that day
> He goes into captivity and slavery.[1]

The virtue of a man is cut in half by servitude. With these words, Odysseus's faithful swineherd, Eumaeus, described the state of affairs which has, since then, shaped world history in multiply changing forms. A slave is only half a human being, inasmuch as human beings have a need for domination. Or vice versa: the slave, subservient to a master, becomes a half-human. Although the quantifying statements can vary, they are not merely to be understood metaphorically.

In the early Middle Ages, depending on gender or degree of freedom, the wergild[2] of an unfree person only amounted to a third or a half of what a free man was entitled to. Likewise, an oath taken by a noble outweighed the oaths of several serfs. In 1787, when the founders of the American constitution failed to manumit the slaves, the voting power of a slave counted as three-fifths of that of their owners (Article I, section 2). And in Prussia, when compulsory services and serfdom were abolished, the liberal school argued that the work output of those liberated would increase by a factor of two-thirds to one. The doctrine of surplus value appropriated by capitalist exploiters can be situated within this series of quantifying statements.

Whether a slave is classified as half, two-thirds, or three-fifths of a human being, whether slaves are completely deprived of their humanity, or whether they are, as slaves, counted as chattel—irrespective of profound historical changes, the structural finding remains the same: human beings owned by other human beings do not count as entirely human. This sort of calculation is the case regardless of whether the intended result was considered necessary and positive or arbitrary and negative.

Generally speaking, it can be said that in view of the prevailing forms of power (*Herrschaftsformen*), the legality of ruling (*Herrschaft*) was not fundamentally contested until the eighteenth century. Of course, despite general consent, the relation between master and slave in terms of its infinite possibility of gradation was seldom accepted in theory without modifications. Stoicism and Christianity, through their doctrines of inner freedom to which all human beings equally have a right or are accorded through faith, also made possible an allowance for slavery, servitude, and subordination of all types. This allowance might have influenced the relationship between master and slave in some places, for instance under feudalism, but this was certainly not the case everywhere. No theological or moral doctrine of inner freedom, of the equality of all human beings before God, or of their equality given by nature ever questioned indentured labor, serfdom, servitude, or slavery as institutions—all of which spread in the most terrible way in the early modern period (*frühe Neuzeit*). De la Boétie is probably the first modern thinker who wanted to show by reference to the element of free will (*Freiwilligkeit*) in every system of servitude that it could also be abolished by free will (*freie Willen*) (1577).

This leads us to another type of argumentation that could be characterized as a doctrine of inversion. It infers a better-grounded system of ruling from the well-understood system of servitude: whether Diogenes assigned to each lord his own slave as the actual master; or whether priests, as slaves to God, claimed to be the supreme rulers in this world or sought to indirectly control power; or whether since Diderot and Hegel, slaves themselves have acquired true power over time because slaves, through their work and reflection, make the masters subordinate and rob them of their function. Thus, for a while, the mutual recognition is forced, and, later, the dissolution of all personal subordination into social functions becomes conceivable. Only since the Enlightenment does the challenge of emancipation emerge, demanding the fundamental eradication of domination by humans over humans.

Only since the Enlightenment does the privilege of exercising power over human beings, a privilege previously limited only to free citizens or lords, become a general right: that rule could henceforth only be self-rule by mature human beings (first men and, then later, women too) over themselves. Out of what was earlier only applied as an ethical principle of self-rule comes a political demand: namely, that inner freedom can only exist if it is also realized outwardly.

What is new about the Enlightenment position is that it no longer permits a way out: neither in the isolated interior nor in a world beyond, two authorities that until then might have worked in a compensatory fashion for either servitude or ignominy that was suffered. This does not mean that these authorities are not applicable to humans in our century. On the contrary, they are strategically omitted or abolished in places where the demand for a complete and total liberation of human beings from human rule is posited. The burden of proof for such a demand—free from logical self-contradictions and morally comprehensible—shifted in the course of the eighteenth century from its contextual grounding in natural law toward a historical future that had been blocked by all previous experience. The transformation from personal rule into rational custodianship may be empirically demonstrated: such an expected, contested, and anticipated liberation of human beings from human subordination, in other words, their redemption within history or the negation of alienation, had hitherto never occurred. Thus I arrive at the point: since the eighteenth century, emancipation turned from a European challenge into a world historical challenge.

I will treat this subject in two stages. First, I will offer a conceptual-historical sketch by reconstructing the meaning and diffusion of meaning of *emancipatio*. Secondly, I will attempt to draw several systematic conclusions from the conceptual history.

I. On the Historical Semantics of "Emancipation"

In the Roman Republic, *emancipatio*, derived from *e manu capere*, described the legal act by which a *paterfamilias* could release his son from paternal power. With this act, the son completely left the family and became, in terms of civil law, *sui juris*. A son who was not yet emancipated still possessed civil rights, the right to trade, and the privilege of marriage —only he was not yet entitled to the power of discretion over property. A legal claim for him to free himself from the father's power did not exist.

Over the course of the late Republic and the imperial period, the rigidity of possible discharge from the power of the patriarchal house became more and more lenient through administrative acts that facilitated the formation of one's own familia.

In the Middle Ages, this technical legal term was also used in the field of German common law. When one reached the age of maturity, when one got married, when one reached economic independence, or gained positions of rank and distinction, civil independence was achieved automatically, so to speak. Thus the term lost the specific meaning from Roman law of a unilateral legal act on the part of the *paterfamilias* and became generally used to designate the naturally attainable state of having come of age and maturity, at the latest after twenty-five years. The linguistic usage became elastic. For instance, only prematurely granted release was characterized as emancipation (or also as *manumissio*, which originally referred only to the release of slaves), while, around 1700, the state of independence thereby already reached could also be described as emancipation. The Roman legal meaning thus lost its conceptual monopoly. The idea that emancipation would arrive automatically when the age of maturity, and hence the status of being legal, was naturally reached already belonged to the principles of numerous doctrines on natural law prior to the Enlightenment. This line of argumentation, from natural pregivens to the status of being legal, remained part of the term from then on.

The actually prevailing differences of rank and legal status—with their dependence on the manor lord or feudal law, or with their estate privileges that extended to the entire political, economic, and social system—could not really be affected by emancipation until the eighteenth century. Any emancipation, whether it was effected unilaterally or arrived naturally, presupposed domination (*Herrschaft*). And so it is not by chance that during the late Middle Ages the term *Knecht* (vassal), at first signifying someone who was still naturally young and had then reached a marriageable, mature age, lost its natural meaning in German-speaking lands: one could remain a *Knecht* all one's life in the feudal system. There was no legal term that could have indicated a general release from domination. Precisely this meaning— in the late eighteenth century—was ascribed to the term "emancipation"; The decisive transformation of meaning was brought about not by legal language but rather by the psychological, social, political, and, above all, philosophical usage of the word. Moving from a civilly and legally circumscribed meaning into the domain of general human relationships and behavior patterns, the expansion of the concept of "emancipation," finally to the point where it acquired revolutionary potential, took place—linguistically and socio-historically—not in the civil sense of the noun form of "emancipation," but first in verb and adverbial usage of our term.

In Latin, the verb *emancipare* was used transitively and could mean, for example, "to sell, to dispose of." After its adoption as a noun and a verb in western European vernaculars—in Italy and France in the fourteenth century, in England and Germany in the seventeenth century—a reflexive usage now came about. It extended from the common law sense of having reached the legal age of maturity and later indicated an act performed on one's own authority, something that was precisely excluded from legal terminology. That one could emancipate oneself was unthinkable in the Roman legal tradition.

The following thesis may be ventured: with the introduction of the reflexive verb "to emancipate oneself" (*sich emanzipieren*), a profound shift of mentality was, for the first time, foreshadowed and then brought about. While initially it was a word used by the cognoscenti, the poets and philosophers, who sought to liberate themselves from all pregivens and dependency, the new active word usage was expanded to increasingly refer to groups, institutions, and entire peoples. One spoke of an emancipated heart that would evade religious vows (René d'Anjou, 1455); Rabelais spoke of people who had emancipated themselves from God and reason in order to indulge their perverse passions, but also in the positive sense of being emancipated from the slavery of ignorance. Montaigne saw the difference between humans and animals embodied in the fact that humans emancipate themselves from the rules of nature so that they can pursue the freedom they fancy. Such anthropologically and psychologically legible shifts were directed against the church, theology, tradition, and authority, and rapidly had an effect in the political sphere as well. Thus one of the reasons for the 1595 religious war in France was that the Third Estate was emancipated too much: all subservience had been shed—two hundred years before the great revolution. Contained within the reflexive word usage was *eo ipso* a thrust against the estates system. In German, this linguistic result—to completely break with obedience or claim improper freedoms—was mostly registered negatively in the lexical administration of the language—which only confirmed the thrust against the estates.

The positive associations of self-liberation apparently spread farthest and fastest in England. From Bacon—"for I do take the consideration in general . . . of human nature to be fit to be emancipated and made a knowledge by itself"—via Sir Thomas Browne, who based belief on reason having emancipated itself from all written testimonies—to Bentham, who saw governments emerging that would have already emancipated themselves from established governments—the act of being declared free was always overtaken by the move toward self-authorization. In certain respects, the Roman law sense turned into its opposite during the early modern period, even though the result, to become free from violence, was covered simultaneously by the transitive and intransitive word usages.

Of course, self-authorization was able to draw on more general means of legitimation, such as nature, reason, or free will, authorities which, since the Enlightenment, went beyond the reflexive concept of emancipation and forced all forms of traditional rule to change and justify themselves. This had repercussions on the newly expanded meaning of "emancipation": the unilateral act of state power, placing someone on an equal footing in terms of civil law through emancipation (which remained rigorously preserved in the legal language of the Napoleonic code), was challenged by the demands of those who knew how to legitimately emancipate themselves. Together, the privileged legal titles of nature, reason, and free will led to a historico-philosophical recasting of our concept.

Kant, therefore, knowing the Roman law meaning, defined Enlightenment not as emancipation but as "man's emergence from his self-imposed immaturity." As the stimulant for and consummation of the process of maturing, Enlightenment thus applied to a time that exceeded the singular legal act of emancipation. Kant could do without the term "emancipation" all the more so because he argued that human beings, in accordance with common law, "*naturaliter majorenn*, nonetheless gladly remain in lifelong immaturity."[3] The transference of natural maturation into a moral and political imperative, not only in keeping with nature but also exceeding nature, was a more exacting and also a more effective linguistic usage than the metaphorics of a juridical emancipation still tied to domination. Maturity, always automatically realized by each succeeding generation, became a historical perspective on the future of a politically self-ruling humanity. Part reality, part goal, a processual event was thus redescribed, for which the term "emancipation" soon came to be used.

In Paris during the revolution, Forster was the first to subsume the Kantian philosophy of history under the new and fashionable concept of emancipation. With this, the term simultaneously became associated in German with the colloquial meaning given to it by its Western neighbors: it was both understood reflexively as self-liberation from all the fetters of tradition as well as expressed a normative claim that had to be legalized through a state-sanctioned act.

In its general usage around 1800, the advantage of the new concept of emancipation was that it not only indicated the recurring and natural degrees of maturation of generations that were growing up but it also designated the legal act of liberation coming to pass with self-emancipation. In this triangle between natural pregivens, subjective or collective self-authorization, and the establishment of legal norms, "emancipation" gained its new historical quality. The concept was legible, at once, normatively, evolutionarily, and self-reflexively: In its temporalization, a processual meaning leading to the establishment of laws was always contained. Emancipation becomes an authentic case of a historico-philosophical process-concept which, primarily during the first half of the nineteenth century, achieved the power of a guiding concept. Even with its resuscitation in the 1960s, no new valences were theoretically added to it. "What is the greatest task of our time?" asked Heine in 1828. "It is emancipation. Not just of the Irish, the Greeks, the Frankfurt Jews, the West-Indian Blacks, and other oppressed peoples, but it is the emancipation of the entire world, especially Europe, which has become mature and is now tearing itself free from the iron yokes of the privileged and the aristocracy." Emancipation has turned into a concept of historical movement, without disavowing its juridical implications. Emancipation provided the common denominator of justice for all demands aimed at the eradication of legal, social, political, or economic inequality. Thus, in every case, the term became a concept that demanded the eradication of personal domination by humans over humans; it was both liberal, in favor of the rule by law, as well as democratic, in favor of the sovereignty of the people; it was interpretable in a socialist fashion, in favor of community of property, as well as being the supposed means of abolishing economic domination. Emancipation became, as Scheidler, the clearest systematist of an emancipatory philosophy of history, formulated it in 1840, "practically the most important of all concepts." However, in the same moment, the term also lost its efficacy because it became multivalent and could signify completely different political meanings without losing its general plausibility. It took on the status and force of a catchword, one that admittedly presupposed or evoked a minimal consensus about the equal rights of all human beings.

As a concept of political struggle, emancipation was, at the latest since 1830, employed everywhere: first, in order to acquire individual and personal equal rights with respect to pregiven civil and legal conditions. Second, it was used for the purpose of making possible equal rights for groups: classes, social strata, women, particular churches and religious groups, entire peoples. Third, emancipation aimed at freedom of rule and equal rights for all of humanity, for the world, or for the emancipating time, as one could empathetically say then.

It is striking that the legal acts and statutes that instituted the legal equality of previously subjugated groups—the emancipation of the Jews in France in 1791, in Baden in 1808, or in Prussia in 1812; the laws for the liberation of the peasants (which were only later given this name); the emancipation of the Catholics in Ireland in 1829; or the emancipation of the slaves in 1865 in the United States—did not employ the term "emancipation" in a juridical sense, although this is the way the laws falling under this designation entered into political language and thus into general consciousness. Given this finding, we can suspect that the strict and narrow Roman law meaning was just as much present to the lawyers formulating the laws as the sense that more claims were expressed behind every emancipation than at the time seemed purely juridically possible to concede. As O'Connell predicted with political intuition after he succeeded by way of his mass Catholic organization in obtaining the right for all Catholics in Great Britain to run for office—the so-called Catholic Emancipation: "How mistaken men are who suppose that the history of the world will be over as soon as we are emancipated! Oh! *That* will be the time to *commence* the struggle for popular rights."[4] The goal of universal equal rights, including freedom from domination, obviously triggered reactions that, with every partial emancipation, were in turn, only mastered by emancipation.

To remain with our English example: Catholic Emancipation forced the Reform Act of 1832; it extended the right to vote but only found its general democratic sanction in 1919. Since then, the welfare state tasks of bringing about a redistribution of wealth and production profits for social justice have followed, without, however, reaching an economic balance— as the precondition of lasting social justice.

Likewise, to mention an example from America, during the War of Independence, the demand for the liberation of the slaves was scaled back so that the war could be won and not be eclipsed by a socioeconomic revolution. As such, an excess obligation remained, which, with the Bill of Rights, was to come back in the future. Following the American Civil War, the legal equality of blacks led—partly foreseen, partly unexpected—to a calcification of socioeconomic and thus also political inequality that even today, despite slow and gradual advocacy for change, still remains a challenge for American domestic and foreign policy.

A certain ex post facto teleology, saturated with experience, corresponds to the objective projected *ex ante* with the Bill of Rights. However, actual history has so far never linearly followed such a clear-cut program. It is obviously an enduring problem that the consequences of a legal emancipation stretch farther and last longer than (indeed often only first surface long after) the mere fact of their being incorporated in a legal act.

This leads to several systematic questions that I shall raise upon concluding. I will proceed to these questions in two steps. First, I will argue with the help of an empirically understood set of facts; second, I will investigate the multivalent use of the concept in order to suggest conclusions to be drawn from it.

II. Limits of Emancipation?

If one follows the history of the ratification of legal emancipation acts, one *first* observes that they are retarded again and again by backlashes. When the Catholics gained the right to run in elections in 1829 and thereby broke the political monopoly of the Anglican state religion, the British parliament, in the same act, raised the property qualification for suffrage from forty shillings to ten pounds. Because of this, the Catholics lost about 60 percent of the parliamentary seats that they were expected to win. What had become absolutely necessary to concede on political grounds became largely undermined again by conditions of economic power—not to mention that the daily bread of the Irish continued to be scarce.

Our other examples from the United States also testify to analogous backlashes. During the Civil War, there were many white workers who simply refused to fight against the rebellious Southern states because they feared that the emancipated blacks would take away their jobs. Political and economic emancipation mutually blocked one another. Later, the equal right to vote finally granted to blacks was nullified by quasi-legal manipulations—through ancestry tests, literacy tests, gerrymandering, tests measuring loyalty to the Constitution and more of the same—taking the advances almost back to the zero point for many decades.

Similar backlashes can be seen in the history of Jewish emancipation. The civil and political equal rights introduced by the French Revolution were again restricted in the economic sphere by Napoleon in the case of the Alsatian and Rhenish Jews. This was also the case, only to a much greater extent, for the Papal State after 1815. Less persistently, although similarly, the history of Jewish emancipation in Germany is a history of retardations. The 1812 civil equality granted in Prussia was not extended to the expanded state after 1815; most notably, Jews were, once again, barred from academic careers by a newly adopted edict. Although civic equality was supplemented by political equality after 1869 (almost taken for granted by this time), the same obstructions remained in effect de facto: obtaining political office remained almost entirely denied to Jews.

An initial conclusion can be drawn from these historical findings. Legal acts of equalization can be a help or an impediment to effecting civil rights: there is no guarantee of this. Social and economic conditions always come into play alongside arguments testifying to restrictive behavior patterns. Legal emancipation is thus a necessary, but never a sufficient, condition for effective equal rights.

A second observation also takes us beyond the limits of strictly legal emancipation. As the first black-ruled colony, French Haiti put into effect, with help from the Jacobins in the motherland, its own sovereign human and civil rights under Toussaint L'Ouverture. He was genuinely imbued with revolutionary ideals, and their realization cost the lives of 95 percent of the former white planters there. A racially and economically motivated civil war erupted, a war of settling accounts and revenge, which only came to an end with the help of Napoleon and Britain, but the horror continued much longer. Here, a historical experience exists whose repetition under analogous conditions represents a hitherto unavertable danger. It can only be averted if the legal principle of equal rights for all human beings around the world is proclaimed not only as a legal norm but practiced as a politically necessary and conscientiously enforced principle of justice—for se-

curing our very survival. Here, we should avoid projecting the empirical result of this conditional prognosis one-sidedly.

The annihilation of the Jews by the Germans cannot be completely
defined as a backlash in the history of emancipation. All parallels or en-
capsulating attempts at explanation in socioeconomic terms or those of critique of ideology do not touch the brutal fact of the annihilation itself. In
defiance of all legal efforts, even an assignment of guilt and sin is eluded.
Trying to understand the victims as active or passive also makes no sense.
In this way, the annihilation of the Jews calls us to remembrance as a possible guarantee of maxims for acting in the future: as is always the case,
without the actual recognition of the equal rights of all human beings, no
organized and peaceful political world order can be reached.

This leads us to a *third* observation in the wake of previous experiences of emancipation. Liberal theory has always related the equal rights of
groups to be emancipated only to the individuals within these groups who,
as humans and citizens, should have the same rights as those held by the
other participants in the pregiven legal community. Any recognition of the
groups as such falls under the suspicion of building a state within a state or
a nation within a nation, whether it involves Freemasons, Jesuits, Jews,
Protestants or Catholics, or estate-based groups. The recognition of individuals as humans and citizens has the advantage of being something that
can be legally granted by a general act. But the historical consequences of
this individualizing perspective have run into a dead end.

Most emancipation theories in the nineteenth century argued that
Jews would have to be assimilated in the long term, whether traditionally,
through conversion to Christianity, or progressively, through the attainment of a supradenominational or nondenominational form of community
that would negate or sidestep the opposition between Jew and Christian. A
minority of Jews even considered both goals worthy of striving for, or at
least acceptable. But the other side of this seemingly evolutionary emancipation process consisted precisely in the fact that it did not emancipate the
Jews *as* Jews. Whether Kant counted on "the euthanasia of Judaism" with
the coming of pure religions based on morality; or whether Bruno Bauer
also expected the Jewish question to be resolved with the relinquishment
of an otherworldly Christian religion; or whether Marx also believed that
the necessity of every further emancipation was eliminated by the emancipation of the working class, resulting in a classless society free from domi-

nation: in these perspectives, the Jews had to disappear *as* Jews in every case. They disappear not as individuals granted equal rights but as a group, as a religious community, as their own nation or race, regardless of how they were understood or had understood themselves.

One of the ironies of the time was that conservative Christian arguments were the very ones most capable of recognizing Judaism as such. Of course, these arguments concealed, only too willingly, reservations of an anti-Jewish and later anti-Semitic nature which, in Germany, prevented the Jewish religious community from being treated in the same way as the Christian church. Here, this equal recognition remained denied to Jews, whereas it became possible in the England of the Dissenters and non-Anglican denominations, and even more so in the United States. And throughout France, such recognition was at least safeguarded by Napoleon's compulsory national organization of the Sanhedrin, something which was not possible in the German Reich.[5]

A further conclusion can be drawn from these historical findings. No emancipation can merely place individuals on an equal footing; it must always include the interhuman relationships within which people actually live. But that presupposes the recognition and equal rights of groups. Without pluralism, whatever its legal status, be it of organizations, religious communities, political parties and associations, or within federal constitutions, no equal rights at all will be realized. Humans always live within units of action, without whose cohesion no individual equal rights seem to be possible. If this historical conclusion is accepted as a diagnosis of the present-day situation, it is particularly difficult, although not entirely impossible, to make prognoses.

The history of the recognition of the role of labor unions in Germany might serve as a partially successful example (although less so today in England where industrialization took place earlier). The legally secured task of unions in social emancipation was pushed aside in view of the apparently structural economic crisis: something that cannot dissolve their rights as a group.

Whether the reclaiming of a particular identity and internal homogeneity by blacks in the United States—"black is beautiful"—promotes general equal rights, or whether it is a hindrance in the long run, I cannot say. To be sure, the admissions quotas for specific groups in schools, colleges, employment, and official positions have produced a drive toward recognition whose intensity probably cannot be curtailed any longer. An analogous issue exists in the State of Israel where Arab citizens individually enjoy full equal rights, but are not recognized as a social or religious group. Their individual rights shrink proportionally to their group identity. Every emancipation of peoples into state-based sovereign units of action continues to provoke questions of minorities demanding not only individual but also group recognition—and only through this are equal rights made possible. Further examples are unnecessary, for they can be found all over the world.

The equality of all human beings as the theoretical presupposition of their equal rights can thus only be preserved if the multitude of concrete units of action is taken into consideration. The universal premise of justice can only be realized as a minimal imperative if particular communities gain relative guarantees of existence in their diversity. Although historical experience certainly demands skepticism, it can, however, be a more effective stimulus for and corrective to action.

As a last example, the second Prussian *Kulturkampf* can be cited. The equal rights of individual citizens secured by the Reich's constitution of 1867/71 at first provoked a clash between groups. The *Kulturkampf* was waged on the part of the Center party and the Catholic church in the name of the same fundamental rights in whose name the liberals strove to eradicate from public law every influence of the churches on education and marriage. This historical situation has (almost) been overcome. The comparatively religiously neutral state asserted itself: both leaving the church (without being forced to convert or join another church) and civil marriage became individual rights protected by the law from then on. But afterwards, the church-linked Center party and the moral weight of the Catholic church remained just as effective—as units of group action in the secular state.

To what do these empirical findings testify? They have led us into four situative aporias, which were only able to be resolved, if at all, in the course of historical time: political, social, religious, and economic demands for emancipation cannot be immediately brought into agreement. In reality, they can block one another again and again. Both individual rights claims and group claims to equal rights mutually buttress one another but can just as well provoke irresolvable contradictions. In the course of time, these aporias have also led to the fact that a legalization of emancipatory demands generates new problems that hinder their realization and, at the very least, keeps open problems that cannot be solved solely through legal means. The absurd conclusion of accepting a seemingly hopeless situation or even declaring it hopeless for the purpose of putting an end to it through the annihilation of the other, leads us into apocalyptic dimensions. Therefore, in concluding our discussion of the concept of emancipation, it appears to be necessary, once again, to evaluate the concept with respect to its legitimacy and its use.

1. *The natural substratum* at the base of the emancipation concept—that every succeeding generation becomes mature—is so long-lasting that it compels of itself the possibility of new emancipations. To this extent, while preserving a common legal heritage, emancipation is a fundamental category for all conceivable histories. With every succeeding generation, corresponding to the generation passing away, the possibility arises for it to liberate itself from hitherto pregiven bonds. Only seemingly does this involve regularly recurring conflict between parents and children, which is explicable in terms of social psychology. Rather, what is naturally pregiven, provided it produces histories, always already moves within social changes. Above all, since the technological-industrial revolution, the formerly unchanging preconditions on the basis of which our lives are institutionally regulated, change constantly. What was customary for the father is no longer necessarily right for the following generations growing up with new challenges. The ecological crisis and the threat of atomic annihilation need to be mentioned here because their prevention will only be possible, if at all, when new behavior patterns are learned and practiced in order to survive. In this sense, emancipation is legitimately understood as liberation from those pregivens obstructing survival on the globe. To be sure, it is not sufficient to simply place our hope and trust in coming generations that naturally succeed the preceding generations and, therefore, appear to be qualified and required to take up the challenges with greater freedom from old assumptions.

2. The apocalyptically interpretable threats to our planet are too close at hand for transgenerational obligations not to be formulated and articulated now. Here, the traditional concept of emancipation plays an ambivalent role as a universal goal determinant. All previous experience speaks against freedom of rule (*Herrschaftsfreiheit*) as something demanded by and derived from equal rights. Therefore, the concept has to be differentiated as a goal determinant. We have no choice but to recognize the diverse pre-

givens of heterogeneous units of action that exist within and among politically oriented powers of decision. Only when the plurality of existing communities is taken into consideration can rational politics take their course. To avert the apocalyptic threat even to some extent, the rules of political calculation cannot be countermanded.

On the other hand, and this poses a new challenge, the situation has intensified to such a degree that the general right of all living human beings to this earth must enter into maxims for action by every political leader, if the atomic threat and the ecological crisis are to be directed along controllable pathways. The utopia of freedom of rule can be reduced to its actual core, namely to achieve the distant goal of equal rights today: the responsibility of everyone for everyone and, to this extent, their equal rights on this globe, have become an implicit condition of any politics. The point is to explicate this. That politics is only possible and can only be mediated via particular and small-scale aggregated units of action, without, however, losing from sight the universal claim of an empirically present humanity, is today's challenge. It is thus necessary to consolidate and render present the goal of freedom of rule, a utopian goal stemming from the Enlightenment, so that the claim contained in it, the claim of all human beings to an equal right just to be able to live, becomes enforceable. The concrete goal of a universal minimal consensus regulating the conditions of possibility for life would then come from the concept's utopian goal of a universal emancipation. Even this presupposes an emancipation, namely from those deep-seated behavior patterns that hinder the attainment of the necessary minimal consensus. The path to this may be long and blocked by nearly insurmountable obstacles, but there is no longer any alternative except atomic catastrophe or the depletion of all our natural resources.

3. The *temporal ambiguity* of the traditional concept of emancipation may be instructive here. Either the concept meant the singular act of the state granting equal rights: in that case enforcement by society, the maturity of everyone, was legally presupposed in order for it to be realized in due time. Alternatively, the concept indicated that long-term process which was supposed to bring about equal rights through adaptation, habituation, or self-emancipation.

Both semantic fields could mutually block one another in praxis. During the German state parliamentary proceedings in the period before the 1848 revolution, when attention was called to the lagging self-emancipation of the subordinated or oppressed, the Jews, the workers, and also women, the proposed legislation was blocked as anachronistic. The anticipated legal act was postponed because future development was believed to bring about an equality anyway.

In England, this historico-philosophical position of evasion could not be adopted because in the English juridical system, every law was enacted as a singular "act" involving definitive and delimitable persons. It did not posit temporally wide-ranging general norms such as the compelling nature of fundamental rights. Only retrospectively can British history, therefore, be interpreted as an emancipatory process of increasing equal rights: in political reality, the social adaptation of different groups always moved through the isolated, limited, and narrow bottleneck of their legalization.

It was different in the United States where general civil rights (unknown in England) received both a wide-reaching and direct practical significance. When he did so at all, Lincoln only tried to effect the emancipation of the slaves in a gradual and evolutionary manner, with the help of legal compensations and institutional learning phases for those to be liberated. General fundamental rights and concrete steps toward legalization were to be brought into accord over time. But the events of the Civil War went ahead of him. Lincoln had to reluctantly pronounce the unique legal act as a general liberation in 1865. The planned way had to be progressively accelerated. Every gradual solution became obsolete over the course of the Civil War. This could not, however, obviate further court decisions and amendments in order to promote the general principle of equal rights. In Lincoln's words, "I claim not to have controlled events but confess plainly that events controlled me."[6]

This temporally multilayered concept of emancipation—both the unique legal act as well as the social process—thus leads in praxis to quite varying combinations. The difference between granting and championing, between "Lord" and "serf," between emancipation and self-emancipation, between legal act and social process, must be defined precisely so that one does not abandon the concept to the multivalency of a catchword. If we apply the patent ambiguity of our modern concept of emancipation to our situation, then the following conclusion can be drawn: the temporal dimension of gradual change and the temporal dimension of unique action evidently move together. Not just the spans of action but also the spans of expectation become shorter. The pressure to act has grown so strong that the legal anticipation of equal rights for all human beings can no longer remain merely a traditional demand of the philosophy of history. Rather, equal rights must become immediate maxims of action for all politics, necessarily interest-directed and minority-oriented. The interdependence of all problems on our globe may help to force this minimal consensus. In this way, the concept of emancipation can only remain effectual if it is thought of iteratively: as a constant challenge to reduce or bridge the hiatus still existing between what is legally and intellectually necessary, what can be legally formulated, and what is socially and politically practicable. In other words, the equal rights of all humans on this earth are more than a theoretical pregiven or a utopian goal: they are the minimum that must be preserved from the traditional concept of emancipation in order to make it possible to remain politically and rationally capable of acting. This presupposes, however, that there can be a historical change in experience which is both effective and knows to forge a virtue out of necessity. Here, we might pay homage to St. Jerome:[7] *Fac de necessitate virtutem.*

Translated by Todd Presner

16

Daumier and Death

I

Birth, death, and love are the anthropological pregivens of human existence. How to represent them and, through their representation, how to interpret them belong among art's enduring challenges. Death has a special status here, for it cannot be visualized. Dying is representable in its infinite multiplicity: the deceased are corpses, the murdered, the dead, the skeleton. But death itself has to rely on allegory to become visible or on the metaphorical power of a picture that necessarily involves a reality only able to be experienced by negation. For death itself eludes human experience even though it is contained in the prospective knowledge of the fact that one has to die.

It is a development of our modern age that the caricature increasingly makes use of death to convey to an observer its moral, political, or social message. There are many reasons for this. If the art of the caricature consists in alienating its object to such an extent that the object—through exaggeration or omission—becomes visible in its own form, then this art faces a double challenge in considering death. It has to figuratively constitute its object at the same time that it caricatures it. For death itself eludes the sensorial transference of experience. The caricaturist is thus forced to make allegories or symbols, signs or signals of death—not death itself—into an object of exaggeration or omission. Today, Siné or Tomi Ungerer are masters of this kind of art. Their images of death evoke laughter only to suffocate it. Thus in their work, death appears physically, so to speak.

Caricatures of death in modern times admittedly involve a special case. Theological or humorous interpretations can likewise make use of parodic means and are in a position to be connected with death in order to relativize or overcome it. One need only think of Wilhelm Busch, most of whose comic strips ended in catastrophic scenes of death—a finale to be laughed at. "Max and Moritz," who are consumed like grain, offer only the most familiar example of a ready-made private eschatology delivered to the door of the German bourgeois. Busch's fantasy of inventing violent kinds of death or of furnishing apparent accidents with deeper meaning hardly had a limit. Ending with death, his comic strips are generally executed in a similar fashion: we are dealing with comic strips as Last Judgments (*Weltgerichte*) in miniature; they adapt Schiller's dictum, "world history is the judgment (*Weltgericht*) of the world,"[1] to the everyday life of peasants and the bourgeoisie. The humorous or sarcastic transposition of formerly theological doctrines which later became those of moral philosophy—with a clearly anti-Catholic, even anti-Christian thrust—jumps out at us. Certainly, Busch had also learned from Daumier, but only stylistically, not conceptually. His comic strips prove themselves to be desired fictions precisely in their explicitness. This is different from political caricatures that are related to reality itself.

The pathos of modern caricature aims less at comic strip sequences than at conveying situations. To the extent that it thematizes the limit case of death—an area where Goya and Daumier must be named as the inaugurators and masters—it is less the inescapability or even the justification of death and more the manner of killing that is of interest. Not death but the killing, violent death, is the subject of the caricature. The caricature wants to expose its causes and especially its reasons—the art and ruse, the guile and technical perfection employed for murdering, annihilating, and obliterating. The power and possibility of prematurely bringing about death is unveiled politically or socially (Daumier) or in universal human terms (Goya).

Modern caricature thus differentiates itself from the pictorial satires during the Reformation period whose representations of death remained embedded within the theological pregivens of heaven and hell that transcended death. Modern caricature thus also differentiates itself from the emblematically and allegorically enriched picture pamphlets of the period of absolutism. Here, too, violent death remained a part of preordained doctrines of justice. The state and its administration of justice made judgments about the legitimacy of death, and the numerous, never-ending pictures of murders and battles left no doubt in an observer as to where right and wrong were to be found.

Only with the historical individualization of events, which was fostered aesthetically precisely by the caricature, could the motivation, the manner, and the act of killing be illustrated in their respective uniqueness —and thus be caricatured.

A technical, a stylistic, and a sociohistorical process correspond to this roughly sketched sequence. One need only refer to one case to demonstrate their mutual interdependence. In the Reformation period, pictorial satires primarily used woodcuts. Their production was slow but cheap. The satires reached a wide audience that was conversant with the theologically preconfigured, enduring, and repeatable topoi and pictorial signals. Death remained framed within apocalyptic and always repeatable expectations that pointed beyond death and that could be evoked by the picture. In the early modern state, the copperplate engraving was primarily used for political indoctrination and polemical defamation. Its manufacture was likewise slow, but also expensive. It mainly reached the upper strata who had money to spend. Despite technical refinements, the array of emblematic classifications remained limited and its recurrent application fixed. Individual death remained bound to a world order whose existence was assumed. All of this fundamentally changed in the revolutionary era with the introduction of lithography. It is simultaneously quick and cheap. With lithography, both the style—from Daumier on, a hastened line became the benchmark of perfection—as well as the audience changed. Sales and turnover likewise increased because everyone could be reached faster and faster. Daily events could be turned into illustrations in no time, and the public could thereby be confronted with them. We thus see a precursor of photography and television, namely the production, or at any rate the facilitation, of a convergence between event and picture and, later, between the event and its pictorial reproduction.

The pregiven, symbolic or allegorical meanings that had previously structured depicted events are now swallowed up by the events themselves. The synchronization of events and their pictorial doubling occasion an entirely new symbolism—a symbolism of action, a historical symbolism in-augurated by Daumier.

Schematically speaking, the following series of oppositions can be de-rived from this roughly sketched development. From an art which knew to typify each individual death with a constantly recallable and pregiven mean-ing came an art which learned to comprehend death situationally. From an art which lived off a reservoir of pregiven signs signaling their repeatability came an art which taught that death be interpreted individually. In other words, the relationship of time to death changed. Previously set within en-during structures, death also, in its omnipresence, left its mark on the prac-tice of violent killing. The individual case pointed to its own repeatability. This changed in modern times. Violent death became capable of being in-dividually classified; it gained historical uniqueness and was interpreted from situation to situation as new, able to be provoked and prevented. Constant, pregiven meanings gave way to historical reasons. But these, too, are sur-passable. The actuality of violence leading to death detached itself from its premises, which were formerly experienced as permanent.

Of course, neither empirical history nor the history of its pictorial representation runs in a straight line from one pole to the other in our op-positional schema. But this schema does offer us an interpretative aid. The specific relationships shift such that the world of signs—for instance, the cross, the skeleton, the sword, the place of execution—can forgo the indi-vidual case without becoming meaningless, but not the other way around. That proves to be the case especially with Daumier.

He showed how lasting structural pregivens from the traditional world of signs found their place in the art of the situation-related caricature. Moreover, without the traditional symbolism of death, the real uniqueness of violent killing would not have been exposed either.

II

Chronologically, the sequence of Daumier's pictures of death is inti-mately intertwined with the course of historical events that he wanted to re-flexively and provocatively influence. First engaged in a domestic political conflict lasting from the July Revolution to the repressive laws of 1835, he dedicated himself to the indirectly political—that is, to social caricature—until 1848. Revolutionary pictures then followed under Napoleon III, which under the pressure of censorship granted a certain priority to questions of foreign policy, and not without national fervor. Toward the end of the Empire, and above all during the war of 1870, domestic and foreign political themes intersected—almost inevitably. No wonder that violent death remained a constant challenge, from assassination to mass death and mass battles. Civil war, revolution, and wars traverse Daumier's entire oeuvre in varying inflections.

If one looks for the signs of death, above all for the signals of a violently caused death, the following finding emerges: to present the scenery of death, Daumier frequently makes use of Western symbolic language and both relies upon the traditional repository of allegories as well as employs empirical signs of his own time. One need only mention the play between light and shadow, the pagan-humanistic Kronos/Chronos and Mars, the Christian Great Reaper and the skeleton, the cross, martyrs, pictures of the Resurrection or the Apocalypse, ghosts of the dead or the mythical-literary Gargantua, the rendering of sayings into pictures ("The Pope shall dig his own grave with the Vatican Council"), or the memorial inscriptions. This leads to equally numerous signs of the everyday, directly visible world of experience, to instruments used for killing, murdering, and executing (ranging from the oldest to the most recent), to coffins and autopsy tables, to cemeteries, ruins, graves, and battlefields, together with the deceased or corpses. These empirical signs finally transfer seamlessly to the actions represented. They range from suicide to murder, from execution to violent killing in war or civil war.

So much for the external finding. What does Daumier achieve when he combines the actuality of killing, the brutal presence of instruments of murder, with the world of signs made up of repeatable and enduring claims? One result might be mentioned right away that Daumier did not always achieve but achieved to an increasing extent and with increasing virtuosity. Daumier knew how to meld the traditional expressiveness of symbols and allegories together with the immediacy of everyday occurrences in such a way that any difference disappears in the picture. The symbolic language, always in need of interpretation and obligatory narration and translation, is divested of its linguistic elements to such an extent that it becomes immediately effective as a picture. However, this is only successful because Daumier seamlessly integrates the symbolism with the picture's empirical context of events. In purely aesthetic terms, the difference disappears between the signals of repeatability and their unique, individualized application (in contradistinction to others who worked on *La Caricature* and *Le Charivari*).

Nevertheless, Daumier thematizes this difference. The effectiveness of the caricature is to be found precisely in the determination of the difference between the signs of enduring claims and the unsurpassability of the unique actions and sufferings illustrated. Be it that the symbols unmask reality, or be it that reality exposes allegorization, or be it that the constant, pregiven meanings and everyday quality of death disavow one another, what appears aesthetically reconciled is precisely what is thereby thematized as difference—difference that can be caricatured.

Distortion, often invoked as a principle of caricature, is thus not merely an element of human representation—although it is that, too—but first and foremost the principle of the composition as a whole. To explain this, let us look at two groups of pictures, the first from the beginning and the second from the end of Daumier's career.

1. *Voyage à travers les populations empressées* (Riding past the attentive population), *La Caricature*, August 14, 1834. The stout Louis Philippe rides with an averted face—the censors forbade showing it—through a field covered with naked corpses encircled by buzzards. Without a break in style, the signs of reality are incorporated into the symbolism of death. The king used to show himself to his people—despite frequent assassination attempts—on horseback, just as here. In the picture, he is confronted with numerous dead people, victims of the quelled workers' uprisings in Lyons and Paris. In a commentary, the journal (*La Caricature*) even identified individual people, but the picture's message, however, would not allow for empirical verification. In the picture, the dead do not appear as identifiable people, for instance as fallen barricade fighters or the random dead from blind police violence, but as naked, plundered cadavers through which the monarch indifferently rides. The symbolism of naked corpses is thus confronted with an empirical king who must take responsibility for a murderous system—without, however, doing so.

The mutual exposure of symbolic and event signals calls upon still deeper layers of meaning coalescing in one another. The monarch on horseback also refers to the old tradition of monuments to the king—one might think of the equestrian statue of Henry IV reerected during the Restoration—whose language of signs is supposed to permanently secure just rule.

FIGURE 16.1. Riding past the attentive population.

Infused with present reality, the monument is now set in motion, so as to become an empirical signal of a deeply unjust rule. The difference between the symbolic world of signs and political reality allows still another horizon of meaning to appear. The naked dead and the horse refer an observer brought up in Christianity to their apocalyptic context. The symbols of the Last Days are alienated from their theological meaning in order to remain in force metaphorically as political signals. The critical effect of the caricature is thus grounded in a multilayered and mutually disclosing language of signs. Enduring symbols become historicized, historical signals symbolized. What is figuratively held together on one level creates a provocative, incongruous element in the caricature.

2. *Les honneurs du Panthéon* (The honors of the *Panthéon*), *La Caricature*, April 23, 1834. This picture, aesthetically less balanced and realized with narrativizing and legible references, nevertheless follows the pattern

FIGURE 16.2. The honors of the *Panthéon.*

of difference developed here. On the empirical level, what is contrasted is the Panthéon, center of the republican cult of the dead, with the figures who have come to power since the July Revolution. In more or less grotesque distortion, their faces and bodies are identifiable. But they are hanging together on the gallows—symbolically. The normative claim, posited permanently and proceeding from the Temple of Virtue, the Republic's monument to the dead, is played out in an ironic inversion with respect to the ministers of this republic. The "great men" to whom the fatherland had to show itself beholden belong where the picture shows them: on the gallows, a lasting sign of ineradicable disgrace. The ministers—who are actually living—disgrace the monument erected for the ages. It is robbed of its symbolic worth. Seen from the other side, the monument's claim provokes the death of these ministers.

It may be possible to place this picture of the gallows into the legal or satirical tradition of hangings in effigy—always an enduring signal of forfeited honor. But seen in terms of the situation, the picture moves within a series of satires, specifically images intended to incite or malign. Their production was skillfully mastered by Philipon, the publisher of the caricatures, and they were not without an effect on the civil war atmosphere of the early 1830s. The picture thus implies a disavowal of the republican cult of the dead through the ruling men and, in a compensatory way, calls for political murder. The call to political murder remains figurative (*bildlich*) in the double sense of the word, visible and metaphorical. Never again did Daumier go so far as to conjure up violent death as an accomplice.

3. *Fieschi dit Gérard* (Fieschi a.k.a. Gérard), *Le Charivari*, August 7, 1835. By 1835, the spiral of repression and terror had intensified rapidly. On July 26, *Le Charivari* reported on the king's return to Paris—"without having been murdered." Two days later, he escaped the shrapnel of an explosion which killed eighteen people. The following day, Philipon presented the other side: a list in red ink of all the dead who were to be credited to the account of the July monarchy. It was the logic of civil war. The picture of the assassin appeared ten days later—the anarchist Fieschi, whom Daumier must have seen alive. Fieschi was only executed on February 16, 1836.

The picture is not a caricature in the strict sense—only metaphorically. For the murderer is represented as a victim, supine and evoking sympathy. The chin bandage testifies to the severe injuries Fieschi sustained with the explosion as well as calls to mind the customary chin bandage placed around the head of a person recently deceased. His fixed gaze is directed toward the darkness of imminent death. The murderer's dubious ways—he was also a police informer—are dissolved into the enduring mark of an innocent victim. The caricature is characterized by inversion and is accomplished according to the same interpretative schema. The real situation is symbolically reinterpreted. Perpetrator and victim are interchanged. The readers of both of Philipon's journals were adept at understanding this kind of art. Already on December 17, 1832, after a failed attempt to assassinate the king, *Le Charivari* had published a picture of Louis Philippe grinning widely, with the title, "The Murdered." Both pictures refer to what the represented is not. As little as Louis Philippe was the victim of an assassination, Fieschi

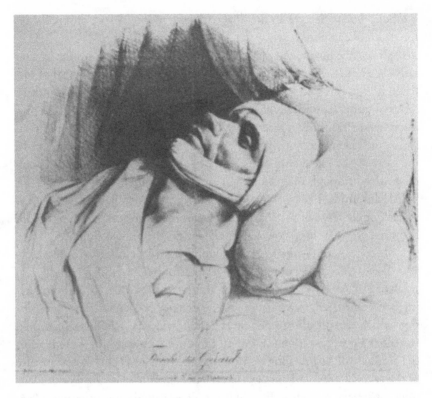

FIGURE 16.3. Fieschi a.k.a. Gérard.

was just as little the actual perpetrator. The symbolic reversal shows him as the victim. On the other hand, Louis Philippe is suggested to be the true perpetrator by his absence. This interpretation may even be strengthened if a reversed replica of David's *The Death of Marat* is seen in Fieschi's portrait. Marat's white turban returns as Fieschi's head bandage, the sign of the prior and now imminent sacrifice.

4. *"C'était vraiment bien la peine de nous faire tuer"* (It's hardly worth the trouble of getting ourselves killed), *La Caricature*, August 27, 1835. This is the last picture from *La Caricature* before the journal came under increased censorship—a caricatured memorial for the past and a provocative monument for the future. In a well-considered manner, the signs of political experience are here folded into the long-term symbols of the death cult in such a way that the temporal dimensions of past, present, and future are

included as interpretative grids. The disappointment over the five years that have gone by since the July Revolution is thematized. The victors of the glorious three days—the workers, the middle class, and the students—were not the ones who profited from the revolution, but the financial bourgeoisie in a new alliance with traditional powers. This is first shown empirically. On the left, a procession moving forward; on the right, one of the massacres caused by cavalry soldiers stampeding fleeing citizens; halfway to the right, a cross crowned with a wreath, like the one dedicated at the Louvre in 1830 to those who died in the civil war. So much for the empirical data. Finally, in the middle, three civil war fighters: a worker who is gigantically stylized in a heroic-realistic fashion, a semi-intellectual citizen, and a long-haired man, perhaps indicating an artist. All three of the civil war dead have disappointment written on their faces. At this point, the empirical anachronism begins: the dead appear to be living, something which is absorbed by and becomes interpretable through the symbolic marks. In the center, the pretended resurrection scene is played out on a burial mound, and the raised burial slab traverses the picture at a diagonal angle.

The picture concerns the paradigmatic case of a secularization. In the Christian language of signs, the raised slab could signal the opening grave, the beginning of the Resurrection. Since the Enlightenment, the picture could change into an automatically closing coffin lid, the sign of irrevocable death. This emerging shift to realism is, in turn, rejected by Daumier, but now with an antichurch, non-Christian thrust. The opening of the slab does not place the dead before the Last Judgment, let alone lead them into Heaven. Rather, the casualties of the July Revolution return to the history they triggered but no longer control. From the symbol of resurrection comes a historical metaphor for permanent revolution—together with the latent resignation that has been a part of this provocative concept since it was coined. The revolution will have to return if its goals are to be reached. Thus the issue is no longer a Christian sign but rather the use of a Christian sign that has been inserted into the iconological horizon of a historico-philosophical interpretation. In iconographic terms, the Christian origin of the stylistic marks is evident. Even Christ's stigma appears on the right-hand side of the worker's breast. However, the iconographic durability of the sign is iconologically recast. Henceforth, the resurrection scene takes on its meaning from secular history itself. The caricature's humor is summed up in the amalgamation of these incompatible levels.

FIGURE 16.4. It's hardly worth the trouble of getting ourselves killed.

That is confirmed by the iconology of both memorials. The Christian cross on the right has been knocked over—and even threatens to fall on the cavalry in the act of butchering. On the left, the republican July Column, which in 1835 was still in its planning stages, rises above the state-sanctioned church procession, strangely floating, without appearing to be anchored in the ground. The political cult of the dead will repress the religious one. Such is the message. Thus we see a reciprocal blockage and an opposing use of empirical data and symbolic signs. The procession, the massacre, and those who fight in the civil war call into question the memorials' message, "fallen for freedom." But even these memorials confer the picture's historical sense in terms that value "republican" as positive and "Christian" as negative. The opening burial plate no longer mediates between this world and the next but between past and future. The symbolic language falls under the temporal pressure of change and is figuratively staged by Daumier as such.

III

If we turn our attention to the pictures from around thirty years later, the motifs and metaphors of death continue to accrue. The series of Napoleonic wars, colonial wars, and, finally, the wars of unification, not to mention the waves of domestic political terror and the vicissitudes of the constitutional struggles until the Third Republic was established, provided Daumier with sufficient material.

Biographically, it can be inferred from the pictures, which exist in large numbers, that Daumier's involvement in party politics diminished. Pictures that celebrate rebellion as the holiest of all duties on a memorial to the dead (*Le Charivari*, May 23, 1834) or which see the printing press as an amusingly cruel death machine for the crushed monarch (*La Caricature*, October 3, 1833) are no longer possible. Not even Cavaignac's 1848 bloodbath or the annihilation of the Communards in 1871 any longer provokes a fighting riposte from Daumier. Regardless of his republican fervor, Daumier holds back political party options in order to confront, according to situation, the general senselessness of battle victims with human, individual, or collective guilt. This will be demonstrated by reference to a series of motifs. Once again, the principle of composition consists of placing signals of reality and newly created or old allegories together in such a way that the unity of the picture thematizes the difference in any particular case.

Thus concrete persons or allegorized agents are confronted with fields of corpses or cemeteries, already familiar to us, and the field of corpses or cemetery itself can also change its significance.

Bismarck is depicted as weighed down by a field of corpses which, in August 1870, had been turned into the reality of a battlefield. Intensified by the scythe-carrying grim reaper, the nightmare prefigures his own death. Death ironically thanks him with "Merci!" (*Un Cauchemar de M. de Bismarck* [*A nightmare of Mr. Bismarck*], *Le Charivari*, August 22, 1870). After his fall, Napoleon was made responsible—in absentia—for all the civil and military victims during the time he ruled. A town square named after him is depicted as the square of death. Numerous crosses and metaphorical gravestones signal the stages of terror and defeat that began on December 2, 1851, the day of the coup d'état in the wake of which ten thousand people were deported. Two stones vouch for this, including the memorial stone for the capitulation after the bloody battle at Sedan (*Square Napoléon*, *Le Charivari*,

November 28, 1870). But not just politicians, also technological innovators, enter into the ranks of those responsible. Thus after the War of 1866, the inventor of the needle gun—Nikolaus von Dreyse had invented the breechloading gun in 1836, which helped the Prussians to victory in 1866—is confronted with a field of the dead and the dying, which yet again, in an ironic inversion, he surveys with a Mephisophelean grin.

But the field of corpses does not only serve as a reference to reality: it also functions as a metaphor, as in the caricatures of the election of May 23, 1869. Before these elections took place in France (*La Mitrailleuse Electorale, Quelle Jonché!* [The election machine gun—what a slaughter!], *Le Charivari*, May 11, 1869), Daumier suggests a victory for the workers who would know how to shoot to "kill" with their votes. Two days after the electoral showdown (*Le Lendemain de la Bataille* [The day after the battle], *Le Charivari*, May 25, 1869), a picture that was apparently conceptualized earlier appeared. It depicted the losers as victims of the voters. The figure in the front may be Napoleon III robbed of his pointed beard; at any rate, the relative majority shifted to the liberal and republican opposition. Through a renewed plebiscite on May 8, 1870, Napoleon was able to regain control and keep this victory of the opposition in check. An enigmatic picture of February 9, 1871, refers to this event. One day earlier, the first election to the republican National Assembly since Napoleon's overthrow had taken place. Daumier is now reminding his viewers that those who had voted for Napoleon the previous year also need to be made responsible for the very real field of corpses that France had become. The allegory of France makes claims to the election from the year before; it embodies the true will of the people (the *volonté générale*), which cannot be recognized by the majority of "yes" votes (the *volonté de tous*). Even the voters are guilty of mass death, of mass killing. The picture, *Ceci a tué cela*, appeared in *Le Charivari* on February 9, 1871, as a forecast of the election that had taken place the day before and resulted in a large conservative majority. The real field of death is thus confronted with a real electoral outcome. Shocked and furious, the true will of the people of France —allegorically—mediates both together: the one killed the other. The "wrong" majority led to death.

Shortly afterwards, as the new Versailles government prepared to quell the Commune rebellion, it was confronted by the allegorized city of Paris with its graveyard: *Voyons, monsieur Réac[tionnaire], il y en a pourtant bien*

FIGURE 16.5. See here, Mister Reactionary, we've had quite enough of this!

assez! (See here, Mister Reactionary, we've had quite enough of this!), *Le Charivari*, March 30, 1871.

Previously, "Francia" was personalized, "shocked over the inheritance," and like Medea, hid her tears from the masses of corpses. Finally, death itself—the living skeleton, bucolically adorned with a wreath—plays a double flute while elegiacally celebrating the skeletons and bones of the killed: *La Paix—Idylle* (Peace—an idyll), *Le Charivari*, March 6, 1871; compare

FIGURE 16.6. Peace—an idyll.

the idyllic Virgilian picture in *Le Charivari*, of December 31, 1842, whose allegory is incorporated in the image of death. The ironic inversion is complete. The sequence of pictures depicts the last possible transposition: the historical victim, France, and the perpetrator, now simply death, replace each other in view of the same dead.

This—almost indiscriminately selected—series of motifs attests to how Daumier took his art, the constant correlation of empirical signals with those of the symbolic world, to the very limit. The field of corpses moves from being a metaphor to a realistic testimony, while the real standards of comparison are increasingly allegorized. Those responsible are concrete, acting persons, smaller or larger units of action, such as governments or the voters. Finally, the field of corpses converges with the allegorized victims who come to stand for it—Paris, the people, or France—until finally death itself comes to stand for everything. The last picture concretizes all the previous slices of experience, so as to remain generally retrievable.

Seen aesthetically, Daumier succeeds in fusing contrasting levels into a picture until they become almost indistinguishable. The structures of violence, the dastardliness of humans and, simultaneously, their helplessness and their responsibility for the fatal and no longer controllable cataclysms of events—all this is empirically and symbolically blended together and incorporated into the picture. Despair and grief both intensify one another and gain an expressiveness that finally outlives all the occasions to which the picture testifies.

One could say that from the 1830s onward, the starting point of Daumier's images of death changed direction, so to speak. The signs of death —formerly comprised of pregiven, suprahistorical symbolism and allegory—were overtaken by events themselves. Now it is the events that generate the symbolic language. With Daumier, the singularity of technological, political, military, and social use of violence in modern history gains a renewed power of permanent and general testimony. And all the more so since Daumier never forswore thematizing the situational and historically enduring causes.

Thus the innovations made in the technical improvement of means of killing are iconographically taken up and iconologically melted together. The seemingly traditional statue of peace is futuristically equipped with the attributes of modern arms technology: *Projet de Statue de la Paix pour l'Exposition Universelle* (Proposed statue of peace for the World Exhibition), *Le Charivari*, January 5, 1867—a prognostic anticipation of a later picture from 1871, *Peace is Death*.

Le Charivari of April 29, 1868, depicts a variant: the inventors of the bomb, the shotgun, and the canon are immortalized on three "monuments of the future." Finally, allegorical time itself trades in its outdated attrib-

FIGURE 16.7. Proposed statue of peace for the World Exhibition.

utes—hourglass and scythe for bayonet and shotgun—in order to progress more quickly thanks to the rising efficacy of killing: *Le Temps éprouvant lui aussi le besoin de s'équiper à la mode* (Father Time, too, feels the need to outfit himself in the latest fashion), *Le Charivari*, January 10, 1867.

The updating of the allegories and the ironic inversion of the memorial messages testify to the same process. All the signs erected for good, above

FIGURE 16.8. Father Time, too, feels the need to outfit himself in the latest fashion.

all those of the modern memorial cult, something that Daumier exposed with an uncompromising gaze whenever he could, are temporalized and depicted in their artifice and infirmity: "peace" points toward "death." In its difference from historical reality, the caricature comes into its own—as a quasi critique of ideology. However, and this is the caricature's counter-claim, this reality is no better than its appearance. The threat of unreality, the production of mass death from the absolute power of human beings themselves, ensconces itself everywhere. With this enduring message, which Daumier drew and learned from modernity, he—like Goya—ran up against the limits of the caricature. No symbol, and still less a memorial, withstands this threat of the always self-surpassing power of annihilation. "The dead die quickly," remarked Gottfried Benn, "and the more who die, the quicker they are forgotten." If anyone succeeded in capturing the constantly changing but lasting and growing power of killing in a picture for the purpose of bearing witness to it, then it was Daumier.

Translated by Todd Presner

War Memorials: Identity Formations of the Survivors

I

In the mid-1970s, three reports on war memorials appeared in German newspapers but apparently were hardly noticed.[1] The first concerned a memorial of World War I; the other two concerned memorials of World War II. In Hamburg, several city officials tried to have an inscription erased that the survivors of the 76th Infantry Regiment had devoted to their dead. The inscription consisted of a saying of Heinrich Lersch in 1914: "Germany must live, even if we must die." By order of the Senate, the inscription was preserved—as a view held by a bygone epoch.[2]

In September 1975, a commemorative ceremony honoring the victims of Stalag 326 VI-K took place in Stukenbrock. In front of the memorial to the sixty-five thousand Soviet prisoners buried in the cemetery and before the eyes of numerous visitors from the Eastern bloc, a brawl erupted, and several people were hurt. Members of the DKP (German Communist Party) and the KPD (Communist Party of Germany) fought with each other over the true legacy of the dead, both claiming it for themselves. The German police intervened only after the "Maoists/Leninists" had been driven out of the cemetery.[3]

In July 1976, one of the huts in the former concentration camp of Struthof in Alsace, which had been turned into a museum, was destroyed by arson. On the camp memorial (figure 17.1)—which, according to its

FIGURE 17.1. B. Monnef. Concentration camp monument, Struthof, Alsace.
A. Rieth, *Den Opfern der Gewalt* (Tübingen: Wasmuth, 1968), jacket photograph.
Photo by Bommer, Strasbourg.

sponsors in 1960, represented the crematorium flames and, in the form of
a rising spiral, called to mind eternal hope—a date was painted: January
27, 1945. On this day, after the Liberation, eleven hundred new prisoners
suspected of collaborating with the Germans were brought to the camp.[4]

All three events point to a common finding. The memorials involved
in these actions evidently do more than just keep alive the memory of the
dead for whose sake they were first erected. In Hamburg, survivors or succeeding generations tried to remove a saying that had been proclaimed to

those who saw the monument since the twenties. In Stukenbrock, two political parties of the present day tried to credit themselves with the memory of the past death of Russians (while denying it to each other). In Struthof, as far as an interpretation is possible, Alsatians protested against a memorial cult that excluded the victims from their own ranks, or at least passed over them in silence.

However different the reactions are, the memorial's challenge is a shared one. As in the examples just mentioned, memorials which commemorate violent death provide a means of identification. First, the deceased, the ones killed, and the ones killed in action are identified in a particular respect: as heroes, victims, martyrs, victors, kin, possibly also as the defeated; in addition, as custodians or possessors of honor, faith, glory, loyalty, duty; and finally, as guardians and protectors of the fatherland, of humanity, of justice, of freedom, of the proletariat or of a particular form of government. The list could be expanded.

Secondly, the surviving observers are themselves put in a position where they are offered an identity: an offer to which they should or must react. The maxim *mortui viventes obligant* (the living are obliged to the dead) is variously applicable depending on the classifications given above. Their cause is also ours. The war memorial does not only commemorate the dead; it also compensates for lost lives so as to render survival meaningful.

Finally, there is the case contained in all the ones mentioned but which, taken in and of itself, means both more and less: that the dead are remembered—as dead.

Memorials to the dead are certainly as old as human history. They correspond to a fundamental state of being, pregiven to human beings, in which death and life intertwine in whatever ways they are referred to one another. Innocent III formulated the nearness of life and death in the following well-known words: "Morimur ergo semper dum vivimus, et tunc tantum desinimus mori cum desinimus vivere" (Therefore while we are living we are always dying, and we cease to die only then, when we cease to live).[5] Whether consciously or not, memorials to the dead presuppose this —what Heidegger later analyzed as "Being toward death."

But it is different with war memorials because they are supposed to recall violent death at the hands of human beings. In addition to remembrance, the question of the justification of this death is also evoked. Here, factors of arbitrariness, freedom, and voluntariness, as well as factors of coercion and violence, come into play. Over and above natural death, so to speak, such deaths stand in need of legitimation and obviously are, therefore, especially worthy of remembrance. The dictum of Innocent III thus ought to be altered: human beings live so long as they are not killed, and only when they can no longer be killed have they stopped living. Or, translated into language that would have made all too much sense in the 1920s: for humans, Being toward death (*Sein zum Tod*) is—in addition—a question of Being toward beating to death (*Sein zum Totschlagen*).

Dying happens alone; killing another takes two. The capability of human beings to kill their own kind perhaps constitutes human history to an even greater extent than our fundamental destiny of having to die.

There is not only dying, but also dying for something. Here, it may remain open for now as to who decides to die for what: the one killing, or the one dying, or the community of agents within which the participants or those affected act, or all of them at the same time, albeit in different ways. There are numerous variants here with which historical anthropology may occupy itself.[6] What is certain is that the meaning of "dying for . . . " as it is recorded on memorials is established by the survivors and not by the dead. For the sense that the deceased may have wrested from their dying eludes our experience. The sense intended earlier can coincide with the meaning established by the survivors, in which case a common identity of the dead and the living is conjured up. The saying that commemorated the battle of Thermopylae[7] was modified by numerous succeeding political entities in accordance with their patriotic morality. But the establishing of meaning ex post facto can just as likely miss the meaning that the deceased may, if at all, have found in their death. For the death of the individual cannot be redeemed.

Thus a double process of identification is contained in the difference between the past death that is recalled and the visual interpretation that a war memorial offers. The dead are supposed to have stood for the same cause as the surviving sponsors of memorials want to stand for. But the dead have no say in whether it is the same cause or not.

Yet over the course of time, and this is what history teaches, the intended identity similarly eludes the control of those who established the memorial. More than anything else, memorials erected permanently testify to transitoriness.

This is a contradiction that will be resolved in the course of this essay. The thesis that I want to demonstrate from history is this: the only identity that endures clandestinely in all war memorials is the identity of the dead with themselves. All political and social identifications that try to visually capture and permanently fix the "dying for . . . " vanish in the course of time. For this reason, the message that was to have been established by a memorial changes.

II. The Transition to Modernity

As the biological causes of death have been scientifically explained and, with such explanations, life expectancies increased, the ways of dying (likewise thanks to the natural sciences) have multiplied and death rates have risen with the violent killing of human beings. That certainly holds true for the last two centuries, whose death statistics can be readily surveyed.[8] It is also during this time that the emergence and spread of war memorials has taken place, with such memorials appearing in almost every community in Europe.

War memorials offer identifications in ways that could not have been offered before the French Revolution. For the time being, let me therefore start by giving two references to monuments to the dead in the prerevolutionary period. First, the otherworldly beyond of death was indicated figuratively, with death being interpreted not as an end but as a passageway. Secondly, in this outlook upon the world, the represented death remained differentiated by estate, even though death became increasingly individualized. Both findings, which roughly involve the period between the twelfth and eighteenth centuries, in no way stand in contradiction to one another. The late medieval *danse macabre* initially was not directed in a revolutionary manner against the existing estates. Each estate is judged individually in terms of its human quality that becomes visible before death, the great equalizer. The diversity of the estates is marked in this world before the equality of death swallows it up in the next.

This becomes especially clear with the gradual spread of double tombs (figure 17.2) in France, England, and Germany during the fifteenth and sixteenth centuries.[9] The worldly but transpersonal official position is indicated on the upper level where the ruler is represented lying down in his official dress, adorned with the insignia of power. Below, his body deteriorates so as to release the individual soul to eternal judgment. As a ruler, he rep-

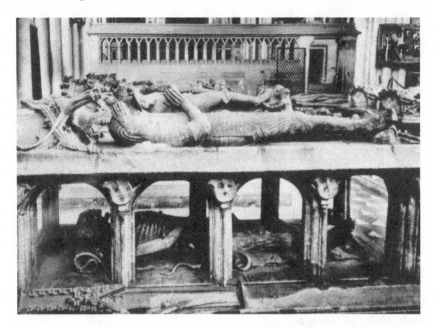

FIGURE 17.2. L. Juppe. Tomb of Count Wilhelm II of Hesse, Elisabethkirche, Marburg/Lahn. Bildarchiv, Marburg.

resents his office which is not subject to mortality, but the ruler is also representative as a human being—for human mortality, for everyone.

Such tombs, which present the official position and the individual separately or sometimes blended together, were reserved for rulers and the rich. Until the eighteenth century, soldiers appear everywhere on victory monuments but not on war memorials. Within the society of estates, mercenaries or soldiers recruited by the state remained relegated to the lowest level, unworthy of a monument. In 1727, a German handbook for the estate of soldiers (*Kriegerstand*) argued against soldiers being burned like witches or counterfeiters.[10] And "old Fritz" (Frederick the Great) counted them among the scum of the earth. Even at Königgrätz, that is, at a time when soldiers were already worthy of memorials, the dead were deposited in mine tunnels and, after Sedan, they remained where they fell, barely covered.[11] However, in places where commemorative monuments or memorial chapels for the fallen were erected, for example those that have come down to us from the Thirty Years' War, such monuments stood as tokens of expiation for human crimes. Thus the Christian transcendence of death and the estate-based leveling of empirical death were connected with one another. Death was a link between this world and the next; this allowed death to be defined both in its earthly sense and in its otherworldly context. Here a tension prevailed in which great personages were monumentally transfigured, but for the masses of fallen mercenaries, buildings could be erected as tokens of expiation without the death of individuals having to be remembered.

The shift to modernity can likewise be conceptualized in two ways. First, while the transcendental sense of death fades or is lost, the inner-worldly claims of representations of death grow. Notwithstanding the point that Christian images of death also always had an inner-worldly function (one need only to think of the tombs of the archbishops of Mainz), the definition of commemorative monuments now begins to change. Their inner-worldly function turns into an end in itself. The bourgeois memorial cult emerges,[12] and within this cult, there originates the independent genre of the war memorial. Since the French Revolution and the Wars of Liberation (1813–14), the number of memorials dedicated to soldiers killed in action has steadily increased. Not only do they stand in churches and cemeteries, but they have also moved from the churches into open spaces and into the landscape. It is not only the death of soldiers itself that serves political purposes, but the remembrance of it is also put to political service. The war memorial is intended to fulfill this task. It shifts the memory of the death of soldiers into an inner-worldly functional context that aims only at the future of the survivors. The decline of a Christian interpretation of death thus creates a space for meaning to be purely established in political and social terms.

Second, as war memorials become more widespread, they are divested more and more of the traditional differences of the society of estates. The physical memorial, previously reserved for great personages, was to include everyone and to do so in the name of all. The individual soldier killed in action becomes entitled to a memorial. Democratization is brought together with functionalization. With this, the equality of death, formerly only related to the Christian world to come, also gains an egalitarian claim on the political entity in whose service death was met. The names of all the dead become individually inscribed, or at least the number of dead noted, on memorial plaques and monuments to soldiers killed in action, so that in the future no one sinks into the past. This kind of democratization includes all the states in the European community of culture and tradition, regardless of their particular constitutional forms.

Compulsory military service certainly furthered the general entitlement of all those killed in action to a memorial, but it was not a necessary prerequisite. This is shown in Great Britain, a land without conscription, by the numerous memorials erected to honor heroes in overseas wars and wars in the colonies, culminating in Boer War memorials, which prefigured the type of memorials of the world wars.

The process of functionalization and democratization thus characterizes the historical succession of war memorials. They are supposed to attune the political sensibility of surviving onlookers to the same cause for whose sake the death of the soldiers is supposed to be remembered. This can certainly only be described as a long-term process, which is ramified in many different ways according to national and denominational patterns and can only be shown with many Christian overtones, accoutrements, signs of renewal, or relics.

But methodologically, it is especially difficult to distinguish the Christian and the national elements from one another. The recourse to the classical and Egyptian arsenal of forms, customary since the Renaissance, and later the use of natural and geometrical signs, gains a claim to exclusiveness in the late Enlightenment, figuratively countermanding the Christian interpretation of death. If, in the nineteenth century, numerous Christian symbols surface again, this iconographic finding can nevertheless refer to a context that is to be read differently in iconological terms. The context of classical figural elements in the baroque period is usually purely Christian, while the context of Christian figural elements in the nineteenth century can point in a different direction, primarily at the safeguarding of identity for a national future. In other words, the iconographically visible finding permits no immediate conclusion with regard to its iconological interpretation. In any case, war memorials themselves are already a visual sign of modernity (*Neuzeit*).

The extraordinary mausoleum of Maurice of Saxony by Pigalle (figure 17.3) may be taken as a signal of this change.[13] The earthly end is accepted without reference to any otherworldly perfection. The marshal, who is marching into the grave, leaves behind pyramids as a sign of eternal virtue, trophies as a sign of his glory, and survivors as mourners. They are moved by the death of their leader, lamenting his passing without being able to draw any hope from it.

FIGURE 17.3. J.-B. Pigalle. Tomb of Marshal Maurice of Saxony, Thomaskirche, Strasbourg. Photo by Hans Naumann.

The increasing thematization of mourning on tombs is part of the visual signature of the new age, for instance, in unsurpassed fashion by Canova in Vienna or Rome. Since then, the meaning of death is forced back to the survivors; since then, non-Christian symbols rival Christian symbols, completely eclipsing them in some places. The representation of subjective mourning is only the private mode of expression for a reinterpretation of death, a reinterpretation that allows death to be placed fully in the service of particular units of action in the political world of images.

III. The Functionalization of the Representation of Death in Favor of the Survivors

It goes without saying that every death at the hands of a human being in foreign or civil war has always had a political function. But in the horizon of the Christian doctrine of two worlds, death was deprived of its inner-worldly finiteness. Only when the otherworldly meaning of death disappeared could the political definition of its function gain the claim to a monopoly. War memorials refer to a temporal vanishing line in the future in which the identity of the particular community of agents who had the power to commemorate the dead with monuments was supposed to be safeguarded. That goes primarily for those halls of fame, temples of honor, and supermemorials whose costs exceeded the financial resources of a community or veterans' association of soldiers.

The many large memorials of the nineteenth and twentieth century were given a theoretical justification in 1808. It came from William Wood who suggested erecting a giant pyramid near London to stimulate heroism among business-minded Englishmen.[14] Wood maintained that only the extraordinary dimensions of a pyramid could steer the minds of the English people in the right direction, namely to support the cause of their native country. Wood's fundamental diagnosis was that "the ordinary feelings of men are not adequate to the present crisis." To extricate the population from its lethargy and egoism, the casualties of war would need to be transported into an earthly immortality so as to secure "unceasing fame, long duration" for them. The only means for doing so would be a gigantic memorial serving "to delight, astonish, elevate, or sway the minds of others through the medium of their senses." The costs incurred in constructing such a memorial would be minuscule when measured against the benefits expected: only three days of war outlay would be required to secure, by way of the memorial, a lasting motivation for heroic death.[15]

Certainly, a war memorial's psychological task of control has seldom been formulated so openly as to obviate any decoding through critique of ideology. It was only after the war that Wood's plan found its first realization at Waterloo where a pyramid was erected, together with British lions, by the citizens of Liège. Today, it is still a tourist destination for thousands upon thousands of visitors. The bygone demand for identification—to emulate the dead—has long since disappeared. The Napoleonic cult, in the meantime, established itself in the iconographic landscape of the Belle Alliance with its numerous memorials and monuments, and all of it is commercially exploited. In other words, the political space of experience of the Napoleonic wars has already been forsaken, and the original functional context of the memorials has been broken apart.

At the same time as William Wood, August Böckh devised a formula for Frederick William III that was to be read over and over again by Prussian subjects. It first appears on commemorative monuments of the Wars of Liberation, then much more frequently and with slight variations on memorials of the Wars of Unification: "In memory of those killed in action, in recognition of the living, for the emulation of future generations."[16] The obelisks, plinths, columns, spheres, cubes (figure 17.4) or the Gothic-inspired tabernacles (figure 17.5) upon which such admonitions were inscribed elude as far as the text is concerned—like Wood's pyramids—any transcendence of death in the Christian other world. The text and the post-Christian language of architectural forms aim at the earthly future of particular nations or peoples which, by virtue of such memorials, was supposed to be set for good.

This did not change when both the classical and the romantic arsenal of forms were obscured by specifically Wilhelminian and Victorian forms in the last third of the nineteenth century. Since about 1880, figures, heroines, and heroes appear more and more frequently on memorials—in Germany, they were supposed to commemorate the Wars of Unification, and in England, they were intended to commemorate the numerous colonial wars to safeguard the future of the Reich or the empire, respectively.

Of course, sayings like those of Wood or Frederick William III could no longer be quoted unconditionally after World War I when losses numbered in the millions, "for the emulation of future generations." Nonetheless, memorials still maintain their political function after 1918: they, too, promulgate a demand for identification. The dead embody an exemplary status; they died for a reason, and survivors are supposed to find themselves in accord with this reason so as *not* to allow the dead to have died *in vain.*[17] This is true across the board, and, therefore, it is not surprising that the arsenal of forms can be found in all countries, apart from characteristic diachronic displacements between enemy nations. If one disregards specific signals of identity on uniforms and helmets, the memorials' stock of motifs remains amazingly constant.

This can—in some places—even be demonstrated with respect to the separate situations in which the victors and the defeated find themselves. If the victors may *eo ipso* lay claim to glory and honor for themselves because they are shielded by success, the same is no less true for the losers. In Sedan, there is a memorial—one of comparatively few in France of the War of 1870–71—that stylistically resembles in its entirety the Ger-

FIGURE 17.4. Memorial to the fallen in the War of Liberation, 1813, Silesia.
Volksbund Deutsche Kriegsgräberfürsorge e. V.

man victory memorials of the same war (figure 17.6). A guardian spirit
crowns a gallant soldier with a wreath, and on the plinth, there is the assurance: "Impavidus numero victus" (Undaunted in defeat) (figure 17.7).
Theodor Mommsen could not yet have known the inscription when, in
1874, he acknowledged regarding the Romance peoples that "in the absence of victory and victors, they celebrate the anniversaries of defeats and
those gloriously defeated with such frenzy."[18] We Germans would not have
been very good at this. Mommsen presumably failed to recognize the po-

FIGURE 17.5. K. F. Schinkel. Memorial of Prussian soldiers, Waterloo.

litical function that inhered at this time in the frenzy for monuments. In any case, the Sedan memorial helped make it possible to morally come to terms with defeat; it could, by virtue of an inverse logic, raise a challenge to identify, precisely out of defeat, with the fatherland for whom the fallen had given their lives.

After 1918, the creators of German memorials followed this course. Even if no more victory angels were erected, the naked youths of the *ver sacer* (sacred spring) and the prone or mourning soldiers in uniform were still occasionally placed under the well-known motto, "in the battlefield,

FIGURE 17.6. A. Croisy. Monument to the fallen French soldiers of 1870, Sedan. Erected in 1897 by national subscription.

undefeated," as it was expressed at Oerlinghausen.[19] This was certainly not an inscription that could be displayed in the cemeteries of the former enemy states. Thus, there is a characteristic dichotomy between the heroic depictions produced after 1918 at home and the memorial themes and cemetery inscriptions that were permitted to be displayed in the former enemy countries: "Here lie German soldiers." The same death was identified in different ways, and the shared space of remembrance was shattered—depending on which memorial was erected where and how it spoke. Finally, it becomes clear (something which after 1945 has become obvious) that de-

FIGURE 17.7. Monument inscription, Sedan.

feat disposes one more toward remembering death as such than toward loading it with additional meanings. This also betrays the end of a long chain of national identifications. Today, a figural memorial for war cemeteries on foreign soil is often rejected for political and moral reasons, not to mention the costs involved.

Even if, as was mentioned above, the stock of motifs of war memorials (regardless of the causes and the enemies) has remained surprisingly uniform since the French Revolution, this betrays a common visual signature of modernity. This signature is found throughout most European countries whose memorials have emerged from the pregiven requirement of forming

FIGURE 17.8. J. Schilling. Memorial of the 76th Infantry Regiment, War of 1870–71, Hamburg-Eppendorf. Erected in 1877. Fritz Abshoff, *Deutschlands Ruhm und Stolz* (Berlin: Verlagsanstalt Universum [shortly after 1901]).

or preserving nation-states. Often the figural shapes of the memorials are so similar to one another that only the inscription itself permits an interpretation. For example, numerous Swiss memorials for soldiers who died during the world wars completely resemble their contemporaneous German counterparts, partly because there was no victory to be celebrated and partly because the Swiss helmets were very similar to those worn by the Germans.[20] Only the inscription makes it possible to establish the specific meaning when the stylistic features are identical.

On the other hand, there are formal similarities that last over time but jump from country to country. The history of memorials, then, runs in diachronic phase shifts. Depending on where victory came, war memo-

FIGURE 17.9. 1914–18 victory monument, Béziers.

rials emerged as victory monuments whose wealth of forms—regardless of their dates of origin—remains amazingly constant (figures 17.8–17.12). Stylistically, too, time seems to have almost come to a standstill. There is a diachronic series of analogous, almost identical war memorials, extending from Germany in 1871, via England in 1902 and 1918 and France in 1918, to Russia in 1945. Again and again, the same guardian spirits, heroines, eagles, cocks, or lions emerge along with palms, torches, helmets, and trophies of every sort; they not only recall the victory and the victims it cost but are at the same time supposed to establish an intuitive pattern of political education.

Evidently, the repertoire of European victory symbols is limited, leading to similar manifestations of taste from country to country that can be called upon independently of other developments in the plastic arts. Cer-

FIGURE 17.10. Regimental memorial of 1870, Wörth. Volksbund Deutsche Kriegsgräberfürsorge e. V.

tainly, a politically sensitive receptivity, one which remained comparatively homogeneous during the preceding 150 years, must be posited as a precondition for the series of victory memorials to be effective.

Altogether, victory monuments surely facilitate the identification radiating from them. Enemies are not remembered, unless as the defeated, and then their defeat is mostly concealed behind allegorical attributes or general platitudes. Even the death of one's own relatives is swallowed in such cases: "Death is swallowed up in victory," as it says, quoting 1 Corinthians 15:54, on victory memorials in British towns and villages after

FIGURE 17.11.   1914–18 municipal memorial, Hinderwell, England.

1918. Here, the national and the Pauline variants entered into an indissoluble connection.[21]

Regardless of the wide-ranging formal commonalities between all war memorials, there are certainly a number of national particularities whose special identity is supposed to be evoked by most of the memorials. As slight as the distinguishing criteria in the formal language of memorials may be, they become effective through their particular deployment and statistical frequency. It is striking that not only does Joan of Arc often appear in France as a masculine-feminine symbol (something for which there is hardly a counterpart in the voluminous Germanias or Bavarias), but France went

FIGURE 17.12. Soviet 1945 victory monument, Torgau. Institut für Denkmalpflege in der DDR, *Gedenkstätten* (Leipzig: Urania Verlag, 1974), fig. 92.

even further after World War I. Here, the fate of whole families (figure 17.13), the stricken wife (figure 17.14), the widowed and the orphaned, those left behind, and the parents of those killed in action are often chiseled in stone or cast in bronze and put on pedestals. Similar representations (figure 17.15) that trace the effects of war back to the home are to be found less often in Germany[22] and are erected in less obvious ways, for instance, on narrative relief plates.

To be sure—and this is true of all countries—different social and political groups make use of memorials to safely preserve their own partic-

FIGURE 17.13. E. Peynot. 1914–18 municipal memorial, St. Mihiel.

ular tradition by laying claim for themselves to the meaning of the death which has taken place. Thus the gray ossuary at Fort Douaumont, an amalgam of crypt and bunker, expresses the hagiography of the Catholic church that figuratively assures fallen soldiers of their ascension to heaven. On the other side, the historicizing and fortification-like great monument in the city of Verdun serves the republican tradition, once again in contradistinction to the memorial built by the city, which has its soldiers represented as joined together in an impenetrable wall.

In Belgium, the demands for identification emerging from the most important memorials are completely divergent. The Walloon ensemble of

FIGURE 17.14. 1914–18 municipal memorial, Peronne.

church, tower, and place of assembly at Liège—erected to commemorate World War I—is today overgrown with grass and weeds and is obviously no longer used for state rituals (figure 17.16). By contrast, the memorial at Dixmunde, razed after World War II by the Walloons, was rebuilt bigger and higher in 1965 (figure 17.17). With robust persistence, the Flemings succeeded in having their memorial not only appeal to their identity as a people but also serve as a pledge to pacificism, at once commemorating and uniting all minorities of the world. This is an offer of identification that goes beyond the boundaries of a nation-state and makes possible a further ritual development beyond the monument's occasion, World War I.[23]

Conversely, in East Germany, the Russian victors of 1945 represented themselves as liberators, and, consequently, the German soldiers killed in

FIGURE 17.15. 1914–18 municipal memorial, Schapbach/Schwarzwald. Siegfried Scharfe, *Deutschland über Alles: Ehrenmale des Weltkrieges* (Langewiesche, Königstein, 1938), fig. 58. Photo by Mauritius Verlag, Berlin.

World War II are thought of only by negation. A double function of war memorials becomes clear, namely to continue the history of the victors in such a way that they become the protectors of the defeated, consigning their former status to oblivion. This goes so far that even the monument for the victims of the concentration camp at Buchenwald—by Cremer (figure 17.18) —thematizes survival but not mass death.[24] Among the survivors, members of the Communist party predominate, while the other prisoners, who were far more numerous, are relegated to the background. Thus in the memorial, the inequality of the survivors dominates over the equality of the dead, something to which the entire complex testifies. The death that has

FIGURE 17.16. Inter-Allied memorial to the defenders of 1914, Liège. Erected in 1937.

taken place becomes fully a function of the victory that is supposed to be permanently set by means of a historical screen. Thus we are dealing with a conscious exclusion of others by obfuscation or silence—a practice more or less observed in all victory memorials.

American commemorative monuments distinguish themselves foremost by their shimmering finish and use of expensive materials. In this respect, they contrast with those of other nations, and are most similar to post-1918 British memorials.[25] In terms of their content, the memorials depict on marble plaques in crypts and memorial halls (figure 17.19) how the bygone conflict was strictly Manichaean, a struggle only between good and

FIGURE 17.17. Tower of the Yser, Dixmunde. Razed in 1946, rebuilt after 1952.

evil. There are victory monuments without a visible enemy; the enemy is bathed in the nothingness of the color black, displaced and outshone by the gold of the victors.

Enough of the examples of national particularities, which, despite the limited arsenal of forms common to all, still facilitate a sufficient identification for particular peoples.

Admittedly, it cannot be denied—across all national differences and in spite of the distinction between triumphant and nontriumphant war memorials—that no monument is completely absorbed by its political function. No matter how much dying for a cause is thematized in order to de-

FIGURE 17.18. Fritz Cremer. Concentration camp memorial, Buchenwald. Rieth, *Den Opfern der Gewalt*, fig. 33. Photo by Schäfer, Weimar.

rive a particular group identity, dying itself is also always a major additional theme.

Viewed generally, it is striking, however, that the process of dying is often omitted on memorials. Objections may be raised that memorials are directed precisely against a sculptural rendition of the transitional; however, for numerous memorials, it can be surmised that the memory of the "dying for . . . ," of having to die, provokes stylistic self-restraints. There is always a general legitimation of the soldiers' death, which transcends the death of the individual, even though the dying itself is rarely, if at all, recorded on the memorial. For most of the time, death is transfigured but not as the death of individuals; rather, it is their death in great numbers, numbers that are placed in a politically functional context. So and so many set out into battle and so and so many did not return home again. This is how the inscription was often stylized in Germany after 1918, particularly on regimental memorials erected with the intention of preserving an additional identity that was military in nature.

FIGURE 17.19. U.S. World War II military cemetery, Neuville-en-Condroz, Ardennes.

But what did such constructions of continuity, whose effect on future generations cannot be underestimated, matter in regard to the spontaneous mourning for the child, son, or husband whose memory needed to be kept alive by relatives? Death still remained the death of individuals, mourned for by survivors. Therefore, memorials could emerge like the one by Käthe Kollwitz (figure 17.20), who had lost her son in Langemarck and who belonged among the losers from then on, irrespective of how the war might turn out. After nearly twenty years of meditation and work, she created a memorial[26] whose message is capable of outliving its own raison d'être be-

FIGURE 17.20. Käthe Kollwitz. *Mourning Parents,* 1914–18 military cemetery, Vladslo.

cause it thematizes survival in relation to death itself, not in relation to dying for something.

IV. The Democratization of Death

When at the beginning of modernity (*Neuzeit*)—in the sense of the experience of a new time—the desire arose for war memorials that were supposed to commemorate the pioneers of the future, Goethe had already formulated the "demands on modern sculptors."[27] He pointed out how earlier memorials were considered to have been intelligible so long as the front lines and the viewpoints of the opponents stirred clear partisanship. For instance, to see a Christian victorious over a Turk would only reinforce justified hatred for slaveholders. However, this would become difficult in modernity (*Moderne*), in present-day Europe, where conflict is said to have originated in industrial and trading interests but where the equality of both sides in terms of religion and morals could hardly be denied. In cases where the two sides could barely be differentiated by their uniforms, as with the French and the Germans, the representation of the fighting opponents could not be expected to have an unambiguous sense anymore. Eventually, when represented without any clothing—it is the sculptors' right to represent their fighters in this way—both sides become "completely the same: there are handsome people murdering each other, and the fateful group of Eteocles and Polynices has to always be repeated like destiny—only becoming meaningful with the presence of the Furies."

With political detachment, Goethe refers to the moral agreement of the opponents and to their common economic situation of conflict, an interpretation that was hardly accepted by the jubilant victors and the afflicted losers after 1815. This kind of historical-structural commonality where the Furies presided was not intended by the founders of memorials who instead aimed at an inner uniformity, at a national homogeneity that excluded others. The extent to which they sounded a common tone beyond national borders, however, is shown by the numerous homologies in the memorials' stock of forms.

The equality in death of those who were killed in action became a motif received with less and less favor. During the Wars of Unification, there were still memorials—such as the one in Kissingen in 1866—that commemorated both sides together. This happened in southern Germany, a region divided between Berlin and Vienna. Even common graves for German and French soldiers can still be frequently found on the battlefields of 1870–71. The reburial of the bodies of French soldiers killed in the Metz region happened later with the help of both French and German troops. In 1915, Wilhelm II had an honorary monument erected near St. Quentin, in front of which two figures cast in bronze represented young and old. It was part of the enclosing walls of a cemetery where soldiers from both sides were buried together. After 1918, the bodies of fallen French soldiers were exchanged for German ones who since then rest under French names. From then on, joint burial only occurred sporadically. After 1945, the separation of the dead has, in general, remained customary—to the point of exhuming all fallen Americans from German soil.[28]

There is thus a trend to be taken into account that increasingly demands the separation of enemies killed in action. The enmity is supposed to reach even beyond death so as not to forfeit the identity of one's own cause. Equality in death is revoked in favor of an equality safeguarding national homogeneity: it is the homogeneity of the living and the survivors, in their particular political grouping. The construction of memorials takes place through political entities that by this very act define themselves against others. Therefore, already the functionalization of war memorials tends toward a *religion civile* in Rousseau's sense, and helps to establish democratic legitimacy. In the memorial, such a legitimacy creates an equality of those who died for the fatherland which is directed inward but not outward. Compared to the feudal past, the position of individuals on war memorials is transformed on the basis of the nation-state.

Still in the hierarchical tradition, a long series of memorials depicting victorious generals exists without their deaths at the hands of the enemy—as in the case of Scharnhorst—necessarily being a prerequisite for a monument. Even living generals remain worthy of memorialization: for instance, in the Prussian military tradition, Blücher or Moltke; or in the hagiographic tradition, Maistre at Nôtre-Dame de Lorette (figure 17.21); or in the tradition of republican pathos, Kellermann; or in the monumental tradition of giving prominence to a leader, General Patton. It is well known that the egalitarian tendency does not preclude the cult of the leader that emerges from the tradition of military rank in the hierarchical series of memorials to individual heroes.[29]

What is really new is the long-term trend to abolish the estate-based hierarchical system in order to emphasize the equality of all soldiers' deaths, irrespective of rank. The East Prussian Senior President von Schön sneered at a memorial erected in honor of General Karl von Bülow: it would have been better to immortalize the reservist (*Landsturmmann*) who shouted "Kiss my . . . " at the general when he ordered the retreat to be sounded.[30]

In the name of the Prussian reserve forces, Schön opposed every memorial devoted to commanders. He lived off the republican pathos that fell back on revolutionary models during the Wars of Liberation. Thus as early as 1798, an antimonarchic memorial was conceived: it was to be dedicated

FIGURE 17.21. Monument to General Maistre and the 21st Army Corps, Nôtre-Dame de Lorette, 1927.

to the emperor and the Prussian king, and the inscription was supposed to end with the sentence: "Sorrowful thanks from the mourning Fatherland! To all those whose names do not appear on this column."[31]

In this satirical testimonial, the entitlement of all the hitherto un-named to a memorial is asserted. And without doubt, the political cult of memorials for the war casualties dovetailed with a monarchical-estates tra-dition that is perpetuated but also recast. With this, the equal status of all war casualties is effected in terms of the layout of both their graves and their war memorials. The two are connected with one another, even if the fallen soldiers' entitlement to a memorial preceded their right to their own resting places.[32] In what follows, both will be treated in juxtaposition.

The transition from a monarchical memorial to a memorial for the people (the hybrid forms of which have been clearly established by Nipperdey)[33] finds its counterpart in the increase in the politically motivated layout of graves. Taken as a whole, the representative grave for the ruler is first complemented by the representative war grave, then—temporally speaking—overtaken by it. On the consecrated tombs, the identity of political protagonists—first of the dynasties and then of the nation to be created—was supposed to find its manifest expression. Not only do the living vouch for the dead in front of the memorial, but the dead are also supposed to vouch for life. Which life is politically intended is delimited by the layout of the grave, the memorial, and the cult attached to it.

To what extent both war graves and the soldiers' entitlement to a memorial owe their origin to a revolutionary impulse initially directed against the estates-monarchic tradition can be shown by literary examples.

Toward the end of the eighteenth century, a first critique is directed at the tombs of rulers. The later cemeteries for soldiers and other places of burial had to compete with these tombs as sites of identification, finally displacing them as a symbol of national representation. For Klopstock, one of the initiators of the bourgeois memorial cult, it was no longer birth that counted but only merit:

> Birthright to immortality
> Is unjust to posterity. As soon as history does one day
> What it is obliged to do: it will bury through silence and
>   no longer set
> The kings themselves up as mummies.
> After death, they are what we are.
> If their name remains, only merit will save it,
> Not the crown: for it, too,
> Fell with the head of the dying.[34]

Embittered and with Christian-revolutionary pathos, Schubart exclaimed: "There they lie, the proud ruins of rulers, / Formerly the gods of this world!"[35] He directs his hatred and scorn at the rulers' tombs, against those places in St. Denis that were cleared away during the revolution.

The political function of the rulers' tombs, however, was to be adopted and used in the service of democratic ends. The burial sites and commemorative memorials for fighters killed in action during civil wars later on served new claims to legitimacy. In 1830, Béranger demanded a holy place for the fallen barricade fighters: "Place wreaths on the graves from our days in July, / Perform, innocent children, the holy rite; / Here flowers and palms to these sarcophagi, / Memorials for the people, not just royal might."[36] In Brussels, the appeal found its fulfillment in the Place des Martyrs, while in Berlin, the "Appeal of the Central Board of the Committee on Burials" on behalf of those killed in March 1848 went unheard after the revolution's failure.[37] Instead, the government troops killed in action—just like those at Rastatt—received their own memorial.

The political cult of the dead, to the extent that it depends on the building of war memorials, remains under the victors' control—as long as they are in a position to exercise their power. But irrespective of the changing political situation, the demand for equality for all war memorials has gained acceptance since the revolution. In addition, the same visual tone is sounded regardless of forms of government. The tombs of the "unknown soldier"—one for all—are the last step in this democratization of death. Some of the visual documents testifying to this path will be traced below.

From 1815 to 1918, the equality of all those killed in action is increasingly recognized, regardless of the military ranks and positions that led to their death. Although Hanoverian officers still erected a monument at Waterloo that only commemorated commissioned officers and not the noncommissioned officers and common soldiers who had lost their lives, such memorials were the exception. By and large, it becomes customary, especially after the Wars of Unification, to list commissioned officers, noncommissioned officers, and soldiers separately on regimental and municipal memorials—but on the same plinth. The use of depictions of officers to represent common soldiers is a stylistic device that comes to emphasize this equality. In Poznan after 1866, four soldiers are portrayed with the features of four generals (figure 17.22); or at Navarin, General Gouraud and Roosevelt's nephew, a lieutenant when he was killed, are depicted as assault soldiers (figure 17.23). Thus the upper ranks participate in the glory of everyone, a glory that they at the same time represent and exemplify.

In the war cemeteries themselves, an absolute equality is certainly introduced. The rule that officers are to be buried individually is generalized for everyone. The idea that every soldier deserved his own grave and gravestone was for the first time legally instituted by the North in the American

FIGURE 17.22. S. Fenque. Memorial of the 5th Army Corps at the Battle of Nachod (1866), Poznan. Abshoff, *Deutschlands Ruhm und Stolz.*

Civil War, even though Southerners remained, at first, excluded from the commemorative ceremonies.[38] This democratic norm, anticipated by the Peace of Frankfurt of 1871, was generally followed in World War I by the Western and Central powers. The individual "right to rest in peace" has, in the meantime, become a norm of international law;[39] however, Russia would not endorse it for reasons whose ideological and realistic components are hard to distinguish.

But at the same time that this democratic rule was instituted to individually memorialize every soldier, it became impossible to comply with it. For the dead who were each supposed to have their own grave were often-

FIGURE 17.23. Réal del Sarte. Allied 1914–18 memorial and ossuary Navarin-Ferme near Reims. From a postcard by C. A. P., 44 rue Letellier, Paris. © S. P. A. D. E. M., Paris.

times not found or they could no longer be identified. In the battles of the summer of 1916, seventy-two thousand of the casualties on the German side were identifiable and eighty-six thousand were missing or their corpses were mutilated beyond recognition. Similar statistics occurred in Flanders or at Verdun on both sides of the front. The technical means of annihilation had been perfected to such an extent that it was no longer possible to find the dead or lay them to rest, as the law stipulated. Individuals were swallowed up by mass death. This fact evoked two kinds of responses, both expressed in the commemorative monuments.

The first was that the sites of death were simply transformed into memorials themselves by leaving them as they were found after the armistice took hold. Hill 60 at Ypres was a battlefield that was later declared a cemetery because approximately eight thousand combatants were physically annihilated on a few acres of land and never found. With this, a postulate of Giraud's in the French Revolution was fulfilled in an ironic reversal: Giraud planned a cemetery operation for Paris that would mold the calcined bones of the deceased into medallions or pillars so that, as a result, the dead would be identical with their commemorative memorial.[40] This purely inner-worldly postulate aimed at immortalizing the dead in this world by turning the corporeal remains into the gravestone. The postulate, certainly still enjoying a certain magical quality during the eighteenth century, was realized in World War I. In Fort Douaumont, about seven hundred German soldiers suffocated and were immured: the wall is their gravestone—an event that was to repeat itself in the bombing raids of 1939–45, affecting everyone regardless of age and gender.

The second response was to erect massive monuments, such as those at Ypres, Vimy (figure 17.24), Thiepval, or Navarin, to mention only a few. On these monuments, the names of all the fallen who could never have a grave but whose names were never to be forgotten were written. "Their name liveth for evermore," as the biblical saying chosen by Kipling goes. Promising earthly immortality, the saying is engraved on monuments in all British cemeteries.

Thus the category of the monumental victory memorial from the nineteenth century turned into an unequivocal memorial to the dead. The nation, which had previously shored up its identity by way of victory monuments, now remembered all the dead individually so as to let a *volonté générale*—in Rousseau's sense—arise from a *volonté de tous*. Additionally, the formerly Christian judgment metaphor does not allow any souls to escape and guarantees a fatefully enriched earthly eternity now.

Perhaps the following appraisal can be made. Almost all the memorials of World War I distinguish themselves by the fact that they compensate for helplessness by pathos. The death of hundreds of thousands on a few square miles of contested earth left an obligation to search for justifications that were hard to create with traditional metaphors and concepts. The desire to salvage continuities or identities that were everywhere torn apart by death all too easily fell short. In Great Britain, there are several memorials that incorporate a timepiece, the ancient symbol of death—be it a sundial or an electric clock—in order to remember, through the death of soldiers, the fact of death itself. In this move back, there is nevertheless the attempt to evoke a new identity, for instance when the maxim is added—as in Hinderwell (figure 17.11): "Pass not this stone in sorrow but in pride / And live your lives as nobly as they died."

FIGURE 17.24. W. Allward. 1914–18 Canadian National Memorial, Vimy.

World War II brought with it a transformation in the iconographic landscape of memorials that also changed political sensibility. The simple expansion of memorials by the addition of plaques for those who died between 1939–45 was still a fresh and generally customary tradition. In France, it was decreed by the state in order to mark a new beginning solely through memorials of the Resistance. But the style of heroic realism, the style in which most of the monuments by the Russians or those for the Resistance in France or Belgium were erected, often barely differs in its formal features from the official art of National Socialism. Over and above that, however, there are recognizable innovations that forgo a visual appeal to political or social identification with the sense of past death.

FIGURE 17.25. Christian Klepsch. 1939–45 memorial, Zell, Lower Bavaria, 1972. [The inscription reads: "In memory of the fallen and missing."—trans.]

The annihilation not only of the living but also of physical bodies during air raids and even more in the German concentration camps necessitated the renunciation of the old arsenal of forms for war and victory memorials. Victims condemned to senselessness required, if at all, a kind of negative monument.

Thus, in a Bavarian town, a dead person is symbolized as a hollow form between three basalt blocks (figure 17.25). In Rotterdam, the destruction of human bodies appears, in Zadkine's work, as despair and accusation, even though the gestures of the dying man seeking help may, perhaps, provide a shimmer of hope. Lastly, there are numerous nonrepresentational monuments with no direct reference to the human body (figure 17.26).[41]

FIGURE 17.26. F. Duszenko and A. Haupt. Detail of concentration camp memorial, Treblinka, 1964. Rieth, *Den Opfern der Gewalt,* fig. 2. Photo by Bommer, Strasbourg.

Their political function boils down, if at all, to the question of their meaning, without being able to sensibly convey a visual answer. Certainly, the formal language of resurrection often remains preserved here, but in the words of Max Imdahl, it is no longer a metaphor of resurrection, but rather a metaphor of this metaphor.

Finally, during the Vietnam war, Edward Kienholz created the anti-memorial, a parody of the victory monument in Arlington. He constructed an ordinary scene within which a portable war memorial is placed. Next to it there is a plaque upon which, depending on the new beginning of a war, the dead can be recorded with chalk so that the memorial is not blamed for the oblivion of death but rather human beings who shirk the memory of the dead.[42] Although not everywhere and not universally, a tendency has thus grown in the Western world to represent death in foreign or civil war only as a question and no longer as an answer, only as demanding meaning and no longer as establishing meaning. What remains is the identity of the dead with themselves; the capability of memorializing the dead eludes the formal language of political sensibility.

V. Concluding Remarks

The history of European war memorials testifies to a common visual signature of modernity. But it just as much attests to an optical transformation of experience. This transformation involves social and political sensibility, which has its own history and has had a productive as well as receptive effect on the language of memorials.

The connection between a demand for meaning in political and social terms and its visual expression is established by the formal language of memorials that is supposed to reach the sensibility of observers. Both the forms and the sensibility are subject to historical transformation, but they apparently change along different temporal rhythms. Hence the identities that a memorial is intended to evoke melt away—in part because sensory receptivity eludes the formal language presented and in part because the forms, once shaped, begin to speak another language than the one from which they were initially fashioned. Memorials, like all works of art, have a surplus potential to take on a life of their own. For this reason, the original meaning of countless memorials is no longer recognizable without recourse to inscriptions or other empirically comprehensible reference signals.

Since the French Revolution, the historical experience begins to emerge that war memorials lose their original emphasis with the passing of the generations responsible for their construction. Numerous memorials from the nineteenth century have not only acquired an external patina; they have fallen into oblivion, and if they are maintained and visited, then only rarely is it to reassert their original political sense. Even in the victor countries of 1918, the celebration of the armistice of November 11 draws fewer and fewer people. The political cult at the old war memorials dries up as soon as the last survivors pass away.[43] One might trace this result back to the natural succession of generations, without having to call upon the fast pace of the modern age. Political experiences or messages can only be passed down beyond the death of a particular generation with great effort. To this end, societal institutions are required. In any case, the memorial, the supposed guarantor of sensory transmission beyond death, does not appear to be capable of achieving this task by itself. A conscious adoption of the message is always necessary.

For this reason, there are exceptions, especially where national memorials are concerned. Their maintenance is taken care of by particular political associations. In this case, it becomes possible for the cultic acts of which they are the focus to last for a longer time.

The dismantling of memorials testifies to how long the inscriptions and signatures of war memorials speak to future generations. Such dismantlings take place for the most part when the founding generation has neither entirely passed away nor can be fought as a direct political opponent. In 1918, after a half century had gone by, the French were able to afford to leave untouched the German war memorials of 1870–71 in Alsace-Lorraine—as monuments of those who were now the defeated. Memorials are taken down when they are felt to be a threat or when a tradition that is still living is intended to be suppressed. To mention a few intervals between commemorated dates and the dismantling of memorials: in Celle, a monument commemorating 1866 was already dismantled in 1869; in Düsseldorf, a 1918 monument or in Weimar, one from 1920—both dismantled in 1933; in Luxembourg and Compiègne, ones from 1918—dismantled in 1940; and monuments of 1918 in many other places in Germany—removed after World War II. In all cases, the intention was to annul political demands for identification.

Memorials long outlasting their immediate occasion may be preserved for historical or traditional reasons, but, even then, their expressive power gradually changes. All over Europe, there is a diachronic line of victory memorials whose formal similarity holds out regardless of particular countries and victors. They move together structurally. It is, then, only victory as such, no longer any particular victory, that is brought to mind. The formal language specific to war memorials is obsolete without ceasing to speak. Evidently, this language outlives its unique, politically and socially determined causes, so that the signs are no longer understood politically but remain comprehensible nonetheless. This difference, this gap, is filled, so to speak, by aesthetics; it interrogates the forms in terms of their own "statement." In other words, the "aesthetic" possibilities for a statement, connected to the sensory receptivity of observers, outlast the political demands for identification that they were supposed to establish. If one investigates war memorials by asking which "aesthetic" signals have outlasted their immediate occasion and which signs have endured throughout the changes in form, one is clearly referred back to symbols of death. Whether dressed in hope or cloaked in grief, symbols of death last longer than any individual case. Although the individual case of death may fade, death is nonetheless still in store for every observer.

Translated by Todd Presner

Afterword to Charlotte Beradt's *The Third Reich of Dreams*

> But does it really matter then whether it was a dream or not,
> if this dream revealed the truth to me?
>   —Dostoyevsky

A subtle but irrevocable change is presently taking place in the research on the Third Reich. The generation of the contemporaries of the Third Reich and its accomplices, of those directly affected and of eyewitnesses, is slowly passing away while the next generation has grown up. With the succession of generations, the subject under examination is likewise changing. Against the experience-saturated present past of the survivors comes an unadulterated past that has become remote from experience—however much we still live in its shadow today. This change has methodological consequences. The eyewitnesses are slowly disappearing and even the earwitnesses are passing away. With the dying memories, the distance not only becomes greater but its quality changes, too. Soon, only the files will still speak, enriched by pictures, films, and memoirs. The research criteria are becoming more austere, but they are—perhaps—also less vivid, less saturated with the empirical, even though they promise to recognize or appreciate more in their objectivity. The moral consternation, the disguised protective functions, the accusations and the designations of guilt by historiography—all these techniques of mastering the past (*Vergangenheitsbewältigungstechniken*) lose their quality as existential political matters; they fade in favor of individual academic research and analyses controlled by hypothesis, even if their intentions as political scholarship remain unmistakable.

It is in this context that a collection of source material of unique and astounding quality has appeared, namely the dreams compiled by Charlotte

Beradt.[1] With courage and foresight, Charlotte Beradt began in 1933 to ask approximately three hundred people about their dreams. In order to save them, she took them abroad into her American exile in 1939. Here, once again, a generation of those involved has the chance to speak in a manner that cannot be more powerfully imagined. With a careful, sobering interpretation, Beradt introduces the social and political milieu of the dream reports, helping us unlock the dreams with the multilayered knowledge of a contemporary. To leave no doubt about the matter, this collection of dreams in no way replaces social-scientific or historical investigations, or economic, political science, or biographical research strategies. But it achieves something offered by no other genre of sources. We experience an amazing change in perspective that helps us see further and recognize new things. Reading this book, for example, throws a bright light on the present-day controversy over the question—which is based on the premise of a false alternative—to what extent was Hitler and, with him, German National Socialism, a singular case, or whether Hitler was only an epiphenomenon of general social or economic conditions that were not limited to Germany but received a particular expression there. Anyone who has read Beradt's collection of sources will quickly realize that one mode of posing the question can in no way be answered without the other. The sources presented testify to how Hitler was inseparable from the preconditions that nurtured him, and how these preconditions were incorporated in himself. Hitler appears in the dreams about twenty times. The other major figures of the day (of these, Göring the most frequently) appear more seldom, and it becomes clear where the psychic disposition of the German population was inseparable from Hitler as their charismatic leader (in the sense used by Max Weber).

For a historian working on the history of the Third Reich, Beradt's documentation of dreams represents a first-rate source. It opens up layers not even reached by diary entries. The narrated dreams have the character of events that precede the writing of them, despite the fact that they were written down ex post facto. In an exemplary fashion, they lead us into the recesses of the apparently private realm of the everyday, to where waves of propaganda and terror penetrate. The dreams bear witness to an initially open terror that then turns insidious, and they even anticipate its violent crescendo.

For whatever the reasons—be it out of methodologically expedient caution or be it for the plausible reason that they are inadequately accessible—dreams do not comprise part of the canon of sources used in the historical disciplines. Of course, this was not always the case. Therefore, we are permitted to take a quick look back to help us open the buried access to this realm of sources.

Since the beginning of historical reports and narrations, dreams have belonged to the permanent stock of those things that seemed worthy of handing down. For dreams maintained their fixed status in high cultures as they did, of course, in so-called primitive cultures. Rulers often required their interpretation in order to be able to act. Dreams had their official, priest-like interpreters in political or religious institutions. After all, dreams about everyday life found their interpreters everywhere. These interpreters ritualized their patterns of interpretation, which, in turn, affected the field of action and the behavior patterns of the population. Whether dreams were caused by magical customs, whether they were experienced as sent from the realm of spirits and demons, whether they were understood as the result of telluric or cosmic influences mediated through the air, or whether they appeared in the Judeo-Christian tradition as revelations from God (in whose place there could be an angel or even the devil)—in all of these cases, humans have tried over and over again to process disclosures from the world of sleep that defy control and integrate them into everyday life.

Precisely where we appear to be completely alone, by ourselves asleep, we are ambushed. Thus we have developed coping mechanisms to rationalize most of the visions experienced as threats. All interpreters had their empirical procedures that could be substantiated through the frequent repetition of dream images. And when the dream images had a surprising newness to them, they provoked unique answers. The point was always to squeeze a meaning—their meaning—out of every dream. Over the centuries, numerous dream books have conveyed the collected empirical knowledge needed for interpreting dreams. In their seeming atemporality, dreams tied together all the temporal dimensions. They were considered as nocturnal doublings of a particular day's activities, as the processing of the past that is left behind, and, even more than this, they were regarded as beacons to the future. And according to the degree of comprehensibility exhibited by the dream images, techniques were developed to decode symbols beyond their directly plausible message—indeed Artemidorus already canonized interpretations later found by Freud to be worth investigating.

Of course, parallel to this institutionalized mastery of dreams, the history of high cultures is also acquainted with an equally strong strand of critique of them. One of the first steps of elucidation was to reduce dream images to physical stimuli. Dream critiques were passed down from the Sophists via the Epicurean school, finally gaining a decisive cogency with Fontenelle and Bayle. Since then, instead of interpreting dreams, it has been part of the educational habitus (*Bildungshabitus*) of enlightened minds in modernity to dismiss dreams as psychologically explainable phenomena and, therefore, as inconsequential fantasies. But already within the Christian tradition, dream interpretations were historicized and theologically rationalized. Supernatural dreams that were said to be sent from God or the angels remained primarily reserved for the past, the times of the two testaments. Later dream revelations and visions, for instance those of saints, were possible but could, just as likely, fall under suspicion of heresy. At any rate, it still remained disputed in Lutheran circles whether the great dream vision of Frederick the Wise that anticipated the Reformation was to be understood as divinely sent or as a legend. The educated of the eighteenth century traced all dreams back to natural causes. Since then, any dream inspiration was to be repudiated—and not just for theological reasons. Dream inspiration, whether divine or not, belonged to the past.

Certainly to the extent that the rationalistic technique of reduction trivialized all dreams, the need for interpretation of dreams remained an open question. The romantics already began to consider them again. And not even Ranke shied away from reporting the dream of an animated duchess at the court of Louis XIV because, in the sense of the moral world order, he was himself ready to adopt the dream's death-portending interpretation by a Capuchin friar.

Historians seeking to write a history of mentalities and behavior patterns as well as their respective self-interpretation will be well advised to also include that counterworld of dreams passed down to us from earlier times. As Peter Burke has demanded, they can draft a social history of dreams. Up until now, this has certainly remained a postulate, but to fulfill the demand would at least correspond with the self-understanding of earlier times when dream occurrences were still used to interpret the everyday. And the history of dream criticism, then, belongs just as much to this project. Beradt's collection attests to how helpful the inclusion of dream experiences can be to researching the history of the everyday.

In the history of dream interpretation, Freud has become a trailblazer;

after him, paths have diverged again in a strange way. It was precisely the critical Enlightenment impulse that led Freud to distill old, but also newly discovered, horizons of meaning from dreams within the framework of his scientifically grounded anthropology. Since then, the traditional criticism of dream interpretations can no longer one-sidedly credit itself with pure rationality. Following Freud, there is rather a demonstrable rationality in-hering within dreams. To deny this would be contrary to reason.

Beradt's text is, indeed, amenable to questions arising out of the Freud-ian school, but it is in no way reliant on them. Nowhere were the dreams narrated with a therapeutic intention. And even if such an intention was harbored in silence, it was not a question of evoking associations that would have, in a diagnostic fashion, referred the dream interpretation back to one's private life. Nor was it a question of dream witnesses whose dreams arose in the context of psychopathology, clinics for mental illnesses, or the psy-chiatrist's couch. Rather, it is a question of normal dreams, so to speak, of everyday life whose very normality and everyday quality render transparent precisely what is so difficult to grasp about events after 1933.

Theoretically, three levels can be defined at which dreams become methodologically useful for the historian. First of all, as individual dreams, they can help to unlock a particular life history. In this area, there have been several exciting attempts to combine psychoanalytic approaches with historical description. Secondly, dreams can also be read as the transper-sonal medium of social and political relationships and conflicts, extending from the family to political forms of organization. This context obviously has some influence on psychoanalytic therapies, but it can also be method-ologically isolated. Beradt's text shows us that there are dreams that do not necessitate such isolation at all because they recast social and political con-flicts directly into dream-like pictorial histories and into their image world. Finally, dreams can be read with regard to their symbolic language, a lan-guage that may lay claim to having validity more or less throughout all times. On this level, questions of continuance and duration are treated.

All three levels are usually interwoven and are thematized differently depending on the direction taken by a given analytical school. For thera-peutic purposes, one level can certainly not be understood without reference to another level. For the social historian, this method, however, is in no way compulsory. Seen from a dogmatic point of view with regard to Freudian theory, the dream interpretations presented by Beradt have been abbreviated. There are certainly consequences which thus arise, namely that specifically social and political points are missed only because dreams can also be interpreted in an individual-psychological way—because vehement anxiety dreams, for instance, are legible as truncated wish dreams able to be traced back to unresolved childhood conflicts. As the editor of the collection, Beradt, in a methodologically consistent decision, refrained from presenting the dreams as testimonies of private conflicts. In order to make apparent the political content of the dream experiences, she left aside all the dreams whose erotic content did not stretch beyond the dreamer's private life history. By contrast, such erotic dreams whose manifest content can clearly be related to political figures, for instance, to Hitler, were included. Charlotte Beradt likewise refrained from presenting purely violent dreams and sheer nightmares because they can appear anywhere and everywhere without being able to say anything specific about the time of National Socialism.

A usage of the testimonials presented by Beradt that is true to the sources therefore stands and falls with the following thesis, as simple as it is compelling. In the dreams—regardless of their psychogenesis—direct experiences of the Third Reich find their expression, experiences that remained specifically bound to the period of six years from 1933 to 1939 and the National Socialist rule. This can in no way be doubted.

The references to the Berlin of that time are numerous since this is where most of the witnesses came from. References appear to the Kurfürstendamm, the Reichstag and its burning, the city railway, the Kaufhaus des Westens (department store of the West), the tourist cafés along the Havel—or border paths in the Riesengebirge—to mention only some locales. And this native ambience is reshaped by the signs and signals of the new time. They clap themselves over the everyday: the banners, slogans and flags, badges and insignia, collection boxes and marching columns. Above all, in half the dreams, the Party organizations emerge in uniform: the Hitler Youth, the SA, the SS, and twice, the concentration camps as well, although the latter were outside the dreamers' direct experience. The political distinctiveness of the scenes of that time is expressed in all the dream images.

Just as numerous are the empirical occasions that can be derived from the dreams themselves or that are elucidated by the editor: for example, the arrest of a relative, or a fund-raising campaign for the *Winterhilfswerk*,[2] or the breaking-off of an engagement to a German Jew—and whatever else the occasions were that evoked the dream images.

Whoever asks about the representativeness of Beradt's sources will necessarily be referred to suppositions. However, some conclusions can be freely drawn. Charlotte Beradt lets approximately fifty witnesses report their dreams *in extenso*. She frequently reviews an entire series of dreams following upon one another in order to make especially clear the variations in experience as well as their complexity. Around twenty people are given the chance to speak multiple times about their dreams so that the repetitions of certain political dream scenes gain a formative power and characterize an experiential type.

The social status of the dream witness can be frequently derived from the dream itself. But the content of the dream is in no way interpretable solely from the initial professional, social, or political position involved in the private life history. In any case, Charlotte Beradt mentions the occupations to present a wide range for our inspection, extending from a factory owner to a housemaid, from skilled manual laborers and produce dealers to students, doctors, and civil servants. Frequently, homemakers of all ages are given the chance to speak. To be sure, the circle includes only a limited number of people and, indeed, people who did not exactly sympathize openly, if at all, with the new regime. Among them, we find a group of Jews, and with significant variations in the dreams, people who, according to the Nuremberg Laws, had been classified as "crossbreeds" (*Mischlinge*) of varying degrees. Thus it can at least be said that our witnesses stand for those bourgeois, lower middle-class, and semi-middle-class strata that were outside of the Party and its organizations. The dreams come from a situation in which the majority of the population initially found itself. The dreamers are not National Socialists but rather citizens who could be identified in the party spectrum of Weimar as middle-of-the-road with a spread toward the Left, and, among them, some people are given the chance to speak who consciously pursued the path of resistance.

Without wanting to anticipate the perceptive interpretations of the author, permit me just a few references to the form and content of the dreams. What is the formal source status of the dreams presented? Although dreams cannot be deliberately produced, they nevertheless belong within the realm of human fictions. Rather than offering a realistic representation of reality, they instead throw a particularly glaring light on the very reality from which they come.

After they are written down, dreams are accordingly counted among the genre of sources of fictional texts. In Beradt's collection, three groups of dreams can be formally distinguished: pure image visions, sheer epigrammatic texts, or dreams of action. The latter outweigh the other two by far. They are, as it were, picture stories in which people speak, or ones in which language is lost. In their internal structure, they are often shaped like short stories, with a beginning and an ending. The density and succinctness of their message moves these dreams close to tales by Kleist, Hebel, or even more, by Kafka. Some passages can be found again, verbatim, in contemporary writers. But our author rightly indicates that the short stories frequently already anticipate paradoxical situations that have only been depicted later by Beckett, Ionescu, or Orwell. No one would dispute the poetic quality of the dreamed short stories. In this, they resemble poetry which—to use Aristotle's words—does not report what has happened but rather what could happen. Many of the dream stories contain a verisimilitude that reaches further than what appeared empirically provable at the time they were dreamt. They anticipate the empirically improbable, which later, in the catastrophe of destruction, became reality. To this extent, they had a prognostic content.

Of course, the prognostic content does not have to be exclusively related to the personal future of the dreamer, as in traditional dream interpretations. For the custom of divinely deriving from dreams private decisions to be made in the future or coming disasters was not taken up again here in a naive manner, as it were. Rather, it was a question of assimilating generalizable experiences with implications for the future that articulated possibilities of totalitarian rule not imaginable until then.

It is precisely this poetic quality of the dreams that allows us to obtain messages from our genre of sources that cannot be captured through factual reports. No one can prevent historians from turning any possible evidence into a source by methodically investigating it. In the way in which historians can adduce any genre of fiction, in a more or less mediated fashion, as evidence for facticity, they can also interrogate the dream. The reality made strange in dreams gains an inscrutable dimension, a dimension that cannot be ascertained from other sources. From these stories, first dreamed and then narrated, conclusions can be drawn and from them insights can be gained for reconstructing the reality of the emergence of the Third Reich.

To this extent, the dreams belong in the vicinity of political jokes or political cabaret, or they refer to the sort of refraction of experience that seems to come from a madhouse or that is practiced today in black humor. Reading the dreams always requires an art of interpretation able to relate fictional texts to the history of that which is supposedly only factual. Because every history (*Geschichte*) of the factual turns into a historical (*historische*) construct as soon as it is written down, this approach gains in importance. The work of the dream is itself a "fact" sui generis. Precisely because the dreamed stories never took place in the way in which they are reported, they throw light on that which must be understood as factual. This facticity then gains a multilayeredness in which the epistemological work of dreams is contained.

With this, we arrive at the content itself. It concerns dreams that are reacting to an enormous outside pressure. This outer pressure is produced through propaganda and terror. Open terror was directed against individuals and against groups that could be identified as different. It struck selectively so as to better exert pressure on the masses. Its echo resounds from every dream. What is decisive, however, is less the open terror mentioned here and more the insidious terror initially effected via propaganda that concealed threats behind its use.

The message content of the dreams is accordingly double-layered. The narrated dream stories testify—as fictional texts—to terror; at the same time, however, they are modes of performance of terror itself. Terror is not only dreamed, but the dreams themselves are a part of the terror. They are dictated upon the body. All the stories convey an experience that got under someone's skin; they supported an inner truth that was not only confirmed by the later reality of the Third Reich but was immeasurably outstripped.

The insidious conformity to the new regime, the submission caused by a guilty conscience, the spiral of anxiety, the disabling of resistance, the interplay between executioner and victim—all this arises in the dreams, often in a directly realistic way, with images that are barely removed. The result is overwhelming.

The dreamers see the entire technical apparatus of modern civilization set in motion as it besieges them in order to control, change, or deform their own behavior. Here, the ministries surface, as well as customs offices and their guards, schools with their report cards and examinations, barracks, prisons, the post office or the electricity plant, hospitals and police headquarters, superiors and technicians, and whatever else helps to facilitate or regulate modern daily life but also to cause humans beings to lose their personal integrity. How this took place with the help of the National Socialist organizations becomes oppressively clear in dreams. There is the coercion to participate in the singing, the saluting, the speaking, and the marching, coercions which the dreamers seek to evade by submitting to them. One's own thoughts become estranged when they adjust to or become completely absorbed by the tenor of propaganda slogans. There are all the variants from the compulsion to speak to imperatives of secrecy and silence all the way to the final consequence of terror in the medium of dreams: the prohibition of dreaming.

These are dreams of victims of persecution, but even more so, they are the dreams of those who conformed or wanted to conform but were not allowed to do so. People are isolated and, so as not to be shattered by it, they submit to a pressure to conform that lets them survive, even at the cost of their inner freedom. One seemingly spares oneself individual despair and a split personality by adapting to the system of madness. In this fashion, it becomes possible to survive while living right in the midst of the perversion. The dream discloses all of this. It thus does not expose the outer reality as it presents itself in the everyday, but rather a structure hidden within it. The dreams disclose those secret driving powers and compulsions to assimilate that set in motion the waves of enthusiasm that at one time carried people or swept them away. And, at the same time, they mercilessly present a fatal opposing account that cannot be settled. To this extent, our dream witnesses were truly realists.

Thus the dreams disclose an anthropological dimension beyond their status as fictional sources, something without which the terror and its effectiveness cannot be understood. As mentioned, they are not simply dreams about terror but are, foremost and above all, dreams dreamed in terror. The terror pursues humans all the way into sleep and insidiously changes them. It is evident that in the dream stories described by Charlotte Beradt, the latent and the manifest dream contents, to use Freudian terminology, virtually coincide. The political significance of the dreams, even if socially determined private destinies are concealed behind them, remains immediately comprehensible. The experiences and threats, to continue with the psychoanalytic metaphors, washed over the gatekeeper and flooded unobstructed into the so-called unconscious. Here, they allowed visual stories to emerge whose political meaning must have been immediately evident to consciousness.

The abolition of walls by fiat divests private space of every protection. The loudspeaker leaves no doubt for the dreamer: his house is forced open in favor of a control that can be exercised by each over anyone in the name of the national community (*Volksgemeinschaft*). The oppressive compulsion of the Jewish lawyer forced to clean up garbage, and to do so even voluntarily, requires no interpretative translation for those who experienced this part of history. In the form of a self-propelling paralysis, the improbable becomes reality. The victims of persecution resign themselves to an absurdity that is as existential as it is banal before this absurdity itself is forced upon them. There is evidently a rationality of the body that reaches beyond where anxiety permits the people dreaming to act while they are awake. With this recognition, the dreamers could change their situation.

The political-anthropological dimension is reduced, if one wanted merely to refer such dream stories back to a dreamer's childhood disposition that had not been adequately worked through. Seen ex post facto, these types of therapeutic patterns of interpretation are inconsequential because they are no longer applicable, and, on top of that, they fail to afford the spontaneous insight that could be gained from the political and social contents of the dreams. A common signature of the dreams collected by Beradt is that they make known a truth which is concealed in reality but has not yet become empirically intelligible. All temporal modalities flash up in them: the Wilhelminian and Weimar past, the presence of an ever more densely organized daily life, and the prognostic potential laid bare by dreams. As oppressive as the content of the dreams was, the perceptive ability of the dreamers remained intact. The temporal dimensions of the experiential world were still ordered to the extent that a conceivable space of action was disclosed. What may be interpreted in an individual and psychological fashion as a disguised wish dream or an open nightmare can, from a political perspective, have fully been an admonitory dream. Many of these dreams were understood in this way by potential victims. It was from the capacity of letting secret anxieties and muted wishes appear visually in stories (*Geschichten*) fraught with political symbols, that the imminent loss of the freedom gained can be seen racing before the eyes of those dreaming. The foreigners who occasionally entered into the dreams as ideal and independent figures of contrast were then, so to speak, the better ego of an inner or outer emigration. In every case, the dreams were suited to set free possible action beyond the register of terror. Evidently, agency was still possible for the witnesses, allowing them to have perceptions charged with prognoses. What appeared as paralysis in dreaming thus contained the power to confront it upon awakening. For what use is an interpretation in terms of individual psychology if it was possible for the dreamers to elucidate political conflicts in this manner and resolve them within themselves? For to be subjected to terror in dreaming meant to be able to potentially withstand it in everyday life.

This changes completely if one examines the dream reports handed down to us from the concentration camps. Charlotte Beradt tells of a young man who only dreamed of rectangles, triangles, and octagons "because it is forbidden to dream." Jean Cayrol, who himself escaped from a concentration camp, has passed down similar dreams to us, dreams both devoid of people and abstract. It is a characteristic common to all concentration camp dreams that the actual terror could no longer be dreamed. Here, the fantasy of horror was surpassed by reality. Thus the dreams gained a changed anthropological dimension.

Cayrol differentiates between future-oriented dreams which, full of hope, remain connected to a pre–concentration camp memory, and dreams of being saved that leave behind all previous experience. Dreams about the future could become dangerous because they nourished an illusion. They opened a moving picture of home beyond the electrified barbed wire, an image of home sought and recalled by the prisoners but from which they were irrevocably cut off. The sheer facticity of the camp is blanked out, and the past is recast as a wish for the future. Such dreams were often harbingers of death. Viktor Frankl tells of a fellow prisoner who had dreamed the date of his release: it became the day he died in the camp. Precisely the wish dream that seemed to promise the security of home life and hope became the sign of destruction.

Cayrol confronts such future-oriented dreams with abstract dreams and ones destitute in plot that he has experienced and understands as dreams of being saved. Lacking every temporal dimension, they correspond to the experience of the camp. What is considered a harbinger of schizophrenia in everyday life—the egocentric destruction of the intersubjective world of experience, ending in utter anachrony—takes on a surprising meaning under the inverted constraints of imprisonment within a concentration camp. In the camp, conditions prevailed which mocked all previous experience, which appeared to be unreal but were nonetheless real. The necessity of de-realizing oneself in order to be able to hold out at the final stage of existence within the coercions of the SS-system also led to an inversion in the experience of time. Past, present, and future ceased to be a linear framework for orienting behavior. This perversion, dictated upon the body, had to be suffered in order for a person to be liberated from it. Dreams of being saved bear witness to this. These dreams no longer desired to anchor the person dreaming in reality and, therefore, became, seemingly paradoxically, the sign of the chance for survival. Such dreams contain no signals of reality that were immediately legible in a political or social way. If you will, the political point of such dreams was precisely to be apolitical. With Cayrol, one must even go so far and see the dream of being saved as one that masks acts of resistance.

These references must suffice to identify the spatial and temporal limits within which the dreams collected by Beradt can be used as sources for a political-historical anthropology. The intertwining between dream and reality as they refer to one another changes with respect to the place and time of events. But precisely in this respect, the historically unique source value of our dream testimonials shows itself. If the agony and unparalleled horror of coming events were wrapped up in the jubilation and the intoxication of today, if ever a future was present, then this was what was revealed in the dreams collected by Beradt.

Translated by Todd Presner

Notes

CHAPTER 1. ON THE NEED FOR THEORY IN
THE DISCIPLINE OF HISTORY

These thoughts were presented in the Workshop for Modern Social History in 1969 and were published in the collection *Theorie der Geschichtswissenschaft und Praxis des Geschichtsunterrichts* (Stuttgart, 1972).

1. Heinrich von Treitschke, *Deutsche Geschichte im neunzehnten Jahrhundert*, 5 vols. (Leipzig, 1889–94)—trans.

CHAPTER 2. SOCIAL HISTORY AND CONCEPTUAL HISTORY

1. H. G. Meier, "Begriffsgeschichte," in *Historisches Wörterbuch der Philosophie*, ed. Joachim Ritter, vol. 1 (Basel, 1971), cols. 788–808.

2. Rudolf Eucken, *Geschichte der philosophischen Terminologie* (Leipzig, 1879; reprint ed., 1964).

3. Otto Brunner, *Land und Herrschaft*, 2d ed. (Brünn, 1942), p. xi.

4. Cf. W. Conze, "Zur Gründung des Arbeitskreises für moderne Sozialgeschichte," *Hamburger Jahrbuch für Wirtschafts- und Gesellschaftspolitik* 24 (1979): 23–32. Conze prefers the term "structural history" to avoid the narrowing down to "social questions" that "social" suggests. Otto Brunner adopted the term "structural history" to avoid any linkage, inevitable in the period, to a "history of the people" (*Volksgeschichte*) which, as early as 1939, would attach to "structure" from his theoretical pregivens. Cf. the second edition of *Land und Herrschaft* (1942) and the fourth, revised edition (Vienna, 1959), p. 164: a good example of how even politically determined cognitive interests (*Erkenntnisinteressen*) can lead to theoretically and methodologically new insights that survive their initial position.

5. Cf. Hayden White, *Tropics of Discourse*, 2d ed. (Baltimore, 1982).

6. Cf. D. Schwab, "Familie," in *Geschichtliche Grundbegriffe: Historisches Lexikon zur politisch-sozialen Sprache*, ed. Otto Brunner, Werner Conze, and Reinhart Koselleck (Stuttgart, 1972–), 2:271–301; E. Kapl-Blume, "Liebe im Lexikon" (M.A. thesis, University of Bielefeld), 1986.

CHAPTER 4. TRANSFORMATIONS OF EXPERIENCE
AND METHODOLOGICAL CHANGE

1. Eduard Fueter, *Geschichte der neueren Historiographie* (Munich, 1936; reprint ed., New York, 1969), treats methodological procedures as part of historiography, without distinguishing precisely between rhetoric and method; Jerzy Topolski, *Methodology of History* (Dordrecht, 1976; originally published in Polish. Warsaw, 1973), is systematically organized, includes historical perspectives, and integrates the theoretical premises as implicit elements of its methodology.

2. Jacob and Wilhelm Grimm, *Deutsches Wörterbuch* (Leipzig, 1862; reprinted: Munich, 1984), vol. 3, col. 789.

3. Ibid., col. 790.   4. Ibid., col. 790.

5. Ibid., col. 794.   6. Ibid., col. 793.

7. "With regard to empirical practice," Kant goes so far as to define experiences as judgments, "which are constantly checked by experiment and success"; Immanuel Kant, *Anthropologie in pragmatischer Hinsicht*, 1.6, in *Werke*, ed. Wilhelm Weischedel, vol. 6 (Darmstadt, 1964), p. 424. For the semantics of the concept "experience" in Kant, Rudolf Eisler, *Kant-Lexikon* ([Berlin, 1930], Hildesheim, 1964), 123–31, is still useful. For the relation between history and experience during the early modern period, see Arno Seifert, *Cognitio Historica: Die Geschichte als Namensgeberin der frühneuzeitlichen Empirie* (Berlin, 1976).

8. Cf. the work of Thomas Luckmann, most recently "Lebensweltliche Zeitkategorien, Zeitstrukturen des Alltags und der Ort des 'historischen Bewußtseins,'" in *Grundriß der romanischen Literaturen des Mittelalters*, vol. 11.1 (Heidelberg, 1986), 117–26.

9. "Erstens kommt es anders, zweitens als man denkt" (German saying).

10. "Erfahren wir's nicht neu, so erfahren wir's doch alt." Karl Simrock, comp., *Die deutschen Sprichwörter* (Frankfurt a. M., 1846; reprint ed., Dortmund, 1978), no. 2105, p. 97.

11. Edward, Earl of Clarendon, *Selections from the History of the Rebellion and Civil Wars*, ed. G. Huehns (Oxford, 1955), 7.

12. Fritz Ernst, "Zeitgeschehen und Geschichtsschreibung," *Welt als Geschichte* 17 (1957): 137–89; Reinhart Koselleck, "Das achtzehnte Jahrhundert als Beginn der Neuzeit," in *Epochenschwelle und Epochenbewußtsein*, ed. Reinhart Herzog and Reinhart Koselleck (Munich, 1987), 269–82 (translated in this volume as "The Eighteenth Century as the Beginning of Modernity").

13. Cicero *De oratore* 2.15.63.

14. Cf. Manfred Schlenke, "William Robertson als *Geschichtsschreiber des europäischen Staatensystems*" (Diss., University of Marburg, 1953). I am grateful to Georg G. Iggers for this reference.

15. Thucydides 2.48, cf. Lucian *Hist. conscrib.* 39, 41.

16. Leopold von Ranke, *Geschichte der romanischen und germanischen Völker*

von 1494 bis 1514 (Leipzig, 1872), vii. Cf. the classical differentiation between "What" and "How": "A strict representation of the fact, however compromised and ugly it might be, is undoubtedly the first principle. Secondarily, I was concerned with conveying the unity and development of the events." Konrad Repgen has shown that Ranke's dictum is a translation of Thucydides's phrase, "egō de hoion te egigneto lexō." "Über Rankes Dictum von 1824: 'Bloss sagen, wie es eigentlich gewesen,'" *Historisches Jahrbuch* 102 (1982): 439–49.

17. Herodotus *Hist.* 7.139; Montesquieu, *Considérations sur les causes de la grandeur des Romains et de leur décadence*, ed. Henri Faguet (Paris, 1951), chap. 18, p. 475.

18. Herodotus *Hist.* 2.113–21.

19. See the textually immanent structural analysis of medieval historiography by Gert Melville, *Der Zugriff auf Geschichte in der Gelehrtenkultur des Mittelalters: Vorgaben und Leistungen*, in *Grundriß der romanischen Literaturen des Mittelalters*, II.1:157–228.

20. See the provocative remarks of Hayden White, who does not, however, pose or answer the methodological question of truth: *Tropics of Discourse: Essays in Cultural Criticism* (Baltimore, 1982).

21. Polybius *Hist.* 1.3–4, 5.31, 8.4.

22. Christian Meier, "Geschichte, Historie," in *Geschichtliche Grundbegriffe: Historisches Lexikon zur politisch-sozialen Sprache*, ed. Otto Brunner, Werner Conze, and Reinhart Koselleck (Stuttgart, 1972–), 2:605.

23. Hermann Strasburger, *Herodot als Geschichtsforscher* (Zurich, 1980), esp. 39ff.

24. Herodotus *Hist.* 3.80–82.

25. Just as an example of the structural analogy discussed here, the correlation between unique, concrete constitutions, and medium, or long-term experiential data, see Wilhelm Roscher, *Umrisse zur Naturlehre des Cäsarismus* (Leipzig, 1888), and *Umrisse zur Naturlehre der Demokratie* (Leipzig, 1890). Because of this, Marx nicknamed him "Wilhelm Thucydides Roscher" (Karl Marx, *Das Kapital*, vol. 1 [Berlin 1955], 225; vol. 3 [Berlin, 1956], chap. 7, n. 30).

26. Aristotle *Pol.* V 1303a; Polybius *Hist.* 3.7; Tacitus *Ann.* 4.32.

27. Pierre Bayle, *Dictionnaire historique et critique*, vol.4 (Amsterdam, 1730), 789: "Révolutions d'Etat, les plus grandes n'ont la plupart du temps pour principe qu'une bagatelle" (vol. 2 [Amsterdam, 1730], 321b). Cf. also Reinhart Koselleck, *Vergangene Zukunft* (Frankfurt a. M., 1979), 161ff.; (*Futures Past*, trans. Keith Tribe [Cambridge, Mass., 1985]).

28. Condorcet, *Esquisse d'un tableau historique des progrès de l'esprit humain* (1793), ed. Wilhelm Alff (Frankfurt a. M., 1963), 38.

29. Cf. Polybius *Hist.* 12: Criticism of Timaeus.

30. Cf. Christian Meier, *Die Entstehung des Politischen bei den Griechen* (Frankfurt a. M., 1980), esp. pt. C, "Das Politische und die Zeit." Cf. also Meier, "Die Entdeckung der Ereignisgeschichte bei Herodot," *Storia della Storiografia: Rivista Internazionale* 10 (1986): 5–23.

31. Hermann Strasburger, "Die Entdeckung der politischen Geschichte durch Thukydides," in *Thukydides*, ed. Hans Herter (Darmstadt, 1968), 412–76.

32. Herodotus *Hist.* 5.55–56, 6.109, 123f.; Thucydides 1.20, 6.54, 59.

33. Hans Jürgen Diesner has critically reviewed the variously biased historical understandings of Thucydides' interpretation of tyrannicide in "Peisistratidenexkurs und Peisistratidenbild," in Herter, *Thukydides*, 531–45.

34. Meier, *Entstehung des Politischen.*

35. Cf. the informative study by James Boyd White, *When Words Lose Their Meaning: Constitutions and Reconstitutions of Language, Character, and Community* (Chicago, 1984), esp. chap. 2, "The Dissolution of Meaning: Thucydides' History of his World."

36. Barthold Georg Niebuhr, *Römische Geschichte*, vol. 1 (Berlin, 1811), preface: "The history of the first four centuries of Rome is generally known to be uncertain and falsified. It would be absurd to criticize Livy for this . . . the excellence of his narrative is his justification. . . . But we have a different conception of history . . . we have to undertake a very different enterprise than a necessarily misguided recounting of what the Roman historian regarded as certain history. We must strive to distinguish between fiction and fraud and train our perception to recognize the features of truth, stripped of those masks. This—the segregation of fable, the destruction of fraud—might be sufficient for the critic: he only wants to unmask a deceiving history, and he is content to state single suspicions, while the whole remains for the most part in ruins. But the historian needs something positive: at the very least he must recognize probability, context, and a convincing narrative in place of what he renounces."

37. Thucydides 3.82.

38. Polybius *Hist.* 3.6

39. Julian H. Franklin, *Jean Bodin and the Sixteenth-Century Revolution in the Methodology of Law and History* (New York, 1966), esp. 137ff.; Erich Hassinger, *Empirisch-rationaler Historismus: Seine Ausbildung in der Literatur Westeuropas von Guicciardini bis Saint-Evremond* (Berne, 1978); Fritz Wagner, "Die Anfänge der modernen Geschichtswissenschaft im 17. Jahrhundert," *Bayerische Akademie der Wissenschaften*, Phil.-hist. Kl. (1979), 2.

40. Ranke, the learned student of Thucydides, still knew how to generate suspense through the introduction of original speeches and letters; a tension always emerges anew between the linguistic interpretation *in actu* and the action itself and only in this way generates a history. Cf., for example, bk. 11, chap. 4, of his Prussian History: Leopold von Ranke, *Zwölf Bücher preußischer Geschichte*, in *Werke: Gesamtausgabe der deutschen Akademie*, vol. 3, ed. Paul Joachimsen and Georg Küntzel (Munich, 1930), 165–85. Ranke masterfully intertwines all the above-mentioned dimensions of experience, the long-, the middle-, and the short-range, and simultaneously thematizes the interplay of the linguistic self-interpretation of participants and the events not to be contained by it.

41. Notker Hammerstein, *Jus und Historie* (Göttingen, 1972).

42. Cf. the political-theological but not yet methodologically confirmed reservations concerning the Donation of Constantine in Otto of Freising, *Chronica sive Historia de duabus civitatibus*, ed. Walter Lammers, vol. 4.3 (Darmstadt, 1960), 306; and Horst Fuhrmann, "Konstantinische Schenkung und Sylvesterlegende in neuer Sicht," *Deutsches Archiv für Erforschung des Mittelalters* 15 (1959): 523–40—a brilliant example of the use of firmly grounded philological and textual criticism for proving forgery.

43. Horst Dreitzel, "J. P. Süßmilchs Beitrag zur politischen Diskussion der deutschen Aufklärung," in *Ursprünge der Demographie in Deutschland*, ed. Herwig Birg (Frankfurt, 1986), 29–141.

44. Ibid., 124.

45. François Guizot, *Histoire générale de la Civilisation en Europe* (1927; reprint ed., Paris, 1842).

46. Gustav Droysen, *Geschichte der preußischen Politik*, 14 vols. (Leipzig, 1855–86).

47. As far as I can see, only the Greeks and the Jews were able, contrary to all official representations of achieved successes, to also claim defeats for themselves in order to derive knowledge from them. This might help to explain the advanced level at which European historiography has learned to process its history with methodological sophistication. One should also mention Islamic history, such as the one by Ibn-Khaldun, which can be derived from the same heritage.

48. Hippolyte Taine, *Les origines de la France contemporaine: La Révolution*, vol. 1: *L'anarchie* (Paris, 1893), iii.

49. Meier, *Entstehung des Politischen*, 434.

50. Herodotus *Hist.* 1.5.

51. Thucydides 5.26, 4.102–8.

52. Plutarch later praises Philistus by saying that Clio had finished the work of the author with the help of his banishment. See Renate Zöpffel, "Untersuchungen zum Geschichtswerk des Philistos von Syrakus" (Diss., University of Freiburg, 1965), 65.

53. Lucian *Hist. conscrib.*, 41.

54. Tacitus *Ann.* 4.33. Cf. recently Albert Dihle, *Die Entstehung der historischen Biographie, Sitzungsberichte der Heidelberger Akademie*, Phil.-hist. Klasse, 3 (1986): 46.

55. See the introduction to the *Histories* by Viktor Pöschl (Stuttgart, 1959) and Reinhart Koselleck, "Revolution," in *Geschichtliche Grundbegriffe*, 5:69.

56. Fritz Ernst, "Philippe de Commynes," in, *Gesammelte Schriften*, ed. Gunther G. Wolf (Heidelberg, 1985), 279.

57. Rudolf von Albertini, *Das florentinische Staatsbewußtsein im Übergang von der Republik zum Prinzipat* (Bern, 1955); a title that rightfully points to the fundamental parallel with Roman history, which both exiles had made part of their method. Cf. more recently Gisela Bock, "Machiavelli als Geschichtsschreiber," *Quellen und Forschungen aus italienischen Archiven und Bibliotheken* 66 (1986): 153–91; she points out "that the technique of fictive speech brought him perhaps

closer to historical truth than the modern technique of quotation used by later historians" (187).

58. Cf. Hans Medick, *Naturzustand und Naturgeschichte der bürgerlichen Gesellschaft: Die Ursprünge der bürgerlichen Sozialtheorie als Geschichtsphilosophie und Sozialwissenschaft bei Samuel Pufendorf, John Locke und Adam Smith* (Göttingen, 1973); Medick and Zwi Batscha, introduction to Adam Ferguson, *Versuch über die Geschichte der bürgerlichen Gesellschaft*, trans. Hans Medick (Frankfurt a. M., 1963). Michel Foure, "Le Scottish Enlightenment: Naissance d'une anthropologie sociale," *Revue de Synthèse* 4 (1986): 411–25.

59. "The unfortunate time of Prussia's humiliation influenced the production of my history. . . . I went back to a great, but long-vanished nation, in order to fortify the spirit of myself and my listeners. I suffered the same fate as Tacitus." Franz Lieber, *Erinnerungen aus meinem Zusammenleben mit B. G. Niebuhr*, trans. from the English by Dr. K. Thibaut (Heidelberg, 1837), 199; quoted from Franz X. von Wegele, *Geschichte der deutschen Historiographie* (Munich, 1885), 998. Alfred Heuss's analysis arrives, for example, at the following conclusion: "What had been an instrument for the mastering of a political situation, and had vanished with it, remained a useful instrument in his hands for historical epistemology. A metamorphosis had occurred. Something that had no use for influencing current events acquired autonomous value, and Niebuhr, having lost his position as 'politician,' had in his hand a new weapon as historian: He had discovered a new hermeneutical principle for dealing with history that was henceforth indispensable." Alfred Heuss, *Barthold Georg Niebuhrs wissenschaftliche Anfänge: Untersuchungen und Mitteilungen über die Kopenhagener Manuscripte und zur europäischen Tradition der lex agraria (loi agraire)* (Göttingen, 1981), 455. This is an exciting example of how a political motivation for the search for historical causes and analogies leads to epistemological principles that become autonomous, inasmuch they surpass the starting questions *nolens volens.* For Humboldt's "defeat" as statesman, cf. Siegfried H. Kaehler, *Wilhelm von Humboldt und der Staat* (Göttingen, 1963), chap. 6.

60. See Carl Schmitt, "Historiographie in nuce: Alexis de Tocqueville," in *Ex captivitate salus* (Cologne, 1950), 25–33. Schmitt also cites the dismissively intended sentence of Guizot: "C'est un vaincu qui accepte sa défaite."

REFERENCES TO CHAPTER 4

Coseriu, Eugenio. *Synchronie, Diachronie und Geschichte.* Munich, 1974.
Gadamer, Hans-Georg. *Die Begriffsgeschichte und die Sprache der Philosophie.* Opladen, 1971.
Koselleck, Reinhart, ed. *Historische Semantik und Begriffsgeschichte.* Stuttgart, 1978.
Pocock, John G. A. *Virtue, Commerce and History.* Cambridge, 1985.
Reichardt, Rolf. Introduction to *Handbuch politisch-sozialer Grundbegriffe in Frankreich 1680–1820*, edited by Rolf Reichardt and Eberhard Schmitt, 39–148. Munich, 1985.

Robin, Régine. *Histoire et linguistique*. Paris, 1973.
Veit-Brause, Irmline. "A Note on *Begriffsgeschichte*." *History and Theory* 20 (1981): 61–67.

CHAPTER 5. THE TEMPORALIZATION OF UTOPIA

1. Louis-Sébastien Mercier, *L'An Deux Mille Quatre Cent Quarante: Rêve s'il en fut jamais*, ed. R. Trousson (Bordeaux, 1971).

2. Carl Schmitt, "Die Buribunken: Ein geschichtsphilosophischer Versuch," in *SUMMA* 1, no. 4 (1918): 89–106. [An English translation of Schmitt's essay appears in Friedrich A. Kittler, *Gramophone, Film, Typewriter*, trans. Geoffrey Winthrop-Young and Michael Wutz (Stanford, Calif., 1999), 231–42—trans.]

3. Mercier, *L'An 2440*, 78.

4. Quoted in R. Trousson, "Introduction," in Mercier, *L'An 2440*, 8.

5. Ibid.

6. Mercier, *L'An 2440*, 330.

7. Cf. Ivan Nagel, "Der Intellektuelle als Lump und Märtyrer: Ein Lebenslauf zwischen Ancien régime und Revolution," *Akzente*, no. 1 (1981): 9.

8. Mercier, *Tableau de Paris*, VI, 15; quoted in Trousson, "Introduction," 51.

9. Cf. Reinhart Koselleck, *Kritik und Krise*, 2d ed. (Frankfurt a. M., 1976), 231.

10. Trousson, "Introduction," 51.

11. Mercier, *L'An 2440*, chap. 11.

12. Ibid., chap. 5.

13. For the following, see my article "Fortschritt," in *Geschichtliche Grundbegriffe*, 2:375–78. [For an English version of the argument in this article, see the essay "Progress and Decline: An Appendix to the History of Two Concepts" in this volume—trans.]

14. Mercier, *De J.-J. Rousseau considéré comme l'un des premiers auteurs de la Révolution*, 2 vols. (Paris, 1791); quoted in Trousson, "Introduction," 11.

15. Cf. Trousson, "Introduction," 47.

16. Mercier, *L'An 2440*, chap. 44.

17. Cf. R. Trousson, "*Introduction*," 66.

18. Schmitt, "Die Buribunken," 103.

CHAPTER 8. THE UNKNOWN FUTURE AND
THE ART OF PROGNOSIS

1. Immanuel Kant, *Anthropology from a Pragmatic Point of View*, trans. Victor Lyle Dowdell, rev. and ed. Hans H. Rudnick (Carbondale, Ill., 1978), pt. 1, para. 35, p. 77.

2. [Koselleck is playing on the word *Geschichte*, which can mean both "history" and "story" or "narrative."—trans.]

3. D'Argenson, *Considérations sur le gouvernement ancien et présent de la France* (Yverdon, 1764), 138ff.

4. [The German word for "history" (*Geschichte*) contains the word for "layer" or "stratum" (*Schicht*)—trans.]

5. Diderot, in *Histoire Philosophique et Politique et du commerce des Européens dans les deux Indes*, ed. G. Raynal, vol. 4 (Geneva, 1780), 488ff.

6. Frederick the Great, *Kritik des "Systems der Natur" von Holbach* (1770), in *Die Werke Friedrichs des Großen*, ed. G. B. Volz, vol. 7 (Berlin, 1912), 267f.

7. Herodotus *History* 3.

8. Christoph Martin Wieland, *Der Neue Teutsche Merkur* 2 (March 1798), in *Sämtliche Werke*, vol. 32 (Leipzig, 1857), 53ff.

9. Wieland, *Das Geheimnis des Kosmopolitenordens* (1788), in *Sämmtliche Werke*, vol. 30, p. 422.

10. Letter to Emil Ludwig, quoted in Helmut Kreuzer, "Europas Prominenz und ein Schriftsteller," *Süddeutsche Zeitung*, November 17–18, 1962.

11. Max Domarus, ed., *Hitler, Reden und Proklamationen*, vol. 1/2 (Munich, 1965), 760; translated as *Hitler: Speeches and Proclamations 1932–1945*, vol. 2 (London: I. B. Tauris Publishers, 1992), 968. [Translation modified—trans.]

12. Churchill, Speech to the House of Commons, November 27, 1932, *Parliamentary Debates*, Commons, 5th ser., vol. 272.

13. Cf. Thucydides, *History of the Peloponnesian War*, vol. 2 (Ann Arbor, Mich., 1959), 364–72.

CHAPTER 9. REMARKS ON THE REVOLUTIONARY
CALENDAR AND 'NEUE ZEIT'

1. [Michael Meinzer, "Der französische Revolutionskalender und die 'Neue Zeit,'" in *Die Französische Revolution als Bruch des gesellschaftlichen Bewußtseins*, ed. Reinhart Koselleck and Rolf Reichardt, with Erich Pelzer and Michael Wagner (Munich, 1988).—trans.]

2. ["La moitié de la révolution du monde est déjà faite; l'autre moitié doit s'accomplir." Robespierre, "Speech on 18 Floréal, year II" (May 17, 1794), in *Les Orateurs de la Révolution Française*, ed. Garaudy (Paris, 1940), 77.—trans.]

CHAPTER 10. THE EIGHTEENTH CENTURY AS
THE BEGINNING OF MODERNITY

1. Goethe, *Materialen zur Geschichte der Farbenlehre*, in *Goethes Werke*, ed. Erich Trunz, vol. 14 (Hamburg, 1960), 195.

2. Wilhelm von Humboldt, *Das achtzehnte Jahrhundert*, in *Werke*, ed. A. Flitner and K. Giel, vol. 1 (Darmstadt, 1960), 401f.

3. Ibid., 398.

CHAPTER 11. ON THE ANTHROPOLOGICAL AND SEMANTIC
STRUCTURE OF 'BILDUNG'

1. Goethe, *Zahme Xenien IX*, in *Sämtliche Werke.*, vol. 2: *Gedichte*, ed. Karl Eibl (Frankfurt am Main, 1988), 744.

2. [Werner Conze and Jürgen Kocka, eds., *Bildungsbürgertum im 19. Jahrhundert*, 4 vols. (Stuttgart, 1985–92). This essay was written as the introduction to the second volume of the series: Reinhart Koselleck, ed., *Bildungsgüter und Bildungswissen* (Stuttgart, 1990)—trans.]

3. Ulrich Engelhardt, "Bildungsbürgertum," in *Begriffs- und Dogmengeschichte eines Etiketts* (Stuttgart, 1986), 189.

4. Benjamin Disraeli, *Contarini Fleming: A Psychological Romance* (London, n.d. [1832?]), vol. 2; quoted in Wilhelm Vosskamp, "Der Bildungsroman in Deutschland und die Frühgeschichte seiner Rezeption in England" in *Bürgertum im 19. Jahrhundert*, ed. Jürgen Kocka, vol. 3 (Munich, 1988), 279. [The quotation is in English in the original—trans.]

5. W. H. Bruford, *The German Tradition of Self-Cultivation: Bildung from Humboldt to Thomas Mann* (London, 1975).

6. Richard Wagner, *Deutsche Kunst und deutsche Politik (1867/68)*, in *Dichtungen und Schriften*, ed. Dieter Borchmeyer, vol. 8 (Frankfurt am Main, 1983), 247ff. (in reference to Constantin Frantz). Cf. Jörg Fisch's conceptual history, "Zivilisation und Kultur," in *Geschichtliche Grundbegriffe*, ed. Otto Brunner, Werner Conze, and Reinhart Koselleck, vol. 7 (Stuttgart, 1991).

7. Goethe, *Ideen über organische Bildung* (1806–7), in *Sämtliche Werke*, vol. 24 (Frankfurt am Main, 1987). Dorothea Kuhn, ed., *Schriften zur Morphologie*, 392.

8. On the conceptual history: Hans Weil, *Die Entstehung des deutschen Bildungsprinzips* (1930; 2d ed., Bonn, 1967); Ilse Schaarschmidt, "Der Bedeutungswandel der Worte 'bilden' und 'Bildung' in der Literaturepoche von Gottsched bis Herder," (Diss., Königsberg, Elbing, 1931, reprinted in *Zur Geschichte des Bildungsbegriffs*, ed. Wolfgang Klafki (Weinheim, 1965); Hans Schilling, *Bildung als Gottesbildlichkeit: Eine motivgeschichtliche Studie zum Bildungsbegriff* (Freiburg i. Br., 1961); Ernst Lichtenstein, *Zur Entwicklung des Bildungsbegriffs von Meister Eckhart bis Hegel* (Heidelberg, 1966). Also cf. "Bildung," in *Historisches Wörterbuch der Philosophie*, ed. Joachim Ritter, vol. 1 (Basel, 1971, cols. 921–37); Rudolf Vierhaus, "Bildung," in Brunner et al., *Geschichtliche Grundbegriffe*, vol. 1 (Stuttgart, 1972), 508–51; Günther Buck, *Rückwege aus der Entfremdung: Studien zur Entwicklung der deutschen humanistischen Bildungsphilosophie* (Paderborn, 1984).

9. Genesis 1:27.

10. Cf. Lichtenstein, *Zur Entwicklung des Bildungsbegriffs*, 5.

11. Cf. Schaarschmidt, "Der Bedeutungswandel der Worte 'bilden' und 'Bildung,'" 14.

12. Gottfried Arnold, *Wahre Abbildung des inwendigen Christentums*, 2d ed. (Leipzig, 1733), 250; quoted in Vierhaus, *"Bildung,"* 510.

13. Quoted in Lichtenstein, *Zur Entwicklung des Bildungsbegriffs*, 41 n. 17.

14. Wilhelm von Humboldt, *Über Religion*, in *Werke*, ed. Andreas Flitner and Klaus Giel, vol. 1 (Darmstadt, 1960), 25.

15. [Hermann Timm, "Bildungsreligion im deutschsprachigen Protestantismus —eine grundbegriffliche Perspektivierung," in Koselleck, *Bildungsgüter*—trans.]

16. Moses Mendelssohn, *Jerusalem oder religiöse Macht und Judentum* (1783), reprinted in *Gesammelte Schriften, Jubiläumsausgabe*, vol. 8: *Schriften zum Judentum II*, ed. Alexander Altmann (Stuttgart, 1983), 110.

17. Humboldt, *Werke*, 4:113f.

18. Max Scheler, *Die Wissensformen und die Gesellschaft*, ed. Maria Scheler, 2d ed. (Bern, 1960), 60ff., passim.

19. Kant, "Beantwortung der Frage: Was ist Aufklärung?" (1784), in *Werke*, vol. 6, ed. Wilhelm Weischedel (Darmstadt, 1964), 53; "An Answer to the Question: What Is Enlightenment?" in *Perpetual Peace and Other Essays on Politics, History, and Morals*, trans. Ted Humphrey (Indianapolis, 1983), 41.

20. Johann Ludwig Ewald, *Ist es jetzt rathsam, die niederen Volksklassen aufzuklären?* (Leipzig, 1800), 87. Quoted in Vierhaus, "Bildung," 522.

21. Carl von Rotteck, *"Bildung,"* in Carl von Rotteck and Carl Welcker, *Staats-Lexikon*, vol. 2 (Altona, 1834), 577.

22. Ibid., 578.

23. Hegel, *Die Vernunft in der Geschichte*, ed. Johannes Hoffmeister, 5th ed. (Hamburg, 1955), 58.

24. Lorenz von Stein, *Die Verwaltungslehre*, pt. 5: *Die innere Verwaltung, Das Bildungswesen* (Stuttgart, 1883; reprint ed., Aalen, 1975): 17.

25. Friedrich Schlegel, *Athenäum*, vol. 2, pt. 1 (Berlin, 1799), 26; quoted in Konrad Feilchenfeldt, "Die Berliner Salons der Romantik," in *Rahel Levin Varnhagen*, ed. Barbara Hahn and Ursula Isselstein. Also in *Zeitschrift für Literaturwissenschaft und Linguistik*, no. 14 (1987): 155.

26. Edeltraut Kapl-Blume, "Liebe im Lexikon" (M.A. thesis, University of Bielefeld, 1987).

27. *Henriette Herz in Erinnerungen, Briefen und Zeugnissen*, ed. Rainer Schmitz (Frankfurt am Main, 1984), 198.

28. Goethe, *Dichtung und Wahrheit*, pt. 3, book 15, in *Sämtliche Werke*, vol. 14, ed. Klaus Detlef Müller (Frankfurt am Main, 1986), 692. Cf. Lucian Hölscher, "Die Religion des Bürgers: Bürgerliche Frömmigkeit und protestantische Kirche im 19. Jahrhundert," *Historische Zeitschrift* 250 (1990): 595–630; Gerhard Hergt, "Christentum und Weltanschauung," in *Terror und Spiel, Probleme der Mythenrezeption*, ed. Manfred Fuhrmann (Munich, 1971), 357–68; Trutz Rendtorff, "Die Religion in der Moderne—die Moderne in der Religion," in *Theologische Literaturzeitung* 110 (August 1985): 562–74; Hans Erich Bödeker, "Die Religiosität der

Gebildeten" (manuscript, 1988). For all of this, see the relevant chapters in Thomas Nipperdey, *Deutsche Geschichte 1800–1866* (Munich, 1983); and *Deutsche Geschichte 1866–1918*, vol. 1 (Munich, 1990).

29. Friedrich Schlegel, "Athenäumsfragment 233," in *Kritische Friedrich Schlegel Ausgabe*, ed. Ernst Behler, vol. 2, ed. Hans Eichner (Paderborn, 1967), 203.

30. Goethe, *Zahme Xenien IX*, 737.

31. Hegel, *Phänomenologie des Geistes*, ed. Johannes Hoffmeister, 5th ed. (Leipzig, 1949), 376f.

32. Ibid., 351.

33. Emil Du Bois-Reymond, *Über die Grenzen der Naturerkenntnis*, 2d ed. (Leipzig, 1872), 34.

34. Wilhelm von Humboldt to Friedrich Schiller, April 30, 1803, in *Briefwechsel Schiller-Humboldt*, vol. 2, ed. Siegfried Seidel (Berlin, 1962), 234. Cf. Rendtorff, "Die Religion in der Moderne," 565.

35. Friedrich Ast, *Über den Geist des Altertums und dessen Bedeutung für unser Zeitalter* (1805); quoted in *Dokumente des Neuhumanismus*, vol. 1, ed. Rudolf Joerden (Langensalza, 1931), 23.

36. Schlegel, "Athenäumsfragment 222," in *Kritische Ausgabe*, 2:201.

37. Richard Wagner, letter to H. von Stein, January 31, 1883, in *Dichtungen und Schriften*, 10:168.

38. [Karlfried Gründer, "Die Bedeutung der Philosophie in der Bildung des deutschen Bürgertums im 19. Jahrhundert," in Koselleck, *Bildungsgüter*—trans.]

39. [Dietrich von Engelhardt, "Der Bildungsbegriff in der Naturwissenschaft des 19. Jahrhunderts," in Koselleck, *Bildungsgüter*—trans.]

40. Heinrich von Treitschke, *Die Gesellschaftswissenschaft: Ein kritischer Versuch* (Leipzig, 1859), 26–27.

41. Virchow's Archive II, 1849; quoted in Ludwig Aschoff, *Rudolf Virchow: Wissenschaft und Weltgeltung* (Hamburg, 1940), 86.

42. Thomas Mann, *Betrachtungen eines Unpolitischen*, ed. Erika Mann (Frankfurt am Main, 1956), 103.

43. Adolf Grabowsky, "Die Partei der Gebildeten," *Die Grenzboten, Zeitschrift für Politik und Literatur* (1911) 1533ff.

44. Engelhardt, "Der Bildungsbegriff in der Naturwissenschaft."

45. Fichte, *Reden an die deutsche Nation*, ed. Fritz Medicus, introd. Alwin Diemer (Hamburg, 1955), speech 11, p. 185.

46. von Stein, *Die innere Verwaltung*, 24.

47. Ibid., 28.

48. Eichendorff, "Die deutsche Salon-Poesie der Frauen," in *Geschichte der Poesie*, ed. Hartwig Schultz, in *Werke*, vol. 6 (Frankfurt am Main, 1990), 291.

49. Staatsarchiv Münster, Oberpräsidium 690.

50. Lutz von Werder, "Arbeiter und Volksbildung," in *Die Arbeiter*, ed. W. Ruppert. Munich: 1986. pp. 319f.

51. Wilhelm Wundt, *Erlebtes und Erkanntes.* Stuttgart: 1920. p. 396. Also, pp. 299f.

52. Jacob Burckhardt, *Weltgeschichtliche Betrachtungen,* ed. Rudolf Stadelmann (Pfullingen, 1949), 99.

53. *Wegweiser zur Bildung für deutsche Lehrer,* ed. F. A. W. Diesterweg (Essen, 1844), xiv.

54. Ibid., xx, xxviii.

55. Theodor W. Adorno, *Gesammelte Schriften,* vol. 8: *Soziologische Schriften I* (Frankfurt am Main, 1972), 93–121 (1959).

56. Rahel Varnhagen to Frau von F. Berlin, December 14, 1807; *Rahel-Bibliothek,* in *Gesammelte Werke,* vol. 1, ed. Konrad Feilchenfeldt, Uwe Schweikert, and Rahel E. Steiner (Munich, 1983), 325.

57. Hegel, *Texte zur philosophischen Propädeutik,* in *Werke,* vol. 4, ed. Eva Moldenhauer and Karl Markus Michel (Frankfurt am Main, 1970), 260. Cf. the clear analysis by Karl Löwith, "Das Problem der Bildung," in *Von Hegel bis Nietzsche,* 2d ed. (Stuttgart, 1950), 312–29.

58. Engelhardt, "Der Bildungsbegriff in der Naturwissenschaft," pp. 112–13, provides a good summary.

59. Cf. Karl Löwith, "Jacob Burckhardt," in *Sämtliche Schriften,* vol. 7 (Stuttgart, 1984), pp. 62–65. See also the references to Burckhardt given there.

60. Friedrich Nietzsche, *Nachgelassene Fragmente* (1873), in *Kritische Studienausgabe,* vol. 7, ed. Giorgio Colli and Mazzino Montinari (Munich, 1988), 718.

61. Friedrich Nietzsche, "Vom Nutzen und Nachteil der Historie für das Leben," in *Kritische Studienausgabe,* vol. 1 (Munich, 1967), 273–74.

62. Löwith, *Von Hegel zu Nietzsche,* 457.

63. Friedrich Paulsen, "Das moderne Bildungswesen," in *Die Kultur der Gegenwart,* ed. Paul Hinneberg, 2d ed. (Berlin, 1912), pt. 1, sec. 1, p. 55.

64. Ibid., 60.

65. Ibid., 56.

66. [Ulrich Herrmann, "Über 'Bildung' im Gymnasium des wilhelminischen Kaiserreichs," in Koselleck, *Bildungsgüter*—trans.]

67. Hegel, *Texte zur philosophischen Propädeutik,* §§ 41ff., p. 258.

68. Rudolf Virchow, *Die Aufgabe der Naturwissenschaften* (Berlin, 1872), in *Der deutsche Geist,* vol. 2, ed. Peter Suhrkamp (Frankfurt am Main, 1954), 272.

69. Cf. among others, Erich Trunz, "Der deutsche Späthumanismus um 1600 als Standeskultur," in *Deutsche Barockforschung: Dokumentation einer Epoche,* ed. Richard Alewyn (1931; 2d ed., Cologne, 1966), 147–81; Klaus Schreiner, "Laienbildung als Herausforderung für Kirche und Gesellschaft," in *Zeitschrift für historische Forschung* 11 (1984): 257–354.

70. von Stein, *Die innere Verwaltung,* 24.

71. Alfred Weber, "Die Not der geistigen Arbeiter," in *Die Zukunft der Social-*

politik—Die Not der geistigen Arbeiter: Jubiläumstagung des Vereins für Socialpolitik in Eisenach 1922 (Munich, 1923), 169–70, 181.

72. [Koselleck is referring to the title of the volume to which this is the introduction: *Bildungsgüter und Bildungswissen*, "cultural heritage" and "cultural knowledge," respectively—trans.]

73. [Ulrich Muhlack, "Bildung zwischen Neuhumanismus und Historismus," in Koselleck, *Bildungsgüter*—trans.]

74. Schlegel, "Athenäumsfragment 116," in *Kritische Ausgabe*, 2:182.

75. Richard Wagner, "Die Kunst und die Revolution" (1849), in *Dichtungen und Schriften*, vol. 5 (Leipzig, 1857), 273–309.

76. Erich Weniger, "Kriegserinnerung und Kriegserfahrung," in *Deutsche Zeitschrift* 48 (1935): 403–4; see Klaus Vondung, ed., *Kriegserlebnis* (Göttingen, 1980).

77. [Carl Dahlhaus, "Das deutsche Bildungsbürgertum und die Musik," in Koselleck, *Bildungsgüter*, p. 228—trans.]

78. [Frank Büttner, "Bildungsideen und bildende Kunst in Deutschland um 1800," in Koselleck, *Bildungsgüter*, 273—trans.]

79. [Cf. Werner Busch, "Die fehlende Gegenwart," in Koselleck, *Bildungsgüter*—trans.]

80. [Wolfgang Frühwald, "Büchmann und die Folgen: Zur sozialen Funktion des Bildungszitates in der deutschen Literatur des 19. Jahrhunderts," in Koselleck, *Bildungsgüter*—trans.]

81. Herder, *Über den Ursprung der Sprache*, in *Werke*, ed. Martin Bollacher, vol. 1: *Frühe Schriften*, ed. Ulrich Gaier (Frankfurt am Main, 1985), pt. 2, 770.

82. Herder, *Ideen zur Philosophie der Geschichte der Menschheit*, 2.9.2, in *Werke*, vol. 6, ed. Martin Bollacher (Frankfurt am Main, 1989), 345ff.

83. Wilhelm von Humboldt, *Über die Verschiedenheit des menschlichen Sprachbaues und ihren Einfluss auf die geistige Entwicklung des Menschengeschlechts*, in *Werke*, vol. 3 (Darmstadt, 1963), 293.

84. Ibid., 399.

85. Herder, *Ideen zur Philosophie der Geschichte der Menschheit*, 355.

86. Friedrich Nietzsche, "Über die Zukunft unserer Bildungsanstalten," in *Kritische Studienausgabe*, 1:683, 685.

87. Friedrich Schleiermacher, *Über die Religion: Reden an die Gebildeten unter ihren Verächtern*, ed. Carl Schwarz (Leipzig, 1868), speech 2, 72.

88. Johann Gustav Droysen, *Erhebung der Geschichte zum Rang einer Wissenschaft*, in *Historik*, ed. Rudolf Hübner (Munich, 1943), 395.

89. *Zeitschrift für bildende Kunst* (1876): 264; quoted in Klaus Lankheit, "Malerei und Plastik im 19. Jahrhundert," *RGG* 4 (1960): 687. Cf. Werner Busch's essay, "Die fehlende Gegenwart," in Koselleck, *Bildungsgüter*, 286–316.

90. Kandinsky, *Über das Geistige in der Kunst*, ed. Max Bill, 4th ed. (Bern, 1952), 86, 135, 139. Cf. Peter Anselm Riedl, "Abstrakte Kunst und der Traum von

der rezeptiven Gesellschaft," in *Festschrift Klaus Lankheit*, ed. Wolfgang Hartmann (Cologne, 1973), 67–77.

91. Cf. Carl Dahlhaus, *Analyse und Werturteil* (Mainz, 1970), 21ff., 226ff.

92. Arthur Schopenhauer, *Werke*, vol. 1. (Zurich, 1977), 324; quoted in Albert Menne, "Arthur Schopenhauer," in *Klassiker des philosophischen Denkens*, vol. 2 (Munich, 1982), 217.

93. Wagner, *Religion und Kunst* (1880), in *Dichtungen und Schriften*, 10:117.

94. Joseph von Eichendorff, "Die Poesie der modernen Religionsphilosophie," in *Sämtliche Werke*, vol. 9: *Geschichte der poetischen Literatur Deutschlands*, ed. Wolfram Mauser (Regensburg, 1970), 265.

95. Eduard Spranger, *Das deutsche Bildungsideal der Gegenwart in geschichts-philosophischer Beleuchtung, Sonderdruck aus der "Erziehung."* 2d ed. (Leipzig, 1929), 72.

96. Ibid., 71.

97. Ibid., 72.

98. C. H. Becker, *Das Problem der Bildung in der Kulturkrise der Gegenwart* (Leipzig, 1930), 22, 21.

99. Ibid., 25. 100. Ibid., 33.

101. Ibid., 23. 102. Ibid., 34.

103. Hans Freyer, "Zur Bildungskrise der Gegenwart," *Die Erziehung*, no. 6 (1931): 597.

104. Ibid., 623.

105. Ibid., 625.

106. Richard Benz, *Geist und Reich* (Jena, 1933), 48, 50.

CHAPTER 12. THREE 'BÜRGERLICHE' WORLDS?

1. The following thoughts serve as an introduction to a research program which the author, together with Ulrike Spree and Willibald Steinmetz, is carrying out at the University of Bielefeld.

2. For the entire history of the concept, see M. Riedel's articles "Bürger," in *Historisches Wörterbuch der Philosophie*, ed. J. Ritter, vol. 1 (Basel, 1971), 962–66; and "Bürger," in *Geschichtliche Grundbegriffe*, ed. Otto Brunner, Werner Conze, and Reinhart Koselleck, vol. 1 (Stuttgart, 1972), 672–725. The same articles appear as "Gesellschaft, bürgerliche," in *Historisches Wörterbuch der Philosophie*, vol. 3 (Basel, 1974), 466–73; and Brunner et al., *Geschichtliche Grundbegriffe*, vol. 2 (Stuttgart, 1975), 719–800, respectively.

3. J. Zedler, *Großes vollständiges Universallexikon aller Wissenschaften und Künste*, vol. 31 (Leipzig and Halle, 1742), article "Republik," 656–57.

4. A. L. Schlözer, *Staatsanzeigen* 17 (1792): 354; see also Riedel, "Gesellschaft, bürgerliche," 754–55.

5. *Brockhaus*, 10th ed., vol. 6 (Leipzig: 1852), article "Gesellschaft," 688–89.

6. E. Duclerc and Pagnerre, *Dictionnaire Politique* (Paris, 1841; 7th ed., 1868), article "Bourgeois, Bourgeoisie," 164.

7. Ibid., article "Election," 360.

CHAPTER 13. "PROGRESS" AND "DECLINE"

1. Professor Heinrich Grupe (1878–1976).

2. See the following essays in Reinhart Koselleck and Paul Widmer, eds., *Niedergang: Studien zu einem geschichtlichen Thema*, Sprache und Geschichte, vol. 2 (Stuttgart, 1980), in which this essay appeared as the introduction. Frank W. Walbank, "The Idea of Decline in Polybius," 41–58; Franz Georg Maier, "Niedergang als Erfahrung und Begriff: Die Zeitgenossen und die Krise Westroms, 370–470," 59–78; and Reinhart Herzog, "Orosius oder die Formulierung eines Fortschrittskonzepts aus der Erfahrung des Niedergangs," 79–102. See also Christian Meier, "'Fortschritt' in der Antike," in *Geschichtliche Grundbegriffe*, ed. Otto Brunner, Werner Conze, and Reinhart Koselleck, vol. 2 (Stuttgart, 1975), 353–63.

3. Cf. Maier, "Niedergang als Erfahrung und Begriff."

4. On the following, see my article "Fortschritt," in Brunner et al., *Geschichtliche Grundbegriffe*, 2:363ff.

5. *De Civitate Dei* 10.14.

6. Isidore of Seville, *Sententiae* 2.5.3, in Migne, *Patrologia Latina*, vol. 82 (Paris, 1862), 604.

7. "Sermones de Sanctis: In purificatione B. Mariae" 2.3, in Migne, *Patrologia Latina*, vol. 183, p. 369, and *Epistolae ad dragones monachum*, § 1, in Migne, *Patrologia Latina*, vol. 182, p. 100.

8. Paulinus of Aquileia, *Liber exhortationis, vulgo de salutaribus documentis* 43 (circa 795), in Migne, *Patrologia Latina*, vol. 99, p. 246.

9. For more on this, cf. Gert Melville, "Zur geschichtstheoretischen Begründung eines fehlenden Niedergangsbewußtseins," in Koselleck and Widmer, *Niedergang*, 103–36.

10. Francis Bacon, *Novum Organum* 1.84.

11. Blaise Pascal, *Fragment de préface sur le traité du vide*, in *Oeuvres de Blaise Pascal*, ed. Léon Brunschvicg and Pierre Boutroux, vol. 2 (Paris, 1908), 138–39.

12. Bernard de Fontenelle, *Digression sur les anciens et les modernes, Oeuvres complètes*, ed. G. B. Depping, part 2. Paris: 1818. Reprint, Geneva: 1968, p. 364.

13. From the handwritten posthumous works, quoted in Ernst Cassirer, *Leibniz' System in seinen wissenschaftlichen Grundlagen* (Marburg, 1902), 444.

14. Leibniz, *De progressu in infinitum*, in *Kleine Schriften zur Metaphysik*, ed. Wolf von Engelhardt and Hans Heinz Holz (Frankfurt, 1965), 368ff.

15. Cf. my article "Fortschritt," p. 377.

16. Condorcet, *Esquisse d'un tableau historique des progrès de l'esprit humain* (1794), ed. Wilhelm Alff (Frankfurt, 1963), 364, 382, 388.

17. Lessing to Mendelssohn, January 21, 1756, *Sämtliche Schriften*, vol. 17 (1904), 53.

18. Kant, *Allgemeine Naturgeschichte und Theorie des Himmels*, in *Werke: Akademie-Textausgabe*, vol. 1 (1902; reprint ed., Berlin, 1968), 256, 314. See also Hans Blumenberg, *Die Legitimität der Neuzeit* (Frankfurt am Main, 1966), 182ff., 427ff.

19. Franz Hitze, *Die sociale Frage und die Bestrebungen zu ihrer Lösung* (Paderborn, 1877), 182.

20. Novalis, *Fragmente und Studien, 1799–1800*, in *Novalis Schriften: Die Werke Friedrich von Hardenbergs*, vol. 3 (Darmstadt, 1968), 668.

21. For a more subtly differentiated interpretation, see Jean Starobinski, "Rousseau und die Niedergangsthematik: Einige Bemerkungen zur Prosopopöie des Fabricius," in Koselleck and Widmer, *Niedergang*.

22. Kant, *Das Ende aller Dinge* (1794), *Werke: Akademie-Textausgabe*, 8:334ff.

23. Nietzsche, *The Will to Power*, trans. Walter Kaufmann and R. J. Hollingdale (New York, 1967), no. 1055, p. 544.

24. For more on this, see Bernhard Lypp, "Über die verschiedene Arten Geschichte zu schreiben: Bemerkungen zur Logik historischen Diskurses im Hinblick auf Nietzsche," in Koselleck and Widmer, *Niedergang*, 191–213.

CHAPTER 14. SOME QUESTIONS REGARDING THE CONCEPTUAL HISTORY OF "CRISIS"

1. E. Duclerc and Pagnerre, *Dictionnaire Politique* (Paris, 1839; 7th ed., 1868), article "Crise," 298. For all the following references, see my article "*Krise*," in *Geschichtliche Grundbegriffe*, ed. Otto Brunner, Werner Conze, and Reinhart Koselleck, vol. 3 (Stuttgart, 1982), 617–50.

2. Leibniz, "Konzept eines Briefes an Schleiniz" (September 23, 1712), in *Leibniz' Rußland betreffender Briefwechsel*, ed. Wladimir Iwanowitsch Guerrier (St. Petersburg and Leipzig, 1873) pt. 2, 227–28, quoted in D. Groh, *Rußland und das Selbstverständnis Europas* (Neuwied, 1961), 39.

3. ["Die Weltgeschichte ist das Weltgericht." "Gericht" has a double meaning in both Schiller's dictum and Koselleck's usage: the dictum can be translated as both "world history is the judgment of the world," as in the Last Judgment, and also as "world history is the court of the world," the place where the trial itself occurs.—trans.]

4. Schiller, "Resignation: Eine Phantasie," in *Sämtliche Werke*, Säkular-Ausgabe, ed. Eduard von der Hellen et al., vol. 1 (Stuttgart, n.d.), 199.

5. Richard Rothe, *Die Anfänge der christlichen Kirche und ihre Verfassung* (1837), quoted in Peter Meinhold, *Geschichte der kirchlichen Historiographie*, vol. 2 (Munich, 1967), 221.

6. Karl Barth, *Der Römerbrief* (1918; 5th ed., 1926) (reprint ed., Zollikon-Zurich, 1954), 57.

7. Gustave de Molinari, *L'Evolution économique du XIXe siècle: Théorie du Progrès* (Paris, 1880), 102–3.

8. Quoted in W. Besson, *Die politische Terminologie des Präsidenten F. D. Roosevelt* (Tübingen, 1955), 20.

9. Jacob Burckhardt, *Weltgeschichtliche Betrachtungen*, ed. Rudolf Stadelmann (Pfullingen, 1949), 211.

CHAPTER 15. THE LIMITS OF EMANCIPATION

1. [*The Odyssey*, trans. Robert Fitzgerald (New York, 1961), book 17, lines 288–92, p. 332—trans.]

2. [In ancient Teutonic and old English law, wergild was the price set upon a man according to his rank, paid by way of compensation or fine in cases of homicide and certain other crimes to free the offender from further obligation or punishment (*OED*).—trans.]

3. [Immanuel Kant, "An Answer to the Question: What is Enlightenment?" in *Perpetual Peace and Other Essays on Politics, History, and Morals*, trans. Ted Humphrey (Indianapolis, 1983), 41.—trans.]

4. Correspondence of Daniel O'Connell, ed. W. J. Fitzpatrick, vol. 1 (London, 1888), 176; quoted in Norman Edward, *The English Catholic Church in the Nineteenth Century* (Oxford, 1984), 33–34. For the full references to all sources not cited here, see my article "*Emanzipation*," cowritten with Karl Martin Grass, in *Geschichtliche Grundbegriffe*, ed. Otto Brunner, Werner Conze, and Reinhart Koselleck, vol. 2 (Stuttgart, 1975), 153–97.

5. Cf. Robert Liberles, "Emancipation and the Structure of the Jewish Community in the Nineteenth Century." *Yearbook of the Leo Baeck Institute* 31 (1986): 51–67.

6. Richard Hofstadter, *The American Political Tradition* (New York, 1948), 133.

7. Migne, *Patrologia Latina*, vol. 22 (Paris), 552.

CHAPTER 16. DAUMIER AND DEATH

I am especially indebted to the publications of Werner Busch, Klaus Herding, Werner Hofmann, and André Stoll, and am thankful for the conversations and discussions I have been able to have with them—as well as, last but not least, with Max Imdahl.

1. [On the double meaning of *Weltgericht* in both Schiller's dictum and Koselleck's usage, see above, chapter 14, note 3.—trans.]

REFERENCES TO CHAPTER 16

Grohmann, Will, and Gerhart Ziller, eds. *Daumier.* Dresden, 1947.

Koch, U. E., and P.-P. Savage, eds. *Le Charivari.* Cologne, 1984.

Landschaftsverbände Westfalen-Lippe und Rheinland, Westfälisches und Rheinisches Landesmuseum. *Honoré Daumier, 1808–1879: Bildwitz und Zeitkritik.* 3rd ed. Bonn, 1979.

Langemeyer, G., et al. *Mittel und Motive der Karikatur in fünf Jahrhunderten, Bild als Waffe.* Munich, 1984.

Rheinisches Landesmuseum. *Honoré Daumier: Der bürgerliche Alltag.* Bonn: 1979.

Schenk, Klaus, ed. *Honoré Daumier, Das lithographische Werk.* 2 vols. Munich, n.d.

Searle, R., et al. *La Caricature, Art et Manifeste.* Geneva, 1974.

Unverfehrt, Gerd, ed. *La Caricature: Bildsatire in Frankreich 1830–1835.* Göttingen, 1980.

CHAPTER 17. WAR MEMORIALS: IDENTITY FORMATIONS OF
THE SURVIVORS

1. For references and assistance, I would like to thank the participants in the Colloquium on Identity (whose papers are published in *Poetik und Hermeneutik,* vol. 7) as well as the members of a research group at the Center for Interdisciplinary Studies at the University of Bielefeld who organized the conference *Totenmale und Todesbilder zwischen Kunst und Politik* (Memorials to the Dead and Images of Death between Art and Politics). Among other things, the conference served as the preparation for a comparative investigation of German and French war memorials undertaken by the author, together with Lurz, Riedl, Roques, and Vovelle.

2. *Zeitmagazin,* March 3, 1972.

3. *Neue Westfälische Zeitung,* September 8, 1975.

4. Reported by Nikolas Benckiser, in the *Frankfurter Allgemeine Zeitung,* July 22, 1976. On the history of the concentration camp and the memorial erected there, see *KZ-Lager Natzweiler Struthof,* comp. Comité National pour l'érection et la conservation d'un mémorial de la déportation au Struthof (Nancy, 1966).

5. Pope Innocent III, *De Miseria Humane Conditionis Lotharii Cardinalis* (Innocentii III), ed. Michele Maccarrone (Rome, 1955), c. 23, "De vicinitate mortis," 30.

6. Louis-Vincent Thomas, *Anthropologie de la mort* (Paris, 1976).

7. [Inscribed on the memorial to the Spartan dead: "Tell them in Sparta, passerby, / That here, obedient to their laws, we lie."—trans.]

8. Louis-Vincent Thomas, *Anthropologie de la mort,* 106ff.

9. Ernst Kantorowicz, *The King's Two Bodies—A Study in Medieval Political Theology* (Princeton, N.J., 1957), 419–36; Kathleen Cohen, *Metamorphosis of a Death Symbol—The Transi Tomb in the Late Middle Ages and the Renaissance,* California Studies in the History of Art, 15 (Berkeley, Calif., 1973).

10. Hans Friedrich von Fleming, *Der vollkommene Teutsche Soldat* (Leipzig, 1726), reprint ed., introd. W. Hummelsberger, Bibliotheca Rerum Militarium, ed. W. von Groote and U. von Gersdorff, vol. 1. (Osnabrück, 1967), 375.

11. Half a year later, the bodies were burnt. See Stefan Fayans, "Bestattungsanlagen," in *Handbuch der Architektur*, pt. 4, half-vol. 8, no. 3 (Stuttgart, 1907), 22.

12. Alois Riegl, *Der moderne Denkmalkultus, sein Wesen und seine Entstehung* (Vienna, 1903); "The Modern Cult of Monuments: Its Character and Its Origin," trans. Kurt W. Forster and Diane Ghirardo, *Oppositions*, no. 25 (1982): 21–51. Hubert Schrade, *Das deutsche Nationaldenkmal—Idee/Geschichte/Aufgabe* (Munich, 1934). The discussion here follows the path established by Thomas Nipperdey, "Nationalidee und Nationaldenkmal in Deutschland im 19. Jahrhundert," *Historische Zeitschrift* 206, no. 3 (June 1968): 529–85. In the Thyssenstiftung series, see Hans-Ernst Mittig and Volker Plagemann, eds., *Denkmäler im 19. Jahrhundert— Deutung und Kritik* (Munich, 1972).

13. Cf. Eduard Hüttinger, "Pigalles Grabmal des Maréchal de Saxe," *Neue Züricher Zeitung*, August 3, 1963.

14. William Wood, *An Essay on National and Sepulchral Monuments* (London, 1808). My thanks to Franz Joseph Keuck and Klaus Lankheit for kindly drawing my attention to this reference. [All quotes are in English in the original.—trans.]

15. Wood's calculation became a reality after the First World War. The Imperial War Graves Commission spent about £8 million for British cemeteries. The cost of munitions for one day during the battle of Passchendaele, September 19, 1917, was £3.75 million.

16. Cf. Nipperdey, "Nationalidee und Nationaldenkmal," 541. The saying, first directed by the monarch at the people, became independent of this relationship after the War of 1870 and was attributed, as it were, to the entire nation. The saying appeared for the first time on Schinkel's Kreuzberg memorial in Berlin. It is noteworthy that Kreuzberg was later allowed to be developed despite the national memorial located there. The issue concerned a famous liberal ruling by the Prussian Higher Administrative Court in favor of property rights and against an appeal by the Berlin police headquarters; the latter was denied the responsibility for "upholding and advancing the public welfare" according to paragraph 10, title 17, part II of the General Common Law (*Entscheidungen des Preußischen Oberverwaltungsgerichts*, vol. 9 [Berlin, 1883], 353ff.). The saying, which also obligated future generations to be ready to die, was used in the official dedication of the Niederwald Memorial by William I in the same year (Fritz Abshoff, *Deutschlands Ruhm und Stolz* [Berlin, n.d.], 164). And even Hindenburg used the formula to evoke the unity of all Germans in the past, the present, and the future at the official dedication of the Tannenberg Memorial, saying: "In honorable memory of those killed in action, in solemn reminder to the living, for the emulation of coming generations. May inner discord always be shattered at this commemorative memorial; let it be a place where everyone who stretches their hands toward one another is inspired by love for the Fatherland and for whom German honor matters more than anything" (Karl von Seeger, *Das Denkmal des Weltkrieges* [Stuttgart, 1930], 24). Thus Böckh's saying has outlived all stylistic changes in national memorials. It has

become a sign of the continuous demands for identity that were supposed to come from memorials, even if the makers of these appeals change from the monarch, through city governments, to the nation, and back again to its president.

17. "You did not die in vain"—this cry was often raised after 1918 and can be found, for example, on the war memorial by Kolbe in Stralsund. Siegfried Scharfe, *Deutschland über alles: Ehrenmale des Weltkrieges* (Königstein im Taunus, 1938), 55.

18. Theodor Mommsen, inaugural address as rector, October 15, 1874, in *Reden und Aufsätze* (Berlin, 1905), 6.

19. The Berlin theologian Reinhold Seeberg (1859–1935), a brilliant Latinist, trumped the inscription of Sedan when he created the memorial inscription for the students of Berlin in 1918: *"Invictis Victi Victuri"* (For the undefeated, the defeated ones who will be victorious). The three temporal dimensions of the dedication refer to the inner-worldly demand for identification which admits the defeat but demands that the results of World War I be revised in the future. The ideologically suggestive formula that Karl von Seeger (*Das Denkmal des Weltkrieges*, 146) quotes from the war memorial at the Charlottenburg Technical University is more awkward: "When a thousand strike a man dead, / That is not victory, not glory, nor integrity! / And one of these days it will be said: / To the German army indeed comes victory!" In contrast to Seeberg's postulate, here past history also becomes optative. Compare also the motto on the Eagle Memorial on the Wasserkuppe: "We dead airmen / remained victors / because of ourselves alone / People, you will fly again / and will remain victors / because of yourself alone." The effect of such formulas, which at once seek to conjure up and revise destiny, is difficult to appraise. In general, the formal language of German memorials after 1918 does not permit an interpretation that visibly demands revenge. To what extent they did foster certain invisible drives depends on the intonation of the commemorative celebrations held before the heroic monuments. Memorials that were openly intended to foster unity against the resumption of world war were not built. For more on this, see Dietrich Schubert, "Das Denkmal für die Märzgefallenen 1920 von Walter Gropius in Weimar und seine Stellung in der Geschichte des neueren Denkmals," *Jahrbuch der Hamburger Kunstsammlungen* 21 (1976): 211.

20. E. Leu, ed., *Soldatendenkmäler* (Belp, 1953).

21. The inscription appears, for example, on the town war memorial in Ancrum, Scotland.

22. For the motif of the widowed and the orphaned in Germany, see Seeger (note 16), 78, 125, 202ff., 209f., 247.

23. *40 IJzerbedevaarten* (Dixmunde, n.d.).

24. For the genesis and history of this memorial, designed "to activate . . . a political stance in victors," see Volker Frank, *Antifaschistische Mahnmale in der DDR—ihre künstlerische und architektonische Gestaltung* (Leipzig, 1970), 11ff. In addition, on the subject of the politics of memorials, see Anna Dora Miethe,

Gedenkstätten, Arbeiterbewegung, antifaschistischer Widerstand, Aufbau des Sozialismus (Leipzig, 1974).

25. On Great Britain after 1918, see Fabian Ware, *The Immortal Heritage: An Account of the Work and Policy of the Imperial War Graves Commission during Twenty Years, 1917–1937* (Cambridge, 1937); and Eric Homberger, "The Story of the Cenotaph," *Times Literary Supplement*, November 12, 1976.

26. Käthe Kollwitz, *Tagebuchblätter und Briefe*, ed. Hans Kollwitz (Berlin, 1948): Hans Kollwitz, ed., *The Diary and Letters of Kaethe Kollwitz*, trans. Richard and Clara Winston (Evanston, Ill., 1988). See the diary entries between December 1914 and August 1932, from the first conception of the memorial to its installation in Berlin and Belgium. Without believing in immortality, Käthe Kollwitz lived in a close spiritual relationship to her fallen son. It is this inner vision that made Kollwitz change her mind about her initial plan of representing her son himself. His premature death is thematized—purged of all embellishment—by depicting the parents as remaining behind.

27. Goethe, *Sämtliche Werke in 30 Bänden*, vol. 25 (Stuttgart, 1851), 205–7. Written in 1817 in connection with the erection of the Blücher Monument in Rostock, among whose backers was Goethe.

28. This was the premise of the so-called Bitburg affair (1985). Apart from concentration camp cemeteries, Bitburg is one of the German war cemeteries where handshakes and wreath laying take place, and where Waffen-SS troops, who incidentally were drafted over the course of the war like other soldiers in the Wehrmacht, were usually buried. "Half children," that is, youth called up to serve in fall of 1944, also lie in Bitburg.

29. It is remarkable that at first the English did not build any memorials dedicated only to a single person in London after 1918. In 1928, there were 235 statues, commemorative buildings, plaques, and war memorials in London, of which only two dated back before 1800. One hundred and forty-nine commemorated civil achievements and 86 military ones. Of the military memorials, only 22 (that is, 26 percent) were erected to individual persons, and all of them dated from before World War I (1914–1918). But that would entirely change. The statistics come from C. S. Cooper, *The Outdoor Monuments of London* (London, 1928).

30. Schön to Stägemann, August 30, 1822, in Franz Rühl, ed., *Briefe und Aktenstücke zur Geschichte Preußens unter Friedrich Wilhelm III*, 3 vols. (Leipzig, 1902), 3:600. Schön goes on to ask: where would we be "if all the friends of kings were to have their own statues? Where do we draw the line? . . . If we had built a German cathedral, how very different things would be today!" Schön supported a national memorial, like many at that time. In so doing, he also made use of Christian-humanistic arguments: "Like heathendom in the Christian world, statues in public squares are only tolerable when they represent ideals. Every 500–1000 years one, Luther, and since then, no one" (to Stägemann, July 10, 1822, Ibid., 101). Cf. also Hartmut Boockmann, "Das ehemalige Deutschordens-Schloß Marienburg 1772–

1945: Die Geschichte eines politischen Denkmals," in *Geschichtswissenschaft und Vereinswesen im 19. Jahrhundert*, Max-Planck-Institut für Geschichte, no. 1 (Göttingen, 1972), 99–161.

31. Monument of the Peace of Rastatt, in the year 1798, cited in *Kameleon, oder das Thier mit allen Farben, Eine Zeitschrift für Fürstentugend und Volksglück*, nos. 1–3, 54.

32. An early case of individual burial in rows of graves for common soldiers can be found in 1813 in the Zillertal / Riesengebirge. Cf. *Kriegergräber im Felde und daheim* (Munich, 1917), 155.

33. Nipperdey, "Nationalidee und Nationaldenkmal," esp. 533–46.

34. F. G. Klopstock, *Ode "An Freund und Feind,"* in *Sämtliche Werke*, vol. 6 (Karlsruhe, 1826), 37.

35. Christian Daniel Schubart, "Die Fürstengruft," in *Politisch-soziale Zeitgeschichte*, ed. Edgar Neis (Hollfeld/Obfr., n.d.), 19–21.

36. "Die Gräber der drei Julitage," German translation by Adalbert von Chamisso, in *Werke*, pt. 2, ed. Max Sydow (Berlin), 121–23.

37. Adolf Wolff, *Berliner Revolutionschronik 1849–54* (Berlin, 1898).

38. Fritz Debus, "Blüten in Gottes Wind: Ereignisse und Gestalten aus der Geschichte der Kriegsgräberfürsorge der Vereinigten Staaten," *Mitteilungsblatt "Kriegsgräberfürsorge,"* nos. 1–5 (1958).

39. See the German-Russian Supplementary Treaty of March 3, 1918, or the German-Ukrainian Supplementary Treaty of February 9, 1918, as well as articles 225 and 226 of the Versailles Peace Treaty and the corresponding articles in the other Paris peace treaties. On this whole issue, see Rudolf von Neumann, "Kriegsgräberfürsorge im Sinne der Genfer Abkommen," *Revue Internationale de la Croix-Rouge* 13, no. 11 (1962). See the Statute on the Preservation of the Graves of Victims of War and Despotism ("Graves Statute") of July 1, 1965, *Bundesgesetzblatt*, July 8, 1965. In addition, for the agreement between the Federal Republic of Germany, Great Britain and the Commonwealth countries, and France of March 5, 1956, see ibid., June 13, 1957.

40. Wilhelm Messerer, "Zu extremen Gedanken über Bestattung und Grabmal um 1800," in *Kunstgeschichte und Kunsttheorie im 19. Jahrhundert* (Berlin, 1963), 172–94; and Franz-Josef Keuck, "Politische Sinnlichkeit vor Totenmalen" (M.A. thesis, University of Heidelberg, 1974), 57–67.

41. Hans-Ernst Mittig, "Die Entstehung des ungegenständlichen Denkmals," in *Evolution générale et développements régionaux en histoire de l'Art—Actes du XIIe. Congrès international d'histoire de l'art, Budapest 1969*, 3 vols. (Budapest, 1965–72), 2:469–74, 3:434–37; and Dietrich Clarenbach, "Grenzfälle zwischen Architektur und Plastik im 20. Jahrhundert" (Diss., University of Munich, 1969).

42. Dieter Ronte et al., eds., *Hurra!? Vom Unsinn des Krieges: Sechste Jugendausstellung der Kölner Museen im Wallraf-Richartz-Museum* (Cologne, 1971), 49–59.

43. Clare Hollingworth, "Memory of the Fallen Begins to Fade Away," *Daily Telegraph*, November 11, 1976. Thanks to Fritz Trautz for this reference.

CHAPTER 18. AFTERWORD TO 'THE THIRD REICH OF DREAMS'

1. [Charlotte Beradt, *Das dritte Reich des Traums* (1966; reprint ed., Frankfurt, 1981); *The Third Reich of Dreams*, trans. Adrianne Gottwald (Chicago, 1968).—trans.]

2. [The *Winterhilfswerk* was a relief organization in Nazi Germany providing food, clothes, and fuel for the needy.—trans.]

Cultural Memory | in the Present

Hélène Cixous and Jacques Derrida, *Veils*

F. R. Ankersmit, *Historical Representation*

F. R. Ankersmit, *Political Representation*

Elissa Marder, *Dead Time: Temporal Disorders in the Wake of Modernity (Baudelaire and Flaubert)*

Reinhart Koselleck, *Timing History, Spacing Concepts: The Practice of Conceptual History*

Niklas Luhmann, *The Reality of the Mass Media*

Hubert Damisch, *A Childhood Memory by Piero della Francesca*

Hubert Damisch, *A Theory of /Cloud/: Toward a History of Painting*

Jean-Luc Nancy, *The Speculative Remark: (One of Hegel's Bons Mots)*

Jean-François Lyotard, *Soundproof Room: Malraux's Anti-Aesthetics*

Jan Patočka, *Plato and Europe*

Hubert Damisch, *Skyline: The Narcissistic City*

Isabel Hoving, *In Praise of New Travelers: Reading Caribbean Migrant Women Writers*

Richard Rand, *Futures: Of Derrida*

William Rasch, *Niklas Luhmann's Modernity: The Paradoxes of Differentiation*

Jacques Derrida and Anne Dufourmantelle, *Of Hospitality*

Jean-François Lyotard, *The Confession of Augustine*

Kaja Silverman, *World Spectators*

Samuel Weber, *Institution and Interpretation,* second edition

Jeffrey S. Librett, *The Rhetoric of Cultural Dialogue: Jews and Germans in the Epoch of Emancipation*

Ulrich Baer, *Remnants of Song: Trauma and the Experience of Modernity in Charles Baudelaire and Paul Celan*

Samuel C. Wheeler III, *Deconstruction as Analytic Philosophy*